Jerusalem

Jerusalem, the holy city of three faiths, has been the focus of competing historical, religious, and political narratives from biblical chronicles to today's headlines. With an aura that transcends the boundaries of time and place, the city itself embodies different levels of reality—indeed, different realities altogether—for both observers and inhabitants. There is the real Jerusalem, a place of ancient streets and monuments, temples and coffee-houses, religious discourse and political argument. But there is also the imaginary and utopian city that exists in the minds of believers, political strategists, and artists. The study of this multifaceted city poses complex questions that range over several fields of inquiry.

The multidisciplinary studies in *Jerusalem: Idea and Reality* offer insights into this complexity. Chapters by leading scholars examine the significant issues that relate to the perception, representation, and status of the city at the historical, religious, social, artistic, and political levels. Together they provide an essential resource for anyone interested in the paradoxes that Jerusalem offers.

Tamar Mayer is Professor of Geography at Middlebury College and the editor of *Women and the Israeli Occupation: The Politics of Change* (Routledge, 1994) and *Gender Ironies of Nationalism: Sexing the Nation* (Routledge, 2000). Her research interests focus on the interplay among nationalism, gender, and sexuality, particularly in the Middle East, and on the relationships among nationalism, landscape, and memory.

Suleiman Ali Mourad is Associate Professor of Religion at Smith College, USA. His research focuses on early Islamic history and religious thought, including the sanctity of Jerusalem. He is the author of *Early Islam between Myth and History: al-Hasan al-Basri (d. 110H/728CE) and the Formation of His Legacy in Classical Islamic Scholarship* (Brill, 2005).

Jerusalem
Idea and reality

**Edited by
Tamar Mayer and
Suleiman Ali Mourad**

Routledge
Taylor & Francis Group

LONDON AND NEW YORK

First published 2008
by Routledge
2 Park Square, Milton Park, Abingdon, Oxon OX14 4RN

Simultaneously published in the USA and Canada
by Routledge
270 Madison Avenue, New York, NY 10016

Routledge is an imprint of the Taylor & Francis Group, an informa business

Transferred to Digital Printing 2010

Typeset in Times New Roman by
Taylor & Francis Books

British Library Cataloguing in Publication Data
A catalogue record for this book is available from the British Library

Library of Congress Cataloging in Publication Data
Jerusalem: idea and reality / edited by Tamar Mayer and Suleiman Ali Mourad.
    p. cm.
    Includes bibliographical references and index.
[etc.]
    1. Jerusalem – History. I. Mayer, Tamar, 1952– II. Mourad, Suleiman Ali.
    DS109.95J476 2008
    956.94'42 – dc22
                    2007037619

ISBN13: 978-0-415-42128-7 (hbk)
ISBN13: 978-0-415-42129-4 (pbk)
ISBN13: 978-0-203-92977-3 (ebk)

To Tahl Mayer, Jude Mourad, and Alya Mourad

Contents

List of figures		ix
Notes on contributors		xi
Acknowledgments		xv

1 Introduction   1
TAMAR MAYER AND SULEIMAN ALI MOURAD

2 Jerusalem: one city, one faith, one god   14
F. E. PETERS

3 Jerusalem in Jewish history, tradition, and memory   27
LEE I. LEVINE

4 The Temple Mount in Jewish and early Christian traditions: a new look   47
YARON Z. ELIAV

5 Early Christian Jerusalem: the city of the cross   67
OLIVER LARRY YARBROUGH

6 The symbolism of Jerusalem in early Islam   86
SULEIMAN ALI MOURAD

7 The holy fool still speaks: the Jerusalem Syndrome as a religious subculture   103
ALEXANDER VAN DER HAVEN

8 Sacred space and mythic time in the early printed maps of Jerusalem   123
REHAV RUBIN

9 Seeing is believing: Auguste Salzmann and the photographic representation of Jerusalem   140
EMMIE DONADIO

10 Fayruz, the Rahbani Brothers, Jerusalem, and the Leba-stinian song 155
CHRISTOPHER STONE

11 Jerusalem in the visual propaganda of post-revolutionary Iran 168
CHRISTIANE J. GRUBER

12 Negotiating the city: a perspective of a Jerusalemite 198
SARI NUSSEIBEH

13 Jerusalem in the late Ottoman period: historical writing and the native voice 205
ISSAM NASSAR

14 Jerusalem in and out of focus: the city in Zionist ideology 224
TAMAR MAYER

15 Administering Jordanian Jerusalem: constructing national identity 245
KIMBERLY KATZ

16 The Palestinian political leadership in East Jerusalem after 1967 266
ELIE REKHESS

17 Yerushalayim, al-Quds, and the Wizard of Oz: the problem of "Jerusalem" after Camp David II and the Aqsa *Intifada* 283
IAN S. LUSTICK

18 Negotiating Jerusalem: reflections of an Israeli negotiator 303
GILEAD SHER

Index 321

Figures

1	Map of Jerusalem	xvii
8.1	Seutter's double map of realistic and imaginary Jerusalem	124
8.2	Adrichom's map of Jerusalem	127
8.3	A detail from Adrichom's map of Jerusalem presenting the coronation of King Solomon and the *Pisanorum Castrum* side by side	128
8.4	Villalpando's map of Jerusalem	129
8.5	David and Goliath near the Walls of Jerusalem, a detail from de Pierre's map of Jerusalem (1728)	130
8.6	Eder's map of Jerusalem	131
8.7	A detail from Schedel's map of Jerusalem: The Dome of the Rock as the burnt Temple	134
8.8	A detail from Adrichom: The Idol and the Crescent	135
9.1	Michael Wohlgemut, *Hierosolima*, 1493	141
9.2	Matthaeus Merian, after Erhard Reuwich–Bernhard von Breydenbach, *Jerusalem*, 1497	142
9.3	Francis Frith, *Jerusalem from the Mount of Olives*, c. 1858	143
9.4	Auguste Salzmann, *Jérusalem, enceinte du temple, vue générale de la face Est*, Pl. 2, 1854	143
9.5	Auguste Salzmann, *Jérusalem, enceinte du temple, côté Ouest*, 1854	146
9.6	Auguste Salzmann, *Jérusalem, Birket-Hammam-Setty-Mariam*, 1854	148
9.7	Auguste Salzmann, *Jérusalem, Birket Mamilla*, 1854	149
9.8	Auguste Salzmann, *Jérusalem, Birket Hammam-el-Batrak*, 1854	150
9.9	Auguste Salzmann, *Jérusalem, Porte de Damas, vue extérieure*, 1854	151
9.10	Auguste Salzmann, *Jérusalem, Porte de Damas, intérieure*, 1854	151
9.11	Auguste Salzmann, *Jérusalem, Birket-es-Soultan*, 1854	152
11.1	"The Road to Jerusalem Goes through Karbala," billboard, Mehran, c. 1983	172

11.2 Military procession in Kermanshah, 1987   174
11.3 Maquette of the Dome of the Rock, Kermanshah, c. 1980   176
11.4 Model of the Dome of the Rock, *Maidan-i Azadi* (Freedom
      Square), Kermanshah, 2005   177
11.5 Dome of the Rock Fountain, *Sahn-i Quds* (Jerusalem
      Courtyard), Shrine of Imam Reza, Mashhad, 2005   179
11.6 Dome of the Rock Maquette, *Serah-i Quds* (Jerusalem three-
      street junction), Niavaran, Tehran, 2001   180
11.7 Dome of the Rock Model, *Maidan-i Filistin* (Jerusalem
      Square), Tehran, c. 1990   182
11.8 View of *Maidan-i Filistin* (Palestine Square), Tehran, 2005   183
11.9 Mural of Sayyid 'Abbas Musawi, *Maidan-i Filistin* (Palestine
      Square), Tehran, 2005   184
11.10 The Ensnaring of Holy Sites, *Maidan-i Filistin* (Palestine
      Square), Tehran, 2005   185
11.11 Mural of a Palestinian Martyr and the Dome of the Rock,
      Modarres Highway, Tehran, 2005   186
11.12 Logo of the Palestinian Solidarity Organization, Modarres
      Highway, Tehran, 2005   188
11.13 Ayatollah Khomeini and the Dome of the Rock, 'Abbas Abad
      Street, Tehran, 2005   189
11.14 Ayatollah Khomeini and the Dome of the Rock, 'Abbas Abad
      Street, Tehran, c. 1992   190
11.15 *Starless Night* (*Shab bi-Sitara*) by Iraj Iskandari, c. 1980   192
13.1 The surrender of Jerusalem to British officers, December 9,
      1917   220
14.1 Partitioned Jerusalem   232

Contributors

Emmie Donadio is Chief Curator of the Middlebury College Museum of Art, in Middlebury, Vermont. She has published on a wide range of subjects. An art historian with a Ph.D. degree from Columbia University, her work is primarily in the field of modern sculpture and the history of photography. She has organized numerous exhibitions at Middlebury and has been guest curator of a major retrospective exhibition of works by American sculptor Richard Stankiewicz, which opened at the Addison Gallery of American Art and traveled to New York, San Antonio, and Basel.

Yaron Z. Eliav is the Frankel Associate Professor of Rabbinic Literature and Late Antique Jewish History at the University of Michigan. His research draws on talmudic, early Christian, and classical literatures, as well as on archaeology in order to study the multifaceted cultural environment of Roman Palestine with emphasis on the encounter between Jews and Graeco-Roman culture. His book *God's Mountain: The Temple Mount in Time, Space, and Memory* was published by Johns Hopkins University Press in 2005. It won two national awards, the 2005 American Association of Publishers award for best scholarly book on religion, and the 2006 Salo Baron prize for best first book in Judaic studies from the American Academy for Jewish Studies. Eliav is the co-director of the *Statuary Project*, an interdisciplinary, multiyear research endeavor that takes place at the University of Michigan, and he is the chief editor of a two-volume publication of this project, scheduled to appear in 2008 in the series *Interdisciplinary Studies in Ancient Culture and Religion* (Peeters). Eliav is also working on a new book, *A Jew in the Roman Bathhouse: Daily Life Encounters with Hellenism in Roman Palestine*.

Christiane J. Gruber (Ph.D., University of Pennsylvania, 2005) is Assistant Professor of Islamic Art at Indiana University, Bloomington. She is the author of the online presentation *Selections of Arabic, Persian, and Ottoman Calligraphies* in the Library of Congress (http://international.loc.gov/intldl/apochtml/apochome.html) and also has written a number of articles on Islamic painting and the Prophet Muhammad's ascension. She is currently preparing a monograph on *The Art of Martyrdom in Modern Iran*.

Kimberly Katz is Assistant Professor of Middle Eastern History at Towson University in Maryland. She earned her Ph.D. in History and Middle Eastern Studies at New York University in 2001. Katz is the author of *Jordanian Jerusalem: Holy Places and National Spaces* (University Press of Florida, 2005) and has published articles in *The Muslim World, Comparative Studies in South Africa, Asia and the Middle East*, and *The Journal of Social Affairs*. She is currently working on a previously unpublished Palestinian diary written during the World War II years in British Mandate Palestine.

Lee I. Levine is Professor of Jewish History and Archaeology at the Hebrew University of Jerusalem, where he holds the Reverend Moses Bernard Lauterman Family Chair in Classical Archaeology. He is the author of several books, including *The Ancient Synagogue: The First Thousand Years* (Yale University Press, 2000); *Jerusalem: Portrait of the City in the Second Temple Period (538 BCE–70 CE)* (Jewish Publication Society, 2002), and has edited eleven volumes and written some 170 articles. Levine has excavated in Caesarea and the Horvat 'Ammudim synagogue in Galilee. He has lectured widely in the United States, Israel, and Europe, has been a visiting professor at Harvard, Yale, and the Jewish Theological Seminary, each on numerous occasions, and received an honorary doctorate in 2000 from Lund University, Sweden, for his work on the ancient synagogue. He is currently working on a volume titled *Visual Judaism: History, Art, and Identity in Late Antiquity*.

Ian S. Lustick is the Bess W. Heyman Professor of Political Science at the University of Pennsylvania. Among his books are *Trapped in the War on Terror* (University of Pennsylvania Press, 2006) and *Unsettled States, Disputed Lands: Britain and Ireland, France and Algeria, Israel and the West Bank/Gaza* (Cornell University Press, 1993). Aside from his work on Arab–Israeli relations, Lustick is a pioneer in the use of computer-assisted agent-based modeling in political science. His current research focuses on techniques of disciplined counterfactual thinking, the dynamics of political cascades, and Israel's problematic future as a Jewish state in a Muslim Middle East.

Tamar Mayer is Professor of Geography at Middlebury College, in Middlebury, Vermont. She is the editor of *Women and the Israeli Occupation: The Politics of Change* (Routledge, 1994) and *Gender Ironies of Nationalism: Sexing the Nation* (Routledge, 2000). Her research interests focus on the interplay among nationalism, gender, and sexuality in the Middle East, and on the relationships among nationalism, landscape, and memory.

Suleiman Ali Mourad is Associate Professor of Religion at Smith College, in Northampton, Massachusetts. He specializes in medieval Islamic history and religious thought. His monograph *Early Islam between Myth and History: al-Hasan al-Basri (d. 110 H/728 CE) and the Formation of His*

Legacy in Classical Islamic Scholarship was published by Brill (2005). He has also published extensively on the historian/religious scholar Ibn 'Asakir of Damascus, and on the presentation of Jesus in the Qur'an and Islamic tradition. He is currently working on a project to reconstruct the earliest now-lost Islamic text from the ninth century CE on the Merits (*Fada'il*) of Jerusalem, and also serves as vice-president of Middle East Medievalists. He holds graduate degrees from the American University of Beirut and Yale University.

Issam Nassar is Assistant Professor of Middle East History at Illinois State University. He is the author of *Different Snapshots: Early Local Photography in Palestine, 1850–1948* (Beirut: Kutub, 2005 in Arabic), and co-editor (with Salim Tamari) *of Pilgrims, Lepers and Stuffed Cabbage: Essays on Jerusalem's Cultural History* (Institute of Jerusalem Studies, 2005). He also serves as associate editor of *Jerusalem Quarterly.*

Sari Nusseibeh is President of al-Quds University in East Jerusalem. He has received several international awards and fellowships in recognition for his active role in peace initiatives between the Palestinians and Israel, including, in 2004, the sixteenth Catalonia International Prize (Spain), which he shared with the Israeli novelist and scholar Amos Oz. He holds a Ph.D. in philosophy from Harvard University.

F. E. Peters is Professor of Middle Eastern and Islamic Studies, History and Religion at New York University. He was trained at St. Louis University in classical languages (A.B., M.A.) and in philosophy (Ph.L.), and received his Ph.D. from Princeton in Islamic studies. His most recent books are *The Monotheists: Jews, Christians and Muslims in Conflict and Competition* (2 vols., 2003) and *The Voice, the Word, the Books: The Scriptures of the Jews, Christians and Muslims* (2007), both from Princeton University Press.

Elie Rekhess is Senior Research Fellow at the Moshe Dayan Center for Middle Eastern and African Studies and Head of the Konrad Adenauer Program for Jewish–Arab Cooperation in Israel at Tel Aviv University. Concurrently, he is the Pearlman Visiting Professional Fellow in Jewish Studies and History at Northwestern University. He is one of Israel's leading experts on the Arab minority in Israel, Jewish–Arab relations, Palestinian politics, and Islamic resurgence in the West Bank and Gaza. He was senior consultant on Arab Minority Affairs to the Prime Minister's Office (1993–94), strategic advisor to Prime Minister Ehud Barak (1999), and advisor to the Chairman of the Ministerial Committee on the Arabs in Israel (1999–2000). He is the author of *Islamic Fundamentalism in Israel* (forthcoming) and the editor of *Arab Politics in Israel at a Crossroads* (Tel Aviv University, 1996).

Rehav Rubin is Professor of Geography at the Hebrew University of Jerusalem, Israel. He received his Ph.D. in geography and archaeology at the Hebrew University in 1986. He was a visiting fellow at the University of Maryland (1986–87), Wolfson College, Oxford (1993–94), and the University of Pennsylvania (2006–7). His two main areas of research are people and settlement in the arid regions in late antiquity, and the history of cartography and the mapping of Jerusalem and the Holy Land. He is the author of articles and of the books *The Negev as a Settled Land, Urbanization and Settlement in the Desert in the Byzantine Period* (Yad Izhak Ben-Zvi and the Israel Exploration Society, 1990; in Hebrew) and *Image and Reality: Jerusalem in Maps and Views* (Eisenbrauns, 1999).

Gilead Sher is an attorney. He was the former Israeli prime minister Ehud Barak's Chief of Staff and Policy Coordinator, and acted as co-chief negotiator from 1999 to 2001 at the Camp David Summit and the Taba talks, as well as in extensive rounds of covert negotiations with the Palestinians. He teaches frequently as a guest lecturer at the Wharton School of the University of Pennsylvania, mainly on dispute resolution and negotiations in times of crisis. The English version of his book *The Israel–Palestinian Peace Negotiations, 1999–2001: Within Reach* was published by Routledge in 2006.

Christopher Stone is Associate Professor of Arabic Language and Literature and Head of the Arabic Division at Hunter College of the City University of New York. He received his M.A. (1995) and Ph.D. (2002) in Near Eastern studies from Princeton University, where he specialized in Arabic language, literature, and culture. His dissertation received the Malcolm Kerr Dissertation Award for the Humanities from the Middle East Studies Association in 2003. The book version—titled *Popular Culture and Nationalism in Lebanon: The Fairouz and Rahbani Nation*—was published by Routledge in 2007. He is now working on a project on the role of the actor Ahmad Zaki in contemporary Egyptian popular culture.

Alexander van der Haven is a Ph.D. candidate in the History of Religions at the University of Chicago Divinity School. He is currently working on a dissertation about Daniel Paul Schreber and religion. His focus is on Western religions since 1800.

Oliver Larry Yarbrough is the Tillinghast Professor of Religion at Middlebury College, Vermont, where he has taught New Testament, early Christianity, early Judaism, and Greco-Roman religions since 1983. His early work focused on the family in the social order of early Christianity and Judaism; he is currently working on two projects related to the Passion narrative and early Christian art related to it. He holds graduate degrees from Cambridge, Emory, and Yale.

Acknowledgments

The idea of this collaboration between an Israeli Jew born in Haifa, Tamar Mayer, and a Lebanese Muslim born in Benwati (South Lebanon), Suleiman Ali Mourad, began in June 2003 when we met to chat about research interests and possible collaboration. Soon it became clear that we share many interests and that the idea and the reality of Jerusalem were prominent among them. We decided to organize a symposium on this topic at Middlebury College and to publish the papers in an edited volume.

The symposium convened on April 15–17, 2005 and was made possible by the extreme generosity of Middlebury College. Many of its academic departments and funds, too many to list here, enabled us to bring outstanding scholars to campus, and indeed this symposium was an important college event. We thank all those who contributed to the success of the conference, in particular the Rohatyn Center for International Affairs. We are indebted to Charlotte Tate and Martha Baldwin of the Center, who attended to all the organizational and logistical matters before, during, and after the symposium and were responsible, in many ways, for its great success. We also thank our students Maija Cheung, who served as research assistant for the symposium, and Allison West, who transcribed Chapter 12, our colleague Nichole Grohoski for her cartographic skills, and Mary Bellino for her editorial help.

Most of the chapters in this volume were presented at the symposium, but we solicited a few additional essays in order to cover some topics that were not addressed there. We thank all the contributors for participating in our collaborative efforts.

We also want to thank our editor at Routledge, Joe Whiting, and his assistant, Natalja Mortensen, for their support and for their patience. Finally, a great word of appreciation goes to Nancy Shumate and Rana Knio for their continuous support and encouragement.

Tamar Mayer and Suleiman Ali Mourad

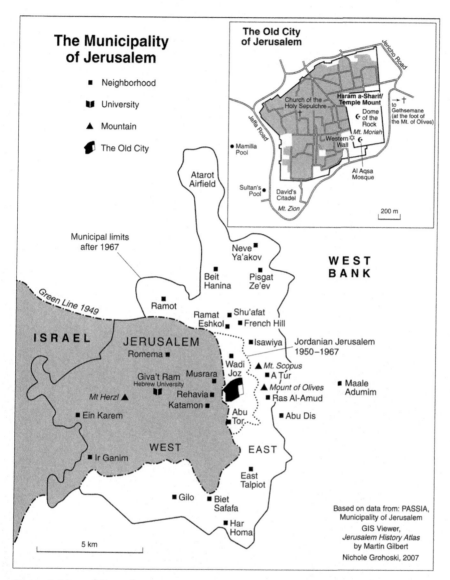

Figure 1 Map of Jerusalem.

1 Introduction

Tamar Mayer and Suleiman Ali Mourad

Very few cities around the world have captured the imaginations of religious scholars, artists, politicians, and lay people in the way that Jerusalem has. Indeed, it is hard to find another city that has been so central to people's identity and has been the focus of so much literary and visual artwork. Its long history, its importance to the three monotheistic religions, and its image as the "heavenly city" continue to make Jerusalem as important a pilgrims' destination in the present as it has been in the past. But Jerusalem is not just a holy city. It is also a place where regular people reside, where people of the three monotheisms live side by side, not always peacefully, and where the national struggle between Israelis and Palestinians has been played out for more than sixty years, reflecting the greater Arab/Muslim–Israeli conflict. Jerusalem thus embodies both the earthly (what belongs to this world) and the heavenly (what belongs to the other world).

Over the centuries, Jerusalem has been given countless names and epithets, among them Shalem, Yerushalayim, City of Melchizedek, City of the Great King or City of David, Aelia Capitolina, Prototype of the Heavenly Jerusalem, Bayt al-Maqdis or al-Quds, and City of Peace. All of these names have illuminated aspects of the "heavenly" and "earthly" Jerusalem. As a destination for pilgrimage and as the city with the oldest continuous history in the western world, Jerusalem has always been an object of longing and a place of great attachment. It has been idealized and immortalized in travel guides, memoirs, novels, poetry, journalism, film, television, and song and has been celebrated over millennia through religious rituals and practices. But over the last century, the deep emotions regarding Jerusalem have also been expressed in national discourses and in an intense national struggle for control over all or parts of the city. Thus Jerusalem as an idea and Jerusalem as a reality converge and diverge constantly, creating countless facets of the city that magnify its aura, yet at the same time setting up irreconcilable opposites that make Jerusalem seem a place at odds with itself.

Much of the *idea* of Jerusalem stems from religious attachment to the city. Mircea Eliade (1987), one of the greatest scholars of the academic study of religion, wrote in his masterwork *The Sacred and the Profane: The Nature of Religion* that when the sacred manifests itself in any hierophany, there is not only a break in the homogeneity of space; there is also revelation of an absolute reality, opposed to the nonreality of the vast surrounding expanse. The manifestation of the sacred ontologically founds the world. In the homogeneous and infinite expanse, in which no point of reference is possible and hence no *orientation* can be established, the hierophany reveals an absolute fixed point, a center.

(Eliade 1987, 21)

Leaving aside the issue of the existence of the sacred, there is no better place on earth to validate Eliade's theory than the city of Jerusalem. For Jews, Christians, and Muslims, the divine has manifested itself in and around Jerusalem, even adopting the city as its earthly abode. Again, whether or not these divine manifestations and residencies actually occurred is beside the point. As long as there continue to be groups who believe that such manifestations took place in Jerusalem, the city will retain its centrality in their religious beliefs and traditions. And, because separate groups with millions of followers believe that the *truly authentic* divine manifestations that took place in Jerusalem relate to them and only to them, and that those of others, if they have any claim to legitimacy, have been superseded, Jews, Christians, and Muslims continue to compete over Jerusalem. In this sense, Jerusalem is unlike any other city.

Religious symbolism

Jerusalem's religious importance is believed to have begun, as far as monotheistic religion is concerned, when a spot of land identified as Mount Moriah, later incorporated into the city, witnessed the divine intervention that saved the child Isaac from the determination of his father Abraham to carry out God's command to sacrifice the boy. Thus it is believed that it was in Jerusalem that the god of monotheism tested Abraham, and that there Israel was saved to live on and receive God's promises and blessings. But Mount Moriah was not yet Jerusalem. What made Jerusalem the city that we know started, as F. E. Peters shows (Chapter 2), when King Solomon carried out the wishes of his father David to build a Temple as a house for the God of Israel. That the Temple was occupied by the *Shekhinah* of God (that is, the presence of God) transformed it from a mere threshing floor with an altar on it into a sacred space, and subsequently transformed Jerusalem from a marginal Jebusite dwelling into the holiest city in monotheism.

Jerusalem has witnessed a plethora of divine manifestations, both positive and negative. Yet, ironically, both are equally powerful. Although God's Temple was destroyed twice and the *Shekhinah* departed from it, and despite the curse made against the Temple by Jesus, the sacred status of Jerusalem was not undermined. One can argue, as Eliav does (Chapter 4), that the Temple Mount and Jerusalem gradually began to gain more sacredness as soon as the Temple was destroyed. Contrary to what Eliade suggests, sometimes it is the withdrawal of divine manifestation that turns a space from a profane into a sacred space. That Christians disregard the Temple Mount is a case that proves the point: Christians rejected the sacredness of the Temple Mount area only after they transferred all of its symbolism to the Church of the Holy Sepulcher. Only then did the "old" Temple and its surroundings lose their significance and centrality—but Jerusalem, as Oliver Larry Yarbrough shows (Chapter 5), did not. With respect to Islam, as Suleiman Ali Mourad (Chapter 6) demonstrates, early Muslim traditions prove that the association of Muhammad with Jerusalem was promoted after the Dome of the Rock was built in 692 CE. Hence, there is every reason to doubt, as many early Muslim scholars did, the historicity of the claims that the cause of Muslims' veneration of the city is Muhammad's journey by night to Jerusalem and his ascension from the Temple Mount area to Heaven. But historicity rarely impacts people's beliefs, because those beliefs originate from a source that is beyond the judgment of history. Ironically, however, such beliefs often determine the course of history.

The centrality of Jerusalem to the three Abrahamic religions was constructed carefully over time. For each group, there was a time-lag between when the constitutive events presumably took place and the time Jerusalem is noted as important. The binding of Isaac, as mentioned earlier, was not known or believed to have taken place on the precise site where the first Temple was built until the building was already there. In considering Jerusalem's religious significance, one has to constantly struggle to distinguish between what is belief and what is history—and, of course, try to do that without ridiculing either one. Peters (Chapter 2) gives us an overview of the religious attachments each of the monotheistic traditions developed regarding Jerusalem. He suggests that while the Jewish attachment has been to the city as a whole, because it was the religious and political capital of biblical Israel, both Christian and Islamic believers have identified and focused on particular sites within it, some of which are biblical (such as the Temple Mount/al-Haram al-Sharif) and some specifically Christian (such as the Church of the Holy Sepulcher). Peters also argues that these notions of attachment to Jerusalem must be viewed against the historical background, and that the existence and promotion of a holy place is fundamentally conditioned by political power—that is, by whoever controls that place. He also maintains that political hostility or political support may define piety and the attachment to place; who worships in Jerusalem, and how, has never been very remote from who rules Jerusalem.

In the case of the Jewish tradition, Lee I. Levine (Chapter 3) shows that Jerusalem's sanctity and centrality did not emerge overnight, but rather were the result of a long and complex process of internal as well as external developments, including the presence of the Temple and the efforts to make it the only venue for the worship of the God of Israel. After the destruction of the city and its Temple in 70 CE, Jews lost control of Jerusalem for close to 1,900 years. During this long period the center of Jewish life relocated many times, but throughout the centuries Jews never lost their attachment to Jerusalem and the hope of restoring their national and religious presence there. Judaism, unlike Christianity and Islam, does not have any other city that equals Jerusalem's sacredness and centrality. To assure preservation of the sacredness and centrality of Jerusalem, Levine argues, Jews expressed, concretized, and reinforced their passion culturally and religiously, through literature, prayer, and distinctive customs and rituals.

Although Jewish attachment to Jerusalem as the center of Jewish life has encompassed the historical City of David, it is the Temple Mount itself that has evoked the deepest of feelings toward the city. The Temple Mount has evolved over the years into a national, cultural, and political symbol, and in the twentieth century it became deeply entrenched in the foundations of both the Jewish-Zionist and the Arab-Muslim ethos. Eliav (Chapter 4) examines the evolution of the sacredness of the Temple Mount. He investigates the origin of its name, the factors that gave it a unique and sacred status independent of the Temple itself, and the types of consciousness the term evoked in the Jewish tradition and the Jews' perception of Jerusalem. Eliav argues for a multifaceted model that encompasses radical changes in the function of the Temple Mount within the urban landscape of Jerusalem over the years. He also points out that some early Christian groups, such as the movement of James, brother of Jesus, found the Temple Mount equally central to their religious activities.

Christianity undoubtedly adopted many of the Jewish attitudes toward Jerusalem, but the city was most sacred to them as the site of the crucifixion of Jesus of Nazareth, the son of God, around 30 CE. Was Jesus really the son of God? Certainly one has the right to raise such a question, but would the answer change the fact that the city is revered as the site of the most sacred Christian events? In the early fourth century CE, Helena, the mother of the Byzantine emperor Constantine, led a team to Jerusalem to discover the places where Jesus was crucified, where he was laid to rest, and from where he rose to Heaven, and those spaces gave the city the status of the holiest city in Christendom. Christian men and women came from far and near to see and touch the holy sites, and they brought the experiences and stories back to their own lands, writing countless accounts of what they saw and felt. Some even left their homelands and came to live near those sacred sites and to serve them. Those who could not make the journey tried to visualize it through art, songs, and stories.

Although Jerusalem did not become a Christian city until the beginning of the fourth century CE, Christians had a long association with it, which is obvious both in their adoption of Jewish scriptures and in their own memories and accounts of events in the life of Jesus and the apostles. Yarbrough (Chapter 5) examines those associations—some mundane and others otherworldly, some of a place, others of an idea. Yarbrough traces the importance of Jerusalem primarily as a place, the place of Jesus' crucifixion and a place in God's history of salvation. But after the destruction of the Temple in 70 CE and of the city itself in 135 CE, Jerusalem became more of an idea than a place. During this period, the notion of Jerusalem as a heavenly symbol was fixed in early Christian life and thought. At this time, too, the claim that God would establish a heavenly Jerusalem on earth to inaugurate his rule began to spread among various groups of Christians. As a result Jerusalem came once more to be thought of as a place, and this shift coincided with the development of the city as a pilgrimage destination, following Helena's visit in the early fourth century CE, and the tremendous interest and investment in the city by the Byzantine emperors.

Islam was the last of the three monotheistic traditions to be introduced to Jerusalem. Here too the earlier two layers—Jewish and Christian—were fundamental. Mourad (Chapter 6) argues that the biblical events that unfolded in Jerusalem represent the foundation upon which the Muslims based their reverence for the city. By examining the earliest work on the merits of Jerusalem by a Muslim scholar, *Fada'il Bayt al-Maqdis* by al-Walid b. Hammad al-Ramli (d. c. 912 CE), Mourad demonstrates that early Muslims, especially in Syria, perceived the religious symbolism of Jerusalem as primarily a continuation of its biblical heritage, and secondarily as the place of Muhammad's night journey and ascension to Heaven. Whereas the first theme arises out of the shared heritage of Jerusalem among the members of the three Abrahamic religions, the second came to be added later, in order to impose an exclusively Islamic dimension on Jerusalem's holiness. Only when the second theme was well entrenched in Muslim religious discourse did Jerusalem become a specifically "Islamic" place. But this was only accomplished when Jerusalem fell under crusader rule in 1098 CE. In order to rally the Muslims to liberate the city, religious scholars and politicians promoted Jerusalem as an exclusively Islamic sacred place, at the expense of its shared heritage.

Jerusalem's sacred aura is most often expressed through conventional religious discourse and culture, and through art. But for a few of the tourists who visit Jerusalem, especially if they are seeking a supernatural experience, being in the holy city is so intoxicating that they suffer religious delusions. Jerusalem's psychiatric hospitals have treated many cases of this form of mental illness, known as the Jerusalem Syndrome. Often temporary, the syndrome has been assumed to be triggered or intensified by a visit to Jerusalem. Contrary to this understanding, however, Alexander van der Haven (Chapter 7) argues that Jerusalem Syndrome is more a religious subculture than a mental disorder, and that Jerusalem provides a rare space where "insane" and religious behaviors not only coexist, but converge. Van der Haven suggests that Jerusalem Syndrome should be seen as an eschatological subculture, consisting of foreigners who believe they are called by God to come to the city. The remarkable similarity between the typical pathological behavior and specific religious functions such as prophetic and redemptive roles and rhetoric has engendered a unique space, and an examination of the Jerusalem Syndrome shows that there are sites in Western culture where expressions of mental illness can become meaningful.

Images and representation

Given the intense emotions associated with Jerusalem as both a religious and national center, it is not surprising that the city has been imagined and represented in many different ways. The representation of Jerusalem for public consumption is neither new nor exclusively the domain of a particular group; the city has been imagined and depicted for millennia, first in mosaics and on vellum, on wall paintings and on small objects, and later in manuscripts and in print, in broadly differing contexts. In premodern times, the majority of those depictions were produced by Christians for a Christian audience, especially when Jerusalem was under Muslim rule. By depicting the glorious past of the city, Rehav Rubin suggests (Chapter 8), the authors of most of the old maps of Jerusalem provided an alternative reality to the impoverished Oriental city. Rubin examines early printed maps, from 1486 to the beginning of measurement-based mapping in 1818. He suggests that the idea of Jerusalem as an imaginary city of Holy Scriptures is expressed well in these early maps, and that specific representations are a reflection of the way Jerusalem looked to their authors. But a map is not simply a representation; it is imbued with ideology and must be read as a text replete with the ideas and values of its time (Harley 1989). A map is also a tool for propaganda (Monmonier 1996) and a weapon that can be used during political conflict. Rubin suggests that in order to understand the ideological messages of Jerusalem's maps we need to look at them as representations of the diachronic concept of time, and realize that they were created as historical encyclopedias or as representations of sacred space primarily for Christians. He also argues that early maps of Jerusalem amalgamated the sacred and the profane; beyond depicting a remote oriental city, they included feelings and beliefs. Thus they represent and express a Jerusalem of spirit as well as a Jerusalem of stone.

With the introduction of photography in the nineteenth century, the representation of Jerusalem became more realistic than ever, but the fascination of early photographers (primarily travelers to the holy land) rarely captured daily life in the city. Early photography functioned as a continuation of the interest in Jerusalem's religious archaeology; the stones of Jerusalem, standing as witnesses to the history that unfolded there, mattered more than its inhabitants. Emmie Donadio (Chapter 9) examines the work of the well-known French photographer Auguste Salzmann, whose collection of nearly 200 photographs of Jerusalem was published in 1856 in Paris under the title *Jérusalem: Etude et reproduction photographique des monuments de la Ville Sainte depuis l'époque judaïque jusq'à nos jours* (Jerusalem: Study and Photographic Reproduction of the Monuments of the Sacred City from the Jewish Period until Our Days). Donadio examines a number of Salzmann's photographs and concludes that his commitment was to the architecture of Jerusalem, and particularly to the city's religious sites. Donadio notes that in fact the first photograph in Salzmann's collection is of the oldest Jewish relic, the Wailing or Western Wall, and this helps to set the tone for the collection's focus. Salzmann's work does not capture the quotidian reality of mid-nineteenth-century Jerusalem, when the city was a lively place on the verge of modernization. Rather, his commitment was to history, religion, and stone—to archaeology. No people appear in his photographs. Salzmann's work, Donadio concludes, provides an important monument to the particular attractions of the Holy City which were, she says, "caught between the elusive past and the tumultuous present."

Jerusalem has been represented in the performing arts as well, and the number of such representations has grown since 1948. In the Arab world, the loss of the western part of the city in 1948, followed by the total loss in 1967, created a sense of nostalgia about the glory of Jerusalem. Christopher Stone (Chapter 10) analyzes the Jerusalem songs of the legendary Lebanese singer Fayruz, who is, for non-Lebanese, associated most closely with the city of Jerusalem. For years the Voice of Palestine radio, broadcasting from Egypt, opened and closed its programs with Fayruz's song "We Are Returning" (*Raji'un*), which had literally become the station's anthem. But as Stone shows, the song's lyrics have evolved dramatically over the years, reflecting the fate of Jerusalem in the eyes of the Arabs. Between 1948 and 1967 Fayruz sang about the city but never mentioned it by name, but after the 1967 war she sang about Jerusalem explicitly, as in her "O Jerusalem" (*Ya Qudsu*) and "The Flower of the Cities" (*Zahrat al-Mada'in*), for which she was awarded the key to the city.

Fayruz does not mention specific sites, but most Muslims around the world are attached to a specific site in Jerusalem, the Dome of the Rock, at the Haram al-Sharif; the Dome that was built over the *sacred stone* from which Muslims believe Muhammad ascended to Heaven. It is perhaps the most famous and easily recognized Islamic site in Jerusalem, and its representations are used by Muslims the world over to symbolize the Islamic tradition. These representations can be found in homes, coffeehouses, mosques, official offices, and even storefronts. The symbolism of the Dome has the potential to break through Muslim sectarian lines, especially Sunnis and Shi'as. Christiane J. Gruber (Chapter 11) examines a number of Iranian murals, paintings, and maquettes depicting the Dome of the Rock. Reading their placement with imbedded political slogans, she argues that such works of visual art were intended by the Islamic regime in Iran to generate a rhetorical medium for political mobilization and to fashion Iranian public opinion in favor of the Palestinian cause. Analyzing the iconography of the murals in tandem with writings on the subject by Imam Khomeini and other Iranian leaders and thinkers, Gruber further reveals a carefully crafted presentation of Islamic "unity" intended for the Iranian people as well as for Muslims worldwide, one that seeks to promote Islamic solidarity across state borders and to endorse a universal rising up against global oppression.

The political struggle over Jerusalem

As important as Jerusalem has been for the religious imagination and the artistic expressions of people of the Abrahamic religions, it has also been a real place, an earthly place, where people live their daily lives, confronting economic problems and engaging in political struggles. In the last two millennia, Jerusalem was under foreign rule until the middle of the twentieth century (and some would argue that it is still under foreign rule). The city's history was shaped primarily by both its religious attributes and foreign domination. The largest and most rapid change occurred in the late nineteenth and early twentieth centuries with the introduction of modernization and nationalism to historic Palestine and with the ensuing British Mandate. The demographic balance and amicable relationship between Jews and Arabs in Jerusalem changed dramatically as immigrant Jews settled in Jerusalem and built new neighborhoods and institutions, and as the British declared Jerusalem their capital in Palestine and became the custodian of the Christian sites in the city. This heavenly city, with its earthly struggles, became the focus of the Israeli/Jewish and Palestinian/Arab/Muslim national and religious struggles. As both sides claim the city as their national and state capital on the basis of their historical connection to it, the struggle over Jerusalem has become a microcosm of the larger Arab–Israeli conflict.

The story of modern Jerusalem is also a tale of lineage and its connection to place. It intertwines with stories of those who were born in the city, Jews and Arabs alike, and of all those who consider themselves Jerusalemites, to form a rich narrative marked by religion and intense national feelings. Personal stories often become political, and the national story becomes personal. Many see their personal history in the city as going back hundreds of years, long before national or political consciousness came about. Sari Nusseibeh, currently the president of al-Quds University and a past PLO representative in Jerusalem, is a good example of this. In a personal narrative, Nusseibeh (Chapter 12) recounts his and his family's connection to the city, which goes all the way back to Mamluk times. Because he is so intimately connected to the history of the city, he identifies first and foremost as a Jerusalemite, and this identity precedes his national identity. As a Palestinian living in Jerusalem and as a PLO official, Nusseibeh understands the Palestinian story in the city at both the personal and the national levels; thus he is in a unique position to analyze the past and the present and to offer solutions for the future. He believes that if the current stalemate between Israel and the Palestinians is ever to be fully resolved, it must include an agreement over Jerusalem. Jerusalem, he argues, holds the key to a better Middle East.

Memoirs and reflections of both locals and visitors are another important way of telling the story of the city. Jerusalem has long been one of the most often-visited cities in the world, and its story has most often been told by travelers—indeed, much of what we know, or think we know, about the city's past comes from outsiders who have visited the city. These accounts may be highly detailed, but they remain incomplete, for no visitor, especially one who does not know the language or understand the culture, can fully capture the vitality of a place, and outsiders often witness only a brief moment in the city's life. Issam Nassar (Chapter 13) shows the importance of using local accounts to provide a different picture of Jerusalem. He argues that many travelers' journals, for example, painted Jerusalem in the pre-modern period as not much more than a small service town with a sterile culture. By examining memoirs and photographs by Arab Jerusalemites in the nineteenth century, Nassar argues, we can recover a Jerusalem that was far richer than outsiders could see. The Jerusalem of the locals was a thriving town, a prosperous province, open and welcoming to all, where local culture throve in a variety of venues that travelers rarely visited. It is the local touch, local understanding, and living the everyday experiences of Jerusalemites in the city that yields the richest picture.

By the turn of the twentieth century Jerusalem was on the verge of modernization, a process which began in earnest in the early 1900s and was the result of two forces, both of European origin. The first was associated with the Jewish immigrants who came to Palestine motivated by their national ideology, Zionism, and the second was associated with British Mandatory rule over Palestine, which followed their conquest of the city in 1917. Over the course of the twentieth century Jerusalem developed from a small town with a clear Arab majority to a city of hundreds of thousands with a clear Jewish majority, and it increased in area from a few square kilometers to well over a hundred square kilometers.

The history of Jerusalem in the twentieth century can be divided roughly into four periods: the last years of the Ottoman Empire in the city, until the First World War; the British Mandate period, from 1917 to 1948; the divided city period, from 1948 to 1967, when the newly established state of Israel controlled the western part of the city and the Hashemite Kingdom of Jordan controlled the eastern part; and the current "united" *coty perdion*, which began immediately following the 1967 war when Israel annexed East Jerusalem, expanded the size of municipal Jerusalem, and quadrupled the number of inhabitants in the city.

The remaining chapters in this book discuss the political struggle over Jerusalem during these periods. Tamar Mayer examines (Chapter 14) the changing importance of Jerusalem in Zionist ideology during the twentieth century; Kimberly Katz (Chapter 15) discusses what happened to Jerusalem, that is East Jerusalem, under Jordanian rule, and Elie Rekhess (Chapter 16) shows what happened to the Palestinian leadership in the city after 1967.

Ian S. Lustick (Chapter 17) and Gilead Sher (Chapter 18) provide analysis and insights into the negotiations over Jerusalem.

As we have seen, much of the struggle over Jerusalem originates in national and religious interests in the city and in historical claims made by both Jews and Arabs. Despite the millennia-old Jewish yearning for Jerusalem, Jewish national sentiments about the city are fairly new. Mayer (Chapter 14) shows that for the first few decades of the twentieth century the Zionist leadership was not terribly interested in Jerusalem, in large part because the city was associated with the Old World, against which the Zionist movement was created. Zionism, as a modern and modernizing movement, was much more interested in establishing productive agricultural communities and new towns as a way to reclaim and rebuild the homeland than in dealing with the existing Jewish community in Jerusalem, which was non-productive and extremely religious, and which rejected the Zionist project altogether. Mayer argues that Zionist interests in Jerusalem were often a response to the interests of others in the city and that on several occasions the Zionist leadership, which never really cared about the Jewish religious sites in the city, was willing to let go of Jerusalem if it meant that a sovereign Jewish state was to be gained. In other words, Jerusalem seems to have been the price Zionist leaders were willing to pay for achieving Zionist goals. Zionist attitudes toward Jerusalem changed after 1967, however, and more precisely after 1977, and this, Mayer argues, follows changes in Jewish nationalism. Nationalism shifted to the right and began to include religious voices and, at the same time, the Settlers Movement gained political and social strength. Both of these factors have made Jerusalem perhaps the most important symbol for Jews in Israel. But it is not Jerusalem per se that is the symbol; it is not the Zionist accomplishments in the city, such as the Hebrew University, the Israel Museum, or the national memorial sites, but rather the Western Wall, which had long been associated with religion rather than with nationalism. At the end of the twentieth century, Mayer shows, the Wall is no longer simply a religious site; it has been imbued with national meaning. It thus serves as a mirror of the changing character of Jewish Israeli nationalism.

The end of the British Mandate over Palestine was followed by UN Resolution 181, which called for the partition of Palestine into two states and for international governance over Jerusalem. Neither the Jews nor the Arabs favored internationalization of the city, and each sought to prevent it. The result of the 1948 war was that both the newly established state of Israel and the Hashemite Kingdom of Jordan controlled the western and the eastern parts of the city, respectively. In her analysis of Jordanian Jerusalem, Kimberly Katz (Chapter 15) asserts that Jordan's interests, and specifically King Abdullah's interests in East Jerusalem, followed Israel's interests in West Jerusalem, and that when Israel declared West Jerusalem its capital, Jordan quickly sought to elevate the administrative status of East Jerusalem to match that of Amman but fell short of declaring it a second capital. In addition, despite international protest, Jordan appoi the custodian of the holy sites in the city.

Katz suggests that the debates about whether or not to make ᴸast Jerusalem the capital of Jordan have produced both internal and international problems for Jordan. It brought to the surface conflicts between Palestinians and Jordanians, between West Bankers and East Bankers. It also produced tension between Jordan and the Arab world, specifically Nasserist Egypt, which was against a unilateral Jordanian move to make Jerusalem Jordan's capital. These tensions threatened King Hussein's authority, and in the end the declarations of Jerusalem as the capital did not amount to much more than a rhetorical exercise. Nevertheless, the Jordanian king referred to the city in his speeches as the "spiritual capital" of Jordan. This move, Katz suggests, indeed re-affirmed King Hussein's authority both in the Arab world and in Jordan at a time of political difficulty.

Soon after 1948, when the debates about the future of East Jerusalem were under way and Arab nationalism was becoming an important force in the Middle East, the voices of the Arabs of Palestine, and more specifically the Arabs of East Jerusalem, some of whom were of very prominent families, were suspiciously absent. Elie Rekhess suggests (Chapter 16) that when East Jerusalem was under Jordanian rule and subsequently, after 1967, under Israeli rule, first the Jordanians and then the Israelis undermined the political power of the city's Palestinian leadership. After 1967, Israel weakened the Palestinian leadership by deporting leaders of Palestinian organizations in East Jerusalem, who resisted Israel's occupation of their city. As the Palestinian leadership in the West Bank and Jerusalem began to change in the 1970s and to become more pro-PLO, their activities became more and more anti-Israel, and Israel responded by exiling them. In turn, the Palestinians created new venues for their anti-occupation activities. The vacuum in Palestinian leadership was finally filled by the PLO, especially after the Oslo Accords were signed in 1993 and the subsequent creation of the Palestinian Authority (PA). Rekhess shows that it was not until the 1990s that the PLO established a strong leadership in Jerusalem, which controlled key Palestinian institutions in education and health, as well as centers of power such as the Orient House, and demanded a voice in the discussion of the future of *their* Jerusalem.

At the same time, post-1967 Israel had its own plans for the future of the "united" city. Ian S. Lustick contends (Chapter 17) that since 1967 Israel has consistently been consumed by the idea of Jerusalem, and that it enacted several laws that would enable the annexation of Yerushalayim and al-Quds—that is, Jewish Jerusalem and Arab Jerusalem—into one city. But he shows why, despite all attempts to fully annex the Arab sections of Jerusalem, the city remains divided, and he suggests that the Aqsa *Intifada* and the concrete barrier wall that Israel has erected around Jerusalem to exclude Arab villages have effectively separated the populations and riven the physical geography of the city. In his view, the lack of agreement about the future of Yerushalayim among Israelis is also responsible for the fact that the city remains divided even today, more than forty years after its supposed unification.

It seems fairly clear that in order for Israelis and Palestinians to achieve a peaceful solution, the future of Jerusalem must be negotiated to the satisfaction of both sides. As Sari Nusseibeh argues (Chapter 12), without an adequate solution to the Jerusalem question the entire region's stability will be at risk—a point that has also been made by Palestinians of all ranks. Because the city remains less integrated than Israel might have wanted, an undoing of the "unification" might actually be easier than has been believed. It seems logical that any new political map of the city should follow the demographic map, but the difficulty of what to do about the holy sites remains the greatest obstacle. In the almost two decades of intermittent negotiations between Israelis and Palestinians, discussion about Jerusalem's future had habitually been postponed until a time when the focus could be entirely on Jerusalem. An opportunity arrived in the summer of 2000, when President Clinton summoned to Camp David both the Palestinian and the Israeli negotiation teams, headed respectively by President Yasser Arafat and Prime Minister Ehud Barak. Gilead Sher, a member of the Israeli delegation, offers his reflections (Chapter 18) on the dynamics of the Camp David meetings, within and between the groups, and the failure of the Camp David Summit to achieve a solution to the Jerusalem problem.

The stakes at Camp David were high for all three sides—the Palestinians, the Israelis, and the Americans. Each side understood that these meetings offered the last possible opportunity for an attempt to achieve stability in the region, specifically in the occupied territories. Israelis realized that it would be better to talk to moderate Palestinians now than to engage with extremists, such as Hamas,[1] later. But neither side was satisfied with the concessions made by the other, because the bottom line was that neither the Palestinians nor the Israelis could agree on who would control the Haram al-Sharif/Temple Mount. The Palestinians demanded full sovereignty over the Haram, and for that matter over the entire Old City, and Israel could not agree because of the historical and religious significance of the site. An Israeli proposal of a joint administration, subject to both a Jewish and a Palestinian municipality, Sher notes, was rejected by Arafat, and the disagreement was so deep that even President Clinton could not broker a solution. Less than three months from the time the meetings at Camp David ended in failure, the Aqsa *Intifada* broke out—almost certainly making a mutually agreeable solution for Jerusalem nothing more than a distant dream. The erection of a wall around Jerusalem separating Jews from Palestinians made unity in Jerusalem an idea rather than a reality.

If Palestinians and Israelis take Sari Nusseibeh's challenge seriously and begin to look into the future to imagine the kind of city they would like to live in, they may be able to solve the Jerusalem problem. By looking ahead to a future Jerusalem that reflects their hopes and dreams for the city, the two sides may be able to craft the blueprint for a solution. By working backwards, Nusseibeh hopes, "one can design a roadmap to achieve that dream."

The essays in this volume touch a variety of issues that relate to the perception, representation, and status of Jerusalem at the religious, social, artistic, and political levels. They examine the past and the present, and include some speculation about the future. The study of Jerusalem is, of course, vast and complex, and no doubt there are many aspects that are not covered here. The city's multifaceted character is the challenge it poses for researchers. Nonetheless, once one reads more than one religious narrative, hears more than one political opinion, and sees more than one artistic representation, it becomes obvious that Jerusalem embodies different levels of reality, or possibly different realities altogether. One can visit the real Jerusalem, walk its streets, rest in its coffeehouses, and pray in its temples. But there is also the imaginary Jerusalem that exists in the minds of believers, political strategists, and artists. Sometimes the two are juxtaposed in an ironic way, to the extent that many do not see the irrationality of adhering to opposite views of the city. But it is the work of those who accept Jerusalem as a city of multiple realities and allegiances that interests us the most, and in putting together this volume we have tried to do justice to the city's richness, both as idea and as reality.

Note

1 At that point, Hamas had neither political power nor a sizeable representation in the Palestinian Parliament.

References

Eliade, Mircea. 1987. *The Sacred and the Profane: The Nature of Religion*, trans. Willard R. Trask. New York: Harcourt.

Harley, Brian. 1989. "Maps, Knowledge, and Power." In *The Iconography of Landscape*, ed. Denis Cosgrove and Stephen Daniels, 277–312. Cambridge: Cambridge University Press.

Monmonier, Mark. 1996. *How to Lie with Maps*. 2nd ed. Chicago and London: University of Chicago Press.

2 Jerusalem
One city, one faith, one god

F. E. Peters

All cities have histories, whether in years or centuries or millennia. Wrapped around the stones and the mortar of the physical settlement, the city's history announces or boasts or reflects a past that should not or cannot be forgotten. For many cities their history is a source of pride; for some, of shame. We are dealing here with one city, Jerusalem, with a very long history, a history so detailed and so dense with memory that it often overshadows, and so obscures, the lives of the people who have lived there. The history of Jerusalem is not merely descriptive or celebratory; it is also argumentative, at times a sword and at times a shield. Nor is it a single story. This city, perhaps above all others, has multiple histories, discordant accounts of what it was and what it is and what it will be. It is easy to understand why.[1] Jerusalem has had many masters and powerful and persistent claimants. Many of them have written the city's history, and many too have used that history to explain why they are, or should be, in possession of Jerusalem.

For all its invocation, history seems, however, to be of limited effectiveness as a weapon; history wounds but only very rarely kills, and one is sorely pressed to point to an instance when contestants have yielded their claims to Jerusalem, or anyplace else, because the other side has made a better historical case—which is not to say that history is unimportant. Jerusalem is, in a sense, its history. As a city it has no future; it has only a past or, to put it somewhat differently, it is its past that has made Jerusalem important, not its future.

That future is certainly of interest, indeed, of great interest to the primary contestants for its possession, who wish to have it, of course, by reason of its past. Those contestants are, and have been since the seventh century of our era, the Jews, Christians, and Muslims and whatever political instruments they have had at their disposal to press their claims to possess the city that once each one of them had as its own.[2]

How is a city possessed? Physically, by occupation, by a Syrian garrison, a Roman legion, a Crusader army. Or politically, by coming under the sovereignty of the state, as when Judea became a Roman province in 6 CE, or the Crusader armies turned it into a Latin kingdom of Jerusalem, or a

British occupation of Jerusalem and Palestine is turned into a Mandate by the League of Nations. These are the types of possession achieved by legionaries, by mailed warriors with crosses on their tunics, and, more recently, by a concert of politicians.

But if such diagnostic terms are appropriate for describing the struggle for possession of a Berlin or Baghdad, they are not particularly so for Jerusalem. Jerusalem is not Baghdad, and its claimants, who seek possession on a far larger scale than can be achieved by armies or garrisons, are not merely states or sovereigns, but entities that we can name but scarcely describe. Shall we call them Judaism, Christianity, and Islam, or the multitude of Jews, Christians, and Muslims who now inhabit the planet? Actually, it is both. It is Judaism that provides the ideology of a Promised Land, for example, but it is Jews who settle in the West Bank in fulfillment of that promise.

It is, then, the first, the often maligned constructs called Judaism, Christianity, and Islam that are of primary concern here. What I mean by them is that combination of ideology and institution produced by the "high tradition" of lawyers, theologians, and, yes, circumstances in each of the faith communities. Islam, for example, is both the Qur'an and what those same lawyers and theologians have unpacked and assembled from the Qur'an and other canonical material and is assented to by Muslims—not always, of course, and never by everyone—over the centuries.

But it is individuals and groups of believers who convert those beliefs into action. Thus, it is both Jews and Judaism that have laid claim to Jerusalem, Christians and Christianity, Muslims and Islam. There was and is ideology behind those emblazoned crosses and Uzis, and some at least of the Palestinian nationalists have died with the cry of "Allahu Akbar" on their lips. The ideology in question is the familiar Christian and Muslim supercessionist one: God's favor, which originally rested upon the Children of Israel, was transferred; to the Christians in the first instance, and then, as the Muslims argued, to the community of the "Submitters," the Muslims.

The supercessionist argument is essentially a theological one, but, like many such, it was eventually converted into a political agenda. Once Christianity joined uncertain hands with the Roman Empire in the fourth century, and Islam created its own churchly state in the seventh, these two latter have had at least the institutions—and the weaponry—to impose their will on their antagonists: first, on the dwindling ranks of the pagans; then on those of their own ranks who did not get it right, the heretics; and finally those incorrigibles who did not get it at all, to wit, the other two members of the Monotheistic Church. The Jews, stateless, and so weaponless in the face of Christian pressures, could only pray for deliverance, which, it seems clear, despite the modern polemics about dhimmitude (Ye'or 1985), was Islam. As far as the Jews were concerned, better the crescent than the cross.

And what did that Islamic Church-State, or that Christian Church with a State, do with or about Jerusalem? Very little, actually. Jerusalem has changed hands a number of times over the course of its post-Jewish history. The Christians never took it from the Jews—the Jews had already long lost the city to Rome by the time Christianity and Rome found each other—and only on two occasions have Muslims and Christians gone to war over it: the Christians in 1099, not to dislodge the Turks or Fatimids or Ayyubids but precisely to take the city away from the infidel Muslims. The First Crusade was rather exactly a jihad, as were Salah al-Din's Jerusalem-centered efforts to take the city back from the Latin Christians in 1187 (Dajani-Shakeel 1986).

The two Crusade-jihads make an interesting contrast (Murphy 1976). A Christian crusade is formally announced by the pope—may *only* be announced by the pope—and then the secular princes and their followers are persuaded to *volunteer* for the conflict, encouraged by the proffered spiritual rewards and certain substantial financial considerations offered by the Church (Brundage 1969). A Muslim jihad, on the other hand, is also formally declared by the Imam of the community, technically the caliph, but rather than a volunteer task it is a religious *obligation*. It is not, however, a *fard ayn*, an obligation which, like prayer, for example, is incumbent upon every Muslim, but rather a *fard kifaya*, an obligation on the community as a whole, which the canon lawyers of Islam in their wisdom decided was fulfilled if one Muslim in eight or ten responded, a percentage that has never been even remotely approached in anything that history might judge as a jihad. More, while the call to Crusade issues entirely from the conscience, or the will, of the pope, the conditions that trigger and direct a jihad are elaborate enough to fill an entire law-book (Khadduri 1955; R. Peters 1996).

But to return to our two actual examples whose objectives were Jerusalem, the Crusaders' conquest and Salah al-Din's reconquest, they both achieved their objectives, though it must be said that Urban II's indulgences had far greater appeal and far more sustained staying power than anything that Salah al-Din had to offer. Christian crusades continued to be fired off randomly and opportunistically for another couple of hundred of years—though only rarely at Jerusalem (Atiya 1938)—and their residue poisoned the Mediterranean for even longer.[3] The Muslims waited another seven and a half centuries before mounting another jihad with Jerusalem as its objective. But this time the enemy was not Latin Christians but Israeli Jews.

Before and after that eleventh-century outburst of religious violence, Jerusalem changed hands the way most cities do: armies caught it up on their way to somewhere else. A number of Muslim armies took it from each other between 635 and 1099, and a couple more between 1187 and 1917, when the British arrived, who were on their way to Damascus and not, in any event, on a religious mission. In 1948 the British declared in effect that they had had enough of the Holy Land, and two other interested parties, the Israelis and the Jordanians, rushed in to claim it (Gilbert 1996, 171–245). Were either of them fighting for the city in the name of religion? It may be debated, but let us leave the debate to the debaters and return to the issue of why the question is even worth considering. Why exactly is Jerusalem such a glittering prize and how glittering is it after all?

The answer, obviously, is that Jerusalem is not just a city but a holy city, and a city holy to three faiths. And not to any three, but those aforementioned communities whose ideologies are both absolutist and supremist: we, and we alone, are God's Chosen, each asserts. And how does the holy city of Jerusalem enter into the equation? To understand that we must first address the question of what exactly is a holy city. The very notion is an odd one. Sanctity and cities do not seem to go together, and traditionally the first thing that most saints do in their quest for self-sanctification is to clear out of the city and head for remote pastures, or better, deserts.

What, then, is a holy *city*? Some cities are holy because they possess a shrine, like Lourdes or Fatima in Portugal or Karbala in Iraq. But many cities possess shrines, perhaps many shrines, without being regarded as holy. New York City, for example, which has been called many things but never holy, possesses shrines to everyone from John Lennon in Central Park to Babe Ruth in Yankee Stadium, and it changes its street names almost daily to keep up with the current saints. No, holy places do not a city holy make.

What then does? I have suggested elsewhere (F. Peters 1987, 76–77) that

> a holy city is one where the principal holy place is of such magnitude or allure that it dominates the city, changes its institutions and creates its own, and draws to the city numbers of people and types and amounts of investment that would not normally be found in an urban settlement of that size or in that place.

Like an athlete on steroids, it grows large in odd places. Holy cities double or triple their population during times of pilgrimage, a touristic windfall, no doubt, and wonderful for the economy but, somewhat like the descent of a rock concert or a political convention upon a city, it is not an unmixed blessing, particularly for the local rulers, who are, in a sense, in competition with an authority higher than themselves. Those rulers respond with their own submissive but self-serving gestures, the investment of state or private funds and resources in the subsidy of those pilgrims and, more particularly, in the architectural adornment, usually monumental and just as often signed, of the principal holy place and its secondary derivatives. Holy cities, like national capitals and Las Vegas hotels, can usually be identified by the architectural statements made in them.

This is true of every holy city, this interplay between the spiritual and the secular, the religious and the political, and it explains why there is so often contention in such cities. Indeed, were the Christians and Muslims voluntarily to withdraw from Jerusalem and all other political claims presently be surrendered to the Israelis, the city would be a no less contentious place. Secular and religious Israelis, reform and orthodox Israelis, the Ministry of

Religious Affairs and the Department of Antiquities all have enough Jewish holy place issues between them to keep them angry for generations.

But Jerusalem is not merely a contentious place, like all holy cities; it is also a *contested* city, for the rather simple reason that it has long since become the focus of interest for those three rival religious bodies joined by common origins, though separated by profoundly differing beliefs, and who have, among them, braided a thick cord of shared political experiences from Spain to the Philippines.

Religious warfare and armed contention in the name of religion we in the West once thought had been eliminated in this ecumenicizing age and in a society where "civil religion" is the politically and socially preferable form of both behavior and ideology. We are not comfortable with the religious issues that underlie these conflicts since our theories of what constitutes a *just* war accepts many legitimate reasons for the use of force, but religion is not one of them, while many people, in many places, believe that religion, the defense of God or God's people, is the *only* real reason for taking the life of another, that the only just war is a holy war (Kelsay and Johnson 1991).

Jerusalem is one of those places, and some of the Jews and some of the Muslims—though no longer, apparently, the Christians[4]—who live in and around that city unmistakably believe in the legitimacy of the use of force in the name of religion. And to return to where we began, we should not be surprised that these three contestants should be contesting for Jerusalem. The three religious communities that we call, by a kind of shorthand, Judaism, Christianity, and Islam, have been for centuries, indeed, for millennia, rival heirs for God's legacy to Abraham, that famous promise recorded in Genesis whereby God granted to Abraham and his descendants His everlasting favor. To put it as succinctly as possible: Jews, Christians, and Muslims each claim that they, and they alone, are the genuine descendants of Abraham. Jews and Christians have been in that posture since the beginning of the Christian era, and the Muslim claim that it was *they* who were the Chosen People was entered into contention some six hundred years later (F. Peters 2004).

What the three have done to each other in the furtherance of that claim is the very stuff of our history, most of it enacted, it is true, in the Middle East, where Muslims have possessed political sovereignty over the other two, and in Europe, where, until modern times, some form of the Christian Church and one or more recognizably Christian states has held sway. Our American past, on the other hand, is a modern one: we find natural the separation of church and state; we believe, by and large, and in direct opposition to the teachings of traditional Judaism, Christianity, and Islam, that religion is a private matter and that Jews, Christians, and Muslims should leave one another severely alone.

Let us leave aside their often troubled history and return to the heart of the dispute among Jews, Christians, and Muslims, the original Covenant made with Abraham. The Christians and Muslims have generally read the Covenant in a "spiritual" sense, as a promise of salvation, but the Jews insist on its original terms, as they are set out in the Bible: you and your descendants will be numerous, God is reported to have said; that is, you will survive in that dangerous world of Bronze Age nomads, and, in addition, you will possess a land, *Eretz Israel*, a land for Israel (Genesis 15:1–6, 18). At first sight this makes sense, a land for a landless people wandering along the margins of the Fertile Crescent. But we know a good deal about nomads, and their dream of felicity is *not* to become farmers; indeed they are strongly resistant to exchanging their herds, and their freedom, for a plow or a hoe. It may be, then, that the Bible's promise of a "Land for Israel" is, like much else in ancient history, and in modern history as well, a myth constructed to explain, and justify, the Israelites' actual, and still contested, possession of the Land of Canaan.[5]

Whatever the case, it is clear enough where that land lay—it is where Israel is today—though its exact extent was not: God was flexible in His Holy Land geography, and the Bible, which tended to follow His lead, even more so.[6] So is the modern historian: the Israelites got whatever territory they could manage to hold by force of arms. It expanded and shrank under different political circumstances, as it still does. But the world, alas, is composed of more than historians. There are at least two other estates at large, politicians and lawyers, and both of them are still deeply concerned with the exact borders of that "land" promised by God, the first because some of them, the religious Zionists, believe that the modern state of Israel is also a fulfillment of that promise of land; and the rabbis, because the Torah laws, chiefly the agricultural laws, can be fulfilled only within the boundaries of the biblical *Eretz Israel*. That combination of land and law has converted generations of rabbis into cartographers.

What God did not promise to Abraham, nor to anyone else, as far as we can see, was the city of Jerusalem. Later authors liked to find indirect references to Jerusalem in the Abraham story—Melchizedek is a priest of *Salem* (Genesis 14:17–20), for example, which might be Jerusalem, and Abraham goes to the "land of Moriah" to sacrifice Isaac (Genesis 22:2), which later turns out to be a hill in Jerusalem—but these are highly problematic. Jerusalem was David's idea, according to the Book of Samuel, and on the testimony of that same biblical source, he conquered it from the Jebusites (2 Samuel 5:3–8) and then simply bought its chief holy place from the Canaanite owner (2 Samuel 24:10–25).

Despite some occasional claims to the contrary, there are no Canaanites left, and certainly no Jebusites, so it may be said that the operative history of Jerusalem began about 1000 BCE, when David chose it as the capital of the Israelites, and that its career as a holy city began when David first brought into the city the portable ark-throne of the once nomadic Israelites (2 Samuel 6:1–5) which his son Solomon permanently enshrined in the grandiose temple he built atop Mount Moriah (2 Samuel 7:1–13; 1 Kings

6:1–27). This, in effect, is why Jews, Christians, and Muslims are all in Jerusalem today and are contesting this somewhat out-of-the-way place in the hills, with a rather pleasant climate and good drainage but no river, no port, and no natural resources, not even the fabled milk and honey.

But for the Jews it had something else, what we may call innate holiness. Mecca enjoys some of this aura because of its *omphalos* quality: the Ka'ba, originally built by Adam, stands on an axis beneath its heavenly prototype (Tabari 1989, 293–294). And Delphi, too, another *omphalos*, because the oracular god spoke through its cleft to the Pythia seated on the tripod above. And finally, Jerusalem, the innately holy city par excellence, holy by reason not of an epiphany like Bethel or Lourdes or Fatima, but by reason of the *continuous presence* of God, at least from the moment David brought the Ark into the city and he and Solomon provided adequate quarters for it. The land was God's own, and Jerusalem stands at the epicenter of its holiness. The rabbis' famous concentric circles proceeding inward from *Eretz Israel* to the Holy of Holies of the Jerusalem temple paint the picture in graphic fashion (*Mishna*, Kelim 1:6–9).

We are merely moving along the surface: Jerusalem is more than a city or even a national capital; it is an idea.[7] And it is safe to say that it is a biblical idea. As the Bible unfolds, it is easy to follow the progressive identification being drawn between the People of Israel, or the Land of Israel, and Jerusalem and its Temple. People, city, temple become one, linked in destiny and God's plan, and then transformed, apotheosized, into the Heavenly Jerusalem. And despite being dragged into exile by the Babylonians or pushed out of their lands by the Romans, even though both the city and the Temple were destroyed, the idea survived. Not as a vaguely conceived and fitfully remembered nostalgia but built like Jerusalem stonework into the thought and synagogue liturgy of Judaism.[8] Rabbis sitting in study halls in Galilee or Iraq two centuries and more after the actual Herodian buildings had disappeared could still cite the physical measurements of the entire complex and debate questions of priestly ritual there with as much vigor and conviction as if the Temple still stood in its glory (*Mishnah*, Middoth 1:1–5:4). As indeed it did, in a tradition more perennial than stones or mortar or golden fretting.

But if Jerusalem was and is holy to the Jews, it is equally so to those other two Children of Abraham, though in a somewhat different sense. Jerusalem is holy for the Muslims and Christians because the city embraces a number of sites of importance in salvation history. But none necessarily so. Muhammad alighted in Jerusalem because it was already holy to the Jews, and Jesus could equally well have been crucified and buried in Caesarea. The presence of the Jesus and Muhammad sites in Jerusalem thus puts a Christian and Muslim overlay on a place that was already holy to the Jews, and that is the real point. To illustrate graphically: in post-Crusade days, when Christian pilgrimage to Jerusalem became exceedingly problematic for the Christian, the Church simply shifted the template of sanctity off the Jerusalem

Jesus sites, together with all the spiritual rewards of visiting them, and put them down on a series of Roman churches, and eventually up and down the aisles of the most modest parish church in Christendom, where anyone could walk in Jesus' steps, with the attendant blessings, through the "Stations of the Cross" (Kubler 1990; Prior 1994; Vogel 1996).

It was Constantine who converted pious recollection in Palestine into a defined Christian landscape, into a Christian Holy Land. Not in any transcendental sense, surely; nor even in a ritual or legal sense, as the contemporary rabbis understood it. But as a *network of enshrined holy places*, with Jerusalem's holy places at its center since there the drama of redemption had come to its conclusion. And it was done, it should be noted, not to counter Jewish claims to that land or that city, claims that would have appeared ludicrous at that moment in history, but to effect the extirpation of paganism (Wilken 1992).

In the mid-seventh century the Muslims took Jerusalem, together with much else around the southern and eastern Mediterranean, Jerusalem almost effortlessly and certainly without bloodshed.[9] They left the Christians there pretty much as they were, but the new Muslim masters of the city seem to have struck up what appears to us as an odd symbiotic relationship with the Jews. A Jewish community was formally permitted to return to Jerusalem, which they did, and they soon moved the yeshiva that directed Jewish legal and religious affairs from Tiberias, where it had been for more than five centuries, back to Jerusalem. More, the Muslims built their first place of prayer in the city not in or by one of the Christian churches or shrines but atop the Temple Mount, a place ignored and neglected by the Christians but obviously still important to the Jews. Indeed, the Jews may have been permitted to pray once again on the Temple Mount.

Within a generation the Muslims had greatly enhanced their first rude mosque and constructed atop that same Herodian platform a magnificent domed shrine over the rock that was said to have been the foundation stone of the Temple. This "Noble Sanctuary" or *Haram al-Sharif* as the Muslims call it, the Herodian platform with the Dome of the Rock and the Aqsa mosque placed atop it, not only dominates the cityscape of Jerusalem to this day; it is probably the single most impressive architectural expression of Islamic sanctity.

Why did the Muslims choose that place? If we are willing to jump forward from the seventh to perhaps the eighth or ninth century, there are answers in abundance, since by then the traditions on the subject were well established. The Jerusalem Haram, it was said, was holy for two reasons. First, there were its biblical associations which, by reason of the Qur'an's certifying them as God's true revelation, became Muslim sacred associations as well. But if the Haram is biblical and so Muslim, it is also "Muhammadan," connected with the life of the Prophet. "By night," Sura 17 of the Qur'an begins, "God carried His servant from the holy sanctuary [of

Mecca] to the 'distant place of worship,'" the latter in Arabic *al-masjid al-aqsa*. The Qur'an says no more about this "Night Journey" or the location of "the distant shrine," but the Muslim tradition identified it with Jerusalem and, more precisely, with the top of the Temple Mount. And it was from this same spot, the tradition continues, that the Prophet was straightway taken up to the highest heaven and granted a supernal vision (Busse 1991).

Both the biblical and the "Muhammadan" associations are sorted out around various places atop the Herodian platform, chiefly clustered about the Dome of the Rock, and the mosque built there by Umar's command in 638 and rebuilt more splendidly later in that same century is called "al-Aqsa," with direct reference to Qur'an 17:1.[10] Jesus traditions too were connected with the Temple Mount, an association that the Christians themselves never chose to make, even though the Gospels put Jesus in Herod's still unfinished Temple on more than one occasion. And finally and predictably, since such motifs collect about every holy place, the cosmological themes appear: the rock beneath the dome is not merely the foundation stone of the Temple; it marks the very navel of the earth.

There is no need to rehearse the First or Jerusalem Crusade, or better, "the Pilgrimage," as those who were participants called it (Phillips 1997; Riley-Smith 1997). The Western knights, most of them French, took Jerusalem in 1099, slew the Muslim survivors down to the women and children—the fate of the Jewish community is less clear; some were doubtless killed but many others were ransomed by their coreligionists in Egypt—and so found themselves in possession of a city that was filled with holy places but had no other inhabitants but themselves. This extraordinary interlude in the history of Jerusalem lasted less than a century, from 1099 to 1187, when the Crusaders were driven out by the armies of Salah al-Din. But for all its brevity it left a broad vapor trail of expectation across Europe where the hope of another crusade ignited new Christian holy wars from Lisbon to Damietta and led to the massacre of Jews in the Rhineland and the slaughter of Greek Christians in Constantinople. The Crusade *sillage* was no less poisonous in the Middle East, where its hostile odor lingers on to this day.

In early modern times the real contest in Jerusalem, beginning with the Crusades, perhaps, but certainly in full vigor when the Ottomans gained sovereignty over the city in 1517 (Ben-Arieh 1994, 104–125; Asali 1990, 200–227), was that among Christians; and to be precise, between the Latin Christians—generally the Franciscans who enjoyed a kind of papally certified monopoly on the Latin side—and the Orthodox Greeks, suffragans of the Patriarch of Constantinople, and each schismatics or worse in the eyes of the other. The turning point here was the fall of Constantinople to the Turks in 1453, which effectively made the patriarch and all his ecclesiastical dependencies subject to the Ottoman Sultan. What it meant with respect to Jerusalem was that the patriarchs of Constantinople now had direct access to the Muslim sovereigns of Jerusalem and so could apply whatever means were at their disposal to check the Franciscans, who were themselves acknowledged agents of European powers.[11]

The two parties' field of combat were the churches of Jerusalem and particularly and preeminently the Church of the Holy Sepulcher (Couasnon 1974). The present-day visitor to that church is generally oblivious of the invisible territorial lines that cross and recross that small enclosed space and separate not only Greeks and Latins but also a great number of other Eastern Christian groups with claim to that holy ground. They have all at last come to rest, stabilized in the famous *status quo* established by a decree of the Sultan in 1852—each sectarian group was to remain frozen in place until a final determination was made (Zander 1971, 53–54),[12] which it never was—but not before they had become a cause célèbre of eighteenth- and nineteenth-century European diplomacy with the Sublime Porte and the predictable subject of a tortuous clause in every pan-European treaty negotiated in that era (Heacock 1995).

Since the Ottoman collapse and surrender in 1917, Jerusalem has had three different masters, the British, the Hashemite Kingdom of Jordan, and the State of Israel. With sovereignty comes, of course, the question of the holy places and, more intriguingly and dangerously, the possibility of altering the state of that question. All three powers were in agreement on one point at least: each in effect reaffirmed the Ottoman *status quo* concerning the Christian holy places, an act of such rare unanimity as to suggest that the question may at last be dead, or at least moot (Eordegian 2003).

In June of 1967, the Israel Knesset passed a "Law for the Protection of the Holy Places," and though its implementation was not, and still is not, spelled out in detail, it guaranteed in principle freedom of access to all the holy places in Jerusalem (Zander 1971; Benvenisti 1976). Access means many things, of course: access to those to whom the place is holy to perform liturgical services there; access to all visitors, since most if not all of the places in question are by now historical sites; and—a very modern preoccupation—access to scholars, including archaeologists, who wish to study those holy places primarily as historical sites. At present there seems to be no question that the appropriate liturgy may be celebrated at each of Jerusalem's shrines and holy places, and though a minority of Israelis might still hold that Jewish prayer *atop* the Temple Mount is just such an appropriate liturgy, their government has ruled firmly otherwise (Benvenisti 1976, 227–304). Equally apparent is that most of the same places are open and available to visitors at regularly posted times. With regard to the third point, the Franciscans, Greeks, and Armenians can likely dig to their hearts' content on their own property, as has been done in the Holy Sepulcher since the early 1960s. But the right of an Israeli archaeologist, for example, to investigate the Haram or even a Jewish holy place is fiercely contested, on the first terrain by the Muslim authorities, and on the second by Israel's own Ministry of Religious Affairs. As no one in Jerusalem has forgotten, the nineteenth century invented appropriation by archaeology (Silberman

1982; Shepherd 1987), the twentieth its counterpart, alleged profanation by archaeology.

It is difficult to discern how precisely we should parse "holiness" in our highly secular and secularized age. Jews and Christians in particular, from their long sojourn in the post-Reform and post-Enlightenment West, have become profoundly de-numenized. While they can still recognize personal holiness in the occasional Brooklyn *tzaddik* or a Mother Teresa, they have grown careless or indifferent to the holiness of places in a way that Muslims have not. Pilgrims have now become, in that long arc from Felix Fabri to Mark Twain, whether consciously or not, tourists; we now want toilet facilities among our indulgences.

Muslims waste little time on the city history of Mecca, which is quite as unlovely as Jerusalem's own.[13] Mecca is still tightly, even rigidly, wrapped in a ritual, the *hajj*, which has in a sense *sealed in* the holiness of the city (F. Peters 1994a). No one has to explain the holiness of Mecca to a *hajji* who is in it. We, on the other hand, are almost all of us historians of one sort or another, and we can all recite one or more chapters in the *history* of Jerusalem's holiness; indeed, we are constrained to do so since we are all sore pressed to describe or explain the numinous present of the city save in the unlovely terms of ownership, or the Realpolitik of sovereignty, or that mantra of the early twenty-first century, *access.* Jerusalem is still an idea, but increasingly, and overwhelmingly, it is a *political* idea. What was once the heavenly Jerusalem has fallen heavily back to earth.

Notes

1 Some notion of the diversity may be gathered from the historical essays collected in Asali 1990.
2 The landscape of attachments and claims, Jewish, Christian, and Muslim, are graphically displayed in the various essays collected in Rosovosky 1996.
3 Remarkably illustrated in Hillenbrand 1999.
4 Roman Catholics, who constitute the one Christian Church with what passes as a Department of State and a foreign policy, were once deeply involved in the question of who possessed Jerusalem, but the Israelis have consistently, and apparently successfully, discouraged the Vatican's interest (Irani 1986; Minerbi 1990).
5 This, and even more radical proposals, are the matter of Dever 2004.
6 Compare Davies 1982.
7 The *idea* of Jerusalem is certainly present by the time of Ezekiel (8 ff.) and in the earliest (Galatians 4:25–26) and the latest (Revelation 21:9–27) works in the New Testament. It is not transparently in the Qur'an; in Islam the *idea* of Jerusalem must await the exegetes' unpacking of the phrase "the distant shrine" in Qur'an 17:1.
8 Texts in F. Peters 1985, 121–122.
9 The legend-laden account is analyzed by Busse 1984.
10 On the Muslim holy places atop the Jerusalem Haram and the liturgy that developed there, see Elad 1995.
11 On the Franciscans in Jerusalem, see F. Peters 1985, 421–425, 459–462, 498–508, 556–581.
12 Text in F. Peters 1985, 178–180. The precise *status quo ante* in question was that of an Ottoman decree of 1757.

13 It does, of course, exist, though after the Prophet it is chiefly political (F. Peters 1994b).

References

Asali, K. J., ed. 1990. *Jerusalem in History.* New York: Olive Branch Press.

Atiya, A. S. 1938. *The Crusade in the Later Middle Ages.* London: Methuen.

Ben-Arieh, Yehoshua. 1994. *Jerusalem in the Nineteenth Century: The Old City.* New York: St. Martin's Press.

Benvenisti, Meron. 1976. *Jerusalem: The Torn City.* Minneapolis: University of Minnesota Press.

Brundage, J. A. 1969. *Medieval Canon Law and the Crusader.* Madison: University of Wisconsin Press.

Busse, Heribert. 1984. " 'Umar ibn al-Khattab in Jerusalem." *Jerusalem Studies in Arabic and Islam* 5: 73–120.

——. 1991. "Jerusalem in the Story of Muhammad's Night Journey and Ascension." *Jerusalem Studies in Arabic and Islam* 14: 1–40.

Couasnon, Charles. 1974. *The Church of the Holy Sepulcher in Jerusalem.* London: Oxford University Press.

Dajani-Shakeel, Hadia. 1986. "Al-Quds: Jerusalem in the Consciousness of the Counter-Crusade." In *The Meeting of Two Worlds: Cultural Exchange between East and West during the Period of the Crusades,* ed. Vladimir P. Goss, 201–222. Kalamazoo: Western Michigan University Press.

Davies, W. D. 1982. *The Territorial Dimension of Judaism.* Berkeley and Los Angeles: University of California Press.

Dever, William G. 2004. *Who Were the Early Israelites?* Grand Rapids: Eerdmans.

Elad, Amikam. 1995. *Medieval Jerusalem and Islamic Worship: Holy Places, Ceremonies and Pilgrimages.* Leiden: E. J. Brill.

Eordegian, Marlen. 2003. "British and Israeli Maintenance of the Status Quo in the Holy Places of Christendom." *International Journal of Middle East Studies* 35: 307–328.

Gilbert, Martin. 1996. *Jerusalem in the Twentieth Century.* New York: John Wiley & Sons.

Heacock, Roger. 1995. "Jerusalem and the Holy Places in European Diplomacy." In *The Christian Heritage in the Holy Land,* ed. Anthony O'Mahony, Göran Gunner, and Kevork Hintlian, 197–210. London: Scorpion Cavendish.

Hillenbrand, Carole. 1999. *The Crusade: Islamic Perspectives.* New York: Routledge.

Irani, George E. 1986. *The Papacy and the Middle East.* Notre Dame: University of Notre Dame Press.

Kelsay, John, and James Turner Johnson, eds. 1991. *Just War and Jihad: Historical and Theoretical Perspectives on War and Peace in Western and Islamic Traditions.* New York: Greenwood Press.

Khadduri, Majid. 1955. *War and Peace in the Law of Islam.* Baltimore: Johns Hopkins University Press.

Kubler, George. 1990. "Sacred Mountains in Europe and America." In *Christianity and the Renaissance: Image and Religious Imagination in the Quattrocento,* ed. Timothy Verdon and John Henderson, 413–441. Syracuse: Syracuse University Press.

Minerbi, Sergio I. 1990. *The Vatican and Zionism: Conflict in the Holy Land, 1895–1925,* trans. Arnold Schwarz. New York: Oxford University Press.

Murphy, T. P., ed. 1976. *The Holy War.* Columbus: Ohio State University Press.

Peters, F. E. 1985. *Jerusalem: The Holy City in the Eyes of Chroniclers, Visitors, Pilgrims, and Prophets from the Days of Abraham to the Beginnings of Modern Times.* Princeton: Princeton University Press.

——. 1987. *Mecca and Jerusalem: The Typology of the Holy City in the Near East.* New York: New York University Press.

——. 1994a. *The Hajj: The Muslim Pilgrimage to Mecca and the Holy Places.* Princeton: Princeton University Press.

——.1994b. *Mecca: A Literary History of the Muslim Holy Land.* Princeton: Princeton University Press.

——. 2004. *The Children of Abraham: A New Edition.* Princeton: Princeton University Press.

Peters, Rudolph. 1996. *Jihad in Classical and Modern Islam.* Princeton: Markus Wiener.

Phillips, Jonathan, ed. 1997. *The First Crusade: Origins and Impact.* Manchester: Manchester University Press.

Prior, Michael. 1994. "Pilgrimage to the Holy Land, Yesterday and Today." In *Christians in the Holy Land*, ed. Michael Prior and William Taylor, 169–202. London: World of Islam Festival Trust.

Riley-Smith, Jonathan. 1997. *The First Crusaders: 1095–1131.* Cambridge: Cambridge University Press.

Rosovosky, Nitza, ed. 1996. *The City of the Great King: Jerusalem from David to the Present.* Cambridge: Harvard University Press.

Shepherd, Naomi. 1987. *The Zealous Intruders: The Western Rediscovery of Palestine.* San Francisco: Harper & Row.

Silberman, Neal. 1982. *Digging for God and Country: Exploration, Archaeology and the Secret Struggle for the Holy Land, 1799–1917.* New York: Alfred Knopf.

Tabari. 1989. *The History of Tabari: From the Creation of the World*, trans. Franz Rosenthal. Albany: The State University of New York Press.

Vogel, Lester I. 1996. "Staying Home for the Sights: Surrogate Destinations in America for Holy Land Travel." In *Pilgrims and Travelers to the Holy Land*, ed. Bryan F. Le Beau and Menachem Mor, 251–268. Omaha: Creighton University Press.

Wilken, Robert L. 1992. *The Land Called Holy: Palestine in Christian History and Thought.* New Haven: Yale University Press.

Ye'or, Bat. 1985. *The Dhimmi: Jews and Christians under Islam.* Montclair: Fairleigh Dickinson University Press.

Zander, Walter. 1971. *Israel and the Holy Places of Christendom.* London: Weidenfeld & Nicolson.

evaluate memory (handwritten)

3 Jerusalem in Jewish history, tradition, and memory

Lee I. Levine

Jews lost control for almost 2 millenia (handwritten)

Jerusalem has occupied a pivotal position in Jewish life and consciousness over the past three thousand years. For one millennium, the city constituted the political and religious focus for Jews,[1] in the beginning for those in the region of the tribe and kingdom of Judah and subsequently, for some 800 years, for Jews everywhere. Even after the destruction of the Second Temple in 70 CE, its memory was ever present despite the fact that the Jews would not regain control of the city for almost two millennia. Countless expressions of the intimate ties to Jerusalem maintained and strengthened their memories of and attachment to the city. Below we will examine these two distinct aspects—history and tradition—which are, in fact, different chronological stages, in order to understand how this centrality and sanctity emerged and how Jewish tradition succeeded in preserving these associations through the ages.

First Temple period

The prominence of Jerusalem in the first millennium BCE did not emerge overnight; it was the result of a long and complex process to which both internal and external developments contributed significantly. By the end of this period, in the first century CE, the city had become the hub of Jewish life, hosting every important national institution and socio-religious group. The change from a totally peripheral role to one of absolute centrality is reflected in the following two sources, themselves separated by a millennium. The first is from Genesis 14:17–20:

Research (handwritten)

> When he [Abraham] returned from defeating Chedor-laomer and the kings with him, the king of Sodom came out to meet him in the Valley of Shaveh, which is the Valley of the King. And King Melchizedek of Salem [Jerusalem] brought out bread and wine; he was a priest of God Most High. He blessed him, saying, "Blessed be Abram of God Most High, Creator of heaven and earth. And blessed be God Most High, who has delivered your foes into your hand."

Acts 2:1, and 2:5–11 have the following to say about Jerusalem in the first century CE, in the days of the nascent Jerusalem church:

Galilean's in brackets in

> The day of Pentecost had come, and they were all together in one place ... Now there were staying in Jerusalem devout Jews drawn from every nation under heaven. At this sound a crowd of them gathered, and were bewildered because each one heard his own language spoken; they were amazed and in astonishment exclaimed, "Surely these people who are speaking are all Galileans! How is it that each of us can hear them in his own native language? Parthians, Medes, Elamites, inhabitants of Mesopotamia, of Judaea and Cappadocia, of Pontus and Asia, of Phrygia and Pamphylia, of Egypt and the districts of Libya around Cyrene, visitors from Rome, both Jews and proselytes, Cretans and Arabs—all of us hear them telling in our own tongues the great things God has done."

The difference between these two texts and the reality that each reflects are striking. In the former, Jerusalem (Salem) had nothing whatsoever to do with Abraham or his family. The city was in the hands of an indigenous population whose king and high priest was Melchizedek. It is interesting to note that Melchizedek went out to greet Abraham with a gift of bread and wine; Abraham, and Isaac and Jacob after him, studiously avoided this city; their peregrinations in Canaan took them from Beersheva and Hebron to Shechem and back, but they never visited Jerusalem. The latter source is one of many indicating how pre-eminent Jerusalem had become to Jews everywhere by the first century, drawing pilgrims not only from its immediate environs or from the entire province of Judaea but from far-flung places in the Diaspora as well. The list of places in Acts is impressive, and even if not accurate historically, it nevertheless reflects many of the areas in which Jews lived as well as the extensive influx to the city on the three annual pilgrimage festivals.

Thus, from a peripheral role, at best, the city became the very warp and woof of Jewish life. How can we account for this astounding change in the Jewish connection with Jerusalem during the first millennium BCE? The first part of this essay will attempt to answer this question.

Jerusalem first entered the Jewish scene (and vice versa) in the days of David. In his quest for real and symbolic gestures that would bind the confederation of twelve tribes into a united monarchy, he established a capital that would command the allegiance of all sectors of the population. David's choice of Jerusalem after having ruled for seven years in Hebron was due to several factors, one of which was its greater geographical centrality, situated as it was between the powerful tribes of Ephraim to the north and Judah to the south. Moreover, having been a Jebusite city up until David's time, it was neutral ground and no tribe could claim preference and superiority because the capital was in its territory. By bringing the Holy Ark and the tablets of stone, the most holy objects of the Jews, into the city, David transcended strictly political considerations by according Jerusalem a more far-reaching status as the spiritual and religious capital of the people. It was this combination of the political and religious dimensions, of the worldly and otherworldly realms, that was to characterize Jerusalem for the next thousand years and beyond. Solomon's building of the Temple on the site where the Holy Ark had come to rest culminated this process.

However, David and his successors enhanced Jerusalem's credentials even further by transforming the city into the most important national and religious site for Jews. Under the patronage of these rulers, historians and poets wrote about the city in glowing terms, the former focusing on its history and traditions, the latter lavishing praise and superlatives on its bulwarks, pilgrims, the Temple, its pageantry, and more. Psalms 48, 122, 125, and 126, for example, describe the spiritual dimension of the city and its unique religious status. Traditions associating the city with Abraham (Genesis 14:18–20; 22:1–19) crystallized with the purpose of demonstrating the Jewish people's ties to the city from earliest times. So successful were these efforts that Jerusalem became known as the City of David and soon became inextricably intertwined with Israel's present and future. As a result, Mount Zion replaced Mount Sinai as the focus of Jewish attention (Japhet 1999, 3–8; Zakovitch 1999, 16–35).

Jerusalem's political and religious prominence in the First Temple period peaked in the late eighth and seventh centuries BCE. Beginning with the reign of King Hezekiah (727–698 BCE), the city's status and population increased dramatically owing in part to Assyria's destruction of the northern kingdom of Israel and its capital Samaria. Hezekiah's efforts to enlarge and fortify his capital were accompanied by attempts to achieve administrative centralization and religious reform. Jerusalem's stature was further heightened in 701 BCE by the sudden flight of the Assyrian king Sennacherib's forces besieging the city, an event that was interpreted by many as proof of God's protection of the city (Borowski 1995; Tadmor 1985; Hallo 1999). The prophet Isaiah expresses the increased pride in Jerusalem's centrality and importance at that time when he depicts the city in universalistic and quasi-messianic terms as a veritable second Mount Sinai; the Torah was now given to all the nations gathered there, and not—as before—just to the children of Israel in the desert:

> In the days to come, the Mount of the Lord's House shall stand firm above the mountains and tower above the hills; and all the nations shall gaze on it with joy. And the many peoples shall go and say: "Come, let us go up to the Mount of the Lord, to the House of the God of Jacob; that He may instruct us in His ways, and that we may walk in His Paths." For instruction shall come forth from Zion, and the word of the Lord from Jerusalem. Thus He will judge among the nations and arbitrate for the many peoples, and they shall beat their swords into plowshares and their

spears into pruning hooks: nation shall not take up sword against nation; they shall never again know war. (Isaiah 2:2–4)

The final stage in the evolution of Jerusalem's religious and political prominence during the First Temple period came in 622 BCE, with King Josiah's sweeping reforms revolving around the centralization of all cultic worship in the city. Previously, shrines and altars had existed throughout the country and sacrifices to the God of Israel could be offered anywhere. Josiah's reforms established Jerusalem as the sole legitimate site for all such cultic activity (Bright 1972, 295–300).

Second Temple period

Jerusalem's enhanced stature in the Second Temple period was the result of both internal and external developments, and its international recognition as a temple-city from the Persian era onward accorded the city a distinguished position in Jewish and non-Jewish eyes alike.[2] As the capital of an extensive kingdom under the Hasmoneans and Herod, Jerusalem became the seat of all major national institutions—political, social, and religious— as well as the home of important priestly and aristocratic families and a variety of religious sects. Extensively and lavishly reshaped during Herod's reign, the city bore an impressive physical appearance. The Temple and Temple Mount, both of which were enlarged and rebuilt, formed an especially imposing public domain. Jerusalem's renown spread throughout the Roman world as ever-increasing numbers of pilgrims visited the city. It is to these developments that we now turn.

Under Persia

The Persian, or Restoration, era witnessed the renewal of Jewish life in Judaea following a hiatus of some fifty years. The primary and almost exclusive sources for this era, the books of Ezra and Nehemiah (henceforth Ezra–Nehemiah), inform us of the return to Jerusalem of thousands of exiles from Babylonia who, despite innumerable obstacles, succeeded in rebuilding the city and its Temple. Their numbers were significant enough (and what they lacked in numbers they gained in imperial support) to initiate social, political, and religious renewal. The fact that they returned at all should not be taken for granted. In 722 BCE, the northern kingdom of Israel was destroyed and its inhabitants dispersed. Lacking a strong leadership, a well-defined communal framework, and presumably the possibility of returning to their homeland, these exiles eventually became fully assimilated into their new milieu.

Both external and internal factors favored the Restoration. One that contributed to the successful return of the Judaean exiles under Cyrus was that Jerusalem had never been resettled by the Babylonians after the conquest of

586. Thus, there was no foreign body in the city that might have obstructed their return, a situation that obviously facilitated the returnees' repossession of the city a half century later (Bickerman 1962, 3–10).

Of more consequence, however, was the dramatically innovative Persian policy that allowed, and even encouraged, subjected peoples to return to their homelands and restore their national and religious institutions. Persian authorities aided in their return—safe passage, regular communication with those remaining behind via the Persian royal road system, and the frequent appointment of Jewish leaders (such as Nehemiah) as Persian officials, or at least the lending of official support for their missions (as in the case of Ezra). The Persian government also extended financial aid for the construction of temples, helped pay the costs of sacrificial offerings, and even granted tax privileges to temple personnel. The Jews, for their part, responded to all this support by expressing confidence in the imperial government and fully cooperating with it. Their close ties with the Persian authorities had a profound impact on Jerusalem's character and destiny.

However, the role of the Persian government in the shaping of Jewish policies and directions at this time may have been even more far-reaching. Blenkinsopp has suggested that the initiative for the return stemmed from imperial circles that sought a loyal group to organize and govern the province of Yehud and chose the local (i.e., Babylonian) Jewish elite to represent them (Blenkinsopp 1991, 50–53). The result was the emergence, in the early decades of Achaemenid rule, of a semiautonomous temple-community controlled by the dominant societal stratum of Babylonian immigrants, *bnei ha-golah* of Ezra–Nehemiah.

Hasmonean Jerusalem

With the establishment of the Hasmonean regime in the mid-second century BCE, Jerusalem entered a new stage as the capital of an independent state. While the city had already enjoyed this status for some four hundred years in the First Temple period, it was reduced to a modest temple-city in the first four hundred years of the Second Temple era (c. 540–140 BCE), serving as the "capital" of a small and relatively isolated district. All this changed under the Hasmoneans; as Jerusalem became the center of a sizeable independent state, the city's dimensions and prosperity were affected as well. Replacing the district of Yehud of the Persian and early Hellenistic eras, the Hasmonean realm expanded considerably, encompassing an area roughly the size of David's and Solomon's reputed kingdoms and becoming a significant regional power by the beginning of the first century BCE. Under the Hasmoneans, Jerusalem grew fivefold—from a relatively small area in the City of David with some five thousand inhabitants to a population of twenty-five to thirty thousand inhabitants.

The important events in Jerusalem and the development of the city in this period were inextricably intertwined with the Hasmonean leadership. The cultural creativity and religious ferment that became part and parcel of Jerusalem society were in large measure a reflection of the political leadership wielded by this dynasty. The Hasmoneans were instrumental in providing the economic means for Jerusalem's growth and constituted the decisive factor in shaping the city's social, religious, and cultural agendas no less than its political and geographical ones. The dynamic growth of the city was undoubtedly a response to the traumatic events that had taken place in previous decades. Having been subjected to Greek rule for almost two centuries, with the memories of the religious persecution still fresh in their minds, the population probably felt relief and salvation on the one hand and a sense of pride and self-confidence in having achieved independence on the other. These forces released enormous energies that, in turn, fueled the city's growth and creativity. Nevertheless, without the firm and vigorous political leadership that the Hasmoneans provided and the territorial expansion resulting from their assertive foreign policy, it is doubtful whether such energies would have been fully harnessed or the means would have been found to support such a wide range of literary and institutional activity.

There can be little question, then, that with all the expansion and growth of Jerusalem, the Temple remained the central focus of the city. Before the Hasmoneans, the Temple's physical prominence was ensured by its location on the highest point of the eastern ridge, where the city was then located; but, with the expansion of Jerusalem westward, the newly enclosed area was, in fact, on much higher ground. Nevertheless, even without its topographical prominence, the Temple continued to command center stage. This prominence was further enhanced by the fact that the Hasmoneans themselves regularly officiated there and were able to mobilize the funds necessary for the ongoing maintenance, refurbishing, rebuilding, and expansion of its facilities. Moreover, the Temple was revered as Judaism's single most holy site, not only by an ever-growing population in Judaea (partly by natural increment, partly by forced conversions), as noted above, but also by the fact that it was the subject of much attention and debate among the newly established sects, each of which, in its own way, emphasized the centrality of Jerusalem's sacred site. For all their differences, no group denied the sanctity of this site, even though some might have been critical of the way the Temple was being managed.

An intriguing religious development during this period is the appearance of unprecedented purity concerns among a wide variety of Jews. Already noted in the apocryphal books of Tobit, Judith, and the Letter of Aristeas, purity issues are noted in a Seleucid edict from the beginning of the second century BCE (Josephus, *Antiquities*, 12.145–46). The most concrete expression of this emphasis is evidenced by the introduction at this time of ritual baths, or *miqva'ot*, which were to be found in domestic quarters often associated with priests and alongside agricultural installations (olive and wine presses) throughout Judaea. The large number of stone vessels used at this time by a broad segment of Jerusalem society is a further indication of this concern, as stone was reputedly impervious to defilement.

We can only speculate as to why such purity concerns became so important in this period. Perhaps it was the desire to emulate priestly purity, a response to the growing influence of the Temple and its punctilious observance of purity, the striving of increasing numbers of people to attain holiness and sanctity, or a combination thereof. This emphasis indeed took hold, and one can thus readily understand the relevance of the talmudic statement, "Purity burst forth in Israel" (B Shabbat 13a).

Another significant change during this period was in the field of art. Beginning with the Hasmonean era, and continuing for some three centuries, a dramatic shift took place in the attitude of the Jews toward figural art. In the latter half of the second century BCE, figural images all but disappear from the Jewish scene. Hasmonean coins are aniconic, as are almost all the archaeological remains from this period. The tombs and small finds from Jerusalem, along with those from Jericho and Qumran, point to an almost universal observance of this prohibition.[3]

Together with the above developments that emphasized the unique characteristics of Jerusalem, there is no question that Hasmonean society had also adopted many aspects of Hellenistic culture. Judah Maccabee had already exhibited an openness to the surrounding world. Holidays were introduced on the Greek or pagan model, and Greek-named emissaries were dispatched to Rome to conclude an alliance. Simon's official public appointment in 140 (1 Maccabees 14) was suffused with Hellenistic influences—from convening the population to approve such a decision (reminiscent of the political convocations of Greek city-states) to wearing purple and recording the decision on bronze tablets to be set up in the Temple area; the document itself reflects Hellenistic format and style. Moreover, inspired by contemporary architectural models, Simon erected a monumental tomb in his ancestral home of Modi'in, where all members of the family were interred.[4]

Hellenization becomes even more evident under the second-generation Hasmonean ruler, John Hyrcanus. The name "Hyrcanus" is the first instance of Greek nomenclature in this dynasty, and although it is not the first time such a name appears in a Jewish context, it is nevertheless a striking advance over the preceding generation of Hasmoneans, all of whom bore distinctively Jewish names. Hyrcanus was the first in his family to hire foreign troops, as was customary among Hellenistic rulers, and the first to mint coins that, inter alia, used foreign symbols. He also initiated the building of a palace complex in Jericho exhibiting Hellenistic architectural and artistic designs, including swimming pools and an impressive pavilion nearby.

Although little is known about Aristobulus's one-year reign (104–103 BCE), it is noteworthy that he bore the title of Philhellene, that is, lover of Greeks (Josephus, *Antiquities*, 13.318). Following Aristobulus, Alexander Jannaeus continued the tradition of relying on foreign mercenaries, and he further expanded the Jericho palace complex. He was the first, as noted, to use his Greek name and royal title on coins.

Besides the Hasmoneans themselves, Hellenism had a significant impact on the upper echelons of Jerusalem society as well. The Greek names borne by the various emissaries to Rome and elsewhere are clear evidence of this. The two monumental tombs from this period, Jason's to the west of the city and Bnei Hezir to its east, belonged to priestly families and were built according to standard Hellenistic models.

Hellenistic influence also permeated sectarian groups; for example, the Pharisaic adoption and adaptation of concepts such as resurrection, the Oral Law, and a framework for advanced study appear to have been borrowed from surrounding cultures. Even more poignant is the specific innovation attributed to Simeon b. Shatah in the marriage document or *ketubah*. This Pharisaic sage purportedly altered the ceremony and document so that the arrangements and obligations were between the bride and groom, and not her father, with the groom agreeing to give her his choicest property in case of divorce, without designating something specific beforehand. Such a change in practice is also attested in Egyptian marriage contracts from the fourth and third centuries BCE, and it is possible that this practice had first crystallized in Egypt and was adopted by the Jews several centuries later (Geller 1978, 227–245; Levine 1998, 116–119). Alternatively, it is possible to view this development as part of a more general Aramaic common law that prevailed throughout the Hellenistic and Roman worlds.

Herodian Jerusalem

During the 130 years of Roman rule over Jewish Jerusalem, the city's fortunes ebbed and flowed. Soon after Pompey's conquest in 63 BCE, Gabinius, the Roman governor of Syria, divided Judaea into distinct regions, stripping the city of all claims to political preeminence owing to its drastically reduced territory. Soon after, however, Jerusalem began to regain its prominent position. After a period of transition (63–37 BCE), during which the Hasmonean dynasty was effectively eliminated and the family of Antipater and his son Herod assumed full control of the city, Jerusalem entered an era of relative stability and calm (37–4 BCE).

Herod's unswerving loyalty to Rome gained him a large measure of autonomy; the Romans rarely intervened in matters concerning Herod's relations with his subjects and family or with regard to policies and programs pursued within the borders of his kingdom. Moreover, Herod's political and cultural proclivities, i.e., integration into the imperial system, contributed to some far-reaching internal changes in Judaea. Herod cultivated the country's non-Jewish population to a far greater extent than did his Hasmonean predecessors, and the adoption of Greek as well as Roman models and styles became more prevalent than ever. Moreover, Herod undertook sweeping changes in the social and organizational structure of his kingdom, much as he did in its political and cultural spheres. The ruling classes in his kingdom now came to include new elements while most of the previous leadership circle, especially the Hasmoneans and their supporters from among the Jerusalem aristocracy, was removed (if not physically eliminated) from power. Herod can be credited with a tripartite allegiance—to the Roman political structure (*pax Romana*), to Greco-Roman culture, and to the stability and prosperity of his kingdom and its capital, Jerusalem.

For Herod and other contemporary rulers, from Augustus down to the least of the client kings, building projects constituted a benchmark of their rule, enabling them to shape their respective societies and honor their gods and patrons while creating impressive monuments to perpetuate their reign (Sullivan 1990). For rulers like Herod, such building also expressed a desire to become integrated into the Roman Empire and its culture. Moreover, many of these projects had an important public relations component, as they were meant to win the hearts and trust of the people. In Herod's case, these projects should also be regarded as an attempt on his part to rehabilitate his stature in the eyes of both Jews and pagans who might have viewed his origin, Jewishness, or political leadership with disdain.

We are in a most fortunate position to determine the nature and extent of Herod's refashioning of Jerusalem's landscape. Much is known about the material culture and architectural evolution of the city from Josephus's historical works and the archaeological discoveries over the past 150 years. The two prominent buildings that stood at the highest points of the city's eastern and western ridges defined Jerusalem's skyline. The former was the greatly expanded Temple Mount, with its spacious plaza, porticoes, and monumental basilica, the latter was Herod's sumptuous palace. Both of these magnificent complexes were given special protection—the three towers on the western ridge just north of the palace, and the Antonia fortress that guarded the Temple. In addition to these structures, Herod introduced major entertainment institutions into, or just outside of, the city (theater, amphitheater, and hippodrome) and provided Jerusalem with an expanded aqueduct system as well as sophisticated sewage facilities. He may have been responsible for the Jerusalem *bouleuterion* (council building), the Xystus (a place for assembly, possibly with some sort of gymnasium facilities as well), major streets, and marketplaces. Herod erected several family tombs north and west of the city, in addition to his own grand mausoleum at Herodium, some seven miles southeast of the city. He also provided a façade for David's tomb.

The rebuilding of the Temple and Temple Mount was a project of unparalleled size and magnificence, constituting the crowning jewel of Herod's reign, certainly vis-à-vis his Jewish subjects. All sources describing this complex agree that it was most impressive; Josephus notes that he, as well as Herod earlier on, was of this opinion: "For he (Herod) believed that the accomplishment of this task would be the most notable of all the things achieved by him, as indeed it was, and would be great enough to assure his eternal remembrance" (Josephus, *Antiquities*, 15.380). Even rabbinic literature, which either ignores or disparages Herod, is most complimentary about his undertaking: "Whoever has not seen Herod's building (i.e., the Temple) has not seen a beautiful building in his life" (Babylonian Talmud: Bava Batra 4a).

Popular imagination had conjured an aura of sanctity around the construction of the Temple, conferring on it a divine hand that facilitated the project. Both rabbinic literature and Josephus cite essentially the same tradition in this regard; the former preserves the following:

> And thus we have from the days of Herod, that when they were working on construction of the Temple, rains would fall at night. On the morrow, the winds would blow and the clouds dispersed and the sun would shine and the people would proceed with their work, and they knew that they were doing God's work.
>
> (Babylonian Talmud: Ta'anit 23a)

In the same vein, Josephus writes:

> And it is said that during the time when the Temple was being built, no rain fell during the day, but only at night, so that there was no interruption of the work. And this story, which our fathers have handed down to us, is not at all incredible if, that is, one considers the other manifestations of power given by God.
>
> (Josephus, *Antiquities*, 15.425)

Such buildings throughout the Greco-Roman world were multifunctional; there must have been times when the basilica and other parts of the Temple Mount hummed with activity. One of its functions was to serve the city's political agenda. Although Jerusalem's city council (*boule*) met in its own building (*bouleuterion*) just west of the Temple Mount, meetings of smaller groups (e.g., members of a sect) and assemblies of the people at large were held in the Temple Mount's outer court. Upon returning from one of his trips abroad, Herod convened the people to report the results and announce the order of accession to the throne among his sons after his death (Josephus, *Antiquities*, 16.132–135); following the mourning ceremonies for his father in 4 BCE, Archelaus heard the greetings, acclamations, and grievances of his subjects in the Temple precincts while seated on a golden throne placed on a high platform (Josephus, *Antiquities*, 17.200–209).

Often packed with pilgrims during the festivals, this court also served as a convenient venue for the exchange of political views and the airing of declarations, criticisms, and grievances. Sometimes a particularly impassioned speech would be delivered, stirring fervor and sparking violence. Josephus describes riots that erupted among the crowds, as in 4 BCE, after the death of Herod; during the procuratorship of Cumanus; and under the last procurators. It is not surprising, then, that the Antonia fortress in the northwestern corner of the Temple Mount was designed to provide military units with direct access to its porticoes. From Herod's reign onward, soldiers were posted on the rooftops around the Temple Mount during festivals to demonstrate their presence and, it was hoped, to prevent trouble (though, in fact, these soldiers sometimes incited it).

Judicial bodies met on the Temple Mount and possibly also in the basilica hall. We read of one court of appeals that met near the steps leading to the Temple Mount from the south, and another that sat in an open area just outside the Temple courtyards. The supreme court (at times referred to as the *sanhedrin* in rabbinic literature)[5] met in the Chamber of Hewn Stone, immediately south of the Temple building itself.

One of the largest marketplaces in Jerusalem was on the Temple Mount. It focused on the needs and requirements of the Temple and most probably was located in the basilica. This activity was substantial and carefully supervised: animals had to be supplied for sacrifices and grain for meal offerings, while Jews coming from foreign lands had to convert their native money into local currency or tokens. These functions increased immeasurably during the three pilgrimage festivals, when people thronged to the city.

No less ubiquitous in these precincts was the religious activity (instructional and otherwise). It was here that the spiritual leaders of the people congregated, taught their disciples, and preached to the masses. With respect to the earlier, Hasmonean, era, Josephus mentions the presence of Judas the Essene on the Temple Mount together with "his disciples." Later, Luke speaks of teaching on the Temple Mount, and of Jesus and some of the apostles preaching there (Luke 2:46–47, 21:37; Acts 2–3). The early Christians appear to have favored Solomon's Portico to the east for their gatherings (John 10:23–30; Acts 3:11–26, 5:12–16). Rabbinic literature knows of many Pharisees who frequented the site. Rabban Gamaliel the Elder responded to the questions of Yo'ezer Ish-Habirah from the School of Shammai when standing by the Eastern Gate, and R. Yohanan ben Zakkai "taught in the shadow of the sanctuary" (Mishnah: 'Orlah 2, 12; Babylonian Talmud: Pesahim 26a). Many debates and discussions between the Pharisees and Sadducees probably took place in these areas as well.

As much as the Temple functioned as Jerusalem's urban center, it served first and foremost as a religious focal point for Jews in Judaea and the Diaspora throughout the Second Temple period. This sacred dimension is reflected in the various privileges granted to Jews by foreign rulers from Cyrus through Julius Caesar and Augustus; in fact, it was the Temple's very existence that often served as the raison d'être for privileges accorded Jews by foreign rulers, and in descriptions of the city written by non-Jews the Temple's centrality is underscored.

Recognition of the Temple's sanctity among non-Jews is only an echo of the importance it held for the Jews. By the late Second Temple period, Jerusalem's

Temple had come to symbolize the Jewish *locus sanctum* par excellence. Here was where God dwelled, this was the cosmic center of the universe (*axis mundi*), the navel (*omphalos*) of the world that both nurtured it and bound together earth and heaven as well as past, present, and future (Eliade 1961, 20–67; 1986; 1959). For Judaism, no less than other religions of antiquity, space was not a homogeneous entity. There is the sacred in the midst of the profane (i.e., the ordinary) and the former, of course, is directly related to the presence of the divine.

Jews everywhere demonstrated loyalty and support for the Temple by contributing a half shekel annually. This donation was intended to help pay for the maintenance of the Temple, the purchase of animals for the required daily offerings, the renovation of the walls and towers, the water-supply systems, and other municipal needs. Another means of identification was through pilgrimage, and Jerusalem was regularly filled with visitors during the three festivals—Passover, Shavu‘ot, and Sukkot. As "the navel of the world," one could actually sense the holy dimension of the city as tens of thousands of pilgrims, from Judaea and Galilee and from Transjordan and throughout the Diaspora, gathered there for a few days or several weeks. They played an important role in forging the city's character and economy, and thus one can appreciate Philo's enthusiasm when he wrote:

> Countless multitudes from countless cities come, some over land, others over sea, from west and east and north and south at every feast. They take the Temple for their port as a general haven and safe refuge from the bustle and great turmoil of life, and there they seek to find calm weather.
>
> (Philo, *Special Laws* 1, 69)

Jerusalem became the hub of all Jewish life on these occasions, and many languages and dialects commonly spoken by Jews at the time could be heard in its streets. Philo, however, true to form as a philosopher and religious thinker, emphasizes a somewhat different perspective. Speaking of the uniqueness of the Jews in having only one temple for their God, he says:

> But he provided that there should not be temples built either in many places or many in the same place, for he judged that since God is one, there should also be only one temple. Further, he does not consent to those who wish to perform the rites in their houses, but bids them to rise up from the ends of the earth and come to this Temple. In this way he also applies the severest test to their dispositions. For one who is not going to sacrifice in a religious spirit would never bring himself to leave his country and friends and kinsfolk and sojourn in a strange land, but clearly it must be the stronger attraction of piety which leads him to endure separation from his most familiar and dearest friends who form, as it were, a single whole with himself.
>
> (Philo, *Special Laws* 1, 67–68)

In the latter part of this quote, Philo commends the courage and commitment behind a pilgrim's decision to leave house and home and endure the trials and tribulations of a long journey as well as the inconveniences of a sojourn in a foreign land. In the first part, however, he focuses on a cardinal distinction that set pilgrimage to Jerusalem apart from similar phenomena throughout the ancient world. In general, each deity in the Roman world had many shrines, and his or her worship could take place in one of countless locales throughout the empire. Judaism, however, had but one God, and this God had but one shrine. Therefore, those wishing to visit His earthly abode and participate in public sacrificial ceremonies in His honor had to go up to Jerusalem. Josephus phrases this same idea more succinctly: "In no other city let there be either altar or temple; for God is one and the Hebrew race is one" (Josephus, *Antiquities*, 4.201). Only Jerusalem could provide the most complete worship experience to the God of Israel, and the centripetal pull of the city was a significant, perhaps the most significant, bonding factor for Jews everywhere. Much as Rome functioned as the *urbs* par excellence for the empire as a whole, so, too, did Jerusalem cement the various disparate Jewish communities of Judaea and the Diaspora.

Ironically, Jerusalem was destroyed precisely at the moment it had reached its zenith religiously and spiritually. Such a coincidence had all the makings of a Greek tragedy. According to the Greeks, only someone who had reached a high and exalted position could truly experience tragedy; the greater the fall, the greater the magnitude of the tragedy. First-century Jerusalem was at the height of its influence and prestige, and it was at this point that the city was enveloped in turmoil, gradually descending into anarchy. The internal crisis was compounded by a series of confrontations with the Roman authorities and the neighboring pagan population, which resulted in a direct armed conflict with the greatest military power of the time.

In concluding the first edition of his *Jewish War*, to which a seventh book was later added, Josephus raises a profound issue in the face of the painful historical reality of Jerusalem in ruins. His rumination is laden, inter alia, with far-reaching theological and social implications:

> How is it that neither its antiquity, nor its ample wealth, nor its people spread over the whole habitable world, nor yet the great glory of its religious rites, could aught avail to avert its ruin? Thus ended the siege of Jerusalem.
>
> (Josephus, *Jewish War*, 6.442)

The post-70 era: the formation of traditions

With the destruction of the city and its Temple in 70 CE, the Jews lost control of Jerusalem for close to 1,900 years. Their presence in the city throughout these several millennia was negligible, at best, as Jerusalem—beginning in 135—became a pagan, Christian, Muslim, Crusader, Mamluk, Turkish, and finally, in the early twentieth century, British city (Peters 1985). Whatever Jewish community was to be found there was at the mercy of the prevailing authorities; in a profound though ironic way, the Jews of Jerusalem also lived in *galut* (lit., exile). As for the overwhelming majority of Jews, their everyday focus as a people and religion was elsewhere, as the center of Jewish life relocated many times, at first to Galilee and then to different parts of the Diaspora—from Babylonia to Spain and northern Europe, to eastern Europe, and in modern times to western Europe and America. Despite these peregrinations and migrations and the absence of direct contact with Jerusalem, the Jews never lost touch with their memories of the city nor with the longing to return one day and restore their national and religious presence. Retaining this hope was facilitated by the creation of an extensive network of symbols and customs, reinforced through literature, song, prayer, and art. Not only did these "triggers" span the entire life cycle from birth to death, but they surfaced regularly in the annual cycle of Sabbaths, holidays, and days of commemoration.[6]

The synagogue, an institution that assumed a more central position in the religious realm in the centuries following 70 CE, played a major role in preserving these memories. Three major components stand out in its liturgy: prayer, Torah reading, and *piyyut* (religious poetry).

Prayer

Although the major prayers crystallized by the end of antiquity, many others were added in the course of the next thousand years, and some continue to be added on special occasions up to our own day. Below I discuss two of the most salient examples of the centrality of Jerusalem and hopes for its rebuilding that find expression in several of the most important prayers in Jewish liturgy.[7]

The *'Amidah* (lit., Standing [Prayer]), or *Shemoneh Esrei* (lit., Eighteen [Benedictions]), is the basic prayer in Jewish liturgy recited three times a day in every service, and even more on Sabbaths and holidays. The longest of its three weekday sections (the other two being a standard introduction and conclusion) includes thirteen paragraphs divided into two parts. The first contains prayers of a personal nature wherein one asks for wisdom, forgiveness, the removal of distress, health, and prosperity. The next six blessings focus on the Jewish people and its restoration in the Land of Israel. Among the subjects mentioned here are the ingathering of the exiles, the establishment of national institutions, the removal of groups that threaten national unity, the welfare of scholars, the rebuilding of Jerusalem, and the restoration of the Davidic dynasty. Thus, three times a day (almost one thousand times a year) these hopes are rehearsed through recitation of the *'Amidah*.

In the sixteenth and seventeenth centuries, the mystics of Safed in Galilee created a wide-ranging literature that included an entire prayer service for the onset of the Sabbath, known today as *Qabbalat Shabbat* (Greeting of the Sabbath). The central prayer is *Lekha Dodi* (Come, my beloved [to greet the Sabbath Bride]). It is composed of nine stanzas, the first and last two of which are devoted to the Sabbath and its quasi-messianic repose. However, the middle five stanzas address Jerusalem, its destruction and ignominy, and the fervent hope for its restoration in the near future.

Torah reading

A central feature in the public prayer service is the reading of Scriptures, which emphasizes primarily the Torah, or Pentateuch, but regularly includes selections from the Prophets as well. Although Jerusalem is never mentioned by name in the Torah, much of the text is geared toward settlement in the Land of Israel. This is the backdrop of the Genesis stories, the goal of the Exodus and desert narrative, the core assumption underlying many of the laws recorded in the books of Exodus and Leviticus, and, of course, foremost in Deuteronomy. The prophetic readings (*haftarot*), on the other hand, often emphasize Jerusalem, either in describing the sins of the people or in the hopes of its rebuilding. For example, for ten consecutive weeks, from before the fast day of the Ninth of Av (see below) until the High Holidays, the subject of Jerusalem's future role in Jewish history is highlighted. In fact, on all holidays a special section is read describing the sacrifices that were once offered in the Temple on that particular occasion.

Piyyut (religious poetry)

In late antiquity (sometime during the fourth or fifth centuries), a new genre appeared in Jewish liturgy, the *piyyut*, and thousands of such poems were composed in the centuries following its appearance. *Piyyutim* might have been written for weekdays, but most were geared for Sabbaths and holidays; the High Holidays (Rosh Ha-Shanah and Yom Kippur) were particularly propitious for such compositions. While the subjects of these poems are varied, a prominent theme is messianism. The destruction of the Temple and other calamities that befell the Jewish people often provide a background for poetic renditions of the hopes and aspirations of returning to and rebuilding the Temple and Jerusalem. Two of the most famous *piyyutim* are recited on Yom Kippur, generally regarded as the holiest day of the year. One describes the martyrdom of ten sages (*Eleh Ezkarah*) and the other, the *'Avodah* (i.e., the Temple service), is a poetic rendition of the ritual of the High Priest in the Temple on that day, when he prayed for forgiveness on behalf of the Jewish people. It should be noted that *piyyutim* play a role in home ceremonies as well, the most prominent among which appears in the Haggadah used during the Passover seder.

The custom of mourning the destruction of Jerusalem and its Temple and praying for their restoration recurs throughout the Jewish calendar, and while many of these moments are celebrated in the synagogue, they also find expression in other settings. A series of fast days commemorates the destruction (or impending destruction) of the Temple, and besides the fast itself special prayers, *piyyutim*, and Scriptural readings are invoked to underscore the significance of this ritual. Before the most important of these fasts, the Ninth of Av, there is a three-week period wherein special prophetic readings are recited in the synagogue; weddings are forbidden, as are hair-cuts and other amenities[8] such as the abstention of some Jews from eating meat on the first eight days of Av.

There are also several times during the year when the hope of returning to Jerusalem is publicly pronounced with the words *L'shanah haba'ah b'Yerushalayim* (Next Year in Jerusalem). On one occasion, this declaration concludes the Passover seder, and on another it is recited by the entire congregation at the conclusion of the Yom Kippur fast.

The home provides another setting for the remembrance of Jerusalem and the Temple on a regular basis, and that is the Grace after Meals. This prayer consists of four basic blessings relating to the following themes: thanksgiving for food; gratitude for the Land of Israel that produced it, along with the Covenant, the Torah, and its commandments; hopes for the rebuilding of Jerusalem; and, finally, thanks for all God's goodness. Thus, two of the four sections, and especially the third, focus on memories of the past and specifically of Jerusalem.

Another important area of Jewish life in which Jerusalem figures promi-nently is that of the life-cycle events that punctuate the lives of individuals and families. I will address two of the most central ones—the wedding ceremony and the funeral.

Weddings

Although the wedding ceremony itself is rather brief, several customs relat-ing to Jerusalem are quite central, particularly toward its conclusion. The seven benedictions recited in honor of the bride and groom begin with the universal themes of God the Creator and prayers for the happiness of the newlyweds; this, is then expanded to include the ingathering of the exiles, alluding to the joy thereby bestowed on the bereft mother, Zion. The long-est and concluding benediction associates the joy of the newly married couple with the concomitant atmosphere of celebration that now permeates the cities of Judah and the streets of Jerusalem.

The official ceremony ends with the breaking of a glass in memory of the destruction of Jerusalem, reminding all present that even in times of great happiness, the sorrows and misfortunes of the past should not be forgotten. This custom is often accompanied with the recitation (sometimes sung) of Psalm 137:5–6:

If I forget you, O Jerusalem,
Let my right hand wither;
Let my tongue cleave to my palate
If I cease to think of you,
If I do not keep Jerusalem in memory
Even at my happiest hour.

The customs noted above are universally practiced by Jews. This, however, does not preclude individual communities from embellishing them. A late medieval European custom had brides wearing an additional large, ornate ring that represented the Temple, or grooms placing ashes on their heads in memory of Jerusalem. One Hasidic custom (followed by some even today) includes the following in the wedding announcement: "The wedding shall take place, God willing, in the Holy City of Jerusalem. But if, Heaven forbid, because of our sins, the Messiah will not have come by then, the wedding shall take place in Berdichev" (Charif and Raz, 1977, 70).

Funerals

Funerary customs as well have incorporated statements to remind the Jews of Jerusalem. The most prominent is the words of comfort given mourners, both at the cemetery and when visiting their home: "May God comfort you among the mourners of Zion and Jerusalem." This sentence is also recited by the entire congregation when a mourner first enters in the synagogue for the Friday evening service. In addition, there is the custom of burying people with their feet in the direction of Jerusalem, so that when the Messiah comes and the ingathering begins, the deceased will rise and be able to commence their journey to the Holy City immediately. A story is told about a small, pious elderly woman who was to be buried in Bnei Brak (just east of Tel Aviv); her request was that her grave be placed a bit before the others, as she was small and needed more time than others to get to Jerusalem! While the account itself may well be apocryphal, it nevertheless reflects the reality among many Jews of the desire to return to Jerusalem at the first opportunity.[9]

The above instances are only a sampling of the rich and varied ways that Jews tried to preserve the memory of Jerusalem and its Temple while also giving expression to their hopes for their rebuilding. Not only are the categories discussed above only partial treatments, the evidence being far more extensive than what can be included in an article such as this, but there are also many other types of expressions that have not been studied adequately. Responsa literature—discussions of particular aspects of Jewish law in response to specific queries—deal at length with questions related to our topic, and many other literary genres (e.g., poems, lamentations, eulogies, sermons, etc.) also address it. Moreover, we have entirely ignored other phenomena that revolve around specific events and actions taken by groups of Jews throughout the ages. Messianic movements surfaced from time to time, each having a component that included the return to Jerusalem. The most famous of these is, of course, the seventeenth-century phenomenon of Shabbetai Zevi, when countless Jews all over the world were ready to pack their bags (and some, in fact, actually did) to return to Jerusalem and the Holy Land. In addition to these more or less major upheavals, there are innumerable instances of Jews, either individually or in groups, who picked up and returned to the Land of Israel. The famous Spanish poet Judah Ha-Levi, Maimonides, and Nahmanides all did so, as did a group of some 300 German rabbis in the early thirteenth century.

In more recent times, this hope was given expression in song, plays, belles lettres, and essays by Jews in many lands. Despite the new vistas and opportunities opened by the Emancipation and Enlightenment, and the acceptance of Jews as citizens in democratic countries, many never relinquished the hope of return. Such expressions are myriad but perhaps none so poignant as that of A. J. Heschel, who gave expression not only to the longing of Jews for Jerusalem but also to Jerusalem's need for the Jews (Heschel 1967). Behind such sentiments is an awareness that other religions also lay claim to the city as a spiritual center. Nevertheless, there remains a difference between the Jews on the one hand, and Christians and Muslims on the other. While the latter two religions regard Jerusalem as holy, each has other holy sites that are of no less significance for all or most of their followers, Rome for the Christians and Mecca and Medina for the Muslims. But for the Jews, there is no other city. Their allegiance, past and future, is to this one place and no other. It is an exclusive relationship—with all that entails—not only from the Jews' perspective but, as Heschel suggests, from Jerusalem's as well:

> For centuries we would tear our garments whenever we came into sight of your ruins. In 1945 our souls were ruins, and our garments were tatters. There was nothing to tear. In Auschwitz and Dachau, in Bergen-Belsen and Treblinka, they prayed at the end of Atonement Day, "Next year in Jerusalem." The next day they were asphyxiated in gas chambers. Those of us who were not asphyxiated continued to cling to Thee; "Though He slay me, yet I will trust in Him" (Job 13:15). We come to you, Jerusalem, to build your ruins, to mend our souls and to seek comfort for God and men.
>
> (Heschel 1967: 17)

> We, a people of orphans, have entered the walls to greet the widow, Jerusalem, and the widow is a bride again. Jerusalem is not divine, her life depends on our presence. Alone she is desolate and silent, with Israel she is a witness, a proclamation. Alone she is a widow, with Israel she is a bride.
>
> (Heschel 1967: 14)

Notes

1 I will use the term "Jew" and "Jewish" throughout the essay for convenience, even though, in this early period, the term Judahite, Judaean, or Israelite would be more accurate.
2 For a fuller treatment of the city in the Second Temple period, see Levine 2002.
3 This sudden shift in practice has merited little scholarly attention. In truth, there is precious little to go on since our sources simply ignore this matter. Was it due to Sadducean influence, given their dominance for long periods and their possibly more restrictive interpretation of the Second Commandment? Or was it perhaps due to the religious persecutions of Antiochus IV in 167 BCE, the centerpiece of which was the introduction of idolatrous images into the Temple? The subsequent ban of all images in Jewish life thus would have constituted a reaction to this. Such a drastic step may also have been part of the overall Hasmonean religious ideology, modeled after Deuteronomy, that dictated a complete disengagement from idolatry and everything associated with it. Just as Ezra took Deuteronomy 7 one step further, placing all gentiles in the category of the seven nations, so, too, the Hasmoneans may have considered all figural images as extensions of idolatrous behavior and thus prohibited any and all representations. Certitude in this matter is elusive, but the reality created—i.e., the studious avoidance of figural art—is undeniable. It served as a unique assertion of Jewish self-identity in a world where the use of images was ubiquitous.
4 See 1 Maccabees 13:27–29:

> Over the tomb of his father and his brothers Simon constructed a monument impressive for its height, built of hewn stone on both its front and rear sides. He set up seven pyramids, one in front of the other, for his father, his mother, and his four brothers. For the pyramids he contrived an elaborate setting: he surrounded them with massive pillars on which he placed full suits of armor as a perpetual memorial; besides the full suits of armor, there were carved ships, intended to be seen by all who sailed the sea.

5 On the nature of this institution, see Levine 2002, 267–269.
6 Two fine anthologies relating to this material are Holtz 1971 and Hammer 1995.
7 A more detailed discussion of this topic can be found in Reif 1999.
8 It should be noted that the three-week period of abstinence from these activities is an Ashkenazic (i.e., European) custom; Sephardic Jews usually restrict such observances to the beginning of the month of Av only.
9 More material on these and other customs can be found in Golinkin 1999.

References

Bickerman, E. 1962. *From Ezra to the Last of the Maccabees: Foundations of Post-Biblical Judaism*. New York: Schocken.

Blenkinsopp, J. 1991. "Temple and Society in Achaemenid Judah." In *Second Temple Studies, I: Persian Period*, ed. P. R. Davies, 22–53. Sheffield: Sheffield Academic Press.

Borowski, O. 1995. "Hezekiah's Reforms and the Revolt against Assyria." *Biblical Archaeologist* 58: 148–155.

Bright, J. 1972. *A History of Israel*. Philadelphia: Westminster.

Charif, R. and S. Raz, eds. 1977. *Jerusalem the Eternal Bond: An Unbroken Line with the Jewish People*. Tel Aviv: Don Publishing House.

Eliade, M. 1959. *Cosmos and History: The Myth of the Eternal Return.* New York: Harper & Row.

———. 1961. *The Sacred and the Profane: The Nature of Religion.* New York: Harper & Row.

———. 1986. "Sacred Architecture and Symbolism." In *Symbolism, the Sacred, and the Arts,* ed. D. Apostolos-Cappadona, 105–129. New York: Crossroad.

Geller, M. 1978. "New Sources for the Origin of the Rabbinic Ketubah." *Hebrew Union College Annual* 49: 227–245.

Golinkin, D. 1999. "Jerusalem in Jewish Law and Custom: A Preliminary Typology." In Levine 1999, 408–423.

Hallo, W. W. 1999. "Jerusalem under Hezekiah: An Assyriological Perspective." In Levine 1999, 36–50.

Hammer, R. 1995. *The Jerusalem Anthology: A Literary Guide.* Philadelphia: Jewish Publication Society.

Heschel, A. J. 1967. *Israel: An Echo of Eternity.* New York: Farrar, Straus & Giroux.

Holtz, A. 1971. *The Holy City: Jews on Jerusalem.* New York: W. W. Norton.

Japhet, S. 1999. "From King's Sanctuary to the Chosen City." In Levine 1999, 3–15.

Levine, Lee I. 1998. *Judaism and Hellenism: Conflict or Confluence?* Seattle: University of Washington Press.

———, ed. 1999. *Jerusalem: Its Sanctity and Centrality to Judaism, Christianity, and Islam.* New York: Continuum.

———. 2002. *Jerusalem: Portrait of the City in the Second Temple Period (538 B.C.E.–70 C.E.).* Philadelphia: Jewish Publication Society.

Peters, F. E. 1985. *Jerusalem: The Holy City in the Eyes of Chroniclers, Visitors, Pilgrims, and Prophets from the Days of Abraham to the Beginnings of Modern Times.* Princeton: Princeton University Press.

Reif, S. 1999. "Jerusalem in Jewish Liturgy." In Levine 1999, 424–437.

Sullivan, R. D. 1990. *Near Eastern Royalty and Rome, 100–30 BC.* Toronto: University of Toronto Press.

Tadmor, H. 1985. "Sennacherib's Campaign to Judah: Historical and Historiographic Considerations." *Zion* 50: 65–80. (In Hebrew.)

Zakovitch, Y. 1999. "First Stages of Jerusalem's Sanctification under David." In Levine 1999, 16–35.

4 The Temple Mount in Jewish and early Christian traditions

A new look

Yaron Z. Eliav

Holy sites have always been inseparable from religion (Eliade 1959, 20–65; Smith 1987).[1] One of the more famous places is the flat, walled trapezoid located on the eastern edge of Jerusalem's Old City. In English, it is commonly referred to as the Temple Mount, but the literal translation of the Hebrew would be the "Mount of the House." Judaism and Islam in particular, but Christianity also, still revere the site as holy. Consequently, the faithful are careful to observe special religious strictures and practices there.

The Temple Mount's stature, however, has long exceeded the bounds of its specifically religious significance. Over the years, it has been transformed into a national, cultural, and political symbol, deeply entrenched in the foundations of both the Jewish-Zionist and Arab-Muslim ethos. Poets have elegized it, writers have extolled it in essays and stories. The Mount has inspired spiritual leaders and has furnished countless images for artists belonging to many and varied schools and traditions. At the same time, however, it has, especially in recent times, cost political leaders many a sleepless night.

But what is the origin of the Mount's name, and what are the factors that have fashioned its physical and religious fabric? This chapter investigates the Temple Mount's origins and sketches out the formative stages of its unique status. It follows two basic principles. One is the fundamental ground rule of historical research, in that historians do not automatically accept statements found in ancient texts as historical truths, but rather strive to discern the entire range of factors that shaped the composition of ancient texts, including the complex, and at times contradictory, dynamics influencing them. The second is more concrete: to distinguish between the physical site referred to today as the Temple Mount, and the terms and names which signify this physical structure. Today, in using the term Temple Mount, we project onto the site all the ideas and images such an appellation evokes, which have varied over time.

A two-pronged question will thus accompany this entire discussion. First, what are the roots of the designation "Temple Mount," when was it coined, and what were the reasons for its appearance? Second, and more significant than the terminology, what consciousness does it represent? Was the site always the Temple Mount in people's consciousness, or did it enter the public lexicon at a particular point in time, suggesting a change in their consciousness and in the way they grasped the reality of Jerusalem? If there was this kind of shift, then its nature, boundaries, and significance need to be determined.

The First Temple period

The word "House" in the literal translation of "Temple Mount" refers to either of the Temples that successively stood on the site in the ancient past. This was no ordinary house but rather "The House of God." According to biblical chronology, King Solomon built the First Temple around the middle of the tenth century BCE. The Second Temple, which can be dated more accurately, was erected during the return of Jewish exiles from Babylon in the second half of the sixth century BCE, and was destroyed by the Romans in 70 CE at the climax of the Jewish rebellion. The very nature of the Temple Mount is firmly connected to these two Temples, as it is considered the hallowed ground on which they stood.

However, according to the books of Samuel and Kings, the earliest existing documents that relate the history of the Davidic dynasty, the location David and eventually Solomon chose for the Temple had no special prior status. The authors use no particular name for the site, nor do they associate it with any illustrious tradition. All that can be inferred from these accounts is that the Temple site lay above the City of David (e.g., 1 Kings 8:1). Mount Zion, which later would become one of the celebrated names for the Temple Mount, is not mentioned even once in the books of Samuel. In the books of Kings it appears only once, in the form of a quotation from the prophet Isaiah (2 Kings 19:31; Isaiah 37:32), but only as a synonym for the city of Jerusalem, and without any reference to the location of the Temple.

Another designation used by later generations to refer to the site of Solomon's Temple, lending it a special aura, was "Ornan's threshing floor." This appellation never actually appears in the book of Kings. Its source is in the book of Samuel (2 Samuel 24:18–25): David, heeding the instructions of the prophet Gad, purchases the plot from Ornan to build an altar for God in the aftermath of a deadly pestilence. Although the site of the threshing floor is described as being located above the city, there is absolutely no indication in the text that it is the same site where Solomon would later build the Temple. Moreover, scattered references indicate that the place in which Ornan did his threshing had no independent value in the eyes of these authors: the Ark of the Covenant and the venues at which sacrifices were offered were definitely located inside the City of David, both before David's purchase of the threshing-floor (2 Samuel 6:17–18) and afterwards during Solomon's time (1 Kings 2:28). According to a later source, the place was used to thresh wheat, just like any other threshing floor (1 Chronicles 21:20).

The books of Kings and Samuel (and Deuteronomy, which is closely related to their outlook) place enormous significance on the establishment of Jerusalem as the Jewish nation's sole ritual center. According to the views promoted by these books, sacrifice is not legitimate in any other location, even if intended for the God of Israel. This is closely connected with the House of David's desire to establish in perpetuity the political hegemony of both its capital and its dynasty. Pointed expression is given to this conception, which ties together the city, the Temple, and the House of David, in Solomon's prayer at the dedication of the Temple. There he cites the words of God: "Since the day that I brought forth my people Israel out of Egypt, I chose no city out of all the tribes of Israel to build a house, that my name might be therein; but I chose David to be over my people Israel" (1 Kings 8:16).

Such a conception does not, however, endow the Temple Mount with any independent status. As noted, the Temple's location in Jerusalem is of utmost importance, and is in fact essential, to the Davidic ideology. Its location on this hill or that, however, is inconsequential. The significance of Solomon's Temple as the ritual center for the God of Israel is similarly beyond doubt. It is quite possible that some of the kingdom's governing institutions—such as the "House of the King" (1 Kings 9:1–10), the "House of the People" (Jeremiah 39:8), and the "House of the Forest of Lebanon" (1 Kings 7:2; Isaiah 22:8)—were situated close to the Temple or even on the territory presently referred to as the Temple Mount. From that generation's point of view, however, these buildings were situated there not on account of the importance of the mountain itself, but by dint of their proximity to the Temple.

The literary image of the Temple's location as a holy mountain first emerges in Psalms and in the prophetic books. Woven repeatedly into these works are names and descriptions reflecting the idea that the Temple is located on a "mountain" possessing special qualities. For instance, the famous prophecy of peace at the end of days, in the books of Isaiah and Micah, describes the "mountain of the Lord's house" as "established in the top of the mountains and exalted above the hills." The gentiles that stream to the place proclaim, "Let us go up to the mountain of God ... and he will teach us of his ways and we will walk in his paths" (Isaiah 2:2–3; Micah 4:1–2). This verse crystallizes the visual impressions that existed in the consciousness of the authors and their audience. Along these same lines, the place of the Temple is frequently represented in the works of the prophets in a series of appellations in which the common element is the mountain image: "holy mountain," "mountain of God," and, combining them both, "My holy mountain."[2] These works are also the first to designate the Temple's location "Mount Zion," whereas in Samuel (2 Samuel 5:7) and Kings (1 Kings 8:1), "Zion" was the name of the City of David. Moreover, in these latter books the image of the mountain is not to be found at all in reference to Zion.

The same tendency to exalt the Temple's location and represent it as a special mountain—as Mount Moriah—is also found, somewhat later, in the book of Chronicles' retrospective description of Solomon's Temple project: "Then Solomon began to build the house of the Lord at Jerusalem in Mount Moriah, where the Lord reappeared unto David his father, in the place that David had prepared in the threshing-floor of Ornan the Jebusite" (2 Chronicles 3:1). In what appears to be a brilliant intertextual maneuver, the author is obviously linking the name "Moriah" to the only other place where it appears in the Bible—the narrative about the binding of Isaac (Genesis 22:2).

In the binding of Isaac story, however, there is absolutely no mention of a specific mountain. All that is noted is that there is a region known as the "land of Moriah," and God commands Abraham to sacrifice his son on "one of the mountains" in that region. Certainly there is no indication in the sacrifice story, or in any other of the early traditions of the Bible, that this site was in any way related with the territory on which the future Temple would be erected. This attempt by the author of the book of Chronicles to bind Moriah with the site of the Temple and Ornan's threshing floor clearly reveals the hidden, interpretive trend embodied in this verse. The Temple, according to this writer, was located on the site of the binding of Isaac, which is also the site of Ornan's threshing floor that David bought. Underlying all three is the cultic concept of sacrifice as the ultimate manifestation of the encounter between God and his people. According to the author of Chronicles' interpretation, the binding of Isaac presents the primordial prefiguration of this ritual model.

The pair of words "Temple Mount" also debuted in the works of the prophets. The "copyright" for this name is reserved to the prophet Micah, who incorporated it into his famous admonitory prophecy: "Therefore shall Zion for your sake be plowed as a field, and Jerusalem shall become heaps, and the *mountain of the house* as the high places of the forest" (Micah 3:12). It is quite doubtful, however, that the book of Micah preserved a concrete name that was actually used in the day-to-day lexicon of the prophet's generation. A close-reading of this passage shows that the phrase "Mountain of the House" is a literary variation of a longer term, the "mountain of the House of the Lord" (three words in Hebrew), which appears in verse 4:1. The author places the complete term in the middle and "plays" with its constituent parts (both pieces come out to two words in Hebrew) in the previous and subsequent verses (3:12; 4:2). In verse 4:1 the name Lord is deleted, leaving the term "Mount of the House," or Temple Mount.

This, then, is not a case of terms taken from the vocabulary of daily life but rather variations characteristic of the common literary diction used by the prophets. Furthermore, nearly one thousand years will pass from the alleged time of Micah until the specific term "Temple Mount" reappears in the Mishnah. In the interim, the term "Temple Mount" is not used in even one of the numerous existing sources, except in works quoting and using the entire phrase from Micah. This is conclusive evidence that the name "Temple Mount" was not used in earlier periods, even though the image of a mountain as a place for a temple was both known and probably, at least to some degree, widespread.

The image of a mountain as the proper location for temples has its roots in the ancient Semitic idea of the "cosmic mountain": a lofty place where the heavens and the earth meet and at which the "divine" manifests itself in the universe (Clements 1965; Clifford 1972). The concept of the cosmic mountain was prevalent in different forms throughout the ancient Near East: from Mesopotamian and Ugaritic cultures, and as far as Egypt and Greece. One of its central aspects is the congruence between "mountain" and "temple" (Parry 1990). It is reasonable to assume that this notion inspired the beliefs and values that fashioned the biblical images of the holy mountain.

It is in this light that the idea of the mountain is employed in the language of the biblical poets and functions in eschatological and apocalyptic visions of that time. It is only natural, then, that the prophets' hopes for the future, as expressed in their poetry, should be uttered as a longing that has political connotations with reference to the Temple's mountain. The Psalms provide us with examples of these aspirations: "Yet have I set my king upon Zion my holy hill" (2:6). The mountain is even linked to acts of worship, as found in Isaiah's vision: "Even [the gentiles] will I bring to my holy mountain, and make them joyful in my house of prayer: their burnt offerings and their sacrifices shall be accepted upon mine altar ..." (Isaiah 56:7). However, the mountain itself does not constitute a concrete political term in the world of the First Temple period nor is it a palpable factor in the ritual framework of those days.

The Second Temple period

The special status of Jerusalem and the Temple during the First Temple period takes on redoubled significance in the days of the Second Temple. In fact, Jerusalem and the Temple took on as many shades of meaning as there were groups and sub-groups of Palestine and Diaspora Jews at the time. There is, for example, a wide gap between Josephus, who highlighted the building's detailed physical dimensions, and Philo, who "stripped" the Temple and its constituent elements—such as the priesthood and the hallowed curtain—of their tangible form and fashioned them into allegoric motifs in his concept of the logos. The common denominator of such varied and conflicting attitudes is that they all pointed to Jerusalem and the Temple as being the focal points of Jewish consciousness in this period.[3]

The Temple rounded out Jerusalem's centrality by giving it a "religious" dimension. It was the primary ritual center for Jews in the land of Israel and throughout the world, as well as the spiritual focus of their worldview. The "half shekel," a levy that all the Jews of the ancient world collected and sent to the high priesthood in Jerusalem, was one practical expression of the central status of the Temple. The large number of pilgrims who flocked to Jerusalem and the Temple for the three major festivals from throughout the Roman and Persian empires is a further indication of this same inclination. The city and the Temple occupied, along with other fundamental elements of Jewish thought and symbolism such as the House of David and the messianic idea, a leading position in the cluster of terms that shaped the historical image, as well as the hopes for the future, of Jews of all sects in the Second Temple period. They were also transformed into spiritual motifs that came to define the Jewish experience in its entirety.

And what of the Temple's mountain during the Second Temple period? How was this mountain crest conceived, if at all, by that generation? Are there Second Temple sources that point to a prevalent mind-set regarding this site? If so, what was this perception? Furthermore, from a terminological standpoint it was Micah, as noted above, who coined the term "Temple Mount," but what of its further historical development? Was the expression in use during the Second Temple period? How was it related to the other, popular terms that existed in the period's lexicon? From a more functional angle, what was the status of the location on which the Temple stood, its surrounding space?

Much of the writing of the Second Temple period was conducted within the contours marked out by the literature of the biblical period. Those acquainted with the texts of the Bible (which had not then reached their final form as we know them today) and writing under its influence could hardly conceive or imagine Jerusalem in any but mountainous terms. This mountainous picture is also supported by the topographic reality with which many of these writers were familiar. Anyone who has ever climbed from the bottom of the hill—the area known as the City of David, or the Lower City—and ascended to the peak where the Temple stood knows by the weariness of their feet that this is a mountain. It is no wonder, then, that images of mountains are sprinkled over many of the texts that deal with Jerusalem (Judith 5:19; Fourth Baruch 3:21; Josephus, *Jewish War* 5:137 and 184).[4]

Terms from the "mountainous lexicon" of the biblical period, both borrowed from the ancient texts and created during the Second Temple period, continue to appear in the literary works of that era in many descriptions of Jerusalem and the location of the Temple. For example, in the apocalyptic chapters of the book of Daniel, the term "Thy Holy Mountain" (9:16) is synonymous with Jerusalem.[5] The author of the text known as the Apocryphal Psalm borrowed the term "the mountain of the height of Israel" from the book of Ezekiel, where it appears several times. Similarly, the term "Thy Holy Mountain," found in the Wisdom of Solomon (9:8) and 1 Maccabees (11:37), refers to the location of the Temple. In the book of Jubilees (1:2, 18:7), however, the term "Mountain of God" refers to both Jerusalem and Mount Sinai. The term "Mount Zion" was routinely used throughout

the entire period, from books written at the height of the era such as Jubilees (1:28) and 1 Maccabees (4:37), in which it was the usual toponym for
the Temple's place, to books written after the destruction such as Syriac
Baruch (13:1) and Fourth Ezra (13:35).

The reliance of Second Temple-period authors on ancient biblical texts
goes beyond terminology, and many ideas conceived during the First
Temple era or in the early generations that followed it were adopted and
elaborated. A prime example is the identification of the site of Isaac's
binding, "Moriah," with Mount Zion. As mentioned above, this idea first
appeared in Chronicles, but it was widely adopted by the authors of the
Second Temple period and developed even further (Jubilees 18:13; Josephus,
Jewish Antiquities 1:226). Similarly, the biblical idea of the cosmic mountain
also resonates in some early Second Temple works. The most prominent
example is the Epistle of Aristeas (83–84). There the author related the
impressions of an Egyptian delegation with whom he arrived at Jerusalem:
"We saw the city which sits in the center of the entire land of the Jews and it
is a high and lofty mountain." On top of the mountain sits nothing less
than a "magnificent temple."

That said, did the mountain on which the Temple stood receive some sort
of political or ritual status in the Jewish world and consciousness of the
Second Temple period? The very existence of an idea in the ancient books
that came to be the Bible, even one that receives some attention in the
Jewish writings of the Second Temple period, does not automatically imply
that it is fully espoused by the people of that time or that it functions in any
substantive way in their world. For example, from sources indicating how
people spoke and thought of the Temple, laws they passed regulating it as
an institution and molding its related activities, accomplishments they
associated with it, the way they acted on its behalf, and the way they criticized it—all these serve as the basis for our conclusions concerning its
status. Indeed, Second Temple liturgy (sacrifices, festivals, laws of purity
and the like) is almost entirely based on Jerusalem's Temple, and thus
affirms its ritual status. The Temple's political centrality is indicated by the
plethora of political events, involving external factors from the Roman
world or internal elements from within the Jewish world. All of the above
could be said of Jerusalem as well.

Were there, however, similar notions and emotions regarding the
mountain on which the Temple stood? The answer is no. The fact that there
are sporadic echoes of biblical expressions and literary phrases does not
prove that the mountain in and of itself had any political or ritual status.
An integral part of the Jerusalemite experience is, as noted above, its
mountainous scenery, and as part of that landscape the Temple's location
was on one of the city's hills. A clear distinction must be made, however,
between a physical reality that is essentially neutral and the existence of an
ideological posture that may be granted to any particular component of
that reality.

The claim that the mountain itself was not an independent category in the consciousness of Second Temple Jews is based primarily on a methodical examination of all the places in the texts from that time in which Jerusalem and its related sites are mentioned (Eliav 2005a, 12–23). Jewish writing during this period was prolific and extremely varied. Jerusalem and the Temple appear in these texts hundreds, if not thousands, of times. These sources, despite and perhaps due to their diversity, demonstrate that the mountain on which the Temple stood was devoid of any significant stature. The name "Temple Mount" appears but once throughout the multitude of available sources (in 1 Maccabees, which will be discussed below). Even there, it operates only as a literary construction, inspired by the biblical verse in Micah. This is a decisive finding, which proves that the term "Temple Mount" was not an integral part of the Second Temple period's lexicon.

The absence of the Temple Mount from the works of the period is especially pronounced when examining the manner in which the territories surrounding the actual Temple were conceived in the era's consciousness. The Temple structure never stood alone. From its earliest days there were always adjacent walled courtyards, and perhaps even buildings; the area was bursting with diverse and vibrant activity.[6] Some of this action was naturally connected to the Temple, such as the sale of sacrificial animals and the exchange of currency for the half-shekel levy. The site also attracted other activities that were not directly linked to the Temple. Sources such as Josephus and the New Testament's Gospels and Acts portray an array of events, among them preachers giving sermons and individuals and groups decrying the regime. Some gathered there to study the Torah, while others came to close business deals. There were periods when the court system operated on the Mount, or nearby.

The most important question, however, is: how was this surrounding territory perceived by those living at the time, and how did it rank, if at all, in their world-view? It seems to me that throughout most of the period, the area did not possess any independent identity and was considered an integral part of the Temple itself. From a semantic standpoint, the various names given to the compound—*hatser* (courtyard) in Hebrew, or the Greek *peribolos* and *temenos*—describe a space that surrounds another architectural element. The Temple, then, was perceived as an architectural complex containing different components. Just as the altar was part of the Temple structure, so were the surrounding elements—courtyards and galleries. This is not to say that all these parts shared an equal status or degree of holiness. There was a definite, hierarchical system: the outer enclosure was not on a par with the inner court, and the inner court was not equivalent to the Holy of Holies. They were all grasped, however, as parts of a whole, which together formed the Temple.

The sacredness of these territories is almost self-evident and is certainly no surprise. The expression "my holy courts" appears already in early, First

Temple texts (for example, Isaiah 62:9), and it is only natural that the areas that form part of the Temple should possess some of its holiness. For example, the codes of purity were strictly enforced in these courts, in order to prevent the penetration of defilement into the inner sanctuary. The compounds surrounding the Temple, then, did not possess an independent character, and constituted an integral part of the Temple. People didn't refer to these areas as the "Temple Mount," and they were not even perceived in their consciousness as a mountain.

The origin of the "Temple Mount" concept

The seeds of the Temple Mount concept may be found in some Second Temple sources; the earliest of these is 1 Maccabees. For the most part, this book remains faithful to the usual representations of Jerusalem during this period, which accentuate the dual centrality of city and Temple and neglect the mountain on which the latter stood. In several instances, however, a new, third element is introduced into Jerusalem's landscape, and given the traditional appellation "Mount Zion" (4:37, 5:54). It is clearly referring to the venue of the Temple. On other occasions, the author uses designations such as the "holy mountain" (11:37) and "mountain of the Temple" (16:20). In one instance he even assigns the site the actual phrase "Temple Mount" (4:46).

There are serious doubts, however, concerning the authenticity of the terms "holy mountain" and "mountain of the Temple" in 1 Maccabees. These terms were apparently later additions, most likely from the period after the destruction of the Temple, whereas the name "Temple Mount" was borrowed from the collection of literary images found in the book of Micah (Eliav 2005a, 29–33). Nevertheless, there is no denying that time and again 1 Maccabees conveys the image of a mountain when depicting the Temple's location.

The area's independent status is also reflected in the works of Josephus, at the end of the Second Temple period and thereafter. Josephus (*Jewish War* 4:388) describes the atrocities committed in the civil conflict that raged within the walls of Jerusalem, and includes a short quasi-prophecy whereby he views these sorts of events as foreshadowing the imminent catastrophe of the destruction. Included in this prophecy is the defilement of the area around the Temple by some of the local residents. One aspect of this account sets it apart from other descriptions of the Temple precincts: Josephus uses the expression "*Temenos* of God." In the common formulations referring to Jerusalem's Temple, the "*Temenos*" is subordinate to the Temple, not to God. In Josephus' expression the Temple itself loses its central role, and the *Temenos* is directly partnered with the source of holiness.

In the eyes of Josephus, then, spiritual and moral impairments to the *Temenos* bear their own negative weight and may at the end of the "prophetic accounting" bring tragedy upon the defilers as well as upon the

Temple and the city as a whole. To the best of my knowledge, this marks the first time that a writer of the Second Temple period attributes such an independent value to the area surrounding the Temple, and in which this area plays a self-sufficient literary role. Consciousness and terminology thus go hand in hand. With the rise of a new consciousness, a new term sprang forth—"*Temenos* of God."

A second source that sheds light on the inception of the concept of the Temple Mount as possessing an independent status is the New Testament. The city and its sanctuary rank quite highly in the writings of the New Testament, playing a leading role in its narrative that is unmatched by any other city or holy place.[7] Various passages of the New Testament use the images of the Temple and Jerusalem, whether to express the "Heavenly Jerusalem" or, on occasion, as a label for the actual community. And what of the Temple Mount? The word combination "Temple" and "Mount" is never to be found throughout the entire corpus of the New Testament. The term "Mount Zion," absent from the works of Josephus, appears only rarely in the New Testament—the Gospels do not mention it even once. All of this is true despite the fact that mountains do turn up in these texts, some of them quite intrusively: Mount Sinai, Mount Gerizim, and the anonymous mountain that is the site of the Sermon on the Mount. This is consistent with the world of Second Temple Judaism—Jerusalem in this context is the exclusive location of God's worship. The Temple is indeed the city's essence, but the mountain on which it stands has no function or status.

Nevertheless, the New Testament, like the works of Josephus, contains the seeds of the phrase "Temple Mount" and the concept it embodies. One example is Jesus's well-known prophecy, "there shall not be left one stone upon another, that shall not be thrown down" (Mark 13:2), which was understood by many scholars to refer to the Temple itself. Originally, however, the verse pointed to the territory that the disciples encountered as they exited the Temple—the surrounding plateau, later to be called the Temple Mount.[8] In the description of Stephen's execution found in Acts (6:13–14), "holy place" replaces the usual expression "shrine." Additionally, in Revelation (11) the Temple court is given an independent and separate life from both the city and the Temple.

To conclude, these sequences from Josephus and the New Testament, and to some extent 1 Maccabees, are worthy of being considered as the nascent stages of the term "Temple Mount." Why nascent? Because the sources in which they are found are not unambiguous. On the one hand, they share many of the traits of the "classic" city-temple image found in the other sources of the Second Temple period; on the other hand, they indicate a change from the usual manner in which the area surrounding the Temple is treated. It is given new names, and it is apparently no longer portrayed as solely dependent on the Temple that stands at its center. This indicates the beginning of a change in the perception of reality. These accounts reflect a kind of intermediary stage, in which the previous consciousness is still felt, but—be it consciously or unconsciously—they express a new concept as well.

Herod's project

What brought about the change in the way the Temple's surrounding area was perceived? The answer is to be found in the close interdependency of reality and idea, whereby a significant modification of the physical sphere entails a series of new perceptions, which in turn affect the way people visualize the new reality. What triggered such dynamics was the huge transformation of the Temple area during the last one hundred years of the Second Temple era. This project is entirely bound up with the inspiration and work of one man, King Herod, who more than anyone else was responsible for the present form of the compound we now call the "Temple Mount."

As part of Herod's efforts to beautify and glorify (and in fact to rebuild) Jerusalem's Temple, he expanded the area around it. In fact, he more than doubled its size, converting it into the largest temple complex in the eastern part of the Roman Empire at the time. Herod thus established an artificial topographic entity in the shape of a trapezoid, of an area and height never before seen in Jerusalem.

From an architectural perspective, not only did Herod strengthen and glamorize the Temple, but his project also gave a new look to the entire surrounding complex. Colonnades decorated the open courts that surrounded the Temple, and two huge buildings sheltered the Temple: to the south, Herod's royal basilica, which Josephus considered to be the most spectacular building on the face of the earth; and to the north, the Antonia—not quite fortress and not quite palace—held the entire area in thrall.

The area adjacent to the Temple compound also received a facelift during Herod's reign. Around the enormous walls of the Temple compound, which were made of huge stones, flattened and smoothed, a new urban multiplex was created. This enterprise had no equal in the land of Israel of those days: avenues of up to 23 meters wide were paved with large stones and bordered with curbstones; beneath the streets lay a drainage and sewage system, and above them piazzas, fabulous stairwells, and—a rare sight before Herod's time—an impressive interchange that sat atop arches, leading to the royal basilica (Ben-Dov 2002, 103–126).

This monumental architectural accomplishment was superimposed on the likewise newly-created topography, and together formed a new landscape for the city of Jerusalem. Change was flung at a population unaccustomed to such enormous dimensions, and consequently it radically transformed the physical reality in which they lived and worked. It is only natural, then, that this grandiose creation would engrave its markings on their innermost consciousness. It is these events that provided the concrete foundation for the change in consciousness, the seeds of which are to be found in Josephus and the books of the New Testament. Paradoxically, this process would be fully concluded in the period following the destruction.

After the days of the Second Temple

The destruction of the Second Temple by the Romans in 70 CE opens a new chapter in the annals of both Jerusalem in general and the Temple in particular. Little is known about what transpired within the ruins of Jerusalem in the sixty-year period that followed the Great Revolt and ended with the initiation of Emperor Hadrian's building project in the beginning of the 130s CE (perhaps as late as 135). According to Josephus (*Jewish War* 7:1–2), the Tenth Legion was bivouacked next to the three towers that Herod constructed in the western part of the upper city (presently referred to as "David's Citadel"). Except for this note, there are no other written sources or archaeological discoveries that provide significant information, which may shed some light as to the site's characteristics during these years.

After the Bar-Kokhba revolt (132–135) Jerusalem was turning into a pagan city, at times practically off-limits to Jews. Indeed, its idolatrous image must have disgusted them. Further, their Temple's territory was left in its desolation outside the city limits.[9] These elements provided, in my view, the great impetus for the elevation of the Temple Mount's status. This development took place simultaneously among the various Jewish groups who still resided in Palestine. Ample information about two of these groups enables us to reconstruct part of this process.

The community of James brother of Jesus

The persona known as James brother of Jesus, as well as the characteristics of the group that banded around him, are shrouded in mystery. Over the years, the group came to be known as the "Jerusalem Church of the Circumcised." It was one of many Jewish factions that were active in Palestine in the days before the destruction of the Temple and in the first generations thereafter. In a previous detailed study, I argued that the "Temple Mount" played a significant role in this group's world (Eliav 2004).

The tradition that gave rise to this community's ethos recounts James's murder at the Temple court, where he was publicly preaching his faith. According to this account, one of the priests pushed him off what is called the Temple's *Pterugion* (usually translated as "pinnacle"), which formed part of the massive walls that bounded the Temple and separated it from the surrounding compound (the Temple was essentially a fortified unit within a fortified compound). The hostile mob pelted James's body with stones, and someone crushed his skull with a club. The tradition concludes with James's burial in the compound, in close proximity to the Temple. In the second century CE, about two generations after the destruction, the tombstone was still a gathering place for members of this community.

Given the lack of sources, it is difficult to verify whether or how these events unfolded. Was James really buried on the mountain? We cannot know, and for the purposes of this study it is irrelevant. Although it is hard to believe that the Jewish Temple authorities would permit the burial of anyone so close to the Temple, the fact remains that members of the so-called Judeo-Christian community revered James's tomb on the desolate compound of the destroyed Temple (whether or not he was actually buried there) as a holy place. Additionally, there are many other traditions linking persons who were venerated by the Judeo-Christian communities to events that took place on the Temple's territory: for example, Satan's seduction of Jesus at the same Temple's *Pterugion* and the murder of the prophet Zechariah next to the altar. These memories indicate that holy relics existed in the immediate area of the ruined Temple (such as the large cornerstone and the ruins of the *Pterugion*), which attracted worshipers and pilgrims.

The territory adjacent to the Temple appears, in the consciousness of the creators of the James tradition, as a site of religious significance. Not the Temple, but the "area next to it." The fragments of these traditions indicate the birth of a new location: not the Temple itself but the expanse on which it stands. The status of this place does not rely on Temple rituals, with their related laws of purity, nor on the classic objects that represent the Temple—the altar and the Holy of Holies. In this new spatial arrangement there are different corners and new objects: the *Pterugion*, a large stone, the grave and tombstone of James brother of Jesus. These elements reveal a new facet of the Temple Mount's history.

Rabbinic literature

Rabbinic literature is the largest—and to a great extent the only surviving—corpus of texts written by the Jews of Palestine (and Babylon) in the first centuries of the common era (a rough estimate dates these works to the second through the sixth centuries). These are the first sources that represent the Temple Mount as a fully and clearly defined physical entity possessing unique characteristics that give it an independent status in the Jewish experience of the time.

Tractate Middot (1:1–3, 2:1–2) of the Mishnah, one of the earliest texts of this literature, represents the Mount as a recognized territorial constituent within the Temple complex. Its location is clear, its dimensions are defined ("The Temple Mount was five hundred cubits by five hundred cubits"), and the names of its gates are known ("The Temple Mount had five gates"). Various guidelines are provided concerning the route pedestrians are to follow when entering this place and the manner in which people are to address one another while there. The tractate even recalls the "Temple Mount person," whose responsibilities included the rotation of the Levites who manned the five gates.

These examples are sufficient to ground the impression that the *Tana'aim*, the earlier rabbis who lived in the centuries that followed the destruction and produced, among other texts, the Mishnah, inherited this term from their predecessors of the Second Temple period. Similarly, many sources in rabbinic literature which seem to document rituals and celebrations that took place in Jerusalem during the Second Temple period frequently mention the Temple Mount as an operative reference point in such procedures and take for granted its familiarity to everyone.

According to the Mishnah (Parah 3:3), the Temple Mount served as the last station on the course of the bulls that bore the ritually pure children, who carried water from the Siloam fountain for the ritual slaughter of the red heifer. It also served as a starting point for the entourage that attended the heifer on its way to the Mount of Olives led by the priest who was to burn the slaughtered animal.

Another example is found in the description of the pageantry that marked the bringing of the first fruits (Mishnah, Bikkurim 3:4). The pilgrims' route and various phases of this ceremony are described in detail, including the verses recited, the people involved, and the customs observed. According to the itinerary laid out by the Mishnah, the Temple Mount was one of the stations along the route of this festive occasion, which the pilgrims would reach upon arriving in Jerusalem, after entering the city and before arriving at the inner Temple Court: "The flutes were played before them until they reached the Temple Mount. When they reached the Temple Mount even King Agrippa would take the basket on his shoulder and enter." On a different note, but consistent with the above portrayal, was the *halakha* (rabbinic law) stipulating that when the first group—out of three—finished slaughtering the Passover sacrifice, "the first group left and sat in the Temple Mount" (Mishnah, Pesahim 5:10).

Moreover, Tannaitic literature recounts a significant number of customs and policies pertaining to the Temple Mount during the Second Temple period. First and foremost is the ruling that set the Temple Mount's dress code. It lists the articles that may not be brought in (shoes, sticks, and more) and even sets several restrictions on those entering. The visitor's feet must be clean of dust, and one may not use the Temple Mount as a shortcut (Berakhot 9:5). Another example deals with the case in which the first day of the Feast of the Tabernacles falls on the Sabbath. According to the Mishnah, "they would bring their Lulavim [palm branches] to the Temple Mount and the Temple attendants received them and placed them in order on the top of the portico" (Sukkah 4:4). There were also special additions to the prayers that were recited on public fasts. The Sages linked these prayers to the customs on the Temple Mount before the destruction (Ta'anit 2:5). Other ordinances were concerned with the site's upkeep, such as the prohibition on planting trees on the Mount (Sifre Deuteronomy 145).

In addition to the array of laws and customs associated with the Temple Mount, the Mishnah also depicts actual scenes that occurred on the Mount during the Second Temple period. On other occasions the Tannaitic Sages go so far as to represent the Temple Mount as a part of the Jerusalem reality of much earlier periods. For example, the deeds of the colorful figure known as Honi the circle-drawer are placed by the Mishnah on the Temple Mount (Mishnah, Ta'anit 3:8 and Nedarim 5:5). Many other rabbinic laws anchored the Temple Mount at the hub of day-to-day life in Jerusalem while the Second Temple still stood.

The status of the Temple Mount in Tannaitic literature reaches its zenith in the well-known passage in tractate Kelim (1:8), which classifies the ten levels of holiness: the structure of the Temple Mount is found between the city ("within the walls") and the Temple. "The Temple Mount is more sanctified than this [city], for males and females who have discharged, and women who have menstruated or given birth may not enter there." This affirmation should come as no surprise, and in fact logically reflects the Temple Mount's status in Tannaitic literature. To the Sages, the Mount was an integral part of the Jerusalemite reality of the Second Temple period, which preceded their time, and is consequently ranked among the period's sacred venues.

These circles of sanctity reflect a picture of the Temple as extant and active, as the focus and summit of holiness. This was not some spiritual-abstract idea, but a concept deeply rooted in practical life, which was the source of religious prohibitions such as the laws of contamination and purity that applied to visitors. At first glance, then, the post-70 CE Sages present a picture of the Temple Mount as an essential part of the earlier Second Temple period and an inseparable part of reality as perceived in that generation's consciousness. This literature suggests that the Jews of that time were both familiar with and used the term Temple Mount. They abided by customs linked to the Mount as well as the laws governing the area. People were also familiar with its physical details. According to rabbinic sources, the Temple Mount was deeply anchored in Jewish experience of the Second Temple period.

All this, however, is only ostensibly true. A more careful examination of the traditions regarding the Temple Mount in rabbinic literature—one that investigates the various versions of and changes in the texts over time—reveals formidable gaps in the picture that emerged in the above discussion. These call into question the very validity and historical authenticity of this picture, at least in relation to the existence of both the term and concept "Temple Mount" in the Second Temple period.[10]

A close reading of this material can detect a literary process in which the term "Temple Mount" was added to earlier traditions of the Second Temple period. The essence of this phenomenon has to do with the insertion of the term "Temple Mount" by rabbinic Sages into their back-projected presentation of the earlier reality of the Second Temple. In so doing, the rabbis redesigned Second Temple appearances on both physical and conceptual levels. One who reads the dozens of sequences in which the "Temple

Mount" appears in rabbinic texts is likely to come away with the impression that it was an integral part of the reality of the Second Temple period. This, however, is false; the term was an integral part of the world of the rabbis.

Thus, the development of the concept that took form under the rubric "the Temple Mount" is an absorbing phase in the evolution of Jewish consciousness during the post-destruction generations. It is a process in which a new term, although with ancient roots, took shape and gradually captured an important position in the world-view of the Sages and, apparently, in that of other Jews as well. One aspect of this development is the growing independence of the term "Temple Mount" and the nature of its relationship with the Temple (now destroyed). In many rabbinic texts, the Mount is not just a plot of land that happens to be subordinate to the Temple. It rather enters the picture as an independent force that even occasionally shunts the Temple aside. At some point, for example, the ancient *halakha* that had directed all prayer toward the Temple and the Holy of Holies was rephrased. Instead of the Temple, the Mount became the focus; the Palestinian Talmud termed it "the mount to which all mouths pray" (Eliav 2005a, 179–180). It is in this light that one must understand the better-known sources unfolding the notion that God's divine presence (*shekhina*) never left the locality of the Temple, even after its destruction, hence the site's holiness is not dependent on the existence of the Temple.

The Foundation Stone

One of the clearest examples indicating the rise of the Temple Mount's independent status is the increased attention given to the so-called "Foundation Stone." The first mention of this stone is innocent enough and appears in the Mishnah's tractate Yoma (5:2), which describes the high priest entering the Holy of Holies: "After the Ark was taken away, a stone was there from the time of the early Prophets, called 'foundation,' three fingers above the ground, and upon it he would put [the incense]." In the Tosefta (2:14), the tradition of the stone is recounted nearly word for word, but its conclusion includes a passage that is absent from the Mishnah: Rabbi Yose interprets the name "foundation stone," claiming that "from it the world was carved." Many scholars see in Rabbi Yose's statement a manifestation of the well-known Omphalos concept—the "navel of the earth"—which glorifies the centrality of certain places. This idea can be found, in different forms, in ancient Semitic and Greek cultures. It was adopted by some Second Temple Jewish authors, such as the author of the Epistle of Aristeas and Josephus, and perhaps appears even earlier in the book of Ezekiel.

Rabbi Yose crafted his shrewd explication well. It plays on the ancient name of the stone, by taking the noun *shetiyah* (foundation) and changing it into the verb *shatat* (to found or create). There is no mention of a "navel" or a "center"; the stone is, however, where the world was created. Admittedly, in ancient times all these expressions were members of the same family of ideas, and the Omphalos was defined as both the center of the world and the place of the creation. Despite this, one cannot ignore the fact that Rabbi Yose created a different terminological and ideological scale. The value attributed to the stone is what essentially differentiates the idea inherent in Rabbi Yose's position from the idea found in the Mishnah. Although in the latter, the stone is granted a certain significance—after all, the Ark was placed on it—this importance is measured within the framework of the Temple and the hierarchy of its articles. In contrast, Rabbi Yose's idea removes the stone from its Temple context and grants it a value in and of itself, measuring it in relation to the entire universe. This is the most important stone in the world.

This transition from the "Temple" stone to the "cosmic" stone signifies the conceptual process discussed above. The Temple's territory, and in this case a natural, physical element that occupied the area, replaces the actual edifice of the Temple, and is endowed with its own value. Although in some later rabbinic commentaries the stone is still associated with its function in the Temple (for example, with matters concerning the Day of Atonement), at other times, however, it is completely detached from its past. It is furnished with new substance and linked to new ideas: the foundation stone which is the navel of the earth.

The independence of the stone reached its apex among the Christians during the Byzantine era. The gist of the stone and the scope of ideas and imagery associated with it remained similar to its Jewish counterpart, but its actual spot was relocated to Golgotha, in the Church of the Holy Sepulcher. Early Muslim traditions embraced these notions as well but "restored" the stone to its original location.[11]

Jewish sources also contain more explicit liturgical information: even after the destruction, Jews, although naturally on a diminished scale, maintained their visits to Jerusalem, either to fulfill the biblical requirement of the festival pilgrimage or simply to come and pray. One tradition speaks of Tannaitic rabbis "who reached the Temple Mount and saw a fox leaving the Holy of Holies." A later tradition, dating to the fourth century CE, similarly recounts the visit of Sages who left their sandals "under the gateway to the Temple Mount" (Safrai 1981; Wilken 1992, 105–108). Additionally, there are detailed descriptions of the mourning customs that the visitors observed, mainly the tearing of clothing, and perhaps even fasting. Some scholars have suggested that for some time after the destruction Jews continued to perform some of the Temple rites, such as offering sacrifices and bringing the second tithe and eating it within Jerusalem. The majority of scholars, however, have correctly rejected these conjectures (Safrai 1981, 376–385). The sources, then, do indicate some sort of Jewish liturgical activity on the Temple Mount, but the picture remains incomplete, as many of its details remain a mystery.

Conclusion

The history of the Temple Mount and the growth of its religious and political eminence are more complicated than is commonly thought. In contrast to the widespread view, there is no homogeneous sequential process—from the ancient days of the Bible through the Second Temple period and up until the Late Roman and Byzantine periods—in which the essence of the Temple Mount's status remains more or less the same. The point of this study is to refute this convention. As was presented above, the process was a complex and dialectic one, of which only some of the contributing features are known.

Surprisingly, it was only in the aftermath of the Second Temple's destruction, when Jerusalem lost its own role as a political and religious center, that the Temple Mount gained prominence. Here, too, different factors combined or collided within the process. Paradoxically, Herod's massive building project and the destruction of the Temple, which prima facie would seem to cancel out each other, joined forces to shape both the Temple Mount's physical infrastructure and its consciousness as a sacred space independent of the Temple.

Notes

1 This article is based on my monograph (Eliav 2005a). Extensive comments and bibliographical references may be found there.
2 This generalization does not apply to later prophets. In the book of Jeremiah, for example, none of the terms appears even once, and an expression like "holy mountain," which in most of the prophetic writings almost always refers to the location of the Temple, is used in Jeremiah as a neutral name for the entire Judean mountain ridge (Jeremiah 31:22).
3 The research on Second Temple Jerusalem is too vast to be fully incorporated here. For an exhaustive bibliography, see Purvis 1988–91.
4 Mountainous scenery appears in other texts as well, but it is not always possible to pinpoint their source. For example, the beginning of 1 Enoch, also known as the "Book of the Watchers," takes place against the background of mountains, and Jerusalem is apparently alluded to. Yet it is difficult to establish the source from which the writer drew this scenery.
5 Also see the expression "holy mountain of beauty" (Daniel 11:45), which signifies the entire territory of Judah.
6 See, for example, the words of the Greek author Hecataeus of Abdera, in a fragment preserved in Josephus, *Against Apion* 1:198. See also Nehemiah 13:7–9, 8:16; Jubilees 49:20; Epistle of Aristeas 100. These territories, their components and contents, were frequently described in many of the studies dedicated to the Temple and its reconstruction (Busink 1970–80, 2:904–1016 and 1178–2000).
7 In the Gospel of John many of Jesus' deeds in Galilee are relocated to Jerusalem. For a detailed and updated summary regarding Jerusalem and the Temple in the New Testament, see Walker 1996; Eliav 2005a, 46–50.
8 The focus here is too narrow to discuss the parallels of this passage in the synoptic Gospels (Matthew 24:1–2; Luke 21:5–7) and the extensive research that has been published on this topic (Eliav 2005b).
9 According to the testimony of several sources, it is possible that the Roman legions that were stationed in Jerusalem in those days erected some statues in the

ruined compound. This, however, is not enough to alter the urban picture represented in this study (Eliav 2005a, 83–94). For a summary of scholarly opinions regarding the location of the Temple of Jupiter see Tsafrir 1999; Eliav 2005a, 76–100.

10 A significant portion of my earlier study is aimed at supporting this claim (Eliav 2005a, 189–236). It is obviously impossible to present all the evidence here.

11 For examples of Muslim traditions regarding the sanctification of that stone, see Chapter 6 by Suleiman Ali Mourad in this volume.

References

Ben-Dov, Meir. 2002. *Historical Atlas of Jerusalem*. New York: Continuum.

Busink, Th. A. 1970–80. *Der Tempel von Jerusalem, von Salomo bis Herodes*. 2 vols. Leiden: Brill.

Clements, Ronald E. 1965. *God and Temple*. Philadelphia: Fortress Press.

Clifford, Richard J. 1972. *The Cosmic Mountain in Canaan and the Old Testament*. Harvard Semitic Monographs 4. Cambridge: Harvard University Press.

Eliade, Mircea. 1959. *The Sacred and the Profane: The Nature of Religion*, trans. Willard R. Trask. New York: Harcourt Brace Jovanovich.

Eliav, Yaron Z. 1997. "Hadrian's Actions in the Jerusalem Temple Mount According to Cassius Dio and *Xiphilini Manus*." *Jewish Studies Quarterly* 4: 125–144.

——. 2004. "The Tomb of James Brother of Jesus as *Locus Memoriae*." *Harvard Theological Review* 97: 32–59.

——. 2005a. *God's Mountain: The Temple Mount in Time, Space, and Memory*. Baltimore: Johns Hopkins Universty Press.

——. 2005b. "A New/Old Reading of the *lithos epi lithon* Prophecy and the Role of the Temple Mount in the Jesus Movement." In *The Beginnings of Christianity: A Collection of Articles*, ed. Jack Pastor and Menahem Mor, 325–347. Jerusalem: Yad Ben-Zvi.

Josephus, Flavius (d. c. 100 CE). 1926. *Against Apion*, trans. Henry J. Thackeray. Cambridge: Harvard University Press.

——. 1927–28. *The Jewish War*, trans. Henry J. Thackeray. Cambridge: Harvard University Press.

——. 1930–65 *Jewish Antiquities*, trans. Henry J. Thackeray, Ralph Marcus, and Louis Feldman. Cambridge: Harvard University Press.

Parry, Donald W. 1990. "Sinai as Sanctuary and Mountain of God." In *By Study and Also by Faith: Essays in Honor of Hugh W. Nibley*, ed. John M. Lundquist and Stephen D. Ricks, 2 vols., 1: 482–500. Salt Lake City: Deseret.

Purvis, James D. 1988–91. *Jerusalem the Holy City: A Bibliography*. Metuchen: Scarecrow Press.

Safrai, Shmuel. 1981. "Pilgrimage to Jerusalem After the Destruction of the Second Temple." In *Jerusalem in the Second Temple Period: Abraham Schalit Memorial Volume*, ed. A'haron Oppenheimer, Uri'el Rapaport, and Menahem Shtern, 376–393. Jerusalem: Yad Yitshak Ben-Tsevi. (In Hebrew.)

Smith, Jonathan Z. 1987. *To Take Place: Toward Theory in Ritual*. Chicago: University of Chicago Press.

Tsafrir, Yoram. 1999. "The Topography and Archeology of Aelia Capitolina." In *The History of Jerusalem: The Roman and Byzantine Periods (70–638 CE)*, ed.

Yoram Tsafrir and Shmuel Safrai, 115–166. Jerusalem: Yad Yitshak Ben-Tsevi. (In Hebrew.)

Walker, Peter W. L. 1996. *Jesus and the Holy City: New Testament Perspectives on Jerusalem*. Grand Rapids: Eerdmans.

Wilken, Robert L. 1992. *The Land Called Holy: Palestine in Christian History and Thought*. New Haven: Yale University Press.

5 Early Christian Jerusalem
The city of the cross

Oliver Larry Yarbrough

The fall of Jerusalem

At the beginning of the seventh century CE, a Persian army swept across the eastern Mediterranean, seizing city after city from Byzantine control. In 614 it captured Jerusalem. Apparently, however, Jerusalem meant little to the Persians, since they do not mention its conquest in any literature of the time, and they seem not to have established any presence in the city. But if the seizure of Jerusalem meant little to the Persians, it meant a great deal to those who were defeated—the Christians who had controlled the city for almost 300 years. Its loss was a devastating event that demanded explanation.

Antiochus Strategos, a monk of the St. Sabas monastery located in the Judean desert, took up this task in *The Capture of Jerusalem by the Persians*.[1] An eyewitness himself, Strategos sought to explain the loss of Jerusalem by claiming that the Persians were instruments of God, who was punishing the Christians for their sins. He supports his interpretation with frequent allusions to biblical stories. For example, alluding to Ezekiel's vision of God's abandoning Jerusalem before the Babylonians destroyed the Temple in 587 BCE (Ezekiel 10–11), Strategos says the Persians were able to capture Jerusalem only because its guardian angels had withdrawn their protection (Coneybeare 1910, 505). At the same time, however, Strategos seeks to encourage his readers by praising the martyrs of the city who remained faithful in the face of the persecution inflicted on them during the battle for the city and the deportation that followed.[2] Finally, in what may be a later addition to the manuscript, Strategos glorifies the Byzantine Emperor Heraclius (610–41), who returned "the life-giving tree, the Cross of Christ" after defeating the Persian king and retaking Jerusalem some 17 years later.

Mapping the imperial city

Though Strategos' account clearly stretches the story in the service of his larger purposes, it allows us a glimpse of Jerusalem at the beginning of the seventh century.[3] In the aftermath of the battle, Strategos reports, the survivors surveyed the city to count (and bury) the dead. Most of the bodies were found at holy sites. The churches Strategos mentions include Holy Zion, the New Church, St. Sophia, Sts. Cosmas and Damian, St. Kiriakos, St. Jacob, the Anastasis, St. Serapion, Holy Golgotha, and St. George. Two monasteries are also mentioned: Holy Anastasis and St. John, the latter apparently of considerable size, since Strategos claims 4,219 bodies were found there. Other sites include the Mount of Olives, the Large and Little Assemblies, the Tower of David, and two hospices established for the elderly. Combining Strategos's list with other reports and the results of recent excavations, Oleg Grabar reckons that at the time of the Persian conquest there were some fifty Christian buildings in and around Jerusalem, with seventeen to twenty-one within its walls. Thus, he concludes, "sanctuaries commemorating the narrative of the Gospels and the presence of saints and of holy men and women in Jerusalem were everywhere and gave a special cachet of piety and spiritual wealth to the entire city" (Grabar 1996, 37). No wonder then that Strategos has the king of the Persians refer to Jerusalem as "the great city of the Christians" (Coneybeare 1910, 512).

The Madaba map, a sixth-century mosaic depicting the biblical world from Egypt to Syria, provides graphic confirmation of Jerusalem's Christian status. The city stands at the very center of the map, thus representing it as the "navel of the universe."[4] Identified as "The Holy City of Jerusalem" and shown in an aerial view from the west, Jerusalem appears as a walled city, densely packed with monumental buildings. Readily identifiable among them are some of the sites mentioned by Strategos: the Anastasis,[5] the New Church, and the church on Mt. Zion. Others appear to be Sts. Cosmas and Damian, St. Sophia, and the Church at Siloam. Also notable on the map are prominent gates and the main Roman streets. Notable for a quite different reason is the difficulty in identifying the site of the Temple Mount. Michael Avi-Yonah sees it in the upper quadrant, on the colonnaded street just below the Golden Gate (Avi-Yonah 1954, 59). But since this area has the same architectural features one finds on the rest of the street, which leads back to the Damascus Gate, its identification as the Temple Mount seems doubtful. Its absence, moreover, should not really be surprising, since at least from the time of Julian (361–363), and probably before, the Temple Mount was a dead zone in the Christian city, an architectural wasteland of scattered stones and columns. Keeping it undeveloped apparently served to emphasize the splendors of the monumental basilicas, rotundas, and shrines that made up the Byzantine city (Tsafrir 1999, 144).

The Jerusalem described by Strategos and illustrated on the Madaba map was some 300 years in the making. Throughout the period many bishops, abbots, and patrons from around the Christian world founded churches, monasteries, and shrines in Jerusalem, adding to the modest Christian sites that already existed. It was imperial patronage, however, that did most to create the Christian city the Persians found when they overran it. Constantine and his mother Helena, Eudokia (wife of Theodosius II), and

Justinian were the primary imperial patrons of Christian Jerusalem. Each presented the city with impressive monumental churches and other ecclesiastical buildings.

As we will see, Christian pilgrims had been visiting Jerusalem's holy sites long before Constantine took an interest in the city. So it is clear that he did not begin the notion of Jerusalem as a special place for Christians. Nonetheless, his efforts contributed significantly to the rise of its status. The Council of Nicea, for example, could not have elevated the status of Jerusalem's bishop (as it did in Canons 6 and 7) without the Emperor's consent. Constantine's greatest contribution to the Christianizing of Jerusalem, however, was his inclusion of it on the list of cities to which he made significant grants for the erection of churches.[6] Although Constantine's architectural contributions to Jerusalem included additions to the church his mother Helena had endowed on the summit of the Mount of Olives during her pilgrimage, his most important gift was the Anastasis—a complex built over and around the reputed tomb of Jesus.[7]

Ordaining that the central basilica should exceed all other buildings in the empire, Constantine provided both the grand vision and the funds for its erection.[8] Although he left the final design and construction to the Bishop of Jerusalem and local architects (directing civil authorities from the province to provide whatever workmen and materials the project required), the letters he wrote concerning its construction suggest that Constantine took great personal interest in the project. The final complex included the basilica, a monumental rotunda over the site of the tomb, an atrium leading to the rotunda, and a large baptistery. The result was a sacred precinct that, although not in the center of the city, was nonetheless at its heart.[9]

Eudokia, wife of Theodosius II (408–450) and one of the most cultivated women to reign in the Eastern portion of the Empire, spent considerable time in Jerusalem, first on pilgrimage in 438 and then in residence from 443 to the time of her death in 460. During her pilgrimage, Eudokia was associated with the discovery of the relics of Stephen, the proto-martyr. She built a church over the site and took the relics to Constantinople to establish a shrine there. In addition to building numerous other churches and monasteries in Jerusalem and throughout Palestine, Eudokia also funded the building of a wall around Mount Zion, thus bringing it within the city's precincts (Burman 1991).

Justinian's reign (527–565) may well represent the flowering of Byzantine culture. Following his conquest of the Western Empire, which had been lost in the previous century, Justinian, like Constantine, undertook a major building program throughout the Empire to establish his reputation and secure his reign. Jerusalem was one of the primary beneficiaries of the emperor's largess. He presented to the city a monumental new church of imperial size and grandeur. Dedicated to the Theotokos, locals referred to it simply as "the Nea," the new [church]. According to Procopius, our major source, this church was an architectural wonder, due mainly to the innovative engineering required to provide for its foundation, which was "part on solid rock and partly on air."[10] Although Procopius' description of the church itself is minimal, modern excavations provide enough information to confirm his view of its monumental proportions. Procopius had noted that the columns in front of the main doors may have been the largest in the world and that "the magnificent doors" to the precincts gave passers-by a sense of the grandeur inside. The excavations suggest that the basilica was in fact 116 meters long and 52 meters wide. Thus, though it may not have been the largest church in the world, it was the largest in Palestine (Avigad 1993). At the Nea's completion, at any rate, Justinian claimed to have surpassed both Constantine and Solomon, providing a place of worship that eclipsed the Temple itself (Amizur 1996).[11]

In addition to the churches, monasteries were another prominent architectural feature of Christian Jerusalem. As noted above, Strategos mentions two: Holy Anastasis and St. John. Procopius' long list of the monasteries that Justinian founded or rebuilt includes the names of four others—St. Thaleleus, the Iberian, St. Mary, and the Spring of St. Elisha.[12] The monasteries, which were of various sizes and established for both men and women, contributed significantly to the city's ecclesiastical and social life, not to mention its economy. Their inhabitants took part in the numerous synods and other meetings held in Jerusalem during the theological debates of the period, serving as both participants and hosts for visiting clerics. Indeed, showing hospitality was a fundamental purpose for the monasteries, so that they came to play a significant role in the pilgrimage enterprise, which helped define Jerusalem's reputation as a Christian city.

The pilgrims' city

We have already seen in Helena and Eudokia two of the most prominent pilgrims to Jerusalem. They were clearly not the only ones. Early notable pilgrims include Melito of Sardis, Alexander, Sextus Julius Africanus, and Origen (Wilkinson 2002b, 4–5). After Constantine established Jerusalem's status as a sacred city for Christians following the years it was under direct Roman rule (135–325), the flow of pilgrims increased dramatically. Though the list would come to include most of the important clerics of the fourth to the sixth centuries, the vast majority remain nameless (Wilkinson 2002a, 124–125).[13]

Fortunately, we have several firsthand accounts that, though sometimes difficult to interpret, give us a good indication of what pilgrimage to Jerusalem entailed. The first is the Pilgrim of Bordeaux, who showed up in Jerusalem not long after Constantine's building program began (c. 333). The Pilgrim's account lists some twenty-five sites in Jerusalem, most dealing with biblical scenes. In the sparse style of a Michelin Green Guide, the Pilgrim mentions the tower where Jesus was tempted, the cornerstone that the builders rejected, the site of the house of Caiaphas, the column against which Jesus was scourged, the house of Pilate, a palm tree from which children took branches to spread before Jesus on his triumphal entry to the city, the hill of Golgotha, the rock where Judas betrayed Jesus, and the tomb where Jesus was laid. In a rare comment, the Pilgrim says Constantine's church over the tomb was *mirae pulchritudinis* ("wondrously beautiful"), but gives no description. On the Mount of Olives, the Pilgrim noted the basilica raised over the site where Jesus taught and the circular shrine on the hill where Jesus was transfigured. These are the expressly Christian sites. The Pilgrim also mentions sites referencing heroes and places from earlier biblical history. These include the Temple Mount (now a plowed field), the chambers where Solomon recorded his wise sayings, the house of Hezekiah, the site of David's palace, an ancient synagogue, and memorials to Isaiah and Hezekiah.

Although attempts have been made to find theological/liturgical concerns in the Pilgrim's account, they seem strained.[14] The visit to Jerusalem occurred during a period of transition and major imperial building, yet there is little, if any, notice of their significance. Thus, the description of the Anastasis is hardly different from the treatment of the other sites in the city and its environs. Quite notably, the Pilgrim describes the memorials to Isaiah and Hezekiah with the very same words used for the Anastasis— *mirae pulchritudinis*. Much the same point could be made about the Pilgrim's treatment of Jerusalem itself, in comparison to description of the other biblical sites on the itinerary. They are treated with essentially the same brief notices, devoid of substantive comment. Perhaps we should not read too much into all this. The terse descriptions may reflect nothing more than a laconic style. Nonetheless, it is striking that the Pilgrim could see so much and have so little to say.

A second account of pilgrimage to Jerusalem offers a distinctively different perspective. It comes from one Egeria, a noblewoman from western Europe.[15] From 381 to 384 Egeria toured biblical sites throughout Palestine, participating in local liturgies at the various holy places. Her account, in contrast to the Bordeaux Pilgrim's, does treat Jerusalem differently from the rest of the sites she visits. Indeed, like the author of the Gospel of Mark, she slows the pace dramatically when she writes of her time in Jerusalem. Egeria lists five major Christian sites in Jerusalem, noting both the local name and the events related to it: the column where Jesus was scourged, the basilica of the crucifixion, the Anastasis, the place of the Ascension, and the church on the Mount of Olives. In the surviving manuscript, Egeria never gives a systematic description of any of these buildings. She goes into great detail, however, in describing the liturgies that take place in and around them throughout the Christian year, suggesting that they were designed to recall the events of Jesus' last days. Egeria thus describes Jerusalem as a holy place comprising holy places, all recalling holy events. It is as if the liturgies were designed to reenact the events and bring history to life.[16]

Jerome, who spent much of his life in Bethlehem, also uses the notion of pilgrimage bringing history to life. In a letter of consolation to his protégée

Eustochium, Jerome recalls her pilgrimage to Jerusalem with her mother Paula, pausing over their visit to the Anastasis. He reminds Eustochium that while they were in Jerusalem her mother

> fell down and worshipped before the Cross as if she could see the Lord hanging on it. On entering the Tomb of the Resurrection, she kissed the stone which the angel removed from the sepulcher door; then like a thirsty man who has waited long, and at last comes to water, she faithfully kissed the very shelf on which the Lord's body had lain.
>
> (Epistle 108.9.2)[17]

Thus, although Procopius may have been struck only by the city's architectural grandeur and the Bordeaux Pilgrim could see the sites with little emotion, some pilgrims were deeply moved by what they saw, recalling events of biblical history and bringing them to living memory. And while the whole of biblical history was noted, it was the passion of Jesus that ultimately came to dominate Christian imagination, focusing on the cross, the tomb, and the resurrection.

A city among cities

The fascination with holy sites notwithstanding, Christians were divided about the significance of Jerusalem, and had been from the very beginning. Some of the debates, which I will examine below, had to do with theological issues and the interpretation of scripture, especially prophecies concerning the city's future. Others had to do with ecclesiastical politics and issues of status. In the first of the debates about Jerusalem's status, the conflict reflected tensions between the episcopal sees of Jerusalem and Caesarea. Because Caesarea was the provincial capital, its bishop had primacy throughout the region. But Canons 6 and 7 of the Council of Nicea (325) decreed that the bishop of Jerusalem should have status commensurate with the city's standing as an apostolic city (Walker 1990). Whatever its immediate effect may have been with regard to diocesan politics, Jerusalem soon outstripped Caesarea in every way. Consequently, at the Council of Chalcedon (451), Jerusalem was elevated still further, now receiving patriarchal status. But while this move may have confirmed its standing over Caesarea, it put the bishop of Jerusalem in a totally different circle of players. Indeed, the tensions between Jerusalem and Caesarea were minor compared to those that governed relations among the patriarchs of Antioch, Alexandria, Rome, and Constantinople. The leaders of these churches would challenge each other time and again, forming and reforming alliances, excommunicating one another, and in various ways seeking to protect their own status (and that of their churches) at whatever the cost to rivals. The maneuvering would end only with the fall of Antioch, Alexandria, Jerusalem, and, finally, Constantinople to Muslim forces, leaving Rome as the sole survivor.

There were also tensions arising from Jerusalem's status as a pilgrimage site. Gregory of Nyssa (c. 330–c. 396) and Jerome (c. 345–420), for example, argued that the holy places there were no more sacred than anywhere else, although both had been pilgrims to Jerusalem and Palestine. As Jerome would put it to Paulinus of Nola, "Access to the courts of heaven is as easy from Britain as it is from Jerusalem" (Epistle 46.3). Gregory was more negative in his assessment of Jerusalem's status as the holy city, decrying its immorality and claiming that his own Cappadocia had more holy places than Palestine. Thus, he argued, Cappadocia could be said to have an even greater portion of the Holy Spirit (Epistles 2 and 3). Here again, however, theology and scriptural interpretation were counterbalanced by other concerns. Jerome, after all, lived in Bethlehem, not Jerusalem; and the strained relations that developed between Gregory and the bishop of Jerusalem clearly shaped his memories of the time he spent there (Bitton-Ashkelony 1999, 188–201).[18]

These problems notwithstanding, Jerusalem's status as a Christian city was well established for the period we have been examining. Its historical significance, its imperial patronage, and the resulting importance for pilgrims insured its standing in the minds of Christians around the world. Thus, when Jerusalem fell at the beginning of the seventh century, Strategos reports, "there took hold of all the Christians of the whole world great sorrow and effable grief" (Coneybeare 1910, 510).

When the city belonged to others

At the beginning of the fourth century, however, few, if any, could have foreseen what would transpire in Jerusalem over the next three hundred years, for the opening of that century brought some of the fiercest persecution the Christians had experienced. At the beginning of the second century, the notion of Jerusalem as a Christian city adorned with monumental buildings established through imperial patronage was even further from Christian imagination. Nonetheless, Christians did have a vision of the future and of Jerusalem's place in it. The remainder of this essay will be devoted to examining the vision of Jerusalem in the first three centuries of the Christian movement and how it might have related to what actually transpired. At every step of the way, however, the issues are exceedingly complex and interpretations of the primary texts correspondingly wide ranging. The scope of this essay allows only for brief treatments of the most salient issues, with reference to some of the more important secondary literature.

We divide the first three centuries into two periods: from the life of Jesus to the destruction of Jerusalem (4 BCE–135 CE) and from the establishment of Aelia Capitolina on the site of the destroyed city to the dedication of Constantine's Church of the Holy Sepulcher (135–335). In the first period, the primary sources are the Gospels and Acts, the Pauline letters, Hebrews, and Revelation. In the second period, the writers most concerned with Jerusalem are Justin Martyr (c. 100–c. 165), Irenaeus (c. 130–c. 200), Tertullian (c. 160–c. 225), Origen (c. 185–c. 254), and Eusebius (c. 260–c. 340).

Jesus and the Gospels

Although the differences between and among the Gospels demand caution in using them to determine Jesus' view of Jerusalem, we must at least explore the question. The issues have to do with determining the authenticity of sayings and the interpretation of events. One of the most convincing assessments comes from E. P. Sanders (1985 and 1999), who focuses on Jesus' "cleansing" of the Temple and his sayings about its coming destruction. Sanders argues that these are central to Jesus' self-understanding and calling, concluding that Jesus saw himself as an eschatological prophet called to proclaim that "the end was at hand and that the temple would be destroyed, so that the new and perfect temple might arise" (Sanders 1985, 75).[19] Jesus' words and actions regarding the Temple offended the priestly aristocracy, Sanders infers, causing them to warn the Romans of the dangers such words and actions posed to the peace of the city. The Romans then crucified Jesus for sedition, treating him as a would-be king (1985, Chapters 10 and 11). As an eschatological prophet, Jesus exemplified the "restoration eschatology" of Israel's prophetic tradition as it developed in varying ways during the Second Temple period.[20] Thus, Jesus looked for the coming of the kingdom of God, which meant that "God must step in and provide a new temple, the restored people of Israel, and presumably a renewed social order, one in which 'sinners' will have a place" (1985, 232). Sanders further proposes that Jesus likely held the common Jewish view that "in the last days the Gentiles can be admitted to the kingdom on some condition or other," but that "[w]e understand the debates in early Christianity best if we attribute to Jesus no explicit viewpoint at all" (1985, 221). Nonetheless, Sanders argues, Jesus' disciples and immediate followers understood what Jesus was about and thus continued to expect the coming of the kingdom, even if they also continued to debate its meaning and develop new perspectives over the course of time (1985, Chapter 8 and 334–340). One aspect of this development was further exploration of the meaning of the Temple and, by extension, Jerusalem.[21]

Jerusalem and the Temple are central to the narrative structure of all four canonical gospels, though sometimes in quite different ways. Mark and Matthew are closest in both structure and emphasis, placing most of Jesus' public ministry in Galilee. Only in the last days does Jesus go to Jerusalem, where he is arrested, crucified, and resurrected. While in Jerusalem Jesus curses the Temple, drives out the staff arranging for sacrifices (Mark 11; Matthew 21), and predicts its destruction (Mark 13; Matthew 24). At his death, the veil of the Temple is rent in two (Mark 15:38 and Matthew 27:51), either foreshadowing its destruction or signaling the end of its role in mediating access to God. At the end of both gospels the focus shifts away from Jerusalem and its Temple: the disciples are sent back to Galilee, where they will encounter the risen Jesus (Mark 16:7; Matthew 28:7). Matthew especially emphasizes this movement away from Jerusalem and shows its significance by making Jesus' last words to the disciples, "Go therefore and make disciples of all nations" (Matthew 28:19).

Luke has all of the pericopes in Mark and Matthew just noted, though with changes to each. Luke also places most of Jesus' public ministry in Galilee. He arranges the material, however, so that Jesus' last journey begins pointedly in 9:51, when he "sets his face to go to Jerusalem." Even more pointedly, Luke differs from Mark and Matthew by having the disciples remain in Jerusalem after Jesus' death. They are to wait there "until they are clothed with power from on high" and then beginning *from Jerusalem* are to preach in Jesus' name to all nations (24:47–49). Luke's narrative continues in the Acts of the Apostles, where the story of this mission is recounted. Its programmatic outline is given in Acts 1:8: "you shall be my witnesses in Jerusalem and in all Judea and Samaria and to the end of the earth." Consequently, the first half of Acts takes place in Jerusalem, with the disciples regularly in and out of the Temple to pray. Furthermore, a core of apostles, led by Jesus' brother James, remains based in Jerusalem throughout Acts. Nonetheless, the action of the narrative turns away from Jerusalem, for although many in the city respond to the apostles' preaching (especially those who are present for the holy days), the leadership of the Temple turns against them, so that the second half of Acts recounts a turning to the nations. Though a number of apostles and others take part in this mission, Paul becomes the central figure of the narrative from Chapter 13. Acts ends with Paul's preaching in Rome, after having been challenged by the leaders in Jerusalem and brought before the Roman governor on charges that echo those leveled at Jesus (Acts 28:16–31). Jerusalem is therefore very important to Luke as the site of the Temple and as the seat of the earliest Christians. But the way he writes of those early days makes clear they belong to the past. The Church has moved on; the future belongs to the Gentile mission, which takes place in the cities of the Greco-Roman world.

The Gospel of John intensifies the focus on Jerusalem and the Temple by moving the "cleansing" of the Temple to the very beginning of Jesus' public ministry (2:13–22) and thereby making his conflict with it a running theme throughout the book. John also adds to the story a saying regarding the destruction of the Temple, typically interpreting it for his reader: the Temple to which Jesus refers is not a building but his own body. The effect, of course, is to make Jesus a substitute for the Temple. In a similar way, the narrative structure of the Gospel of John contrasts sharply with the structure of the synoptic gospels, in that it has Jesus journeying to Jerusalem repeatedly and not just at the end. These trips, moreover, are on the occasion of major Jewish festivals, so that John contrasts Jesus to them also. This motif culminates in John's passion narrative. Here, too, the Gospel of

John differs, moving the crucifixion to the Day of Preparation, so that Jesus dies as the Passover lambs are being slaughtered. Time and again, therefore, John presents Jesus as a substitute for the central places and events sacred to Judaism. As with the other gospels, Jerusalem (and all that it represents) is left behind, the climax coming when the Greeks in Jerusalem for the celebration of Passover come to the disciples in search of Jesus (12:20–36). Yet again, the future belongs to the Gentile mission.

In each of the Gospels, therefore, Jerusalem is the site of major events in Jesus' life, especially those related to his death on the cross. In both the Gospels and Acts, however, the story moves on. Jerusalem belongs to the past; the future belongs to the nations. To the extent that Jerusalem is identified with the Temple, the Gospels and Acts do reflect judgment on the city for the events that took place there. But the references to judgment are remarkably reserved, given the significance of the destruction of the Temple in 70. The rhetoric will be highly charged for later Christian writers, with explicit claims that the destruction of Jerusalem was justified because of Jewish responsibility for the death of Jesus. The Gospels, however, show little interest in Jerusalem's fate, focusing their attention rather on what is to come. Even Matthew, who comes closest to making the destruction of the Temple a punishment for the Jews' rejection of Jesus and who alone includes the crowd's acceptance of responsibility for his death (27:25), emphasizes the global aspect of the final judgment, alone noting that the gospel must be preached to the whole world (24:14 and parallels) and concluding the eschatological discourse with the claim that when the Son of Man comes in his glory "*all the nations* will be gathered before him" for judgment (25:31–32).[22]

Paul

The Gentile mission is also central to the letters of Paul, who even styles himself the "apostle to the Gentiles" (Romans 1:5 and Galatians 2:7, for example). This calling took Paul away from Jerusalem and into the cities of the Greco-Roman world. Nonetheless, he kept coming back to Jerusalem; and people from Jerusalem regularly came to him (or followed him) wherever he went. The result is a very complex picture of Paul's relationship to Jerusalem.[23] The primary passages for consideration are Galatians 1:10–2:14; 4:21–5:1 and the references to the ministry for the saints in Jerusalem: Romans 15:25–31; 1 Corinthians 16:3 and 2 Corinthians 8–9;[24] 2 Corinthians 10–13 also bears on Paul's relationship to Jerusalem, since it treats of Paul's opponents the "super-apostles" (the term is highly ironic), who most likely come from Jerusalem.

In all of these passages, except perhaps Galatians 4:21–5:1, "Jerusalem" references the Jewish-Christian community in the city, not the Jews themselves. Galatians 1:10–2:14 contains Paul's account of his relation with the "pillars" of the Jerusalem church: Peter, James, and John. He is at pains to show that he is independent of them, visiting Peter once three years after his revelation[25] and then only for two weeks. Paul adds, with an oath, that he did not see anyone else on this visit, except James, the Lord's brother. Fourteen years later, he went to Jerusalem again, this time with Barnabas and Titus. He was not summoned, he insists, but went as a result of a revelation. The outcome of this meeting, he avers, was the agreement among the participants that Peter would go to the circumcised and Paul to the Gentiles and that Paul would "remember the poor," which, he insists, he was eager to do (Galatians 2:10). The tone throughout this portion of the letter is very defensive, due to the fact that rivals from Jerusalem have raised doubts among the Galatians about the adequacy of Paul's understanding of the gospel. Throughout, therefore, Paul insists on his independence.[26]

The allegory of Sarah and Hagar in Galatians 4:21–25, therefore, must be read in the context of the whole letter. Read this way, the contrast Paul makes between the two figures does not reflect Christianity and Judaism but Paul himself and the segment of the Jerusalem church that is challenging him and his understanding of the gospel (Martyn 1998).[27] Thus, the "present Jerusalem" in Paul's interpretation of the allegory refers to those from Jerusalem who argue that the Gentile Christians in Galatia (and elsewhere) should be circumcised. Extending the allegory, Paul claims that they are nothing less than slaves to the law. Furthermore, they are persecuting Paul just as Ishmael persecuted Isaac. They may claim that Jerusalem is the mother church, but, so Paul argues, it is a mother like Hagar, nothing more than a slave. By contrast, Paul's mother, and the mother of his churches, is the Jerusalem above. Interestingly, and tellingly, the only description Paul gives of the "Jerusalem above" is that it is free. Thus, while he may well have known of biblical and early Jewish traditions that refer to a heavenly Jerusalem that will descend at the end of the age, he makes no reference to them here, even though the comparison with the "*present* Jerusalem" gave him the opportunity.[28] It is Paul's *use* of "the Jerusalem above" rather than its background that determines how we are to read the passage.[29] The watchword here, as in 5:1 and 13, is "freedom."[30]

In spite of the tension between himself and the representatives of the Jerusalem church who insist on circumcision for Gentile converts, indeed perhaps because of it, Paul worked hard to preserve relations between his Gentile churches and the church in Jerusalem. This is abundantly clear in his commitment to completing his ministry to the poor among the saints in Jerusalem, which involved a monetary collection from the members of his Gentile churches. As Romans 15:25–31 shows, he was not at all sure how the collection would be received. Clearly, however, Paul regarded its delivery as extremely important for himself and for his churches. The collection, he argued, was vivid evidence of the interdependence between the Jerusalem church and the Gentile mission. The one shares a spiritual blessing, the other a material one (Romans 15:27). Or, as he puts it in 2 Corinthians, the Gentiles supply the needs of the saints in Jerusalem; the saints pray for the Gentiles (9:12, 14).

Hebrews and revelation

The references to Jerusalem in Hebrews are, if anything, even more complex than those in Paul's letters, for this work has many more allusions to the land, Temple, and the sacrifices of the Temple than one finds in Paul. Furthermore, Hebrews applies both spatial and temporal language to almost every metaphor on which the author draws. Thus, one must constantly examine the overall perspective of the book and individual elements in it. With regard to Jerusalem, 12:12 and 13:14 are indicative of the issues. The former indicates that the readers "*have come* to Mount Zion and to the city of the living God, the heavenly Jerusalem."[31] The latter, however, claims that "*here* we do not have an enduring city, but we see the city *which is to come*." Nor are the readers given any indication of how to construe the coming of the city. The references to the city with foundations designed and built by God in 11:10 and to the city prepared by God in 11:16 point in the direction of Israelite and Jewish traditions regarding a restored Jerusalem, but they are only vaguely allusive. Taken together with the language of "the world to come" (2:5), the "sabbath rest" that yet remains (4:1, 9, 11), the "true tent" (8:2), "the heavenly sanctuary" (8:5), and the "tent [and sanctuary] not made with hands" (9:12, 24), the concern with "the heavenly Jerusalem" and "city to come" points to a reality beyond the present one. As Hebrews 10:1 makes the contrast, it is between the "shadow (*skia*) of the good things to come" and "the very form of things (*aute e eikona ton pragmaton*)." Thus, however one reconciles the phrases "*having come* ... to the city, the heavenly Jerusalem" and seeking "the city *which is to come*," both undermine the significance of the present Jerusalem itself by pointing to a reality out of this world.

The quintessential Christian out-of-this-world references to Jerusalem in the New Testament are the three found in Revelation:

> If you conquer, I will make you a pillar in the temple of my God; you will never go out of it. I will write on you the name of my God, and the name of the city of my God, the new Jerusalem that comes down from my God out of heaven, and my own new name.
>
> (Revelation 3:12)

> And I saw the holy city, the New Jerusalem, coming down out of heaven from God, prepared as a bride adorned for her husband.
>
> (Revelation 21:2)

> And in the spirit he carried me away to a great, high mountain and showed me the holy city Jerusalem coming down out of heaven from God.
>
> (Revelation 21:10)

Christians did not invent this kind of language, or even the specific image of a heavenly Jerusalem. Both had a long history in Israelite and Jewish literature. The history is complex and the language richly nuanced, drawing on traditions referring to Jerusalem, Zion, and the Temple—either singly or in combination. In broad terms, one thinks, for example, of Ezekiel's vision of a new temple (40–48) and Isaiah's plans for Jerusalem after the exile (40–66). Closer to the language of Revelation, however, are the examples from Jewish apocalyptic literature, most notably 4 Ezra 7:26 and 10:40ff and 1 Enoch 90:28f. But the imagery is not limited to apocalyptic literature. Tobit's description of the New Jerusalem, for example, resembles the language of Revelation very strikingly indeed:

> For Jerusalem will be built as his house for all ages.
> How happy I will be if a remnant of my descendants should survive
> to see your glory and acknowledge the King of heaven.
> The gates of Jerusalem will be built with sapphire and emerald,
> and all your walls with precious stones.
> The towers of Jerusalem will be built with gold,
> and their battlements with pure gold.
> The streets of Jerusalem will be paved
> with ruby and with stones of Ophir.
> The gates of Jerusalem will sing hymns of joy,
> and all her houses will cry, "Hallelujah!
> Blessed be the God of Israel!"
> and the blessed will bless the holy name forever and ever.
>
> (Tobit 13:16–17)

The architectural details in Tobit and Revelation may be different, but the utopian vision is the same.

The biblical allusions in the description of the New Jerusalem in Revelation 21:1–22:5 are far too numerous to treat here. One feature, however, is very striking—the seer's claim that there was no temple in the holy city, since "its temple is the Lord God the Almighty and the Lamb" (21:22). This is remarkable, given the importance of the Temple in the prophetic sources on which the author of Revelation draws. It is also remarkable given the urban perspective that permeates the book. It is impossible to imagine any of the cities mentioned in Revelation without temples, not to mention a restored Jerusalem without one. In this regard, at least, Revelation breaks from Jewish restoration expectations, and represents something new. Its prophetic vision, moreover, has had tremendous influence on Christian imagination, from earliest times to the present.

The second and third centuries

For some early Christians, fulfillment of the prophecies in Revelation and anticipation of the New Jerusalem was vivid and immediate. The Montanists, an apocalyptic movement of the mid-second century, looked for the imminent descent of the New Jerusalem in Phrygia, a region in central Asia

Minor (see, for example, Tabbernee 2003). For others (Justin, Irenaeus, and Tertullian, for example), the wait would be longer, and follow the second coming of Jesus and his reign of a thousand years. Significantly, the expectation was for the establishment of a city in time and space, with all the trappings of a Greco-Roman city.[32] For still others, such expectations derived from a too literal interpretation of scripture, a charge Origen leveled at both Jews and Christians who looked for the construction (or descending) of a New Jerusalem. For Origen, it was all allegory. As Robert Wilkins puts it, "For Origen the essential feature of the holy land was not its location but its quality and character" (1992, 77–78). Origen, and others who pursued a more metaphorical reading of the texts held that the New Jerusalem was not a place but an idea, one that emphasized the spiritual and universal aspects of salvation. The treatment of the New Jerusalem was analogous to the treatment of Jerusalem as a pilgrimage site. One did not have to go there to know its benefits.

One of those who followed Origen's line of interpretation, however, was caught up in history, which all too often wreaks havoc on ideas. Shortly after the Council of Nicea, Eusebius of Caesarea wrote a commentary on Isaiah that utilized Origen's allegorical method of interpretation. At the same time, however, it sought to accommodate an historical interpretation of the relevant passages from scripture. Michael Hollerich notes in his study of the commentary that Hebrews 12:22 was especially important to Eusebius, since it "implied an intimate bond between the heavenly Jerusalem and the historical church, which appealed to his desire to equate the church with the city of God." As a consequence, Hollerich adds, Eusebius never mentions Hebrews 13:14, which refers to "the city yet to come" because "[t]he expectancy of this verse may have been too strong, since he tends to see in the godly polity 'an abiding city', the *patris* which Hebrews 13:14 says the Old Testament worthies yearned for" (Hollerich 1999, 174).[33] For Eusebius, therefore, "the eschatological prophecies that speak of a restoration of temple and city" refer to the church, "which he regarded as the rebuilt Jerusalem of texts like Isaiah 54:11–14" (1999, 38). At the same time, however, Eusebius had to deal with Constantine's championing of Christianity and the resultant building program in Jerusalem that he set in place to glorify the city and his empire. In the end, Eusebius would become one of Constantine's most adamant supporters. 1 things that happened in his day," having seen "the profound shift in devotion that was taking place." Thus, Wilkins concludes, Eusebius "was devoted to the 'new Jerusalem set over against the old,' whose center was the tomb of Christ, located not in the heavens but in Judea" (Wilkins 1992, 81).[34]

There is a remarkable image of this "shift in devotion" in the apse mosaic of Sta. Pudenziana in Rome. Crafted shortly after Egeria completed her pilgrimage through the Holy Land, the mosaic depicts Christ in the purple and gold of an emperor, seated on a throne and surrounded by his disciples. Above the image of Christ is a bejeweled cross, flanked by the four beasts of Revelation. Spanning the apse between the upper and lower panels is a cityscape of Jerusalem. Robin Margaret Jensen suggests the mosaic reflects "almost the whole Christian theological program—vicarious sacrifice, victorious resurrection, establishment of the universal church, judgment at the end of time, and the second coming of Christ with the New Jerusalem" (Jensen 2000, 108). She is almost certainly right. But it is especially striking that the image of the New Jerusalem is not the one so vividly depicted in Revelation. It is, rather, Constantine's monumental city. The heavenly Jerusalem of early Christian imagination and the monumental city that Constantine created were united—in the art of a Roman church.[35]

Back to the fall

And this brings us back to the city conquered by the Persians. Though it became a Christian city only at the beginning of the fourth century, Christians had a long association with it, both from their adoption of Jewish scriptures and from their own memories and accounts of events in the life of Jesus and the apostles. Some of those associations were mundane; others were out of this world. Some were of a place; others of an idea.

Although the loss of Jerusalem to the Persians was catastrophic, it was soon overcome. Heraclius retook the city, restored its monuments, and returned the cross to its proper place of honor. Even so, however, the days of Byzantine control of Jerusalem were numbered. In 636 Muslims defeated a Byzantine army at the Yarmuk river in Palestine; two years later the Patriarch of Jerusalem surrendered the city to Omar, Islam's second caliph.

Thus began a new era in Jerusalem's history, one that was to last until the Crusades, when the struggle over Jerusalem was renewed. In 1099 the armies of the First Crusade wrested control of Jerusalem from the Muslims. Yet again, however, the Christians could not hold it, or make much of their victory. Less than a century later, in 1187, Saladin's forces retook the city. Because Saladin allowed Christians to remain in Jerusalem and maintain circumscribed control of their holy places, they continued to belong to the city. Never again, however, would it belong to them. But does Jerusalem ever belong to anyone, at least for long?

Notes

1 I use the translation in Coneybeare 1910, 502–517. It is available online at http://www.tertullian.org/fathers/antiochus_strategos_capture.htm. The Arabic and Georgian versions are in Garitte 1960 and 1973 respectively.

2 Strategos says that the Persians turned Jerusalem over to the Jews and that the Christians refused their offer to save themselves by converting to Judaism (508); later, he says, those who were transported to the Persian capital refused to renounce their faith by trampling on "the Cross of Christ, the tree of our life" (510). The patriarch Zechariah interacts with the Persian king in ways that echo stories of Moses and Daniel, so that in the end "no one any more dared to go near the Lord's Cross, the tree of our salvation, because fear took

possession of all alike" when they saw the miracles Zechariah performed (513).

3 Grabar (1996, 40–44) regards *The Capture of Jerusalem* as fraught with mythical overtones and therefore difficult to use for an accurate reconstruction of what happened. For another treatment of Strategos' motives, see Drijvers 2002, 175–190.

4 On this theme, see Alexander 1999, 104–119.

5 In the West, the Anastasis is more commonly called the Church of the Holy Sepulcher.

6 On Constantine's ecclesiastical building programs, which were modeled on programs undertaken by his predecessors, see Krautheimer 1983 and 1992.

7 Eusebius gives a vivid description of the building and its construction in his *Life of Constantine* III.25–40.

8 For a recent treatment of the Anastasis, with references to earlier work, see Patrich 1993.

9 Although the map locates the Anastasis in the center of the city, it was actually in the northwestern quadrant, just off the cardo (Tsafrir 1999).

10 Procopius, a court secretary, is our major source for all Justinian's building programs. For the full text of his account, see the Loeb edition by Cameron and Dewing (1968–79). For the section on the Nea, see Wilkinson 2002a, 124–28. Discussion, with references, in Wilkinson 2002b, 4–5.

11 Amizur claims that the proportions of the Nea were modeled on Solomon's Temple and that the use of a cedar roof, unusual at the time, was also intended to recall the Temple.

12 For a full list of the monasteries, see Wilkinson 2002a, 127–128. Some of those without geographic reference were probably in Jerusalem also.

13 There is a large body of literature on pilgrimage. Two helpful surveys are Hunt 1982 and Maraval 1985. Augustine is the most conspicuously missing name from the list of pilgrims. For a discussion, see Bitton-Ashkelony 1999.

14 For an intriguing suggestion that the Pilgrim's itinerary is thematically oriented to "the life-giving qualities of water" and thus might be related to baptismal instruction, see Bowman 1999.

15 Translation and commentary in Wilkinson 2002b, 107–164.

16 For studies of the liturgies in Jerusalem, see Baldovin 1987 and Bradshaw 1999.

17 The translation is taken from Wilkinson 2002a.

18 The burial sites of martyrs, which were especially important to pilgrims, were scattered throughout the Greco-Roman world. Not surprisingly, competition developed among their promoters. Thus, critics like Gregory and Augustine did not oppose pilgrimage to Jerusalem in and of itself, but rather denied it special status over local shrines. See Wilkins' wry comment on Gregory's invective directed toward the immorality in Jerusalem: "There may be a smidgeon of Cappadocian chauvinism here" (Wilkins 1992, 118). Bishops, it would seem, are as capable of acting with mixed motives as anyone else.

19 Sanders does not regard the episode in the Temple as an act intended to purify the Temple but to signal its destruction (Sanders 1985, 61–71). The "cleansing" of the Temple is found in Mark 11:12–14 and parallels. References to the destruction of the Temple include: Mark 13:1 (and parallels); 14:15 (and parallels); John 2:18–22; and Acts 6:13.

20 Sanders is very careful to argue that there is no single version of "restoration eschatology" in the Second Temple period, claiming instead that there were sufficiently widespread versions of it to make Jesus' words and actions understandable to both his followers and his opponents (Sanders 1985, Chapters 2–3). More recent treatments of Jesus as an eschatological prophet include Allison 1998 and Ehrman 1999. For a discussion of radically different interpretations, see Sanders 1999, 102n2.

21 On the close relation between the Temple and Jerusalem in the minds of most Jews, see, Sanders 1985, Chapter 2, and Levine 1998, Chapter 2. For an alternative interpretation, see Schwartz 1996.

22 For an interpretation of the gospels that argues for a more pronounced judgment on Jerusalem for the rejection of Jesus, see Walker 1996.

23 I leave aside here the question of Paul's view of the Temple, since it is more complex than space allows for an adequate treatment. Suffice it to say that the references in 1 Corinthians 3:16–17 and 6:19 and 2 Corinthians 6:16 do not of themselves allow one to determine whether Paul thought the Temple in Jerusalem had continuing validity. They simply indicate that the Corinthian community could be compared to "a temple" (not "the Temple") in which God's spirit dwells. (Note that Paul uses several different terms in the Corinthian correspondence for what English translations render as "temple.") In fact, Paul does not explicitly deal with the Temple in Jerusalem anywhere in his surviving letters. Thus, one would have to extrapolate from such passages as Romans 3:24 and 9:4.

24 One might also add Romans 9–11, though the referent point there is "Israel," rather than Jerusalem. But see the references to "Zion" in 9:33 and 11:26.

25 Paul does not refer to his experience as "conversion," a notion that comes from the Acts account of the Damascus road. See Acts 9, 22, and 26.

26 Paul's unusual address (1:1) already signals his independence as a theme in Galatians.

27 For the traditional reading of the allegory as a contrast between Christianity and Judaism, see Wright 1994.

28 Note that Paul switches his metaphor from a temporal to a spatial category.

29 Philippians 3:20 is perhaps the closest analog to "the Jerusalem above" in Paul's other letters, since its reference to citizenship in a commonwealth in heaven is not far from being the child of the mother (Jerusalem) above. Note that Philippians 3 has other echoes of Galatians 4, in that 3:20 concludes an argument about circumcision that began in 3:2 and that the reference "enemies of the cross of Christ" in 3:18 repeats imagery of Paul's handwritten postscript in Galatians 6:11–16.

30 While Paul's own concern may have been freedom from the law, many commentators of the second and third centuries did treat Galatians 4:26 as eschatological. As we will see, they commonly linked it to Revelation 21:2 and Isaiah 49:16.

31 Determining the meaning of Jerusalem here is made even more difficult by the other references in the passage. The author tells his readers they have also come to "a myriad of angels in festal gathering," "the assembly of the first-born who are registered in heaven," "a judge who is God of all," "the spirits of the just who have been perfected," "Jesus," and "the sprinkled blood that speaks better than that of Abel."

32 See, for example, Justin Martyr, *Dialogue with Trypho* 80–83; Irenaeus, *Against Heresies* 5.25.4; 30.4; 34.4; 35.1; and Tertullian, *Against Marcion* 3.24–25. In *Against Heresies* 5.35.1, Irenaeus explicitly argues that the prophecies related to the restoration of Jerusalem were not to be interpreted allegorically. He mentions among these prophecies Isaiah 49:16; Galatians 4:26; and Revelation 21:1–4. For a reconstruction of early millenarian thought that was closely tied to Jewish restoration traditions, see Kinzig 2003.

33 Hollerich notes further that Eusebius does not refer to Revelation 21 for the same reasons. He provides a useful list of Eusebius' references to the city of God and the heavenly Jerusalem in a table (176–178).

34 Hollerich argues that while Eusebius accepted Constantine's commitment to building a Christian Jerusalem, and praised him for it, the *Commentary on Isaiah* reflects Eusebius' real concern—the *church* as the New Jerusalem prophesied by Isaiah, Paul, and the author of Hebrews.

35 Jan Elsner (1998, 232) makes a similar point.

References

Alexander, Philip S. 1999. "Jerusalem as the Omphalos of the World: On the History of a Geographical Concept." In Levine 1999, 104–119.

Allison, Dale. 1998. *Jesus of Nazareth: Millenarian Prophet.* Minneapolis: Fortress Press.

Amizur, Hagi. 1996. "Justinian's Solomon's Temple in Jerusalem." In *The Centrality of Jerusalem: Historical Perspectives*, ed. Marcel Poorthuis and Chana Safrai, 160–175. Kampen: Kok Pharos.

Avigad, Nahman. 1993. "The Nea: Justinian's Church of St. Mary, Mother of God, Discovered in the Old City of Jerusalem." In *Ancient Churches Revealed*, ed. Yoram Tsafrir, 128–135. Jerusalem: Israel Exploration Society.

Avi-Yonah, Michael. 1954. *The Madaba Mosaic Map with Introduction and Commentary.* Jerusalem: Israel Exploration Society.

Baldovin, John. 1987. *The Urban Character of Christian Worship: The Origins, Development, and Meaning of Stational Liturgy.* Rome: Pont. Institutum Studiorum Orientalium.

Bitton-Ashkelony, Brouria. 1999. "The Attitudes of Church Fathers toward Pilgrimage to Jerusalem in the Fourth and Fifth Centuries." In Levine 1999, 188–203.

Bowman, Glenn. 1999. " 'Mapping History's Redemption': Eschatology and Topography in the *Itinerarium Burdigalense*." In Levine 1999, 163–187.

Bradshaw, Paul F. 1999. "The Influence of Jerusalem on Christian Liturgy." In Levine 1999, 251–259.

Burman, Julia. 1991. "The Christian Empress Eudokia." In *Women and Byzantine Monasticism*, ed. Jacques Perrault, 51–59. Athens: Institut Canadien d'Archéologie à Athènes.

Coneybeare, F. C. 1910. "The Capture of Jerusalem," *English Historical Review* 25: 502–517.

Donner, Herbert and Heinz Cüppers. 1977. *Die Mosaikkarte von Madeba.* Wiesbaden: Harrassowitz.

Drijvers, Jan Willem. 2002. "Heraclius and the Restitutio Crucis: Notes on Symbolism and Ideology." In *The Reign of Heraclius (610–641): Crisis and Confrontation*, ed. Gerrit J. Reinink and Bernard H. Stolte (Groningen Studies in Cultural Change 2), 175–190. Leuven: Peeters.

Ehrman, Bart D. 1999. *Jesus: Apocalyptic Prophet of the New Millennium.* New York: Oxford University Press.

Elsner, Jan. 1998. *Imperial Rome and Christian Triumph.* Oxford: Oxford University Press.

Garitte, Gerado. 1960. *Expugnationis Hierosolymae A.D. 614.* Corpus Scriptorum Christianorum Orientalium 203.13. Louvain: Secrétariat du Corpus Scriptorum Christianorum Orientalium.

———.1973. *Expugnationis Hierosolymae A.D. 615.* Corpus Scriptorum Christianorum Orientalium 340.6. Louvain: Secrétariat du Corpus Scriptorum Christianorum Orientalium.

Grabar, Oleg. 1996. *The Shape of the Holy: Early Islamic Jerusalem.* Princeton: Princeton University Press.

Hollerich, Michael J. 1999. *Eusebius of Caesarea's Commentary on Isaiah: Christian Exegesis in the Age of Constantine.* Oxford: Clarendon Press.

Hunt, E. D. 1982. *Holy Land Pilgrimage in the Later Roman Empire, AD 312–460.* Oxford: Clarendon Press.

Jensen, Robin Margaret. 2000. *Understanding Early Christian Art*. London and New York: Routledge.

Kinzig, Wolfram. 2003. "Jewish and 'Judaizing' Eschatologies in Jerome." In *Jewish Culture and Society under the Christian Roman Empire*, ed. Richard Kalmin and Seth Schwartz, 409–429. Leuven: Peeters.

Krautheimer, Richard. 1983. *Three Christian Capitals*. Berkeley: University of California Press.

———. 1992. "The Ecclesiastical Building Program of Constantine." In *Constantino il Grande*, vol. 1, ed. G. Bonamente and F. Fusco, 509–552. Macerata: Università degli Studi di Macerata.

Kühnel, Bianca. 1987. *From the Earthly to the Heavenly Jerusalem*. Rome: Herder.

Levine, Lee I. 1998. *Judaism and Hellenism in Antiquity: Conflict or Confluence?* Seattle and London: University of Washington Press.

———, ed. 1999. *Jerusalem: Its Sanctity and Centrality to Judaism, Christianity, and Islam*. New York: Continuum.

Maraval, P. 1985. *Lieux saints et pèlerinages d'Orient. Histoire et géographie des origins à la conquête arabe*. Paris: Éditions du Cerf.

Martyn, J. Louis. 1998. *Galatians: A New Translation with Introduction and Commentary*. Anchor Bible. New York: Doubleday.

Patrich, J. 1993. "The Church of the Holy Sepulcher in the Light of Excavations and Restorations." In *Ancient Churches Revealed*, ed. Yoram Tsafrir, 101–117. Jerusalem: Israel Exploration Society.

Procopius. 1971. *Of the Buildings of Justinian*, trans. Aubrey Stewart and annotated by C. W. Wilson and Hayter Lewis. New York: AMS Press.

Rubin, Zeev. 1999. "The Cult of the Holy Places and Christian Politics in Byzantine Jerusalem." In Levine 1999, 151–162.

Sanders, E. P. 1985. *Jesus and Judaism*. Philadelphia: Fortress Press.

———. 1999. "Jerusalem and its Temple in Early Christian Thought and Practice." In Levine 1999, 90–103.

Schwartz, Daniel R. 1996. "Temple or City: What Did Hellenistic Jews See in Jerusalem?" In *The Centrality of Jerusalem: Historical Perspectives*, ed. Marcel Poorthuis and Chana Safrai, 114–127. Kampen: Kok Pharos.

Tabbernee, William. 2003. "Portals of the Montanist New Jerusalem: The Discovery of Pepouza and Tymion." *Journal of Early Christian Studies* 11: 87–93.

Tsafrir, Yoram. 1999. "Byzantine Jerusalem: The Configuration of a Christian City." In Levine 1999, 133–150.

Walker, P. W. L. 1990. *Holy City, Holy Places? Christian Attitudes to Jerusalem and the Holy Land in the Fourth Century*. Oxford: Clarendon Press.

———. 1996. *Jesus and the Holy City: New Testament Perspectives on Jerusalem*. Grand Rapids and Cambridge: William B. Eerdmans.

Wilkins, Robert. 1992. *The Land Called Holy: Palestine in Christian History and Thought*. New Haven: Yale University Press.

Wilkinson, John. 2002a. *Jerusalem Pilgrims Before the Crusades*. Warminster: Aris & Phillips.

———. 2002b. *Egeria's Travels*. 3rd ed. Warminster: Aris & Phillips.

Wright, Tom N. T. 1994. "Jerusalem in the New Testament." In *Jerusalem Past and Present in the Purposes of God*, 2nd ed., ed. P. W. L. Walker, 53–77 Grand Rapids: Baker Books.

6 The symbolism of Jerusalem in early Islam

Suleiman Ali Mourad

As soon as the invading Muslims captured Jerusalem in 638 CE, they laid claim to its religious heritage. Their veneration of the city led many Muslims to make pilgrimages to visit its holy sites and to create literature in praise of them. Judging from a variety of later Muslim testimonies, the rituals that were performed on the Temple Mount area ranged from *wuquf* rituals (the customary prayer-while-standing that is part of the pilgrimage ceremony in Mecca) to prayers and liturgical readings associated with specific sites (Elad 1995; Hasson 1996). This veneration may be first displayed in the partly-legendary story of caliph 'Umar b. al-Khattab's trip from Medina to negotiate the terms of the surrender of Jerusalem. 'Umar, escorted by Sophronius, the Patriarch of Jerusalem, toured the many holy sites in the city, and made a point of going up to the Temple Mount area and leading his followers in cleansing it from the manure and dirt that was thrown there, as the story goes, by Christians in order to desecrate it.[1] A few decades later, the fifth caliph, Mu'awiya, who was also the founder of the Umayyad dynasty (r. 661–680 CE) that ruled the Muslim world between 661 and 750 CE, chose to be crowned in Jerusalem (al-Tabari 1987, 6), even though he belonged to one of the most prestigious and powerful families of Mecca. His successors spent lavishly to adorn the horizon of Jerusalem, in particular the Temple Mount area, with distinctively Islamic structures, and they regarded that achievement as the height of their mission to spread the message of Islam.[2]

The two most notable examples of Umayyad sanctification of Jerusalem as one of Islam's holiest cities are the Dome of the Rock and the Aqsa mosque. The Dome of the Rock, which was completed in 692 CE, was built by order of the Umayyad caliph 'Abd al-Malik (r. 685–705 CE). The Aqsa mosque was completed around 710 CE by order of 'Abd al-Malik's son al-Walid (r. 705–715 CE). Although the Dome's architecture is heavily influenced by the architectural style used for Christian churches and martyriums in Palestine (Grabar 1959; Chen 1999), the inscription inside of it, which dates to the time of its first construction, shows the obvious signs of an emerging new religion, the religion of Muhammad; the building was subjected to major renovations and partial reconstructions over the centuries.[3]

As for the Aqsa mosque, it conveys an unambiguously Islamic message. This leads to two questions: why did the early Muslims cherish and promote the religious symbolism of Jerusalem, and why did two powerful caliphs who left their marks on the formation and spread of Islam as a religion invest so much wealth in the city?[4]

It is often taken for granted that the Muslims' reverence for Jerusalem stems from two episodes in the career of the prophet Muhammad.

The first is his Night Journey (*isra'*) to Jerusalem and Ascension to Heaven (*mi'raj*). It is believed that Muhammad was transported by night from Mecca to Jerusalem on a heavenly stallion-like creature—named *al-Buraq*—where he prayed on the Temple Mount and then ascended to Heaven to meet with God. Although it has been believed since the later Middle Ages that these legend-stories in connection with Jerusalem are true, early Muslim scholars were not at all in agreement regarding the reality of the two experiences, their sequence, and whether or nor they occurred in Jerusalem. Some scholars dissociated the two events as separate incidents and did not accept them as real; with particular reference to the Qur'anic material (verse 17.1), there was a disagreement as to whether it was Muhammad's soul or body that made the trip and whether that experience was in Jerusalem, since the Qur'anic text refers simply to an "Aqsa mosque" without any further clarification. Most of those who asserted that Muhammad could have seen Jerusalem—making the connection between the Aqsa mosque and Jerusalem's Temple Mount area—admitted that the vision was in the form of a dream.[5]

The second episode is the adoption of Jerusalem by the Muhammad movement as the first direction of prayer (*qibla*) until the Ka'ba in Mecca was chosen as the final *qibla*. The issue of the direction of prayer (*qibla*) is somewhat similar to that of the Night Journey and Ascension. The reference in the Qur'an 2.142–152, especially the lines *Turn then your face in the direction of the Sacred Mosque. Wherever you are, turn your faces in its direction* (Q. 2.144), does not identify Jerusalem nor allude to it in any way as the first *qibla*, and nowhere else in the Qur'an is there a mention of Jerusalem as the first *qibla*. Yet the practice of praying toward Jerusalem is described in a number of sources, mostly *Sira* (Life and Career of the Prophet Muhammad) books and Hadith collections. There is, however, a disagreement as to where and when the practice started and for how long it remained in effect.[6]

What can be inferred from these observations is that Jerusalem's significance in the first century of Islam did not yet derive exclusively from its association with any episode in the career of Muhammad; the Night Journey and Ascension legends, in particular, were still very fluid narratives and thus could not have been the foundations upon which early Muslims based their veneration of Jerusalem.

The Muslims' veneration of particular towns and regions led to the development of a genre of religious literature called *Fada'il*, meaning "religious merits."[7] Generally, such works were authored by scholars who came from the town or region about which they wrote; almost all *Fada'il* works on Mecca were authored by residents of the city, and likewise with other regions. Jerusalem obviously received its share of these *Fada'il* works. The first examples were written by minor scholars, which is also the case throughout the *Fada'il* works, suggesting that the genre did not establish itself among the notable religious sciences until a much later time—in the case of Jerusalem, until the period of the Crusades.

In this chapter I will examine the earliest Muslim work on the *Fada'il* of Jerusalem in order to identify how the early Muslims recognized and celebrated the sacredness of Jerusalem, how the process of Islamizing the city was achieved, and how it later changed as a result of the capture of the city by the Crusaders. The work that I will be discussing is *Fada'il Bayt al-Maqdis* (literally, the Merits of the Holy House) by al-Walid b. Hammad al-Ramli al-Zayyat (d. 912 CE); the original text is now lost, but it has been almost completely preserved in later works on the same subject.

Al-Ramli and his work

Fortunately, the *Fada'il* of al-Ramli can be reconstructed with great precision as to its size, scope, and arrangement on the basis of two later texts on the same topic written by scholars from Jerusalem: *Fada'il al-Bayt al-Muqaddas* (The Merits of Jerusalem) by Abu Bakr Muhammad b. Ahmad al-Wasiti (d. after 1019 CE), who served as the main preacher (*khatib*) at the Aqsa mosque, and *Fada'il Bayt al-Maqdis wa-l-Khalil wa-fada'il al-Sham* (The Merits of Jerusalem and Hebron, and the Merits of Syria) by Abu al-Ma'ali al-Musharraf b. al-Murajja al-Maqdisi (eleventh century CE), who made a moderate reputation for himself as a transmitter of Hadith.[8]

Al-Ramli came from the town of Ramla, southwest of Jerusalem. He was known in the learned circles of his time as a scholar, albeit a minor one; his other profession was selling olive oil, inferred from his epithet *al-Zayyat* (the oil-seller). He traveled in Syria and visited such cities as Damascus, Jerusalem, and Tiberias to study Hadith, although his main passion was popular history.[9] The assessment of al-Ramli by the Damascene scholar Shams al-Din al-Dhahabi (d. 1348 CE) also points to him as an amateur scholar. Al-Dhahabi describes al-Ramli too as having been very pious (*wa-kana rabbaniyyan*) and adds that he knew of no negative charge against him. But then al-Dhahabi remarks that al-Ramli did his share of transmitting poorly authenticated *hadith*s (al-Dhahabi, 14:79). In the opinion of al-Dhahabi and other medieval critics, popular subjects like storytelling and *Fada'il* attracted minor scholars who often confused factual history with myth, which disqualifies Hadith accounts disseminated in such contexts, since these minor scholars would not have the expertise to distinguish authentic accounts from forged or untrustworthy ones.[10]

The earliest ascription of the work to al-Ramli comes from the same al-Dhahabi. Yet, inferences about its existence can be found in the works of al-Wasiti and Abu al-Ma'ali, both of whom acknowledge that al-Ramli had a book in which he collected traditions regarding the *Fada'il* of Jerusalem (al-Wasiti, 51–52, no. 78; and Abu al-Ma'ali, 98, no. 99). Therefore, there is no reason to doubt that al-Ramli had authored a work on the *Fada'il* of Jerusalem.[11] Moreover, all surviving accounts regarding the sanctity of Jerusalem that were related on the authority of al-Ramli were passed down via one chain of transmission: al-Ramli → al-Fadl b. Muhajir al-Maqdisi → 'Umar b. al-Fadl b. Muhajir al-Maqdisi, which also indicates that we are dealing with an authored text.[12]

Al-Ramli's work was al-Wasiti's principal source; he is quoted for 118 accounts, constituting more than 70 percent of al-Wasiti's *Fada'il*. With respect to Abu al-Ma'ali, he quotes al-Ramli for 110 accounts, slightly more than 25 percent of his material on the merits of Jerusalem, which implies that al-Ramli's work was also a major source for him. What is worth mentioning here is that 24 accounts out of the 110 quoted from al-Ramli by Abu al-Ma'ali do not appear in al-Wasiti's text, so that al-Wasiti did not quote the complete work of al-Ramli. This can be attributed to two possible causes. First, it can be argued that al-Wasiti meant to show that he was not simply copying a previous work, but rather composing his own, so he included reports from other sources. As for Abu al-Ma'ali, his travels for education brought him into contact with a wider network of scholars and information; moreover, his work was not limited to the merits of Jerusalem, but includes reports on the merits of Hebron and greater Syria.

In his accounts on the *Fada'il* of Jerusalem, al-Ramli quotes 37 informants, most of whom were from Syria and Palestine; of these he most frequently quotes four, all of whom came from Jerusalem and the surrounding area. These informants were the following.

Ibrahim b. Muhammad b. Yusuf al-Firyabi. His father, Muhammad, was a well-known scholar of Hadith who moved the family from Iraq to the coastal Palestinian town of Caesarea, where he died in 821 CE. Al-Firyabi moved from Caesarea to Jerusalem and established himself there as a teacher of Hadith. He died some time around the year 860 CE. Al-Ramli quotes 41 accounts from al-Firyabi, whom he almost certainly met in Jerusalem.

Abu 'Abd Allah Muhammad b. al-Nu'man al-Saqati. He originally came from Nishapor in northeastern Iran; he resided in Jerusalem and visited Damascus where he studied Hadith and other subjects with some of the local scholars there. He died in Jerusalem in 881 CE. Al-Ramli transmits 23 accounts from al-Saqati, and must have met him in Jerusalem. Moreover, it appears, as can be determined from the works of al-Wasiti and Abu al-Ma'ali, that al-Saqati developed a particular interest in the *Fada'il* of Jerusalem. Besides the 23 accounts transmitted from him by al-Ramli, 43 other accounts are quoted in the works of al-Wasiti and Abu al-Ma'ali, 40 of which are passed down by one person from Jerusalem, named Muhammad b. Ibrahim b. 'Isa al-Maqdisi. This suggests that al-Saqati might have even authored a work on the topic.

Abu al-Qasim 'Abd al-Rahman b. Muhammad b. Mansur b. Thabit b. Istanibiyadh al-Farisi al-Khumsi. Little is known about al-Khumsi except what can be deduced from the stories he transmitted. They relate to the condition of the Aqsa mosque in the Umayyad and early 'Abbasid periods, suggesting that al-Khumsi's family had inhabited Jerusalem since the time of 'Abd al-Malik and were involved in the service of the Dome of the Rock and the Aqsa mosque. It is very likely that their great ancestor Istanibiyadh was brought to the city as a Persian slave, inferred from the *nisba* al-Khumsi al-Farisi; *al-Farisi* indicates Persian descent, and *al-Khumsi* is derived from *khums*, the tax that early Muslim caliphs levied for the state from military spoils (which included slaves), a practice that was started by the prophet Muhammad. This indicates that, like several other slaves, al-Khumsi al-Farisi was brought to the Temple Mount area by the Umayyads to serve in its upkeep (Elad 1995, 51–52). Al-Ramli transmits from al-Khumsi ten accounts, nine of which feature in their line of transmission the names of al-Khumsi's father, grandfather, and great-grandfather (Elad 1995, 17–18; Mourad 1996, 37–38).

Abu 'Umayr 'Isa b. Muhammad Ibn al-Nahhas al-Ramli. He was a native of al-Ramla and was well known in the Hadith circles of Syria and Palestine as a trustworthy scholar; it is said that many students of Hadith journeyed to Ramla to study with him. He died in 869 CE. Al-Ramli likely knew Ibn al-Nahhas in Ramla, as he transmits from him six accounts.

Besides these four informants who came from Jerusalem and its environs, al-Ramli received some of the accounts of Jerusalem's sacredness by corresponding with a scholar in northern Syria who, in al-Ramli's opinion, had access to important information that could not otherwise be found. This scholar was Ahmad b. 'Abd al-Wahhab al-Hawti al-Jabali (d. 894), a resident of the coastal town of Jabala in northwestern Syria. The fact that he was in correspondence with scholars also demonstrates that al-Ramli was indeed composing a book, and not simply collecting material for no apparent purpose.

The dependence of al-Ramli on 37 informants shows that the traditions about the sacredness of Jerusalem were in circulation in the eighth and ninth centuries CE, although they were primarily disseminated by local scholars, in particular those residing in and around Jerusalem (Mourad 1996). Some of these scholars, especially the five identified above, seem to have developed a specialty in the *Fada'il* of Jerusalem, or at least were known to have access to valuable stories about its sanctity.

Al-Ramli must have finished assembling most of the reports for his book early in the second half of the ninth century CE, which can be deduced from the obituary dates of his informants, most of whom died between 855 and 881 CE (Mourad 1996, 38–39).

The religious symbolism of Jerusalem according to al-Ramli's *Fada'il*

The text of al-Ramli provides us with some information about the religious symbolism of Jerusalem and the foundations upon which the early Muslims based their perception of the city's holiness. Al-Ramli begins with the famous *hadith* that establishes three places as the only destinations of pilgrimage: "The Messenger of God said: 'You shall only set out on pilgrimage for three mosques: the sacred mosque (in Mecca), my mosque (in Medina), and the Aqsa mosque (in Jerusalem)' " (al-Wasiti, 3–4, no. 1).[13] As if in order to explain why Jerusalem merits inclusion in such a prophetic pronouncement, al-Ramli then states that Jerusalem's significance originated with the Temple that once stood there. He relates, among other accounts, the following story regarding the circumstances of the construction of the Temple:

> When God ordered David to build the Temple (*masjid Bayt al-Maqdis*), he asked, "O God, where should I build it?" God said: "In the spot where you see the angel raising his sword." He (David) saw him (the angel) at that spot, so he proceeded with setting up the foundations and building the walls. But when the walls reached a certain height, they collapsed. David asked God: "You commanded me to build for you a house (*bayt*), but when it reached a certain height you caused it to collapse!" God replied: "O David, whom I made my deputy (*khalifati*) among my people, why did you take the land from its owner without restitution? A son of yours will build it instead." So when Solomon's succession came, he negotiated with the owner of the land to buy it . . . , and built (the Temple) . . . Then Solomon appointed from the Israelites ten thousand reciters [to recite the Torah], five thousand during the day and five thousand during the night. Not a single hour passes, whether at night or day, without having someone worship God in it.
>
> (al-Wasiti, 6–7, no. 5; Abu al-Ma'ali, 12, no. 4)

Clearly, this story is a collage of biblical narratives, especially 2 Samuel 7:1–17 and 24, 1 Kings 5:5 and 8:17–21, and 1 Chronicles 21:15–22.1 and 22.6–10. In the case of 2 Samuel 7:1–17, David is told through a prophecy that he is not to build the Temple, but a son of his will build it, and the prophecy is retold to be fulfilled in 1 Kings 5:5, 8:17–21, and 1 Chronicles 22.6–10. As for 2 Samuel 24, which is restated in 1 Chronicles 21:15–22.1, David builds an altar for God on the site where the angel of God, sent to destroy Jerusalem, was standing with his sword unsheathed; the biblical account places this incident in the context of the plague that struck Jerusalem.

Al-Ramli further specifies why David was prohibited from building the Temple:

> God revealed to David: "You shall not build the Temple (*masjid Bayt al-Maqdis*)." He said: "But God, why?" God replied: "Because your

hands are polluted with blood." David asked: 'O God, but wasn't that in your service?" God replied: "Yes, even though it was."

(al-Wasiti, 7–8, no. 6; Abu al-Ma'ali, 15, no. 7)

This legend of David's hands being polluted with blood because of his fighting in the name of God is encountered in 1 Chronicles 22:7–9. But certain details in these stories indicate that they depended on biblical exegesis; for example, the comment that God reprimanded David for taking the land without restitution (1 Chronicles 21:25 states that David paid "six hundred shekels of gold by weight for the site"), and that God replied to David's complaint that shedding blood was in God's service with "even though it was."

Another theme that is addressed in al-Ramli's *Fada'il* relates to the benefits of the pilgrimage to Jerusalem. According to the following report, when the construction of the Temple was completed, Solomon made a prayer that was intended as a blessing to those who come to it:

When the prophet of God Solomon, peace be on him, finished [the Temple's] construction, he ordered the slaughtering of three thousand heifers and seven thousand goats. Then he prayed, saying: "O God, when a sinful person visits it [the Temple] forgive his sin, and when a sick person visits it heal his sickness." No one visits the Temple but receives the blessing of Solomon's prayer.

(Abu al-Ma'ali, 92, no. 87)

This narrative, which is clearly lifted from Solomon's prayer in 1 Kings 8.22–53, concludes with a rather interesting comment, obviously not found in the biblical account, again attesting to exegetical glosses made on the text. It uses the future tense to bestow a certain validity on Solomon's plea for blessing that is associated with the site, irrespective of whether or not the Temple stands there, as if the Temple were synonymous with the Temple Mount area. Hence, what the Muslim redactor meant by quoting this prayer of Solomon is that its value is not time-restricted, and therefore, the "current" visitor to the Dome of the Rock receives the blessing of Solomon's prayer.

Moreover, the pilgrim is encouraged to visit Jerusalem as part of the pilgrimage, for it bestows a level of purity that cannot be attained otherwise. According to Ibn 'Abbas (d. 687 CE), a cousin of Muhammad and one of the major early Muslim authorities on Hadith and Qur'anic exegesis: "He who makes the pilgrimage [to Mecca], prays in the mosque of Medina, and [prays] in the Aqsa mosque in one season, is purified from his sins as if he has just been born" (Abu al-Ma'ali, 161, no. 215).

Leaving aside the issue of authenticity, further accounts in al-Ramli's *Fada'il* share the theme of the importance of pilgrimage to Jerusalem and the need to avoid all those practices that might compromise the experience.

For example, al-Ramli relates that the pilgrim to Jerusalem must avoid visiting Christian sites:

> He who visits the Temple of Jerusalem should also visit David's prayer place on the eastern side, and pray in both of them. He should too submerge himself in the spring of Siloam [Sulwan], because it comes forth from Heaven. But He should not enter the churches nor buy for himself a dwelling-place because the sin in [Jerusalem] equals one thousand sins [elsewhere] and the good deed equals one thousand good deeds [elsewhere].
>
> (al-Wasiti, 44, no. 61; Abu al-Ma'ali, 249, no. 374)

The popular practice of pilgrimaging to Jerusalem, sometimes on the way to Mecca or back, received a categorical rejection and condemnation from a few later Muslim scholars such as the Damascene theologian Ibn Taymiyya (d. 1328 CE), who also argued that praying in Jerusalem is legitimate only if it takes place in the Aqsa mosque (Ibn Taymiyya, 7–17). Ibn Taymiyya was undoubtedly reacting to what he considered unorthodox popular practices. But obviously this was not yet a concern for al-Ramli and his sources, nor for al-Wasiti and Abu al-Ma'ali who quoted the previous account from al-Ramli.

To return to the question of the Temple's sanctity, al-Ramli provides one basis for it: the presence of the Rock (*al-Sakhra*). As if to explain the reason David and then Solomon chose that particular site upon which to build the Temple, al-Ramli relates several accounts regarding the Rock's sacredness, one of which has God praising it as His earthly throne:

> It is written in the Torah that God said to the Rock of Jerusalem: "You are my earthly throne. From you I ascended to heaven. From beneath you I spread the earth, and every stream that flows from the mountains originates from underneath you."
>
> (al-Wasiti, 69, no. 111; Abu al-Ma'ali, 106, no. 113)

Not only did the earthly rivers spring from underneath the Rock, the heavenly rivers do as well: "From underneath the Rock spring four of the rivers of Paradise: Jaxartes (*Sayhan*), Oxus (*Jayhan*), Euphrates (*al-Furat*), and Nile (*al-Nil*)" (al-Wasiti, 68, no. 110; and Abu al-Ma'ali, 106, no. 112). These accounts have a clear biblical foundation and reflect the kind of Jewish legends regarding the Rock's sanctity that were produced following the destruction of the Temple, leaving the Rock its only remaining part.[14] In the particular case of the four rivers tradition, there is an obvious allusion to Genesis 2:10–14, where the river that flows out of Eden divides into four rivers when reaching the Garden of Eden: Pishon, Gihon, Tigris, and Euphrates (the only variation is that in al-Ramli's text the river Nile replaces the Tigris). Moreover, the theme of water flowing out of the Temple is also encountered in the Old Testament, in Ezekiel 47. So it is not far fetched to conclude that the Rock/Temple becomes the earthly Eden, inasmuch as the Temple's most holy section, the Holy of Holies, was believed in biblical times to be God's dwelling place, which was located exactly above the Rock.

The intense sanctification of the Temple Mount area, especially the Rock, in early Islam must have raised some doubts on the part of a group of Muslim scholars, concerning whether or not it is an imitation of Jewish practices and is therefore not sanctioned by the teachings of Muhammad. Either anticipating such worries or in order to directly challenge them, al-Ramli relates the following report, which assures Muslims that Islam validates the veneration of the Rock:

> 'Ubada b. al-Samit and Rafi' b. Khudayj were asked: "You hear what people say about the Rock; is it true so we accept it, or is it something that originated from the people of the book, in which case we should reject it?" Both of them replied: "By God, who in his right mind doubts it [the Rock's holiness]? For God almighty, when he rested in Heaven, said to the Rock of Jerusalem: 'Here is my abode and the place of my throne on the Day of Judgment. My creation will be rushed to it. Here is Heaven to its right and Hell to its left, and I shall erect the scale in front of it.'"
>
> (al-Wasiti, 70–71, no. 115; Abu al-Ma'ali, 109, no. 121)

Indeed, the issue of visiting sacred sites outside the Temple Mount area generated controversy among early Muslim scholars. It is reported, for example, that when the Hadith scholar Mu'ammal b. Isma'il (d. 822 CE) visited Jerusalem from Basra (Iraq), he hired a guide to take him to other holy sites. His son brought to his attention the fact that when the celebrated Hadith scholar Waki' b. al-Jarrah (d. 812 CE) came to Jerusalem from Kufa (Iraq), he refused to do a tour and worshiped only in the Temple Mount area. Mu'ammal answered his son by saying, "Each person does what he pleases" (Elad 1995, 307).

To go back to the tradition quoted above, both 'Ubada (d. 655 CE) and Rafi' (d. 693 CE) were among Muhammad's companions. Even if one doubts the authenticity of this report, especially in light of the fact that both men were not known to have met in Jerusalem ('Ubada resided in Palestine following the Islamic conquests, and Rafi' is not known to have ever visited the city or Palestine), it nevertheless validates and legitimizes the Muslims' sanctification of the Rock. After all, these companions were the only recourse to the teachings of Muhammad; at least this is the pretense for regarding them as irrefutably trustworthy.

The inclusion of the preceding stories, and similar ones, were therefore intended by al-Ramli as background information for 'Abd al-Malik's decision to construct the Dome of the Rock. Al-Ramli argues that 'Abd al-Malik's motives were to shield the Rock as well as the pilgrims who come to pray there:

> Raja' b. Haywa and Yazid b. Sallam said: "When 'Abd al-Malik ordered the construction of a dome over the Rock of Jerusalem, and a mosque, he came from Damascus to Jerusalem and sent letters to his governors throughout his realm that the caliph has ordered the construction of a dome to shelter the Rock of Jerusalem so that the Muslims would not be exposed to the heat or cold [when they visit it]."
>
> (al-Wasiti, 81–83, no. 136; Abu al-Ma'ali, 58–61, no. 47)

Raja' (d. 730 CE) and Yazid (d. c. 730 CE) were the two officials entrusted by 'Abd al-Malik to supervise the construction of the Dome of the Rock, with powers to spend as much money as necessary to finish the task. What their joint report attests to is that Muslims and possibly other monotheists (Jews in particular) were already making pilgrimages to Jerusalem, and going to the Temple Mount area to worship at the Rock. 'Abd al-Malik was told of these worshipers' suffering, especially in the winter season, so he ordered the Dome to be built to cover the holy Rock and as a protection for them.

This Rock that 'Abd al-Malik meant to shield was, according to al-Ramli, the exact location of Abraham's binding of Isaac:

> It is written in the Torah that God said to Abraham: "O Abraham." He replied: "Here I am." [God said:] "Take your only son, the one you love, go to the land of Moriah, and offer him there on one of the mountains that I shall show you." His [God's] saying *the land of Moriah* means Jerusalem, and *one of the mountains* means the Rock. ...
>
> (Abu al-Ma'ali, 115–116, no. 137)

This accurate recital of Genesis 22 is meant to count among the many sacred events associated with the site; needless to say, the association of the location of Abraham's binding of Isaac with that of the Temple was made long before the emergence of Islam, probably as early as 2 Chronicles 3:1 (Solomon began to build the house of the Lord in Jerusalem on Mount Moriah).[15] In other words, it highlights the Rock's many layers of sanctity.

So far we have seen that the biblical dimension, as is evident in the heavy dependence on biblical narratives, was for al-Ramli and his sources the most notable factor that accounts for their understanding of the sanctity of Jerusalem, and this undoubtedly extends to the way early Muslims perceived Jerusalem's sacredness. The next task is to examine what al-Ramli and his sources say about the association of Muhammad with Jerusalem and its significance in relation to the biblical dimension. Al-Ramli was certainly aware of a number of variant reports regarding Muhammad's Night Journey and Ascension; most of what he reports relates to the former. What is interesting about his text is that although the association was important, it was not the reason for the Muslims' sanctification of Jerusalem. For al-Ramli and his sources, that is, for local scholars in Jerusalem and Palestine, these episodes in the career of Muhammad do not make Jerusalem sacred, but rather are powerful testimonies attesting to its sacredness. What confirms this view is that the few accounts that al-Ramli quotes regarding the Night Journey and Ascension occur toward the end of his text.[16] If he believed them to be superior to the biblical accounts, it seems very likely that he would have placed them first. After all, later works on the *Fada'il* of Jerusalem, from the Crusades period onward, begin their display of the city's sacredness with the stories about the prophet Muhammad, clearly making the case that these are the foundations for Jerusalem's importance in Islam.

It might be argued that by placing the stories about Muhammad's Night Journey and Ascension last in the text, al-Ramli was simply adhering to the chronological order of things, and not necessarily showing any preference regarding the significance of the material. Although one cannot entirely dismiss this objection, it does not seem to have been the case. There is only one unique mention of the Qur'anic verse 17.1 (*Glory to Him who made His servant journey by night from the Haram mosque to the Aqsa mosque*), which is the only Qur'anic verse that is often interpreted as a reference to the Night Journey. The way al-Ramli conveys the meaning of this verse, according to a popular storyteller from Jerusalem, suggests that he considered this sole Qur'anic testimony to refer to the future transfer of Muhammad's bones from his burial place in Medina to Jerusalem on the Day of Judgment:

> Khalid b. Hazim said: "Once al-Zuhri came to Jerusalem. I showed him the holy sites, and he prayed in all of them. I said to him: 'We have here an old man who narrates to us from the books; his name is 'Uqba b. Abi Zaynab, let's go and listen to him.' We went there and sat down. He was telling stories about the religious symbolism (*fada'il*) of Jerusalem, and kept going on and on. Al-Zuhri, annoyed by this, [interrupted the old man] and said: 'Old man, aren't you going to mention what God has said [in the Qur'an]: *Glory to Him who made His servant journey by night from the Haram mosque to the Aqsa mosque*' (*Q.* 17.1).' The old man became angry with al-Zuhri and said [to him]: '[The verse means that] the Hour will not come until the bones of Muhammad are transported to it [Jerusalem].' "
>
> (al-Wasiti, 102, no. 165)

Al-Zuhri (d. 742 CE) was a famous scholar of Hadith who developed a specialty in the traditions about the life and career of the prophet Muhammad. He was attached to several Umayyad caliphs, and produced at their request stories about Muhammad and early Islam, all of questionable authenticity. 'Uqba b. Abi Zaynab was a popular preacher in Jerusalem; the medieval biographical sources know nothing about him, which indicates that he was not at all recognized in the scholarly circles. What is shocking about this report is that 'Uqba makes no connection between *Qur'an* 17.1 and Muhammad's ever being in Jerusalem. Even if 'Uqba was not a distinguished religious scholar, this suggests that the legends concerning Muhammad's Night Journey to Jerusalem and Ascension from it to Heaven were still fluid around the beginning of the eighth century CE, at least as far as popular preachers in Jerusalem and its area were concerned. Thus, again, they could not have been the foundation upon which Muslims' veneration of the city was established.

Moreover, we know from later sources that more than one site in the Temple Mount area was identified as the exact location from which Muhammad ascended to Heaven. One such spot was a few meters outside the Dome of the Rock building, on top of which, not earlier than the eighth century CE, a small dome with supporting columns was erected and named Dome of the Ascension (Elad 1995, 48–50 and 73–76). Thus the identification of the Rock as the exact site from which Muhammad ascended to Heaven must have come much later than that.

The last point to be revisited is the issue of 'Abd al-Malik's building of the Dome of the Rock. Al-Ramli tells his readers about how the first Temple was built by Solomon, but does not say anything about its destruction. Interestingly, however, he quotes through one of his sources the famous prophecy of Jesus—which we also find in Matthew 26:61 and John 2:19—that the Temple will be destroyed:

The disciples said to the Messiah: "O Messiah of God, look at this Holy Temple, how beautiful it is." He replied: "Amen, Amen! Truly I say to you that God will destroy the stones of this mosque because of the sins of its people."

(al-Wasiti, 60, no. 95; Abu al-Ma'ali, 230, no. 340)

Al-Ramli then quotes another prophecy, originating possibly from a *midrash* on Isaiah, attributed to the quasi-legendary figure Ka'b al-Ahbar (a companion of caliph 'Umar who converted to Islam from Judaism) that 'Abd al-Malik will be the person to rebuild the Temple over the Rock: "It is written in the Torah: 'Yerushalaym—meaning Jerusalem and the Rock, which is known as the Temple—I shall send you my servant 'Abd al-Malik to build you and embellish you.' " (al-Wasiti, 86, no. 138; Abu al-Ma'ali, 63–64, no. 50). Again, leaving aside the issue of the authenticity of this report, which is said to have been made by Ka'b al-Ahbar, who died long before 'Abd al-Malik reached adulthood (Rabbat 1989), one wonders whether at some point during the construction of the Dome of the Rock some Muslim and Jewish groups in Palestine became convinced that 'Abd al-Malik was indeed rebuilding the Temple, which necessitated that such a prophecy be fabricated and circulated. Moreover, a number of medieval sources argue that 'Abd al-Malik wanted the Dome of the Rock to be used as a pilgrimage site, either along with or in lieu of the Ka'ba in Mecca (Elad 1992). In other words, the superiority of Mecca to other sacred cities in early Islam was not yet fully established (Robinson 2005, 95–100), and such reports attest to attempts on the part of Muslim groups to position Jerusalem favorably.

The transformation in the perception of Jerusalem's sanctity

The primary emphasis with respect to the religious symbolism of Jerusalem, as seen in the case of the text of al-Ramli and his sources, as well as other pre-Crusades compilations on the *Fada'il* of Jerusalem, was placed on the town's biblical heritage—principally as the town that housed God's Temple and as the location of the binding of Isaac. The association with Muhammad was made, but it was not yet the focal point of these works. Starting in the period of the Crusades, there is a clear attempt on the part of Muslim scholars to dissociate Jerusalem, albeit gradually, from its non-Islamic heritage. This process sidelined the biblical dimension and emphasized Jerusalem's association with Muhammad and notable Muslim figures. Once central, the biblical aspect became an afterthought.

The *Fada'il* of Diya' al-Din al-Maqdisi (d. 1245 CE) provides the first example of this transformation. Diya' al-Din was originally from Jerusalem, but his family fled the city when it was captured by the Crusaders in 1099, and moved to Damascus. At the time, the Muslim religious establishment, at the instigation of the political establishment, struggled to rally the Muslims to the defense of Islam and Muslim land. Jerusalem's sacredness could no longer be explained on the basis of its biblical history; rather, this time the "liberation" of Jerusalem required exclusively Islamic legends attesting to its sanctity. There was thus a heavy emphasis on what were perceived to be direct references or allusions to it in the Qur'an and Hadith, including the prophet Muhammad's legendary Night Journey and his Ascension to Heaven, and the several major Muslim figures who visited and prayed in the city, such as caliph 'Umar. In the case of Diya' al-Din, Jerusalem's biblical heritage was completely eliminated, and the city's holiness derived exclusively from particular references to it in the Qur'an and from episodes in the life of Muhammad. One other theme that he emphasizes is the apocalyptic: how Jesus will descend in Jerusalem to kill the Antichrist, how creation will be rushed to Jerusalem for the Day of Judgment, how Mecca and Medina will be brought to Jerusalem at that time, and so forth. This apocalyptic theme is already found in the *Fada'il* of Abu al-Ma'ali and to a lesser extent in al-Wasiti; it is a marginal theme in al-Ramli's work (only seven accounts). It is also encountered in scattered reports relating to the role of Jerusalem at the end of time in such apocalyptic texts as Nu'aym b. Hammad's *Kitab al-Fitan* (Book of Calamities). Therefore, it is clear that in the pre-Crusades period, Jerusalem's apocalyptic role was but one dimension that accounts for the city's sacredness in Islam; the dominant dimension being its biblical heritage. By excluding the biblical accounts, Diya' al-Din gave the apocalyptic dimension much greater prominence.

The biblical heritage could not be a problem, or to put it more accurately, could not become a problem as long as the Muslims' control of Jerusalem was not at risk. The Crusaders wrested Jerusalem from Muslim hands, and it was not regained for almost a century, until Saladin recovered the city in 1187; even then it was not completely Muslim-controlled until the Mamluks ended any Crusaders' presence in the Near East in 1291. While the city was lost, the propaganda that sought its liberation could not have depended or been based on aspects of Jerusalem's sanctity that are "shared" with other monotheists. In other words, the politicians and religious scholars were not interested in promoting Jerusalem's holiness on the grounds that Jews, Christians, and Muslims find it equally sacred. The emphasis on an exclusive Islamic dimension was all that mattered, so that Muslims were being asked to liberate a holy place that was exclusively theirs. This makes it easier to understand why Ibn Taymiyya was so irritated by the emphasis on the "exclusively Islamic" sanctification of Jerusalem at the expense of the other sacred city, Mecca. His *Qaʿida fi ziyarat Bayt al-Maqdis* was intended to clarify, once and for all, that all the traditions regarding Muhammad's association with Jerusalem are legendary, originating from the wild imaginations of story-tellers (Hasson 1996, 374).

Conclusion

As the work of al-Ramli shows, Jerusalem was perceived by the early Muslims as one of Islam's holiest sites, and this situation persisted well into modern times. The city's biblical background was the initial reason for this perception of sanctity, and several legends converged into the creation of a myth that over time became constitutive of the Muslims' veneration of Jerusalem. There the Temple of God once stood. There the binding of Isaac took place. There the most holy Rock stands. And from there the prophet Muhammad journeyed by night and ascended to heaven—although this last theme did not enjoy much authority in the early period. With the advent of the Crusades, Muslim scholars gradually shifted their focus and began to highlight a much more exclusivist heritage for Jerusalem: a purely Islamic one. This meant that Jerusalem's sanctity has to derive entirely from the sources of the Islamic religion, the Qur'an and Muhammad's life and career (*Sunna*). They, and no other sources, were held as the basis on which Jerusalem's sanctity is to be conceived.

Notes

1 On ʿUmar's journey to Jerusalem, see Busse 1984.
2 On Umayyad architectural undertakings in Jerusalem, see Rosen-Ayalon 1996.
3 On the main inscription from ʿAbd al-Malik's time, see Grabar 1996.

4 On caliph 'Abd al-Malik, see Robinson 2005.
5 For a discussion of the various views regarding the Night Journey and Ascension, see al-Tabari 1999, 7: 3–17; and the article on "Mi'radj" in *Encyclopaedia of Islam, New Edition*, 7: 97–105. On the Ascension, see also van Ess 1999.
6 For example, Abu Dawud says it lasted thirteen months (Abu Dawud, *Sunan*, Book 2, n. 507), whereas al-Bukhari says it went on for sixteen to seventeen months (al-Bukhari, *Sahih*, Book 2, n. 39).
7 This genre was not actually limited to places, as a number of *Fada'il* works were written to celebrate particularly significant Muslim figures or groups.
8 The expression *Bayt al-Maqdis* in the title of al-Ramli's work has exactly the same meaning as the Hebrew *bayt ha-miqdash* (The Holy House), which was initially a reference to the Temple, then to the Temple Mount area following the destruction of the Temple in 70 CE; it was applied to the entire city of Jerusalem in the Islamic period. The other name that early Muslims used for Jerusalem was *Ilya'*, from the Latin *Aelia*, that is, Aelia Capitolina, the name the Romans gave to Jerusalem after the Bar Kochba revolt and the destruction of the city in 131–132 CE. The currently-used Arabic name, *al-Quds*, derives from *Bayt al-Maqdis*. There is no difference in meaning between *Bayt al-Maqdis* and *al-Bayt al-Muqaddas*; the grammatical rule is that when the definite article *al-* is introduced, the *d* in *maqdis* (holy) is emphasized and this necessitates a change in the short vowel that it carries (*dda* instead of *di*).
9 On al-Ramli as a transmitter of historical narratives, see Mourad 2000.
10 On popular historians and their evaluation in medieval Islamic scholarship, see Robinson 2003.
11 Elad (1991, 48–49) was the first to suggest that al-Ramli must have authored a book on the *Fada'il* of Jerusalem. The reference in al-Dhahabi was found later, and came to confirm his position.
12 The only partial exception, which in fact further confirms this conclusion, is the quote in the *Fada'il* of al-Raba'i (d. 1052 CE), which features the following transmission: al-Ramli → al-Fadl b. Muhajir al-Maqdisi (al-Raba'i, 26, no. 50).
13 The *hadith* is similarly related by Abu al-Ma'ali, but via an informant other than al-Ramli (Abu al-Ma'ali, 82, no. 70). For an analysis of this prophetic tradition, see Kister 1980.
14 As early as the year 333, the anonymous Christian Pilgrim from Bordeaux noted that the Jews come every year to the Temple Mount to anoint the pierced stone (*Itinerary from Bordeaux to Jerusalem*, 22).
15 In Genesis 22:2, God orders Abraham to sacrifice Isaac on a mountain in the land of Moriah. In Genesis 22:14, this mountain becomes known as the Mount of the Vision of the Lord. For more on Mount Moriah and the Temple Mount area, see the article by Y. Eliav in this volume.
16 This is where al-Wasiti places them. Abu al-Ma'ali also quotes them toward the end of his accounts on the sacredness of Jerusalem.

References

Abu Dawud (d. 889 CE). n.d. *Sunan Abi Dawud*. Ed. Muhammad 'Abd al-Hamid. Cairo: Dar Ihya' al-Sunna al-Nabawiyya.

Abu al-Ma'ali, al-Musharraf b. al-Murajja al-Maqdisi (eleventh century CE). 1995. *Fada'il Bayt al-maqdis wa-l-Khalil wa-fada'il al-Sham*. Ed. Ofer Livne-Kafri. Shafa 'Amr (Shfaram): Dar al-Mashreq.

Al-Bukhari (d. 870 CE). 1987. *Sahih*. Ed. Mustafa D. al-Bugha. Beirut and Damascus: Dar Ibn Kathir and Dar al-Yamama.

Busse, Heribert. 1984. "'Omar b. al-Kattab in Jerusalem." *Jerusalem Studies in Arabic and Islam* 5: 73–119.

Chen, Doron. 1999. "The Façades of the Rotunda of the Anastasis and the Dome of the Rock Compared." In *Bayt al-Maqdis: Jerusalem and Early Islam* (Oxford Studies in Islamic Art IX.2), ed. Jeremy Johns, 191–196. Oxford: Oxford University Press.

Al-Dhahabi, Shams al-Din Muhammad b. Ahmad (d. 1348 CE). 1981–85. *Siyar a'lam al-nubala'*. Ed. Shu'ayb Arna'ut et al. Beirut: Mu'assasat al-Risala.

Elad, Amikam. 1991. "The History and Topography of Jerusalem during the Early Islamic Period. The Historical Value of *Fada'il al-Quds* Literature: A Reconsideration." *Jerusalem Studies in Arabic and Islam* 14: 41–70.

——. 1992. "Why Did 'Abd al-Malik Build the Dome of the Rock? A Re-examination of the Muslim Sources." In *Bayt al-Maqdis: 'Abd al-Malik's Jerusalem* (Oxford Studies in Islamic Art IX.1), ed. Julian Raby and Jeremy Johns, 33–58. Oxford: Oxford University Press.

——. 1995. *Medieval Jerusalem and Islamic Worship: Holy Places, Ceremonies, Pilgrimage.* Leiden: E. J. Brill.

Ess, Josef van. 1999. "Vision and Ascension: *Surat al-Najm* and Its Relationship with Muhammad's *Mi'raj*." *Journal of Qur'anic Studies* 1.1: 47–62.

Grabar, Oleg. 1959. "The Umayyad Dome of the Rock in Jerusalem." *Ars Orientalis* 3: 33–62.

——. 1996. *The Shape of the Holy: Early Islamic Jerusalem.* Princeton: Princeton University Press.

Hasson, Izhak. 1996. "The Muslim View of Jerusalem: The Qur'an and Hadith." In *The History of Jerusalem: The Early Muslim Period 638–1099*, ed. Joshua Prawer and Haggai Ben-Shammai, 349–385. Jerusalem: Yad Izhak Ben Zvi; New York: New York University Press.

Ibn Taymiyya, Ahmad (d. 1328 CE). 1936. *Qa'ida fi ziyarat Bayt al-Maqdis.* Ed. Charles D. Matthews. *Journal of the American Oriental Society* 56: 7–17.

Itinerary from Bordeaux to Jerusalem. 1887. Trans. Aubrey Stewart and annotated by C. W. Wilson. London: Committee of the Palestine Exploration Fund.

Kister, M. J. 1980. " 'You shall only set out for three mosques': A Study of an Early Tradition." Chapter 13 in *Studies in Jahiliyya and Early Islam.* London: Variorum.

Al-Maqdisi, Diya' al-Din Muhammad b. 'Abd al-Wahid (d. 1245 CE). 1988. *Fada'il bayt al-maqdis.* Ed. Muhammad M. al-Hafiz. Damascus: Dar al-Fikr.

Matthews, Charles D. 1936. "A Muslim Iconoclast (Ibn Taymiyyeh) on the 'Merits' of Jerusalem and Palestine." *Journal of the American Oriental Society* 56: 1–21.

——. 1937. "The *'Muthir al-Gharam* of Abu-l-Fida' of Hebron." *Journal of the Palestine Oriental Society* 17: 108–208.

Mourad, Suleiman A. 1996. "A Note on the Origin of *Fada'il Bayt al-Maqdis* Compilations." *Al-Abhath* 44: 31–48.

——. 2000. "On Early Islamic Historiography: Abu Isma'il al-Azdi and His *Futuh al-Sham* (Conquests of Syria)." *Journal of the American Oriental Society* 120.4: 577–593.

Al-Raba'i, Abu al-Hasan 'Ali b. Muhammad (d. after 1052 CE). 1950. *Fada'il al-Sham wa-Dimashq.* Ed. Salah al-Din al-Munajjid. Damascus: al-Majma' al-'Ilmi al-'Arabi.

Rabbat, Nasser. 1989. "The Meaning of the Umayyad Dome of the Rock." *Muqarnas* 6: 12–21.

Robinson, Chase F. 2003. *Islamic Historiography.* Cambridge: Cambridge University Press.

——. 2005. *'Abd al-Malik.* London: Oneworld.

Rosen-Ayalon, Myriam. 1996. "Art and Architecture in Jerusalem in the Early Islamic Period." In *The History of Jerusalem: The Early Muslim Period 638–1099,* ed. Joshua Prawer and Haggai Ben-Shammai, 386–419. Jerusalem: Yad Izhak Ben Zvi; New York: New York University Press.

Al-Tabari, Muhammad b. Jarir (d. 922 CE). 1987. *The History of al-Tabari,* vol. 18. Trans. Michael G. Morony. Albany: SUNY Press.

——. 1999. *Jami' al-bayan fi ta'wil al-qur'an.* Beirut: Dar al-Kutub al-'Ilmiyya.

Al-Wasiti, Abu Bakr Muhammad b. Ahmad (d. after 1019 CE). 1978. *Fada'il al-bayt al-muqaddas.* Ed. Isaac Hasson. Jerusalem: The Magnes Press.

7 The holy fool still speaks

The Jerusalem Syndrome as a religious subculture

Alexander van der Haven

The psychiatric hospitalization of foreigners with religious behavior in Israel has led to the birth of the term "Jerusalem Syndrome." The term is used to represent a pathological phenomenon in which the combination of a visit to Israel—in particular Jerusalem—and religious—in particular Christian—expectations prior to arrival either triggers or worsens a mental illness.

However, mental pathology is not the determining characteristic of the Jerusalem Syndrome, nor do religious expectations combined with an actual visit pose a risk to the mental health of foreign visitors. Based both on fieldwork conducted outside the psychiatric environment and on a critical reconsideration of psychiatric data used for previous analyses, I will argue here, first, that the Jerusalem Syndrome is an eschatological religious subculture of Jewish and Christian foreigners[1] who, on the basis of religious experiences, are convinced that they personally have been called to Jerusalem/Israel (note that the term *syndrome* is used here in a less known sense).[2] Because of the religious topography of the Judeo-Christian scriptures, they attribute central religious significance to Israel (as the Holy Land) and in particular to the city of Jerusalem. Second, rather than the beginning or worsening of mental illnesses, the Jerusalem Syndrome is the site where religious expressions of mentally ill persons interact with similar religious behavior of others to the extent that distinguishing between mental illness and normalcy becomes difficult and, for the political and religious context in which these people operate, irrelevant.

In order to show that one should speak of a religious subculture tolerant to behavior otherwise seen as pathological, rather than as a psychiatric problem, I will present and analyze four cases from fieldwork I conducted in Jerusalem in 1999. As will become clear, not only abnormal sensatory experiences and cultural practices of communication with God intersect in the Jerusalem Syndrome, but also deviant behavior as an outcome of both eschatological beliefs and compulsive pathological behavior. In addition, both outsiders and insiders often regard actions typical of the Jerusalem Syndrome as religious rather than as psychopathological behavior.

This is followed by the ideological contextualization of present notions of the Jerusalem Syndrome and a reconsideration of the data used for them by, among others, matching them with tourist statistics. The analysis will demonstrate that the notion that foreigners' religious (especially Christian) expectations of Israel and Jerusalem pose a danger to their mental health is not more than a product of biased analyses. Instead, a reconsideration of the psychiatric data matched with tourist statistics suggests that the Jerusalem Syndrome should be characterized as a site in which psychiatric hospitalization of mentally ill persons is actually less likely to occur than in other situations.

Four case studies of the Jerusalem Syndrome

The following are biographical descriptions of three persons and one group convinced of having been sent by God on a personal mission to Israel. It will become clear that the distinction between mental illness and normalcy is blurred, and that we are dealing with persons using very similar religious patterns. For the sake of privacy, the names used are fictitious. The fact that all cases are Christian or from a Christian background is related to the limited nature of my fieldwork and does not reflect the Jewish and Christian ratios in the Jerusalem Syndrome.

A Dutch messiah

Gerrit, a 67-year-old Dutchman at the time of the interviews in May and June of 1999, claimed to be the messiah. He lived in a hostel in the Christian quarter of Jerusalem's Old City. He told me that he stopped believing in God at the age of 16. Until 1987 he was the well-off owner of a big publishing company that delivered door-to-door free newspapers containing local news and commercials. He was married to a younger woman and had children with her. He claimed that before he left the Netherlands, enemies tried to kill him because his beliefs had become very close to Marxism, and he had to "hide" in a mental hospital and then left and traveled around the world.

A few years before he arrived in Jerusalem in 1994, he became certain that he was the messiah. Certain events in his life convinced him that he was a descendant of King David. Not remembering exactly when it was, he said that the first supernatural experience he had was that God spoke directly to him and said: "You will not see me." This was the only direct contact with God he ever had, but he still received other revelations that were transmitted to him through sounds, which he compared to the auditive revelations to Nostradamus, who, for example, received a prophecy about a dictator called "Hisler," thus predicting Hitler. Other messages were brought to him through street signs or through names. He claimed that other divine knowledge unfolded in his thought processes, which he stimulated by reading and attending lectures about religion, economics, physics, biochemistry, and computers, and contacting experts in these fields.

Although he admitted several failed predictions, Gerrit claimed that very soon God would prove His own existence and would anoint Gerrit as the Messiah, whose rule would be recognized by everybody. The previous messiah, Jesus Christ, had failed because there had been no organization, but now a benevolent conspiracy had prepared the way for a new world through the Internet, the print media, and movies. Gerrit envisioned a future world as without religion, with few clear laws and with a global economy without banks that would enable the world population to live in prosperity and have plenty of leisure time.

Gerrit told me that he did not like Jerusalem and wished he could go home to his wife and children, but he said he was obligated to stay in the city. According to Gerrit, Jerusalem was no more holy than any other place. Yet he had great plans for Jerusalem of which he claimed he could only reveal a little. First, he claimed, these "cheater-shops" (the Arab tourist shops) had to be "wiped away." In their place, coffee shops, theaters, and movie houses would be built. Tunnels would be constructed under the mountains, for transport, so that your food could come to your place from the supermarket with the touch of a button. Further plans for the world were still secret, but Gerrit could disclose that a Palestinian state would be founded in the Sinai, with a fully irrigated desert that would be turned into an agricultural area and many tourist resorts.

Gerrit was as ambivalent toward the Jews as to the Palestinians, for whom he wished a utopian state, but only after razing their local commerce and removing them from Israel. He claimed that the Holocaust was God's lesson for the Jews, and therefore opposed visiting Holocaust museums. He gave two very different reasons against going to Holocaust museums: his fear of experiencing some enjoyment or pleasure by seeing Jews suffer, and that people who had been in the museum forget the shock within an hour after leaving it.

Gerrit tried to spread his views in several ways. Every day he sent a fax to his "publisher." In these faxes he gave his commentaries on the daily issues he dealt with in the form of humorous text balloons spoken by the cartoon character Garfield he cut from newspapers. He also had just finished a book that he believed God had written through him. In it, he presented the essence of the different sciences simplified for his audience. When "published," he assured me, there would be an enormous amount of media attention and "everything will become clear."

Another avenue for spreading his views was trying to convince experts in the fields in which he wrote, yet he remained unfazed by the ridicule that was often heaped on him—there seems even to be a ritualistic aspect to the way he deals with dismissals. When, for instance, he was silenced during the question-and-answer session after a lecture at the Hebrew University, at which he said that he was "obliged to say some important things about the messiah," he again approached the same lecturer at another lecture with an envelope containing evidence that he was the messiah.[3] Gerrit told me that he was convinced that the aforementioned lecturer would throw away his envelope, and he envisioned a funny movie made in the future about all the rejections of the messiah.

Raising the dead Hebrews

Jim, single and about 35, had worked in many places in the US. Before his travel to Israel he was employed at a K-Mart store in Phoenix, Arizona. When I met him he told me that he had been in Jerusalem for six years already and claimed to have been confined to the Old City all that time on divine orders. He had lived in several hostels and had been in his present hostel in the Muslim quarter for two years, where he pays by cleaning at night. Jim had become Born-Again a few months before he came to Israel.

In his church he was told that God had called him, which he regarded as a sign. Soon after, he saw the sun moving up and down in the sky. Later he was reading the Bible in his apartment, praying for God to tell him what He asked from him. Jim claimed that the air grew thick, and the sounds changed, as if they were coming from further away. He remembered that he experienced fear, astonishment, a profound feeling of being stupid, and all kinds of bodily sensations. He opened the Bible at a random place, which turned out to be Ezekiel 37. It also contained a picture of a "Hebrew priest" raising the dead. Suddenly, in the courtyard of his building complex, seven waves of 2,000 "very fair mourning doves" rose up from the ground in an orderly fashion with the sound of a helicopter. Jim asserted that a neighbor also witnessed it and reported it to the building's janitor.

As he told me, an unknown girl knocked at his door the next day and asked him: "What will you do?" He answered: "I will go to Jerusalem." She told him that he "had to do what he had to do" and disappeared again. Jim was now certain that he was called by God to go to Jerusalem in order to raise the "dead Hebrews and plants and animals, as Jesus did." He put his possessions in storage and left for Israel with the $1,400 he had. He recalled that the absence of cheering crowds and the fact that he had imagined Israel to be quite different were a slight disappointment. For the first three days he stayed at a hotel, after which he moved to the Old City in order to save money. His years in Israel had brought some doubt about the precise nature of his role in the future resurrection, and he said he was bored with waiting.

Since leaving the United States, Jim said, he has not received any more visions. He built his religious worldview by reading about subjects and watching television (he claimed that in the Bible "too much has been changed"). Jim believed that about 40,000 Hebrews would be raised. After that the devil, who would try to lead one race to destroy all the others, would be defeated. These Hebrews, Jim stressed, were not identical to the Jews. Until the coming of Christ, the Hebrews had kept their race pure, but after that they had defiled their blood by mingling with other races, with the consequence that the Hebrew race disappeared. He claimed that a thousand years after the Hebrews were resurrected, the rest of mankind would be raised from the dead, and God and Jesus would return. Jim was obsessed with racial purity. He believed that in Noah's time humans mixed with animals, resulting in the strangest combinations, and although the flood destroyed these mixes, today there are still animal traces in human blood. For Jim, other confusions of categories, such as gender and that of the body and soul, also represented evil. For instance, the souls of transsexuals would not go to heaven, and one should not keep people in a coma alive, because their souls have already left their bodies, which according to Jim can remain functioning for at least two hundred years.

Jim believed that contemporary Jerusalem was not sacred, and he never visited religious sites. He also claimed that anybody who alleges he or she knows where the grave of Christ is is a liar and a demon. However, with the resurrection of the Hebrews, Jerusalem would be a holy place again, the Third Temple—Jim knows exactly what it will look like—will be built, and King David will rule again over a greater Israel.

Although more than willing to explain his views, Jim did not seem too interested in spreading his views and preferred to ignore the hostel's staff and guests. When asked about other people's reactions, he said that most of them are negative, but that he does not care. In contrast to Gerrit, Jim's views, eccentric as they are, are taken from American anti-Semitic Christian beliefs. However, just like Gerrit, he seemed to have no successful interaction with other people. The case of prophet Tim is quite different.

A healing prophet

Tim, around 40 and a New Zealander of mixed Polynesian descent, claimed to have the gift of prophecy. He said he was the son of an "unloving father" and a pastor. He became an alcoholic and drug addict, reaching his lowest point in 1995, when he attempted to commit suicide. He had gone to a church and asked God to help him. He told me that soon after, when a preacher on television put his hands on the screen and asked those watching to touch their TV screens, Tim's knees were pushed to the ground "by the Holy Spirit," and tears drenched his shirt. When "God" asked him "do you accept me completely?" Tim answered yes, and God received the same answer to the question whether he was prepared to give up his family. Tim explained to his relatives that God had commanded him to go to Jerusalem and fulfill the "special plan" He had for him. Since he arrived in Jerusalem, he had lived in a hostel outside the Old City walls, where he pays for his board by doing chores.

On the one hand, Tim claimed that he was just a regular man who had opened his heart to God and that his previous experiences as an alcoholic and drug addict had strengthened his understanding of human failures and limitations and his ability to see potential for change. On the other hand, Tim claimed that God has blessed him with the gift of healing, the gift of voice and the power to exorcise demons. He called himself a "prophet," and said that God had chosen him at the beginning of time to fulfill a certain mission; he would not reveal the details of this mission nor would he share what future prophecies had been revealed to him, apart from a prediction that soon "spiritual wars" would break out that would divide the world, in which "father would turn against father, and son against son." His own plan was to spend a year in Jerusalem and then return to New Zealand to preach at the three largest churches there, after which he would go to Europe, Asia, and Africa, and finally return to Jerusalem.

Like Gerrit and Jim, Tim had a negative view of the religious state of contemporary Israel. He claimed that the Holy Sepulcher was held in bondage and believed that many churches were occupied by evil powers. When attempting to visit the Nativity Church in Bethlehem, he said that the Holy Spirit forbade him to enter, and during a "conversation" with the Holy Spirit at the Western Wall, God told him that the Western Wall was just stone.

Although he compared his stay in the humble hostel to living in the desert, Tim had an active social life. He described the other hostel guests as "family" and the interactions I witnessed showed that he commanded great respect and appreciation from others. Tim claimed that through him God had cured many people in the hostel. For instance, when he prayed in the hostel basement with a confused theology student, the latter was cured of his amnesia and had a vision of Tim in heaven, dressed in a white robe with a gold girdle—Tim claims that others had had the same vision. Tim had told them all that the visions were not of him, however, but of Jesus. He stressed that he could only help those who "received Jesus in their heart," and narrated a failed attempt to cure a possessed Muslim woman because she did not want to believe in Jesus.

Tim did not regard himself as being the only prophet in Jerusalem. According to him, God reveals himself through his prophets, which have never ceased to appear since biblical times, and these prophets communicate with each other. Tim claimed to have frequent contact with prophets in Jerusalem. For example, during a period of "pride," in which he had strayed from the path of humility, he had encountered a prophet at the Jaffa Gate who approached him and said: "What are you doing?" The prophet had a tear in his eye, which instead of downward, ran up on his forehead. Tim said that the prophet claimed that was the pain of the Holy Spirit.

House of Prayer

The fourth case does not concern an individual, but a religious community. Until the group was deported on the eve of the millennium on the suspicion that they were planning collective suicide, the "House of Prayer" offered accommodation for $5.00 a night to Christians who are "born in the spirit" and wanted to stay for a longer time in Jerusalem, "even until the return of

Christ." Under the leadership of Brother Daniel and Sister Susan (who did not use their last names anymore), this group of around 25 evangelical Christians (including the temporary visitors) had formed itself in Israel out of Christian visitors who had drifted into each other's arms and had decided to stay. They first had bought a house in West Jerusalem, and in 1999 they were living in a few adjacent houses in Bethany, on the southeastern slopes of the Mount of Olives. In the past, the group had not only received attention from a group of Orthodox Jews that had attacked the house when the group lived in West Jerusalem, but also from the police and the international press. The police once arrested Brother Daniel on the basis of a list of people they believed he had converted (Christian proselytization is forbidden by law in Israel). In addition, the press was a regular guest in Bethany, where these Christians were awaiting the end times.

I interviewed six persons in the group. Brother Daniel and Sister Susan provided me with their life stories by giving me a copy of an interview with them in the newspaper *Ashland Daily Tidings* (Ashland, Oregon). Brother Daniel worked in the trailer business in upstate New York, and after a conversion experience in which he received the gift of speaking in tongues, Brother Daniel claimed that God started to talk to him through Scripture, and eventually told him that he should go to Israel. He quit his job, sold everything, and bought a one-way ticket, living on voluntary gifts donated by religious groups for whom he served as a tour guide in Jerusalem. Sister Susan had "come to the faith" in 1969 and claimed that one day she asked God what she should do with her life. "Out of the blue, a voice said, 'Well Susan, you've always wanted to go to Israel.' " Within a few months she resigned from her job in California, sold her possessions and also bought a one-way ticket. When she arrived in Israel she traveled to several cities but claims that "nothing seemed right until I came to Jerusalem." She told me that she felt immediately at home there, and the others in the room claimed to have had exactly the same experience. She said that in Jerusalem everything was more intense and more "special things" happen than "back home."

Sister Susan's son, Brother Richard, had been in prison off and on for the 12 years before he had come to Israel. In his mid-twenties, he had come to faith and joined his mother in 1993. He married his wife Kathy, about 40 and from Indiana, two weeks after her arrival in Israel. Claiming to have had visions of God during her childhood, she nevertheless left her faith, became a dancer and, from time to time, a prostitute. She claimed she was almost sacrificed by a Satanist sect and was saved by the cross she was wearing around her neck. Having become more religious under the influence of a religious housemate, she left for Miami Beach, where she started to go to church while doing menial jobs. During the ten years in Florida she became very religious, and eventually God told her to go to Jerusalem to marry. By the time she arrived in Israel, God had told Brother Richard to clean up his apartment to receive his future bride; the two met and got married.

Helen, an Australian woman in her forties, who was there with her two young sons, professed to always have been Born-Again, and came to Israel every time she believed God called her. Her atheist husband had divorced her because he believed she was crazy, and she alienated her family because she rejected the Trinity. Anthony, an American in his forties, had been Born-Again since 1976. He had visited Israel many times and this time had been there for half a year. He referred to Jesus and God only with their Hebrew names, and was preparing tapes with evidences of biblical prophecies.

Pathology and eschatological behavior

Are these four examples clear cases of mental pathology, or are there other issues at stake? The following section will describe how pathological symptoms and common religious experiences overlap.

Hallucinations and divine calls

In the Jerusalem Syndrome, religious discourses are used to describe hallucinations and delusions that originate in mental illness, which justify individual radical religious changes on the basis of private religious experiences to the extent that the two are not always distinguishable. Those who had experiences that were part of the onset or reappearance of a mental illness regard these as religious revelations and learn to place ongoing experiences in a religious framework. Others justify their stay in Israel by narrating what they believe were past communications with God, but it is uncertain whether these are invented later or are based on actual experiences.

Gerrit belongs to the first category, as he was hearing voices and sounds, saw hidden messages and felt that his thought processes were guided by forces outside himself. Although these are typical symptoms of mental illnesses, to Gerrit their content conveyed more than the fact that he was mentally ill. He compared his experiences to the sounds that Nostradamus heard and on which the French seer based his prophecies. Gerrit explained the fact that he alone received these messages by adopting the social role of messiah who had a privileged insight into the invisible side of reality. In the case of Tim, the prophet from New Zealand, it is more difficult to define which came first. Did his rather conventional religious conversion grow into what he believed was direct contact with the Holy Spirit, or did his experience of the supernatural precede his conversion experience? Was his confident control over the dialogue with the Holy Spirit rooted in religious practices that led to hearing the voice of God, or in the gradual control over the interaction with a voice that he later identified as the Holy Spirit?

The narratives of Brother Daniel and Sister Susan suggest that they gradually built up a prayer technique in the form of what they believe is an actual dialogue with God, so that when they were making significant life decisions they could conveniently "discuss" them with "their Maker" in person. Another important element that plays a role in the personal narratives of the House of Prayer is that of rewriting the past. The uniformity of the narratives of the decision to go to Israel and the identical reports of feeling immediately at home when arriving in Jerusalem make it likely that these events and experiences were inscribed onto the past after coming to Israel and jointly developing autobiographical narratives. Studies of the veracity of autobiographical accounts of converts or persons in therapy, for instance, often have indicated that a significant reconstruction of the past takes place, increasing the dramatic elements. There is enough reason to suspect that this is also the case here. For example, Kathy's memory of the Satanist assault on her life has been a very common one in the U.S. over the last decades, but not a single account has been proven to be based on actual events (Hacking 1995, 114–118). In addition, her claim to be Jewish was rejected by the Israeli authorities when she applied for citizenship, and appears to be a later invention to legitimize the close relationship between herself and her newly adopted homeland. Thus, in the Jerusalem Syndrome, the dramatically alien experiences of mental illness intermingle with the dramatic justifications of a personal mission to Israel/Jerusalem.

Religious patterns of deviance

My informants and those who are mentally hospitalized make religious claims in which they challenge the present religious status quo of Israel, and specifically Jerusalem, a city under secular Jewish governance and containing a large number of other ethnic and religious groups. Moreover, they are more committed to the content of their beliefs than to the acceptance of these beliefs by others, and they see themselves as prophetic critics or messianic savers and thus often run into conflict with the authorities. This explains the "impressive amount" of tourists, which according to one of the publications about the Jerusalem Syndrome were referred by authorities for acute worsening of symptoms of a mental illness and for "disrupting public order" (Bar-El, Kalian et al. 1991, 488–489). The tourist who started to "smash idols" in the Holy Sepulcher before he was apprehended did not expect his acts to be appreciated by all (Bar-El et al. 2000, 88).

What the authorities regard as disturbance is for the perpetrator often a way to attract attention to something such importance that it trumps—or abolishes—human laws. For instance, 13 percent of the tourists who are hospitalized for mental illness walk around naked, and this high percentage suggests the influence of Isaiah 20, when the prophet's nakedness serves to warn the Egyptians and Ethiopians of their upcoming fate by the hands of the Assyrians.

The beliefs of the characters in the biographical sketches above closely resemble the kind of radical religious attitudes of those who are hospitalized. Gerrit aimed to abolish all religion, Tim demonized existent churches and expected apocalyptic scenes in the near future, and Jim waited for the present degenerated population to be replaced by a Hebrew theocracy. The members of the House of Prayer mocked the piety of pilgrims at religious sites, attempted to convert Jews (at least in the eyes of the government), and they expected the final apocalyptic battle between Russian, Chinese, and American armies, visible from their own balconies, in the near future. However, in contrast to the attitudes of the hospitalized foreigners, their actions are not always regarded as mentally ill, as we now will see.

Social recognition of the Jerusalem Syndrome as religious

In the Jerusalem Syndrome, experiences that accompany mental disturbances overlap with religious experiences normative to believers such as my informants of the House of Prayer, and religious eschatological beliefs demand the mutual rejection of the holders and the center. Thus, the mentally ill blend in with those for whom dramatic experiences are normative and for whom stigmatization by the social body is a badge of honor. In Israel, those who are part of the Jerusalem Syndrome do not only occupy a social position that might be described as that of the foreign village fool, but also fulfill religious roles in the eyes of others. The Jerusalem Syndrome is not just a matter for district psychiatrists, but for the security apparatus, and within the community of religious foreigners in Israel, they are often seen as religious actors rather than as mentally ill.

An example is the police measures taken to prevent "redemptive acts" at the time of my fieldwork just before the Second *Intifada*: Gerrit was under police order not to approach the Western Wall within a distance of 150 meters, and on the eve of the millennium the members of the House of Prayer, together with a few other religious communities, were deported because of security concerns. Brother Daniel's run-in with the law earlier did not concern issues of mental health but was related to the suspicion that he had violated the law against Christian proselytizing. While one can answer rejection by others with apocalyptic rhetoric, the role of the martyr offers a more public spectacle. The televised arrest of Brother Richard, in which he is seen making the V-sign and shouting "Yeshu" from the police car as it drives away from the camera, had a dramatic quality that eschatological words do not have.

The dense religious atmosphere in Israel also conditions social interactions outside those with the authorities; hence the attack by Orthodox Jews on the House of Prayer, or the anger I once saw displayed during a visit with Gerrit by a fellow hostel guest who accused him of making false prophecies. The attacking Orthodox Jews were invested in expelling the religious outsiders from their neighborhood and not in the mental health of these people, and the anger of the hostel guest showed that he regarded Gerrit as a false prophet rather than as a madman.

The ambiguity of the experiences and behaviors of the Jerusalem Syndrome results in varying interpretations that reflect the worldview and interests of the observers. A famous example is the case of Dennis Rohan, the Australian sheepshearer who set fire to the Aqsa mosque in 1968. The court committed him to a mental hospital because the psychiatric expert witness argued that the underlying cause was "not religious but sexual." Whereas some years later he would have been characterized as a mentally ill "existential tourist," or psychotic as the result of disappointed expectations when arriving in Jerusalem, here the nature of his deeds was seen as sexual. Yet, another view was held in the Arab world where, even after Rohan's trial, the arson was seen as the result of a Zionist plot (Rabinovich 1988, 43), meant to destroy the Haram al-Sharif and rebuild the Temple.

Among the temporary tourist population and others who fall under the umbrella of the Jerusalem Syndrome, positive interaction also takes place. Tourists' greater acceptance of and interest in the out-of-the-ordinary during their vacation or pilgrimage in Israel often leads to a temporary sense of what the anthropologist Victor Turner (1973) called *communitas*. The interactions between Tim and the other guests in his hostel were temporary and *could* therefore be more intense and religiously extraordinary. Tim's encounters, if real, with other prophets could have been those with likeminded spirits, who were able to regard their encounters as those between religiously important actors. In addition, religious communities such as the House of Prayer that are formed by foreigners not only support the extraordinary experiences of their own members, but also welcome those of newcomers. The fact that members of religious communities are rarely hospitalized in Jerusalem not only suggests a correlation between social functioning and mental health, but also implies that these communities provide a shelter to those who otherwise could have been hospitalized.[4] A remarkable example is that of a Swedish woman who, during my visit, knocked on the door of the House of Prayer seeking housing. She recounted her story of having been commanded by God to go to Jerusalem, returning again to Sweden to take care of her son, and consequently being forced again by God with pains, "like birth pangs," to return to Israel. In another environment her case would immediately be recognized as pathological, but on the slopes of the Mount of Olives, her story was received as evidence of the power of God.

Thus far, three elements have been highlighted that support the claim that the Jerusalem Syndrome is an eschatological subculture in which symptoms of mental illness and specific religious behavior blend. First, hearing voices and cultural notions of personal communication with God overlap in the Jerusalem Syndrome. The same can be said for deviant behavior, the result both of eschatological motivations and of compulsive pathological behavior. Lastly, actions typical of the Jerusalem Syndrome are perceived by both outsiders and insiders as religious rather than psychopathological behavior.

But what if this religious subculture in which mental pathology and eschatological behavior successfully mingle is something completely different than the Jerusalem Syndrome as conceived by Israeli psychiatrists, a syndrome which entails the worsening or the sudden genesis of mental illness of tourists in Israel? It will be shown in the following pages that this is not the case. Through the ideological contextualization and critical analysis of the existing theories and a reevaluation of the data on which they are based, two aspects will become clear. First, the assumption that the mental state of foreigners who visit Israel with religious (especially Christian) expectations of the place, especially regarding Jerusalem, is in danger of disintegration is a false one. I will show that not the expectations of the visitors, but those of the people who analyze them, determine the visitors' pathological status in the existing analyses of the Jerusalem Syndrome. Second, a new look at the psychiatric data, matched with statistics from the Ministry of Tourism, shows that the Jerusalem Syndrome should be characterized as a site in which psychiatric hospitalization of mentally ill persons is *less* likely, rather than more likely, to occur than in other situations.

From mad Zionist immigrants to healthy Christian tourists

Although there are some recent arguments for the mental pathologies of some of the older cases, the first reports describing religiously eccentric travelers as insane emerged in the nineteenth century.[5] Whereas nineteenth-century reports are usually worded in mocking terms, Zionist psychiatry took mental illness among newcomers very seriously. Working as a psychiatrist in Jerusalem's Ezrat Nashim hospital, the German émigré Haim Hermann claimed in 1931 that prevalent notions of the beneficial effect of an early release from the hospital on schizophrenics was especially effective in the case of Jews who immigrated to Palestine. A quarter of his immigrant cases apparently did not share this view and decided upon release to return to their former homelands. Nevertheless, Hermann maintained that "the special feeling of freedom of the Jews living in Palestine" brought about a quickened cure (Hermann 1931, 82–92; 1937, 232–237).

Less optimistic sounds were also made. Novelists such as Joseph Brenner exposed the darker sides of the redemptive promise of a Jewish homeland. This was personified in the mentally ill protagonist of his *Breakdown and Bereavement*, who at a certain point in his miserable immigrant existence exclaims: "They say that Palestine is the center of the world ... what a joke! Why, he himself was the center!" (Brenner 1971, 118).[6] Brenner realized better than Hermann that Aliyah (immigration to what is regarded as the Land of Israel) was not the solution to mental problems. Instead of being cured, immigrants with mental problems suffered from the discrepancy between the harsh living conditions and the return of many immigrants to their countries of origin and the optimistic tone of the Zionist ideology.

Three decades after the foundation of the State of Israel, the tourist who was usually represented as a Christian became the new locus of discourses on madness and Israel.[7] This categorization assumed an institutional form in 1979 with the decision to refer all tourists suffering from mental illness to the psychiatric institution Kfar Shaul in Jerusalem. Soon the name "Jerusalem

Syndrome" was coined by a group of psychiatrists in Jerusalem; Yair Bar-El, Moshe Kalian, and Eliezer Witztum were among the most prominent. They had observed a remarkably high frequency of religious claims made by hospitalized tourists and began to collect data from Kfar Shaul. They developed two theories about the hospitalization of tourists that suggested a connection between these tourists' pathologies and their presence in Jerusalem (for the period 1979–84 (177 tourists), see Bar-El, Kalian et al. 1991, 487–492; for 1986–87 (89 tourists), see Bar-El, Witztum et al. 1991, 238–244).

The first theory is reminiscent of the critical connotations of madness in the Yeshuv, such as Brenner's, where personal redemption is unsuccessfully sought in a geographical solution and the subject disintegrates at the destination. It considers mental pathology as the cause of travel to Israel and places hospitalizations of foreigners in the context of "existential tourism"—a term borrowed from sociologist Erik Cohen that entails "travel to an elective spiritual center and that is analogous to pilgrimage" (Bar-El, Witztum et al. 1991, 239).[8] Comparing the Jerusalem Syndrome to tourist hospitalizations in places such as Rome, or non-religious sites of symbolical significance like Florence, the White House, patent offices, and airports, it is seen here as "an aggravation of a chronic mental illness" after the "geographical solution" to personal problems turned out not to be successful. Israel, in particular Jerusalem, serves as the dramatic stage for these private illnesses that take the shape of a pilgrimage (Bar-El, Witztum et al. 1991, 238).

In the other interpretation that these authors proposed, the central aspect of the Jerusalem Syndrome does not lie in the worsening of the situation of a mentally ill person but in the pathological reaction of often quite healthy religious tourists to their arrival in Israel. Thus Kalian explained the impact of travel to Jerusalem in a *Time* magazine interview (17 April 1995): "The thrill of a place previously only known as a sublime dream is in the case of the Jerusalem Syndrome followed by a disappointment that it is also just an earthly town. Unwilling to accept this, the victims withdraw from this reality." Recently, Kalian and Witztum have abandoned the view of Jerusalem as a pathogenic factor and restricted their argument to the first explanation by pointing out that the data suggest that the mental illnesses started before the arrival in Israel (Kalian and Witztum 2000, 492).[9]

Besides being described as a worsening of a pre-existing illness after arriving in "the Holy Land," and as the result of cognitive dissonance, the Jerusalem Syndrome is also identified with Christianity. Many journalists visiting the offices of Jerusalem's psychiatrists have informed their audiences worldwide that the Jerusalem Syndrome, in the words of one news article, "mainly affects Christian pilgrims but is occasionally diagnosed on Jews who tour holy sites" (Siegel-Itzkovitch 1999, 484). The theory of cognitive dissonance has even evolved into the explicit identification of tourist mental breakdowns with Protestant Christianity. Thus in a 2000 article in the *British Medical Journal*, Bar-El and others argued that pious Protestants comprise 95 percent of what they denominate there as the "pure" Jerusalem Syndrome, namely a mental breakdown when there are no pre-existing mental illnesses present. The reason, they claimed, is that very religious Protestants have a greater attachment than tourists of other religions to "an idealistic sub-conscious image of Jerusalem" (Bar-El et al. 2000, 89).

Those who have analyzed the combination of mental illness and visiting Israel had specific ideological expectations of the effect of the land of Israel on the mental health of those who arrive. Hermann saw his patients as *immigrants*, as exiles who come "home," and therefore they benefit from their travel. Bren-ner on the other hand described his character as one who has fallen for a ficti-tious hope and therefore sees immigration for Jews as potentially dangerous for their mental stability. In the two more recent theories, the subjects of interest are classified as *tourists*, especially as Christian tourists. These fail their own category, commonly characterized as uncommitted to the destination of travel, engaged in a ritually failing quest for authenticity (MacCannell 1973), or encouraged to look at different viewpoints rather than imposing a singular (sacred) reality on the visited site (Urry 1995). Since the beliefs and behaviors typical of the Jerusalem Syndrome stand in stark contrast to this disengage-ment toward the travel destination, labeling these foreigners as tourists turns them into tourists gone astray. However, that is not how these people regard themselves. Of all the hospitalized foreigners in 1986 and 1987, almost half came for "reasons of a mystical-religious nature" or to try out a "different life-style" possibly resulting in staying in Jerusalem (Bar-El, Witztum et al. 1991, 240).[10] In the absence of more appropriate visa classifications (a "prophet-visa," a "messiah-visa"), most eschatological travelers have to enter the country on tourist visas. As a result, they become pathological tourists.[11]

The category of Christian tourists is removed from that of Hermann's immigrants not only by tourist status, but also by religion, and therefore is represented as more vulnerable to a mental breakdown. The problem here is that the suggestion of the Jerusalem Syndrome as a predominantly Chris-tian phenomenon is unfounded. Christian cases are presented almost exclusively in the literature on the syndrome, but more than half of the hospitalized foreigners are Jewish. Thus there is a clear misrepresentation, which in none of the publications receives any justification. Moreover, the veracity of Bar-El's statistical elevation of the Protestant sufferer was chal-lenged by Kalian and Witztum, who had access to the same data. This challenge remained unanswered, and the essentializing analysis of a collec-tive Protestant unconscious suggests that there is good reason for that. In addition, an argument not made but probably assumed is that there are simply more Jewish visitors to Israel/Jerusalem, and that therefore the large number of Christian hospitalizations is significant. However, matching tourist data and those from the hospital reveal that if any conclusion should be drawn—which on the basis of these scant data should not be the case[12]—the madness scale tips in favor of Jewish visitors.[13] It seems that the stereotype of the Christian as sufferer of the Jerusalem Syndrome is the result of an exact inversion of the positive effect Hermann believed Zion had on immigrant Jews. The mental health of the mentally ill who arrive and expect a Jewish land undergoes a dramatic improvement, whereas healthy minds that arrive with expectations of a landscape reflecting Christian ideas are in danger of a mental breakdown. In the theory of a mental breakdown, the foreigner is, upon arrival, subject to a swift judgment of madness lest he or she accept the correct religious and territorial true map of Israel (that is, the idealized Holy Land).

The notion of a mental breakdown upon failed expectations itself rests on shaky foundations. Since tourists are hospitalized only *after* this "disappointment," not a single actual description exists in the literature on the Jerusalem Syndrome of how this mechanism of disappointment actually works. The naiveté of the notion is illustrated by studies that describe religious mechanisms that successfully deal with this dissonance, such as Leon Festinger's famous work on the failed prophecies of a UFO cult. In addition, my fieldwork shows the eschatological travelers' ability to cope quite well with a world that doesn't comply to their hopes toward the place—in fact, contrasting ideal and reality is the specialty of eschatology.[14]

We can take this criticism of the idea that the mental health of "sufferers" of the Jerusalem Syndrome disintegrates upon arrival in Israel even further. The data that I presented from my fieldwork make it apparent that those who suffer from symptoms of mental illness can find in Jerusalem a rather hospitable environment in the eschatological subculture, the Jerusalem Syndrome. When placed in a wide context, namely in that of the world outside the hospital walls, the data from Kfar Shaul suggest exactly the same.

Looking beyond the hospital walls: psychiatric hospitalization and religion in the Jerusalem Syndrome

The fact that the present understandings of the Jerusalem Syndrome are based on "tourist" hospitalizations has given rise to three ways in which the picture presented of the Syndrome is skewed. First, because the analyses are based on hospitalized tourists only, it is automatically assumed that psychiatric hospitalization is part and parcel of the Jerusalem Syndrome.

Even though no statistical data exist about the Jerusalem Syndrome besides those from Kfar Shaul, a critical look at the existing data can offer some cautious suggestions when one looks more closely at the relationship between those representative of the Jerusalem Syndrome and the other foreigners within the hospital. One would expect high hospitalization rates among foreigners in Israel based on the arguments that the country attracts pathological travelers with religious fantasies and that Israel poses a danger for the mental health of religious tourists. However, between 1979 and 1987, 100 foreigners underwent psychiatric hospitalization every year, less than half of whom can be identified with the Jerusalem Syndrome, while the yearly tourist population was on average more than a million during that period.[15] This confirms Kalian and Witztum's recent argument that the

Jerusalem Syndrome is actually a very rare phenomenon (Kalian and Witztum 2000, 492).[16]

In the new framework I propose here, we can rephrase Kalian and Witztum's argument to the claim that in the Jerusalem Syndrome, psychiatric hospitalization itself is not a representative phenomenon. This is supported by the data from Kfar Shaul, which suggest that the mentally ill who are part of the Jerusalem Syndrome are less quickly hospitalized than other mentally ill persons.[17] Writing about the hospitalizations between 1986 and 1987, Bar-El, Witztum et al. (1991, 242–243) noticed that there was a significant difference between the self-declared "observant" foreigners and the other hospitalized foreigners in the length of the period between arrival and hospitalization. Whereas 90 percent of the "not observant" to "strictly observant" foreigners were hospitalized within two weeks of arrival, more than half of the religious group remained outside the asylum walls until after that period. The authors explained this difference by giving religiosity the dubious honor of being both the cause of hospitalization and a temporary stabilizing agent for the tourist. When we extend the demographic beyond the hospital population, however, a very different explanation becomes possible: the religious beliefs and behavior typical of the Jerusalem Syndrome tend to prevent mentally ill persons from being hospitalized. If those who are hospitalized were referred significantly later than other tourists, they might only be the tip of an iceberg.

Hence it appears that the relationship between the Jerusalem Syndrome and mental illness is actually that of a negative correlation to psychiatric hospitalization. Some of the mentally ill characteristic of the Jerusalem Syndrome are hospitalized, but it seems that they are the minority rather than the norm. In addition, the sample of hospitalized foreigners represents only those diagnosed with mental illness, not others with behaviors and beliefs characteristic of the Jerusalem Syndrome who are not mentally ill at all.

Conclusion

Thus, instead of a pathological phenomenon, the Jerusalem Syndrome should be seen as an eschatological subculture, consisting of foreigners who believe they are called by God to come to Jerusalem, and in which symptoms of mental illness and religious behavior coexist successfully. Whereas from the academic psychiatric viewpoint the phenomenon is regarded as pathological, on the ground it actually is a religious subculture, and this is of significance for wider arguments about mental illness and Western culture. When comparing the ecstatic experiences of Sri Lankan ascetics to those that are regarded as psychosis in the West, the anthropologist Gananath Obeyesekere, echoing Foucault's famous argument about the silencing of "madness" (Foucault 1965), concluded that in the West, "psychotic fantasy is a private, incommunicable set of images; the afflicted person is trying to represent his inner turmoil in outer images, but the images constructed have little communicative function except to express to the culture the idea that the patient is sick" (Obeyesekere 1981, 102–103). Contradicting Foucault and Obeyesekere, the Jerusalem Syndrome shows that there are sites in Western culture where expressions of mentally ill can become meaningful.

Notes

1 Although existing literature about the Jerusalem Syndrome uses the word "tourists," I prefer to use the more generic term "foreigners," to describe non-Israelis and non-Palestinians, since the word "tourist" has a leisurely connotation that does not adequately describe the self-image of these people and rather represents one of the theories about the Jerusalem Syndrome that I criticize here.

2 The use of the word "syndrome" in non-medical terms and the insertion of the term "subculture" require some justification. Although "syndrome" is commonly used to describe a set of characteristic symptoms, the second entry in the *Oxford English Dictionary* (1989 edition) defines it as "a characteristic combination of opinions, behavior, etc.; freq. preceded by a qualifying word." Since pathology is not a qualifying factor in my definition, the term is employed here in this less-known use. I have chosen the word "subculture" over other terms, such as "movement," because the defined group is constituted of individual actors and groups who display similar forms of behavior and beliefs that, however, differ widely in content. The reason is not only that terms like "movement" suggest a more ideological uniformity that is only the case with groups that represent the Jerusalem Syndrome, but also the word "subculture" entails being at variance with beliefs and behaviors of the general culture of which it forms part, and has a performative quality that sociologist Dick Hebdige called "style" (Hebdige 1979, 133). As will be shown, beliefs and behaviors that are part of the Jerusalem Syndrome are theatrically eschatological rejections of an unredeemed world, including the present religious situation in Israel. (I have not heard of any Muslim cases, but this certainly does not mean that they do not exist. One reason is that their behavior is more likely to be regarded as a matter of security rather than of mental illness. See, for instance, accusations leveled against the Israeli authorities in Siegel-Itzkovitch 1997, 535.)

3 The evidence was that the constellation of stars in Van Gogh's "starry night" indicated a date exactly 40 years before Gerrit's birth, God's humorous variant on the announcement of Christ's birth.

4 Hospitalization of members of religious communities in Israel is rare (Bar-El et al. 2000, 88).

5 For nineteenth-century reports and historical diagnoses, see Witztum and Kalian 1999, 2000; Kalian and Witztum 2002. "Cranks" is the wording of Spafford-Vester 1950. For a convincing case for Sabbatai Sevi's mental illness see Scholem 1973.

6 This work was written in 1914 and first published in 1920.

7 The reasons for this shift are probably local changes in attitude toward immigration and the exponential growth of tourism in Israel.

8 A more specific theory that I do not discuss here is that of Avner Falk (1989, 141–150), who argued that mental illness of tourists in Israel was related to their identification of the landscape with the body of their mother.

9 Kalian and Witztum do not offer numerical data here, but claim that, "If epidemiological data supporting Bar-El, Witztum et al.'s typology exist (1991, 241), it is regrettable that they were not presented in their article. To our knowledge, such data have not been found in previous studies ..." They mention that 82 percent of the tourists hospitalized in 1986 and 1987 had received psychiatric

treatment before their hospitalization in Jerusalem. In addition, the diagnoses made are mostly that of long-term illnesses, such as schizophrenia, personality disorder, and dementia.

10 This half probably coincides with the hospitalized foreigners that represent the Jerusalem Syndrome, who, as I will argue later, make up half of the hospitalization of foreigners.

11 The distinction between pathological and normal tourism suggested by the authors on the Jerusalem Syndrome does not reflect the argument made in Cohen's sociological taxonomy in which he actually stresses the diversity of tourist experiences and the unusual character of some of them (Cohen 1979, 179–201). For an overview of socio-psychological approaches to tourism and to analyses of tourism as modern pilgrimage, see Cohen 1984, 377–378.

12 The raw data from Kfar Shaul have been lost as a result of a recent reorganization of Israel's health services, and the published data are representative only for a segment of the Jerusalem Syndrome (personal communication from M. Kalian, January 31, 2004).

13 Even though more Christians than Jews visit Israel on a tourist visa, more than half of the hospitalized foreigners are Jewish, whereas a little over a third are Catholic or Protestant (Bar-El, Witztum et al. 1991, 240). Two other categories are mentioned: "Other," which accounts for only 2 percent, and "Unknown," 11 percent. Tourist statistics for the periods September–October and November–December 1986 describe respectively that 41 percent and 38 percent of the tourists were Jewish and 52 percent and 51 percent were Christian. My data on foreign visitors use based on the majority of those who entered on tourist visas: *Tourism and Hotel Services Statistics Quarterly* 1987 (special series 813), Table 19.

14 Despite its weakness, the media, from newspapers to tourist guides, have found this theory of "cognitive dissonance" most appealing, and it has inspired other diagnoses of local syndromes, such as the "Paris Syndrome," which describes the sudden depressions of Japanese female tourists in Paris when their expectations are not met: see *The Sunday Tribune* (December 26, 2004); and Festinger et al. 1956.

15 The number of people departing on tourist visas increased from 988,200 in 1979 to 1,333,200 in 1987 (*Statistical Abstract of Israel*, Table 4). The publications on Kfar Shaul show that from 1979 to 1987 around 50 foreigners were referred every year to the hospital (Bar-El, Witztum et al. 1991, 239); an article covering the period 1980–93 (Bar-El et al. 2000: 86) claims 40 people a year were admitted. These are all the tourists in the District of Jerusalem who are in need of hospitalization, which, according to the authors, is about half of the national number of hospitalizations (Witztum and Kalian 1999, 270). Of these 100 tourists, less than half has any relationship to the Jerusalem Syndrome. I base this figure on the assumption that only the 40 percent who claimed to have had religious experiences, the majority of whom identified with religiously important characters, are exponents of the Jerusalem Syndrome (Bar-El, Witztum et al. 1991, 240).

16 They argue that there are almost two million tourists every year.

17 I assume that those hospitalized foreigners who define themselves as most religious roughly coincide with those who have the beliefs and behaviors that we characterize as the Jerusalem Syndrome.

References

Bar-El, I., M. Kalian, B. Eisenberg, and S. Schneider. 1991. "Tourists and Psychiatric Hospitalization with Reference to Ethical Aspects Concerning Management and Treatment." *Medicine and Law* 10.5: 487–492.

Bar-El, I., E. Witztum, M. Kalian, and D. Brom. 1991. "Psychiatric Hospitalization of Tourists in Jerusalem." *Comprehensive Psychiatry* 32.3: 238–244.

Bar-El, I., R. Durst, G. Katz, J. Zislin, Z. Strauss, and H. Y. Knobler. 2000. "Jerusalem Syndrome." *British Journal of Psychiatry* 176: 86–90.

Brenner, Joseph H. 1971. *Breakdown and Bereavement: A Novel*, trans. Hillel Halkin. Ithaca: Cornell University Press.

Cohen, Erik. 1979. "A Phenomenology of Tourist Experiences." *Sociology* 13: 179–201.

——. 1984. "The Sociology of Tourism: Approaches, Issues, and Findings." *Annual Review of Sociology* 10: 373–392.

Falk, Avner. 1989. "Border Symbolism." In *Maps from the Mind: Readings in Psychogeography*, ed. Howard F. Stein and William G. Niederland, 141–150. Norman: University of Oklahoma Press.

Festinger, Leon, Henry W. Reiken, and Stanley Schachter. 1956. *When Prophecy Fails: A Social and Psychological Study of a Modern Group that Predicted the Destruction of the World*. New York: Harper & Row.

Foucault, Michel. 1965. *Madness and Civilization: A History of Insanity in the Age of Reason*, trans. R. Howard. New York: Random House.

Hacking, Ian. 1995. *Rewriting the Soul: Multiple Personality and the Sciences of Memory*. Princeton: Princeton University Press.

Hebdige, Dick. 1979. *Subculture: The Meaning of Style*. London and New York: Methuen.

Hermann, Haim. 1931. "Frühentlassung von Schizophrenen in Palästina." *Archiv für Psychiatrie* 94: 82–92.

——. 1937. "Psychiatrisches aus Palästina." *Folia Clinica Orientalia* 1: 232–237.

Kalian, Moshe, and Eliezer Witztum. 2000. "Comments on the Jerusalem Syndrome." *British Journal of Psychiatry* 176: 492.

——. 2002. "Jerusalem Syndrome as Reflected in the Pilgrimage and Biographies of Four Extraordinary Women from the 14th Century to the End of the Second Millennium." *Mental Health, Religion and Culture* 5.1: 1–16.

MacCannell, Dean. 1973. *The Tourist: A New Theory of the Leisure Class*. New York: Schocken.

Obeyesekere, Gananath. 1981. *Medusa's Hair: An Essay on Personal Symbols and Religious Experience*. Chicago: University of Chicago Press.

Rabinovich, Abraham. 1988. *Jerusalem on Earth: People, Passions and Politics in the Holy City*. New York: The Free Press.

Scholem, Gershom. 1973. *Sabbatai Sevi: The Mystical Messiah, 1626–1676*. Princeton: Princeton University Press.

Siegel-Itzkovitch, Judy. 1997. "Israel Accused of Ignoring Psychiatric Problems in Palestinian Prisoners [news]." *British Medical Journal* 314 (February): 535.

——. 1999. "Israel Prepares for 'Jerusalem Syndrome' [news]." *British Medical Journal* 318 (February): 484.

Spafford-Vester, Bertha. 1950. *Our Jerusalem: An American Family in the Holy City 1881–1949*. Lebanon: Middle East Export Press.

Statistical Abstract of Israel, vols. 31–39 (1980–88). Jerusalem: Central Bureau of Statistics.

Tourism and Hotel Services Statistics Quarterly. 1987. Special series 813.

Turner, Victor. 1973. "The Center Out There: Pilgrim's Goal." *History of Religions* 12.3: 191–230.

Urry, John. 1995. *Consuming Places.* London and New York: Routledge.

Witztum, Eliezer, and Moshe Kalian. 1999. "The 'Jerusalem Syndrome'—Fantasy and Reality: A Survey of Accounts from the 19th Century to the End of the Second Millennium." *Israel Journal of Psychiatry and Related Sciences* 36.4: 260–271.

———. 2000. "The Quest for Redemption: Reality and Fantasy in the Mission to Jerusalem." In *Israel as Center Stage: A Setting for Social and Religious Enactments,* ed. A. Paul Hare and Gideon M. Kressel, 15–29. Westport: Bergin & Garvey.

8 Sacred space and mythic time in the early printed maps of Jerusalem

Rehav Rubin

Through the ages, Jerusalem has been the subject of many treatises and works of art. Among the earlier written works were biblical exegeses, chronicles, and pilgrims' and travelers' itineraries, many of which included graphic images. Depictions of the holy city were presented on vellum and mosaic, on wall paintings and on small objects, in manuscripts and in print, in broadly differing contexts. The earliest known map of Jerusalem is the center part of the famous Byzantine mosaic map in Madaba in Jordan, discovered in 1890 (Avi-Yonah 1954; Piccirillo and Alliata 1999). It presents an idealistic view of Jerusalem in the sixth century, with its walls, colonnaded streets, and churches. During the period of the Crusades a series of maps of Jerusalem were drawn on vellum, and more than a dozen survive today. The majority of them present the city as a circle, although the actual shape was roughly rectangular (Levy 1991, 418–506; Levy-Rubin and Rubin 1996, 352–379). With the advent of the printing press, the number of printed maps of Jerusalem grew, and there are about five hundred known maps dating from the late fifteenth to the mid-nineteenth century, when modern, accurate, measurement-based maps began to be made. In 1818 Franz Wilhelm Sieber, a Czech physician and naturalist, published the first map based on actual field measurements (Sieber 1818), initiating the development of the scientific and precise mapping of Jerusalem (Ben-Arieh 1974, 150–160). This process culminated in 1864–65, when two maps of Jerusalem drawn by Charles Wilson—a large map in a scale of 1:2500 and a smaller one in a scale of 1:10,000—were published by the British Ordnance Survey (Wilson 1864–65). In this chapter, however, I will focus on early printed maps, from the fifteenth to the late eighteenth century.

The first printed map of Jerusalem was the center part of a map of the Holy Land, from the Nile to Damascus, published in 1486 on a large foldout in Bernhard von Breydenbach's *Peregrinatio*, which was based on his pilgrimage of 1483 (Breydenbach 1486). Over the next 350 years, hundreds of maps, small and large, simple and detailed, realistic and fantastic, were printed (Laor 1986; Rubin 1999); a few were based on actual travel to the east, but most were merely copies and imitations of travelers' maps, or imaginary and fantastic images that were largely unrelated to geographical reality.

Previous studies have suggested two primary ways of classifying early maps of Jerusalem. The first is based on content, seeking to distinguish between realistic maps that showed Jerusalem as it appeared at the time and imaginary historical maps. The latter depicted Jerusalem according to the Holy Scriptures and the works of Flavius Josephus, and most had no relation to realistic topography (Ben-Arieh and Alhassid 1979, 112–151). This method tends to rely on the titles printed on the maps themselves, such as "Modern Jerusalem," "Jerusalem in Biblical Times," or "Jerusalem in the Time of Jesus." This distinction is not clear, however, and it cannot be assumed that a map that purports to depict the city as it existed during the mapmaker's time is more factually reliable than one that depicts the sites of legendary events. Imaginary elements are often included in realistic maps, and these maps are sometimes distorted for various reasons. In some cases, a map titled "Modern Jerusalem" does not at all correspond to the reality of the cityscape. Realistic and imaginary maps were sometimes printed side by side on the same sheet or in the same volume (Braun and Hogenberg 1572–1617; Seutter c. 1734; Rubin 1996) (Figure 8.1).

The second classification method is based on the fact that only a very small number of maps, either realistic or imaginary, were original, and that

Figure 8.1 Seutter's double map of realistic and imaginary Jerusalem.

these few originals were repeatedly copied, with minor or major changes. The goal, then, was to identify the original maps and to differentiate between them and the many copies printed after them (Rubin 1991, 166–183), and, where possible, to establish the source–copy relationships and reconstruct them in the form of family trees. This method has identified a second, third, and even fourth generation of copying and re-copying for many maps (Rubin 1990, 31–39). The high ratio between a source map and its copies, among both imaginary and realistic maps, can be explained in part by the lack of first-hand experience of the city; most mapmakers had never made the long, hard, and expensive voyage to the Middle East, and thus found it more convenient to copy the existing maps drawn by the few who had. Imaginary maps were often produced by great scholars, whose authoritative status made their maps worth copying by later mapmakers. In both cases, as these maps were not used by actual travelers, they expressed the spiritual concept of the Holy City rather than a realistic geographical depiction that might include helpful practical details.

Following these two fundamental typologies, this chapter will attempt to identify and define new themes in these early maps, based on a close study of their contents and messages. Many of the maps of Jerusalem were general-ized schematic images that carried little concrete information, but the more detailed maps carried more information about the city and its environs, as they depicted in detail the walls and gates, buildings and sites, roads, and the hills around the city, along with religious symbols and traditions. They often had extensive legends explaining the many sites marked out in the maps.

I should add that it is well recognized by cartographers and historians of cartography (Harley 1988, 57–76; 1989a 1–20; and 1989b, 277–312; Wood 1992a and 1992b, 66–74; Belyea 1992, 1–9) that maps are a medium that often conveys not only objective, factual information, but also ideas and values. It is also well accepted that maps were often used as tools in the struggle over power and control. If it is possible to "lie with maps" in modern times, when maps are supposed to be scientific and accurate, as has been claimed (Monmonier 1996), it was all the more possible with early printed maps.

It is important, too, to note that these maps of the Holy City were made by Christians for a European Christian audience, at a time when Jerusalem was in the hands of the Muslims.[1] Jerusalem has, of course, often been a contested site, and early European mapmakers had to wrestle with the facts that the Holy City had been ruled by the "infidel" Muslims since 1187 and that it included a large Jewish minority. This situation stood in contrast to their ideology and desires. Thus when they depicted this faraway city in the east, which the vast majority of their readers had never seen with their own eyes, they used the opportunity to convey messages, ideas, and values that often contradicted the geographical reality of that remote city. These values hidden in the maps were aimed at serving and promoting the Christian images and concepts of both earthly and heavenly Jerusalem among their readers, among whom the armchair pilgrims far outnumbered the actual travelers.

This study will focus on some of the means and measures used by those western European mapmakers to depict Jerusalem as the "Eternal City," as the "glorious Christian city," the place where biblical traditions were still alive. It will present elements that were used to create an impression of Jerusalem that supported the claim of Christian ownership over the city, or at least hid the fact that Jerusalem was, at that time, a rather small and dusty Oriental town under Muslim rule.

The main themes that will be discussed are the diachronic concept of time as expressed in maps, maps as representations of a sacred space, the role of maps in inter-religion polemics, and maps as reflections of Oriental exoticism and the atmosphere of travel through the Orient. These four themes will help us see how the maps of Jerusalem amalgamated the real with the ideal and the sacred with the profane, depicting a remote Oriental city built of stone, yet casting into it feelings, beliefs, and interests, representing and expressing the Jerusalem of the heart and mind.

The diachronic concept of time: maps as historical encyclopedias

Most modern maps are updated by their editors as an integral and ongoing part of the mapping process. They strive to present what exists currently in the mapped area and delete objects that were present in the earlier editions of the map but have subsequently been destroyed and hence are of no use to the practical map user. Many of the early maps of Jerusalem were designed according to an entirely different concept of time. They depicted, side by side, figures and events from various historical periods, as if the dimension of time did not exist at all. We will see this pattern in both realistic maps and imaginary maps, which were more like illustrated commentaries or historical encyclopedias for reading the Holy Scriptures and the works of Flavius Josephus.

Christian van Adrichom, a Dutch priest who worked in Cologne in the late sixteenth century, published a large map of the Holy Land and a large detailed map of Jerusalem in the time of Jesus (Adrichom 1584, 1590) (Figure 8.2). His map of Jerusalem and its environs is one of the best examples of imaginary maps from this period. It was based on extremely broad scholarship and a deep knowledge of the Holy Scriptures, Josephus, and many other ancient works. On it he marked over 280 sites and traditions, appending to each of them a number, a miniature drawing, and a short phrase. All of these sites were also explained in a booklet. This map was copied in many editions and by many authors, and it had a tremendous influence on the image and concept of Jerusalem.

However, it was more an intellectual theoretical interpretation of historical sources than a geographical map, as it was drawn with no real knowledge, or even consideration, of the actual topography of Jerusalem. Thus, hills and valleys, as well as walls and edifices, which are described in the historical sources, were arranged on the map not according to their real locations, but according to Adrichom's own interpretation of the texts.

In this large map one can find almost any site or event from the time of Kings David and Solomon, through the later kings of Judea, the times of Nehemiah, the Hasmoneans, King Herod, Jesus and his Passion, to the Roman conquest and destruction of Jerusalem in 70 CE. Adrichom even depicted some edifices from much later periods. Events from these disparate periods were depicted next to each other as if they had occurred at the same time. Thus, on Mt. Zion one can see the tent of the Tabernacle, King David's palace, and Bat-Sheba's bath (c. 1000 BCE) next to the house of Annas the High Priest and the Hall of the Last Supper (c. 30 CE). Similarly, the flight of Habakkuk is depicted next to the cave of the Apostles. The most striking example is the coronation of King Solomon, which is depicted next to the Castle of the Pisans (*Pisanorum Castrum*), exhibiting side by side two events that occurred two thousand years apart (Figure 8.3). This is especially disconcerting because the term *Pisanorum Castrum* was used for the Citadel, or David's Tower, by some western travelers only after the time of the Crusades, and thus could not be connected in any way to the times of King Solomon or Jesus.

Juan Bautiste Villalpando, a Spanish Jesuit who worked in Rome in the late sixteenth and early seventeenth centuries, also published a large and detailed imaginary map of ancient Jerusalem as part of his massive book

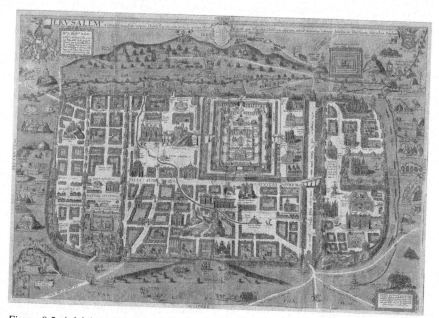

Figure 8.2 Adrichom's map of Jerusalem.

Figure 8.3 A detail from Adrichom's map of Jerusalem presenting the coronation of King Solomon and the *Pisanorum Castrum* side by side.

about Ezekiel (Pradus and Villalpando 1596–1604) (Figure 8.4). Like Adrichom, Villalpando placed buildings, monuments, and place names from various periods next to each other. The City of Shalem of Melchizedek (c. 1500 BCE), mentioned in Genesis 14 and 18, is depicted next to the City of David (c. 1000 BCE), Mt. Acra (second century BCE), Bezeta, and the Theater, Hippodrome, and other Roman edifices from the first century CE.

It is important to realize this map was not drawn out of ignorance; on the contrary, it was the expression of deep and broad erudition, governed by a concept of time that is different than the modern one. These imaginary maps followed the cartographic tradition of medieval times, in which maps were designed as illustrated encyclopedias that presented as much information as possible and therefore depicted events from various periods side by side (Lecoq 1987, 9–49; Barber 1989, 3–8). But the implementation of this diachronic concept of time is far more problematic when it is found in large and detailed maps that were made for pilgrims and used by them as realistic representations of the city in their own time.

Paulus a Milonis, a Franciscan friar who served for many years in Jerusalem, printed his map in Paris in 1687, and it became the source for at least three other versions—one in Greek, one in Latin, and one in German—all printed in 1728 and all extremely rich in miniatures presenting various sacred sites and events (Rubin 2006). On his map, as well as in its copied editions and in other realistic maps, one could see events running throughout history, from the creation of the world to the time of the mapmaker. Among them are the cave of Adam and Eve, Cain and Abel, Abraham and the three angels, the cities of Sodom and Gomorrah in flames, David fighting Goliath, the star rising above Bethlehem when Jesus was born, and Judas hung on a tree. All of these biblical events were drawn around a realistic and a rather reliable view of Jerusalem, with its walls, streets, and the two Muslim edifices (the Aqsa mosque and Dome of the Rock) on the Temple Mount, as they existed in the late seventeenth and early eighteenth centuries.

What was the meaning of this diachronic conception of time, and what purpose did it serve? It seems that the introduction of past events into the current time of the mapmakers and their readers was meant to create a new time dimension. The diachronic concept of time created a "mythic time," a hypothetical period of the great events of the Holy Scriptures, which became an implement in the transformation of earthly Jerusalem into a mythic space, a city where famous miracles occurred in the past, yet where their meaning and spirit are still present (Rubin 2004b, 323–330). Moreover, the depiction of David fighting Goliath next to the camel caravan

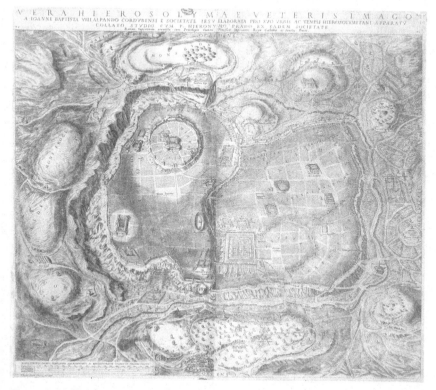

Figure 8.4 Villalpando's map of Jerusalem.

approaching the Ottoman walls of Jerusalem (Figure 8.5), and other sacred events as well, was meant to suggest to the reader that if he were to make the journey to Jerusalem as a pilgrim, he would (almost) be able to see these great events with his own eyes.

Maps as representations of a sacred space

As we've seen, most of the early printed maps were made by Christians for a Christian audience, and they strived to create and promote a Christian image of the Holy City, even though it was under Muslim rule. This target was achieved by various means, some clear and some hidden, some direct—interfering actively with the image of the city as it was—and some indirect, creating an atmosphere around it.

The first and perhaps the most obvious of these strategies was to mark on the maps and in their legends numerous sites commemorating Christian events and traditions. Antonio de Angelis, a Franciscan friar who served for eight years in Jerusalem in the 1570s, printed a large and detailed realistic map of Jerusalem when he returned to Rome (Moldovan 1983, 17–24). In the legend he listed 90 sites in and around the city. Seventy-eight of these sites (or 80 percent) were related to Christian holy places and traditions, while only twelve described the city's daily life, showing such elements as the city's walls, gates, streets, and so forth (Rubin 1989, 100–111; Rubin and Levy 1989, 112–119).

Francisco Quaresmius, another Franciscan friar who served in the Holy Land several years later, published a large book on the holy places, including a detailed map of Jerusalem (Quaresmius 1639). In the legend he listed 115 sites, but only eight items, or about 7 percent, were related to non-Christian history. In his maps, Quaresmius depicted many of the Christian traditions as vivid miniatures. He portrayed events from the life of Jesus

Figure 8.5 David and Goliath near the Walls of Jerusalem, a detail from de Pierre's map of Jerusalem (1728).

and his disciples, such as the star rising over Bethlehem, the arrest of Jesus in Gethsemane, the footsteps of Jesus in the place where he crossed the Kidron Brook, his ascension from the Mount of Olives, the stoning of Stephanos, and the body of Judas hanging from a tree, as if they were part of the actual landscape of Jerusalem.

Like Milonis, de Pierre, and many other mapmakers, Quaresmius situated these miniatures within realistic views of the contemporary city, thus placing—in terms of both time and space—these historical and religious events in the Jerusalem of their own time, and suggesting that pilgrims could actually see these places and experience these events. For the majority who could not undertake the difficult journey, the maps brought Jerusalem's history to life in their minds.

Joseph Eder, an Austrian artist who did not visit Jerusalem, copied Quaresmius' map and printed it around 1800 (Eder c.1800) (Figure 8.6). As he changed almost nothing in the depiction of the city itself, there is no real distinction in terms of scale, details, and focus between his map—a copy made in Europe without knowing Jerusalem—and his source—a Franciscan friar who knew Jerusalem closely. Yet he added much to the atmosphere of piety and devotion of his image of the Holy City by depicting Jesus carrying the cross, accompanied by a group of angels flying over the city. Through this image he furnished the map with a vertical axis connecting the earthly and heavenly Jerusalems.

Figure 8.6 Eder's map of Jerusalem.

Bernhard von Breydenbach, as already mentioned, included in his book the first printed map presenting the Holy Land from the Nile to Damascus (Breydenbach 1486). This map, like most of the illustrations in his book, was drawn by Erhard Reuwich, a Flemish artist who participated in that voyage. The whole map was oriented to the east, but Jerusalem was depicted from the summit of the Mount of Olives, that is, from the east, and was therefore rotated 180 degrees, so it was oriented to the west. Moreover, although the forecourt and the façade of the Holy Sepulcher actually face southward, the image of the church was turned 90 degrees counter-clockwise, and the façade of the church was depicted facing the reader, eastward. This twisted orientation enhanced the impact of the Church of the Holy Sepulcher and depicted it as the central and most prominent monument in the city, although in fact it is not particularly prominent from the Mount of Olives. Breydenbach's distorted map was copied many times, often by artists who had not seen the city but considered his book a high authority, and these mapmakers duplicating his religious message that the Church of the Holy Sepulcher dominates the cityscape.

The Temple Mount occupies about an eighth of the area of the walled (old) city of Jerusalem, and the Dome of the Rock in its center is the most decorated edifice in Jerusalem. When the city is viewed from the summit of the Mount of Olives, as is the case with most early printed maps, the Temple Mount was often depicted in the forefront of the images, realistically occupying a dominant part of the view of the city. Yet Christian mapmakers tried to portray the Temple Mount and its Muslim edifices in a Christian guise. Some, like De Pierre (1728), described both the past and the present, labeling the Dome of the Rock "Solomon's Temple, now a Mosque" (Rubin 2006). Other mapmakers created an anachronistic impression by transferring the Crusaders' name for the Aqsa mosque—*Templum Salomonis*—to the Dome of the Rock, veiling its Islamic function and ownership, and relating it back to the period of the Crusades, when Jerusalem was the capital city of a Christian kingdom.

Hermanus van Borculus went even further (Rubin 1990, 31–39); his map shows three scenes from the Gospels on the Temple Mount: within the courtyard, he depicted the incident of the adulterous woman (John 8:2–7) and the overturning of the tables of the moneychangers (Matthew 21:12). On top of the Dome of the Rock, representing of course the Temple in the time of Jesus, he depicted two figures representing the second trial of Jesus against the Satan (Matthew 4:5–6), and as we might expect he labeled the building *Templum Salomonis*. The same pattern is repeated also in Sebastian Münster's map (Münster 1550, 1015–1018).

Antonio de Angelis depicted the Dome of the Rock in his map (1578) realistically, crowned with a crescent, but decorated the nearby Aqsa mosque with a cross (Rubin 1989). Evidently, this cross was a symbolic one, as no cross could have been there at the time of de Angelis, when the Aqsa was the central Friday mosque of Jerusalem, and when no Christians were allowed to enter the Temple Mount at all. Moreover, as he served as a friar of the Franciscan Order in Jerusalem for eight years, he certainly knew this very well. It may well be, however, that he drew this cross knowing that during the period of the Crusades both the Aqsa and the Dome of the Rock were decorated with golden crosses and wanting to promote and propagate the commemoration of these crosses.

In the map's legend, de Angelis explained this cross as "the place of the presentation of St. Mary," and indeed Christian traditions from the period of the Crusades related the Aqsa mosque to St. Mary. John of Würzburg identified it as her "Presentation in the Temple" (Wilkinson 1988, 245–246), and Theodorich identified it with the "school of St. Mary" (Wilkinson 1988, 289); it seems that both of these associations of Mary with the Temple go back to the second century CE, as is documented in the Christian apocryphal *Protevangelium of James*. In the framework of Muslim–Christian relationship this phenomenon is even more interesting, as it seems that the Christian traditions associating Mary with the Aqsa mosque derived from early Muslim traditions concerning the *Mihrab Maryam* (the place where Mary used to pray as a child), which was located in the southern part of the Temple Mount, adjacent to the Aqsa mosque (Elad 1995, 93–94).

European mapmakers tried to convey through their maps an impression that Jerusalem was a Christian sacred space, even going so far as to show Jesus with his cross over the city. They listed Christian sacred sites in the maps' legends, emphasizing the Church of the Holy Sepulcher as the center of the city and the most dominant structure there, depicted a cross on the Aqsa, and used the anachronistic term *Templum Salomonis* for the Dome of the Rock. When such elements were used in realistic maps, they amalgamated the real and ideal, or the heavenly and earthly Jerusalem, and thus transformed the realistic depiction of Jerusalem into a mythical Christian space.

Maps as implements in inter-religion polemics

Beyond underscoring the Christian holy places in Jerusalem, many mapmakers also sought to undermine Muslim rule and Muslim presence in Jerusalem, and in some cases even to defame Islam and its symbols. This competition between Christianity and Islam over the presence and dominance of the sacred space is reflected in the maps in several ways. The mosques, and especially their minarets, are so prominent in Jerusalem's skyline that most mapmakers depicted them in a rather realistic manner, but many entirely ignored the crescents that decorated the minarets, thus masking the Muslim identity of those elevated spires.

The misrepresentation of the Dome of the Rock sometimes went much further than the use of the anachronistic name *Templum Salomonis*. In his *Liber Chronicarum*, Hartmann Schedel included a map that showed the destruction of Jerusalem and its Temple by the Romans in 70 CE (Schedel

1493, lxiii) (Figure 8.7). In the forefront of this image a large building is depicted on fire, which represents, of course, the Jewish Second Temple. Yet this burning building is actually the Dome of the Rock, with a crescent on its top. The hidden message, or perhaps wishful thought, was that the Muslim sacred edifice would someday be destroyed by fire. Moreover, behind it, standing intact, is the Church of the Holy Sepulcher. It seems quite clear that the author meant to depict on his map not only the historic event of the destruction of the Jewish Temple, but also the victory of the Church over both the Jewish Temple and the Muslim mosque. Ironically, however, when he copied the Church of the Holy Sepulcher from an earlier

Figure 8.7 A detail from Schedel's map of Jerusalem: The Dome of the Rock as the burnt Temple.

unidentified source, he also copied one of the two Mamluk minarets that were built higher than the church on both its sides, and thus—quite unintentionally—emphasized the Muslim presence in Jerusalem.[2]

A clear defamation of Islam and its symbols can be seen in the miniature Adrichom used in his map to depict the infamous idol of the Molech (Figure 8.8). In this miniature the king of Judea accompanied by two drummers and a trumpeter is standing in front of the idol, which is sitting above a fire and holds an infant in his hand. This scene is composed according to the biblical text "and he made his son pass through the fire according to the abominations of the heathen" (2 Kings 16:3). Surprisingly, the top of the idol is crowned with an Islamic crescent. Adrichom seems to have been trying to convey the impression that the crescent is a symbol of idolatry, and to identify Islam as identical to, or at least the successor of, this ancient abominable idolatry.

Maps as reflections of the exotic atmosphere of travel through the Orient

The pilgrimage to the Holy Land was a long voyage to the far and exotic Orient. Like other travelers, those who made the journey to Jerusalem wrote descriptions of their experiences: meeting strange people and animals, observing foreign habits and dress, sampling the local food, and so forth. Mapmakers too depicted people in their local costumes. This practice appears in many maps, both of towns and of larger regions of the world. In the large, six-volume *Civitates* of Braun and Hogenberg, for example, local

Figure 8.8 A detail from Adrichom: The Idol and the Crescent.

people in their typical dress stand in the foreground of maps of different cities around the world (Braun and Hogenberg 1572–1617).

Many maps of Jerusalem, both originals and copies, show local people in their costumes as well as exotic animals. In some cases, as in a group of Italian maps from the sixteenth century, tiny human figures were drawn on the roads leading to Jerusalem from the west, that is, in the background of the city (Rubin 1990). In other cases local people in their costumes are shown with their camels and horses in front of the city. Some maps include depictions of pilgrims walking toward the city. The earliest such image is in a twelfth-century manuscript map from the time of the Crusades; the pilgrims are shown marching, each with a wandering stick and parcel (*pera et baculum*), on their way to Jerusalem (Levy 1991; Rubin 1999). The same idea is represented in Breydenbach's map, on the road between Jaffa and Jerusalem, and later other mapmakers depicted the pilgrims' caravan with horses, camels, and even litters carried by men or beasts. In this way the mapmakers tried to convey the atmosphere of the curious and exotic experience of travel to the Orient, integrating it with specific impressions of the pious and devoted pilgrimage to the Holy Land.

Conclusion

The early printed maps of Jerusalem were much more than "a representation of part of the earth," a common modern definition of a map (Andrews 1996, 1–11). They were drawn and printed with a heavy burden of sentiment and emotion, and they were designed to convey religious messages. Employing a diachronic concept of time, they enhanced the feelings of their Christian readers for the Holy City by emphasizing the holy sites, sacred events, and venerated traditions, and by undermining or even defaming the Muslims and their presence. Although one purpose of these maps was to encourage pilgrims to visit the Holy Land, they were more often enjoyed by armchair pilgrims who stayed safely at home and admired the printed image in their books and on their desks.

The maps aimed at creating the image of an eternal Christian city as an alternative to the reality of a poor Oriental town. By depicting and using the symbolic space, they enlisted the glorious mythic past of Jerusalem as a substitute for its present. They amalgamated the sacred and the profane, rendering a remote Oriental city built of stone as the heavenly Jerusalem of the heart and mind.

Notes

1 Indeed, there is a rather different genre of images of Jerusalem that was common among the Orthodox (Rubin 2004a; Rubin and Levy-Rubin 2006), and only a few Jewish and Muslim graphic images are known from that period (Wientraub and Wientraub 1992; Milstein 1994).

2 On both sides of the Church of the Holy Sepulcher, two minarets were built during the Mamluk period, dedicated to the two great Muslim conquerors of Jerusalem: 'Umar and Saladin.

References

Adrichom, Christiaan van. 1584. *Ierusalem, sicut Christi tempore floruit, et sub-urbanorum, insigniorumque historiarum eius brevi descriptio: simul et locorum, quae Iesu Christi & sanctorum passione gestisque decorata sunt, succinctus commentarius. . . .* Coloniae Agrippinae: Excudebat Godefridus Kempensis.

——. 1590. *Theatrum Terrae Sanctae et biblicarum historiarum: cum tabulis geographicis aere expressis.* Coloniae Agrippinae: In Officina Birckmannica, sumptibus Arnoldi Mylij.

Andrews, John. 1996. "What Was a Map? The Lexicographers Reply." *Cartographica* 33.4: 1–11.

Avi-Yonah, Michael. 1954. *The Madaba Mosaic Map.* Jerusalem: Israel Exploration Society.

Barber, Peter M. 1989. "Visual Encyclopaedias: The Hereford and Other Mappae Mundi." *The Map Collector* 48: 3–8.

Belyea, Barbara. 1992. "Images of Power: Derrida/Foucault/Harley." *Cartographica* 29.2: 1–9.

Ben-Arieh, Yehoshua. 1974. "The Catherwood Map of Jerusalem." *The Quarterly Journal of the Library of Congress* 31.3: 150–160.

Ben-Arieh, Yehoshua, and Naomi Alhassid. 1979. "Some Notes on the Maps of Jerusalem, 1470–1600." In *Jerusalem in the Early Ottoman Period,* ed. Amnon Cohen, 112–151. Jerusalem: Yad ben Zvi.

Braun, George, and Franz Hogenberg. 1572–1617. *Civitates Orbis Terrarum.* 6 vols. Cologne.

Breydenbach, Bernard von. 1486. *Peregrinatio in Terram Sanctam.* Mainz.

De Pierre (1728) "Wahrer und Gruendlicher Abrias der Welt-beruehmten und Hochheiligen Stadt Jerusalem." De Pierre Eques. S.Smi Sepulchri Author, Wien.

Eder, Joseph. c. 1800. *Neuer und Vahrer abriß der Stadt Ierusalem . . .* Wien.

Elad, Amikam. 1995. *Medieval Jerusalem and Islamic Worship, Holy Places, Ceremonies, Pilgrimage.* Leiden: E. J. Brill.

Harley, Brian. 1988. "Silences and Secrecy: The Hidden Agenda of Cartography in Early Modern Europe." *Imago Mundi* 40: 57–76.

——. 1989a. "Deconstructing the Map." *Cartographica* 26.2: 1–20.

——. 1989b. "Maps, Knowledge and Power." In *The Iconography of Landscape,* ed. Denis Cosgrove and Stephen Daniels, 277–312. Cambridge: Cambridge University Press.

Laor, Eran. 1986. *Maps of the Holy Land: A Cartobibliography of Printed Maps, 1475–1800.* New York and Amsterdam: Nico Israel.

Lecoq, Daniel. 1987. "La Mappemonde du Liber Floridus ou la Vision du Monde de Lambert de Saint Omer." *Imago Mundi* 39: 9–49.

Levy, Milka. 1991. "The Medieval Maps of Jerusalem." In *Sefer Yerushalayim: The Crusader and Ayyubide Period 1099–1250,* ed. Joshua Prawer and Haggai Ben Shammai, 418–506. Jerusalem: Yad Ben Zvi. (In Hebrew.)

Levy-Rubin, Milka, and Rehav Rubin. 1996. "The Image of the Holy City: Maps and Mapping of Jerusalem." In *City of the Great King: Jerusalem from*

David to Present, ed Nitza Rosovsky, 352–379. Cambridge, MA: Harvard University Press.

Milstein, Rachel. 1994. "Drawings of the Haram of Jerusalem in Ottoman Manuscripts." In *Aspects of Ottoman History: Papers from CIEPO IX*, ed. Amy Singer and Amnon Cohen, 62–69. Jerusalem: The Magnes Press.

Moldovan, Alfred. 1983. "The Lost De Angelis Map of Jerusalem, 1578." *The Map Collector* 24: 17–24.

Monmonier, Mark. 1996. *How to Lie with Maps*. 2nd ed. Chicago and London: University of Chicago Press.

Münster, Sebastian. 1550. "Ierusalem ciuitas sancta, olim metropolis regni Iudaici, hodie uero colonia Turcae." In *Cosmographia universalis, 1015–1018*. Basel: Henricus Petri.

Paulus a Milonis. 1687. *Legitima Copia Hodierni Situs Almae Civitatis Ierusalem Cum Omnibus Viis Intra et Extra Muros Adiacentibus. Delineavit Reverendus Pater Paulus a Milonico minorita Hierosolimitanus octogenarius 1687, cum privilegio Regis. Parisiis prope majorem conventum P.P. Augustinenstum sub signo duorum globorum, cum previlegio Regis, 1687.* Collections of the Bibliothèque Nationale, Paris. B.N. Estampes Vd 9 Vol. 1, 68 C 35821.

Piccirillo, Michelle, and Eugenio Alliata, eds. 1999. *The Madaba Map Centenary, 1897–1997*. Jerusalem: Studium Biblicum Francescanum.

Pradus, Hieronymo, and Juan Bautista Villalpando. 1596–1604 *Ezechielem explanationes et Apparatus urbis, ac templi Hierosolimitani*, I–III. Roma: 1596–1604. The map of Jerusalem, *Vera Hierosolymae veteris imago*, is in Vol. III, fol. 68.

Quaresmius, Francisco. 1639. *Historica theologica et moralis Terrae Sanctae Elucidatio*. Antverpiae.

Rubin, Rehav. 1989. "The De-Angelis Map of Jerusalem (1578) and Its Copies." *Cathedra* 52: 100–111. (In Hebrew.)

——. 1990. "The Map of Jerusalem by Hermanus Borculus (1538) and Its Copies." *The Cartographic Journal* 27: 31–39.

——. 1991. "Original Maps and Their Copies: Carto-Genealogy of the Early Printed Maps of Jerusalem." *Eretz Israel* 22 (David Amiran volume): 83–166. (In Hebrew.)

——. 1996. "Jerusalem in Braun & Hogenberg's Civitates." *The Cartographic Journal* 33: 119–29.

——. 1999. *Image and Reality: Jerusalem in Maps and Views*. Jerusalem: Magnes Press.

——. 2004a. "Iconography as Cartography: Two Cartographic Icons of the Holy City and Its Environs." In *Eastern Mediterranean Cartography*, ed. G. Tolias and D. Loupis, 347–378. Athens: Institute of Neohellenic Research.

——. 2004b. "Timing the Sacred Space: The Diachronic Concept in Early Maps of Jerusalem." *Ofakim* 60–61: 323–330.

——. 2006. "One City, Different Views: A Comparative Study of Three Pilgrimage Maps of Jerusalem." *Journal of Historical Geography* 32: 267–290.

Rubin, Rehav, and Milka Levy. 1989. "Appendix: The Legend of the De-Angelis Map." *Cathedra* 52: 112–119. (In Hebrew.)

Rubin, Rehav, and Milka Levy-Rubin. 2006. "An Italian Version of a Greek-Orthodox Proskynetarion." *Oriens Christianus* 90: 184–201.

Schedel, Hartmann. 1493. *Liber chronicarum*, p. LXIIII. Nürnberg: A. Koberger.

Seutter, Matthaeus. c. 1734. *Prospectus Sanctae olim et celeberrimae Urbis Hierosolymae opera et impensis*. Augspurg: Matthaei Seutteri.

Sieber, Franz Wilhelm. 1818. *Karte von Jerusalem, und seiner naechsten Umgebungen, geometrisch aufgenomen.* Prague.

Wientraub, Eva, and Gimpel Wientraub. 1992. *Hebrew Maps of the Holy Land.* Wien: Wien Brüder Hollinek.

Wilkinson, John. 1988. *Jerusalem Pilgrims, 1099–1185.* London: Hakluyt Society.

Wilson, Charles. 1864–65. *Ordnance Survey of Jerusalem, 1:2500, 1:10,000.* Southampton: Ordnance Survey Office.

Wood, Dennis. 1992a. *The Power of Maps.* London: Routledge.

———. 1992b. "How Maps Work." *Cartographica* 29.3–4: 66–74.

9   Seeing is believing

Auguste Salzmann and the photographic representation of Jerusalem

Emmie Donadio

Photographs are not narratives, but facts endowed with a conclusive brutality.
Auguste Salzmann, quoted in Solomon-Godeau 1991, 157

Representations of Jerusalem abound in Western art. This is no surprise, since artists in Europe—from Constantine's Rome through the Reformation—served the Church and the states that supported it. One need mention only the ascendancy of Justinian and Theodora, Charlemagne, Otto I, the fifteenth-century Duke of Burgundy, and the papacy to summon up a suggestive succession of patrons whose commissions (both large and small) depicted both the heavenly city and the earthly Jerusalem. In addition to appearing in architectural monuments, symbolic and idealized representations of Jerusalem turn up regularly in European altarpieces, manuscript illuminations, and panel paintings, in images of such subjects as the Passion cycle, Three Marys at the Tomb, and the enthroned Madonna and Child. In fifteenth-century Flemish panel paintings, Jerusalem is often viewed as the town beyond the window of Mary's throne room in heaven. Away in the distance, there is often a river, a walled garden, a church, all in brilliant sunshine. And the city appears in printed books as well. Hartmann Schedel's *Liber chronicarum* of 1493, a compendium of world history, includes a famous and often-reproduced image of Jerusalem (Figure 9.1). Bernhard von Breydenbach made a far more faithful representation in his 1497 woodcut view of the city, reproduced here in a copy form 1645 (Figure 9.2).

Were we to survey in any detail the prodigious number of representations of the Heavenly Jerusalem, we would also need to take into account the mystical and extraordinarily luxurious Beatus manuscript illuminations of Muslim Spain as well as illustrated codices of Augustine's *Civitatis Dei* (Rosenau 1952, 36–40). Such is the rich variety of sources available to us if we seek to trace a history of the visual representation of Jerusalem in Western art.

Surprisingly, for all its promise of a scientific method of recording objective reality, the invention of photography in 1839 did little to change the idealized nature of representations of the Holy City. While sober black-and-white images made by the sun—and "no one could accuse the sun of having an imagination"—could hardly seem to offer exaggerated or fantastical renditions of the landscape and storied buildings, in the end these images too convey the ideologies, expectations, and beliefs of their creators (Jammes and Janis 1983, 246).

Accordingly, over the past few decades, the nineteenth-century photographic representation of Jerusalem has occupied the attention of many scholars working in a range of disciplines. Consideration of the subject lends itself to exploration of such topics as the birth of archaeological and architectural photography, Orientalism in the visual arts, and what may be termed the "imperialist gaze"—an implied corollary of the West's desire to exercise control over, if not colonize, the Levant.

Indeed, one author links the fascination of British photographers with the terrain of Palestine to their overarching goal of mapping the region and establishing control over the land route to India (Howe 1997, 9). Generally speaking, the photographers who journeyed to the Near East during this period often accompanied engineers or archaeologists who were engaged in what some commentators have seen as one of the most rapacious "treasure grabs" in cultural history.[1] By this account, the photographers captured in

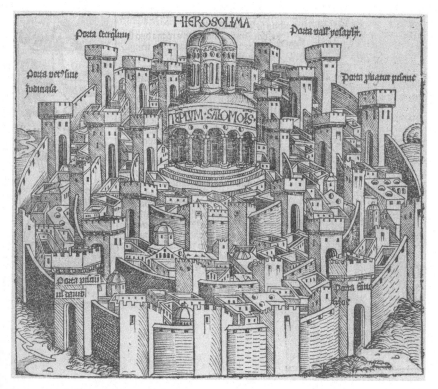

Figure 9.1 Michael Wohlgemut, *Hierosolima*, 1493.

images what the archaeologists couldn't send home to the British Museum or the Louvre.

Issam Nassar, among many other writers, suggests another motivation for European artists' views of Jerusalem. Like painters of the period, they saw the Middle East as the exotic Other and its inhabitants as, if not hopelessly backward, benighted, and unwashed, in any case inferior to Western visitors (Nassar 1997, 25–30). Most authors who treat the subject concur that the early photography of the Middle East reflects the Eurocentric attitude that civilization flourished in the industrialized West while remaining stagnant in the backward Levant.

For his part, Yeshayahu Nir argues that differences between the French and the English photographic images of the Holy Land reflect the contrast between Catholic and Protestant worldviews and, further, that such images may even be said to reveal French national pride in their architectural hegemony and the corresponding British preference for landscape imagery and topographic detail (Nir 1997, 198). In this connection it is useful to recall that the invention of photography itself was a development shared by the French and the British. As a consequence, it seems clear that any subject that photographers of both nationalities chose to pursue must be of

Figure 9.2 Matthaeus Merian, after Erhard Reuwich–Bernhard von Breydenbach, *Jerusalem*, 1497.

special interest to art historians and other scholars seeking to account for and describe the range of assumptions and ambitions revealed by the medium during the first decades of its use.

A comparison between Francis Frith's sweeping view of "Jerusalem from the Mount of Olives" (an albumen print of 1858) and Salzmann's 1854 calotype image of the same site exemplifies this precise distinction (Figures 9.3 and 9.4). While Frith surveys the panoramic spectacle of the ancient city across a valley with verdant vegetation (including an olive tree in the near foreground), Salzmann crops the landscape altogether, focusing instead on the few meters of scrub lying directly outside the city walls. (In fairness it must be admitted that Salzmann visited Jerusalem in the winter months and Frith, as is evident, in the summer.) Yet, as we will see, Salzmann depicted almost exclusively the city's architecture, beginning his photographic essay

Figure 9.3 Francis Frith, *Jerusalem from the Mount of Olives*, c. 1858.

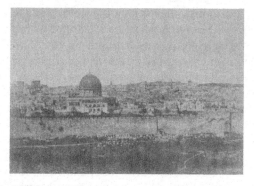

Figure 9.4 Auguste Salzmann. *Jérusalem, enceinte du temple, vue générale de la face Est*, Pl. 2, 1854.

with an image of the western wall of the Temple precinct (the Wailing Wall). He was the only photographer of the nineteenth century to open his book with this particular sight (Nir 1985, 54). And while Frith published extensive volumes of travel literature with his own photographs of the Middle East, it is his mammoth plate images of the pyramids and his panoramic view of Cairo that assured his reputation (Nickel 2004, 79).

This essay attempts to probe some of the implications of the photographs of Auguste Salzmann, whose two-volume *Jérusalem: Étude et reproduction photographique des monuments de la Ville Sainte depuis l'époque judaïque jusqu'à nos jours* is both a landmark achievement in the history of photography and a fascinating case in point, demonstrating that even ostensible accounts of the "brute facts," as the artist referred to his photographs, inevitably conveyed the underlying aims and tacit or explicit beliefs of their creators.[2] With a series of 177 images, the tomes presented a remarkable range of views of the city as well as detailed renderings of its architectural features.

Salzmann traveled to the Holy Land in 1854. The publication of his photographs made use of the most advanced technology of the time—a method of mass production invented by the publishing house of Blanquart-Evrard, in Lille (Jammes and Janis 1983, 29, 152). One of the most celebrated and successful publishers of the mid-nineteenth century, Blanquart-Evrard was a pioneer in the marketing and popularization of travel literature illustrated with photographs. He had perfected a method for the reproduction of images that yielded scores of copies in a day from a single paper negative, or calotype.[3]

Salzmann belonged to a distinguished procession of pilgrims of the era that included, in addition to photographers, painters, novelists, poets, missionaries, biblical scholars, and journalists (Mendelson 2000, 273–296). A consideration of his images of the Holy City offers us an opportunity to explore some of the ways that, in the very first years of its existence, the new art of photography came to serve a remarkably varied range of social, political, and spiritual agendas.

Unlike other travel books that survey the Levant in the mid-nineteenth century, Salzmann's is the only publication illustrated with photographs that focuses its attention solely on Jerusalem and on that city's religious sites. The works by his contemporaries in the new medium include images of Syria and Egypt as well as the outlying regions of the Holy Land. Although they were frequently illustrated with engravings or lithographs, travel books with photographs were still rare in the mid-1850s, and while numerous books of the time were written about travels in Palestine, no other publication, however significant, was accompanied by original photographs. Comparable photographic projects of the period include Maxime du Camp's *Egypte, Nubie, Palestine et Syrie* (Paris, 1852) and Félix Teynard's *Egypte et Nubie* (Paris, 1853–54), with their exotic and haunting photographs of the pyramids (Jammes and Janis 1983, 172–174, 249). Indeed, although the

French photographers of the 1850s were likely to visit both Egypt and Palestine, in calculated sheer numbers of images within the first decades of the invention of the new medium, there was far more widespread and extensive photographic treatment of the pyramids than there was of Jerusalem.

The reason for this lopsided interest may reflect French national fascination with Egypt, where Napoleon met defeat in his ambitious attempt to connect the Occident and the Orient via what ultimately became the British-built Suez Canal. Hence, there were precedents for French scientists and engineers of all ranks to travel to Egypt. And within three months of the publication of Daguerre's 1839 invention, to which the French Government acquired the rights, photographers were dispatched to Egypt to record the legendary sights. The engraved copies of their daguerreotypes were published for an avid audience as *Excursions Daguerriennes* as early as 1840 (Grundberg 2006).

While travel literature about Palestine—and Jerusalem in particular—was already an established industry at the time of his travels, Salzmann's images of the city are unique in both their comprehensiveness and their extraordinary focus on configurations of bricks and mortar—the masonry of the city's ancient remains. There are numerous images in his ambitious publication of isolated columns and lintels, some carved with ornate decoration, some simple and unadorned. And there are also, as we will see, photographic views of the gates to the city and the reservoirs still in use at the time. Salzmann's focus is both panoramic and close-up. He seems to have missed no established site in the city. The photographer's avowed purpose, as he indicates in the text that accompanies his remarkable images, reveals with overwhelming clarity what it is that accounts for his extraordinary— and extraordinarily singular—work.

While other photographers were sent out to capture images of fabled sites, Salzmann traveled to Jerusalem "to render a true service to science"— specifically to illustrate the theories of one Louis-Félicien Caignart deSaulcy, an archaeologist who had published a number of articles stating his belief that the architectural remains of the city predated Christ and the Romans and could, in fact, be as old as the period of King Solomon, who lived in the ninth century BCE (Heilbrun 1982, 135). Accordingly, the order in which Salzmann published these images reflects this presumed chronology: the ostensible site of Solomon's Temple is his first image. This, in turn, is succeeded by other Jewish or Old Testament sites, which precede the Christian sites, which in turn precede the Arab structures. From the start, DeSaulcy's archaeological theories were roundly discredited, and despite their evident exactitude, Salzmann's images were never ultimately successful in proving the validity of the archaeologist's speculations.

Yet such faith in photographic evidence (which may today seem naïve) is characteristic of the initial widespread and enthusiastic reception of photography's presumed claim on the truth. Photographs were said to mirror reality: they were "not merely an instrument which serv[ed] to draw Nature"

but "a chemical and physical process which g[ave] her the power to reproduce herself."[4] We know today that capturing ghosts on film does not prove
the existence of ghosts—though that did not stop a number of late-nineteenth-
century artists from trying to make such claims.[5] Indeed, many photographers
today (Thomas Demand, Jeff Wall, Gregory Crewdson, James Casabere,
and Cindy Sherman, to name but a few of the best known) make their work
by constructing false realities for the camera. But the premise underlying
Salzmann's photographic enterprise was that the camera could tell the truth
merely by recording what it was pointed at.

As a matter of procedure, Salzmann seems literally to have stalked his subject, first from afar, then closer and closer. There are many images of the same
site seen from several vantage points. The twenty-three images of the "Enceinte
du Temple," for example (the Haram al-Sharif, the precinct that houses the
Dome of the Rock, the site of Solomon's Temple), include distant vistas (as seen
in Figure 9.3) as well as close-ups of the Roman masonry marking the Herodian
structure at its base. These latter images reveal an extraordinary degree of close
attention to detail and texture.[6] What other photographers of the period depict
as an image of robed men at prayer at the site of "The Jews' Wailing Place,"
Salzmann renders as a composition of irregularly hewn blocks of stone set off
at their footings by a deep shadow (Figure 9.5).

Indeed, Salzmann seems to have believed that the stones themselves held
powerful mysteries and were invested with a sense of spiritual aura and
sanctity. He wrote that they were "témoignages historiques plus révélateurs

Figure 9.5 Auguste Salzmann, *Jérusalem, enceinte du temple, côté Ouest*, 1854.

que des textes d'archives," or more revelatory than written texts (Heilbrun 1982, 119). The overall effect of his images, accordingly, seems somewhat elegiac, reflecting the knowledge that the city he succeeded in portraying remained a sepulcher. The photographs exude a stillness that we witness again some fifty years later in Atget's haunting images of Paris. One would not know from Salzmann's depictions that there was actually a lively population of some 15,000 people in Jerusalem in 1854 (Ben-Arieh 1975, 262). Like Atget, he seems to have found times to photograph the city when no living soul was in view.[7]

One is tempted to read Salzmann's images of the city as testimony to his piety, or to his aesthetic ambition to render a vision of the timeless, millennial city of God. And, too, like the other mid-century photographers of the city, he was using the new art to "verify scriptural content" (Greenberg 1997, 255). Yet the photographs of his French contemporaries, the fellow masters of the calotype, show the indigenous architecture of their own country with equal reverence and stillness. The new medium, with the long exposure times that it demanded, was perfectly suited to the depiction of immobile stones and deep, quiet reservoirs. Even the texture of the paper negative enhanced the gravelly roughness of the masonry that was the focus of Salzmann's images. The nascent photographic technology was a perfect match for the scientific objectives of the artists who used it. Indeed, if one were to select a mode of depiction that rendered whatever came into its purview as sepulchral, the rich tonalities of the calotype would be a likely choice.

Like the other "painter–photographers" of his time, Salzmann was trained as a painter. He may in fact have exhibited landscape paintings in the Paris Salons of 1847, 1849, and 1850 (Heilbrun 1982, 116–117). Many of the distinguished French photographers of this period, those who were responsible for some of the earliest and most memorable achievements, were artists who had crossed over from the practice of painting or other pictorial mediums (Borcoman 1978, n.p.). Furthermore, Salzmann's photographs demonstrate the mid-century taste for generalized "views" characteristic of both early photography and landscape painting of the period (Galassi 1981). And while there is no record of how, where, or from whom Salzmann learned photography, there is some speculation that it may have been from Henri Le Secq, one of the so-called *primitifs* hired by the French government to photograph churches in the Alsatian region, where Salzmann's family were well established and prosperous (Heilbrun 1982, 122).[8] In this photographic enterprise, then, he was merely following the precedent set by the French government at the time the new medium was launched.

Views of the historic city gates—from within and without the walled citadel—and representations of its reservoirs, key factors in the history of the city's survival throughout the sweep of history, offer a representative survey of the pioneering photographer's accomplishment.[9] From the east we view the Dome of the Rock and the minaret of the Aqsa mosque beyond the

"Birket-Hammam-Setty-Mariam" (The Pool of Mary, Figure 9.6). The apparently empty reservoir appears as a deep triangular blackness at the center of the image. Framed by the St. Stephen Gate in the city wall and a path that cuts the foreground at a downward diagonal, the pool, which is located outside the old city walls near the ostensible site of Mary's birth, is no longer in existence. It has been replaced by a Muslim cemetery. The beautiful twelfth-century Crusader Church of St. Anne, with its extensive archaeological explorations maintained by the White Fathers, is nearby, on the inside of the city wall.[10] It is noteworthy that at the time Salzmann made this photograph, the French were fighting alongside the British and the Ottoman Turks against the Russians in the Crimean War; a primary cause of the conflict was the Russian demand to control access to and oversight of the Christian holy places in Jerusalem that Salzmann captured in images like these (Nassar 1997, 51).

From the west we can view the citadel as Salzmann saw it from the "Birket Mamilla" (The Pool of Mamilla, Figure 9.7), located in what was at the time a Muslim cemetery. This reservoir, surrounded by gravestones, appears to be in use; water is visible within its stone embankments. Today it is the site of "Independence Park," and the view of the walls of the Old City is now obstructed by generalized urban development, which includes the French Consulate and the King David and Palace Hotels. In Salzmann's view of the city from the reservoir, however, the formal pattern of sky, tombstones, and masonry, punctuated by the crenellations of the sixteenth

Figure 9.6 Auguste Salzmann, *Jérusalem, Birket-Hammam-Setty-Mariam*, 1854.

century wall built by Suleiman the Magnificent and the minaret of the Aqsa Mosque provide the dramatic interest.

In the midst of what appear to be residential buildings, the "Birket Hammam-el-Batrak" (The Pool of the Patriarch's Bath, Figure 9.8), which Salzmann viewed from a considerable height, affords us a sweeping vision of the Old City. The Church of the Holy Sepulcher, with its large flattened dome over the tomb itself and another, narrower one to its right—over the main hall of the church—are at the center of the image.[11] These are flanked on either side by the minarets of two nearby mosques. This neighborhood of Jerusalem still contains apartment buildings (perhaps like the one from which Salzmann achieved this view) that surround the reservoir, which is now dry. Like all of Jerusalem's landmarks, this pool has been identified in a number of ways, depending on the Biblical knowledge that the viewer brought to the scene. For Francis Frith it was the Pool of Hezekiah, for example, and deSaulcy identified it with the Amygdalon Pool mentioned by Josephus (*Jewish War*, 5.11.4) (Heilbrun 1982, 152).

Salzmann shot six close-up views of gates of the walled city, which he identified respectively as the Gates of Jaffa, of David, of the Mograbins (or North Africans), of Stephen, of Herod, and of Damascus. In his thorough reportage we can see both the interior and the exterior settings of these still functional routes of access to and from the city. Today the Damascus Gate, constructed by Suleiman the Magnificent, frames a bustling market on its interior and a stepped or terraced approach for pedestrians on the exterior

Figure 9.7 Auguste Salzmann, *Jérusalem, Birket Mamilla,* 1854.

road to the north. In Salzmann's view it was deserted and surrounded by rubble (Figures 9.9, 9.10).

To the southwest of the walled city, the "Birket-es-Soultan" (The Sultan's Pool, Figure 9.11) affords Salzmann an opportunity to portray the dry and rocky landscape at the foot of Mt. Zion. This characteristically stony terrain, a seemingly timeless vision of tranquility through Salzmann's lens, is the most nuanced composition of the works we have surveyed in this capsule overview of Salzmann's project. It brings together a vision of the surrounding, sparsely vegetated hillsides, the ascent to the city gates, and the protective walls of the fortress. (The Jaffa gate and its tower are at the left of the image.) The Sultan's "pool" was no longer in use when Salzmann captured its irregular topography. It still shows the so-called "Turkish Fountain" at its southern extremity (right foreground). Today the city's Cinemathèque sits at the approximate spot where Salzmann must have stood to make this image. And where the scrub and boulders lie, at the foot of the hill, crowds assemble for outdoor screenings of films by the world's most celebrated directors and cinematographers. The very spot Salzmann recorded has become a gathering place for tourists who wish to travel virtually, beyond the world at their feet.

Despite his pioneering accomplishments as an artist, by 1857 Salzmann had rejected the term "photographer" to describe his enterprise, stating that the medium had lost its "nouveauté" and that he preferred to be known simply as an archaeologist (Heilbrun 1982, 121). He spent the remaining

Figure 9.8 Auguste Salzmann, *Jérusalem, Birket Hammam-el-Batrak*, 1854.

Figure 9.9 Auguste Salzmann, *Jérusalem, Porte de Damas*, vue extérieure, 1854.

Figure 9.10 Auguste Salzmann, *Jérusalem, Porte de Damas*, intérieure, 1854.

Figure 9.11 Auguste Salzmann, *Jérusalem, Birket-es-Soultan*, 1854.

years of his life pursuing archaeological research—an activity considerably better documented than is his brief career as a photographer. Yet it is unquestionably his haunting photographs, which tell us as much about the early uses of photography as they do about the topography and sites of Jerusalem in the mid-nineteenth century, that today make Salzmann worthy of our sustained attention. And his careful rendering of the architecture of the city still provides archaeologists, as well as geographers and historians, extraordinarily valuable documentary evidence of the city's past.

By the 1880s there were several photographic firms operating in Jerusalem itself, and soon travelers could purchase picture postcards of the sites and send them home with personal greetings. But the conjunction of the birth of photography and its use by Auguste Salzmann, one of the first pioneers to employ its seeming objectivity in the service of archaeology, has left us an incomparably vivid and solemn monument to the particular and specific attractions of the Holy City caught between the elusive past and the tumultuous present.

Notes

1 On photography and its appropriation by the French government, in particular, see Nassar 1997, 24; Solomon-Godeau 1991, 155–159; Jammes and Janis 1983, 52–56. See also Onne 1980, 19–20.

2 For the most complete biographical presentation of Salzmann and a comprehensive historical study of his project, see Heilbrun 1982, 114–182. The following are also recommended for their illustrations as well as their discussion of the context for Salzmann's works: Solomon-Godeau 1991, 150–168; Jammes and Janis 1983, 246–248; and Borcoman 1978. See also the brief but useful description of Salzmann's project by Nir (1985, 53–58).

3 Before the invention of electricity, it is worth noting, the only light source for the creation of a photograph and its replication was the sun itself, so it was an extremely laborious and time-consuming process to produce hundreds of images. Blanquart-Evrard's invention helps to account for the ubiquity of Salzmann's volumes and their sweeping hold on the market for images of the Holy City.

4 Louis Jacques Mandé Daguerre, "Daguerreotype," quoted in Trachtenberg 1980, 13.

5 See Mahoney 1998 and Goldberg 1998.

6 For good reproductions of those images that capture specifically the textures of the masonry, see Borcoman 1978, and Jammes and Janis 1983, 74 (Figure 54). Heilbrun (1982, 114–182) reproduces the greatest number of Salzmann's images.

7 Given the fact that his photographs required seven-minute exposure times, it is likely that he purposely avoided photographing humans. For an example of an image made by a photographer who did not give such careful attention to the need for long exposure times, see the shadowy, blurred figures in Albert Augustus Isaacs's 1856 image of "The Wailing Place, Jerusalem," in Perez 1988, 43. On the absence of human subjects in mid-nineteenth-century photographs of Jerusalem see Nassar 1997, 35–36.

8 Jammes and Janis 1983, pp. xiv and xviii (n. 10), explain that the "primitives" of photography denote the early French masters DuCamp, Nègre, Le Secq, LeGray, and others.

9 For an account of the history of the city's water supply (a subject of great interest to the nineteenth-century travelers who wrote about the city), see Har'el 1976.

10 Thanks to Rehav Rubin for information about the management of this site. On the White Fathers see http://www.newadvent.org/cathen/15613d.htm, accessed March 1, 2007.

11 The author is deeply grateful to Rehav Rubin for unfailingly kind assistance in the identification of these and many of the sights in Salzmann's images of the city.

References

Ben-Arieh, Yehoshua. 1975. "The Growth of Jerusalem in the Nineteenth Century." *Annals of the Association of American Geographers* 65.2 (June): 252–269.

——. 1979. *The Rediscovery of the Holy Land in the Nineteenth Century.* Jerusalem: Magnes Press; Detroit: Wayne State University Press.

——. 1997a. "Jerusalem Travel Literature as Historical Source and Cultural Phenomenon." In Ben-Arieh and Davis 1997, 25–46.

——. 1997b. *Painting the Holy Land in the Nineteenth Century.* Jerusalem: Yad Izhak Ben-Zvi Press.

Ben-Arieh, Yehoshua, and Moshe Davis, eds. 1997. *Jerusalem in the Mind of the Western World, 1800–1948.* Westport: Praeger.

Borcoman, James. 1978. *The Painter as Photographer: David Octavius Hill, Auguste Salzmann, Charles Nègre: Works from the National Gallery of Canada at the Vancouver Art Gallery.* Vancouver: Vancouver Art Gallery.

Breydenbach, Bernhard von. 1961. *Die Reise ins Heilige Land; ein Reisebericht aus dem Jahre 1483*, trans. Elisabeth Geck. Wiesbaden: G. Pressler.

DeSaulcy, L. F. Caignart. 1955. *Carnets de Voyage en Orient (1845–1869)*. Ed. Fernande Bassan. Paris: Presses Universitaires de France.

Galassi, P. 1981. *Before Photography: Painting and the Invention of Photography*. New York: Museum of Modern Art.

Goldberg, Vicki. 1998. "Of Fairies, Free Spirits, and Outright Frauds." *New York Times*, February 1, AR48.

Greenberg, Gershon. 1997. "Heavenly and Earthly Jerusalem: Pedagogical Perspectives." In Ben-Arieh and Davis 1997, 251–262.

Grundberg, Andy. 2006. "History of Photography." *Microsoft® Encarta® Online Encyclopedia* (http://encarta.msn.com).

Har'el, Menasheh. 1976. "The Ancient Water Supply System of Jerusalem." *Geography in Israel* (23rd International Geographical Congress, USSR), 36–53. Jerusalem: Israel National Committee, International Geographical Union.

Heilbrun, Françoise. 1982. "Auguste Salzmannn photographe malgré lui." In *Félix de Saulcy et la Terre Sainte*, 114–182. Paris: Ministère de la Culture Éditions de la Réunion des musées nationaux.

Howe, Kathleen Stewart. 1997. *Revealing the Holy Land*. Santa Barbara: Santa Barbara Museum of Art.

Jammes, André, and Eugenia Parry Janis. 1983. *The Art of French Calotype: With Critical Dictionary of Photographers, 1845–1870*. Princeton: Princeton University Press.

Mahoney, Robert. 1998. "The Cottingley Fairies and Other Apparitions at Leslie Tonkonow." *Artnet.ComMagazine* (http://www.artnet.com/Magazine/reviews/reviews98.asp).

Mendelson, David. 2000. *Jérusalem ombre et mirage*. Paris: L'Harmattan.

Nassar, Issam. 1997. *Photographing Jerusalem: The Image of the City in Nineteenth-Century Photography*. Boulder: East European Monographs.

Nickel, Douglas R. 2004. *Francis Frith in Egypt and Palestine*. Princeton: Princeton University Press.

Nir, Yeshayahu. 1985. *The Bible and the Image: The History of Photography in the Holy Land, 1839–1899*. Philadelphia: University of Pennsylvania Press.

———. 1997. "Cultural Predispositions in Early Photography: The Case of the Holy Land." In Ben-Arieh and Davis 1997, 197–206.

Onne, Eyal. 1980. *Photographic Heritage of the Holy Land, 1839–1914*. Manchester: Institute of Advanced Studies, Manchester Polytechnic.

Perez, Nissan N. 1988. *Focus East: Early Photography in the Near East (1839–1885)*. New York: Harry N. Abrams.

Rosenau, Helen. 1952. *The Ideal City, Its Architectural Evolution*. New York: Harper & Row.

Schedel, Hartmann. 1493. *Liber chronicarum*. Nuremberg: Anton Koberger.

Solomon-Godeau, Abigail. 1991. "A Photographer in Jerusalem, 1855: Auguste Salzmann and His Times." In *Photography at the Dock*, 150–168. Minneapolis: University of Minnesota.

Trachtenberg, Alan, ed. 1980. *Classic Essays on Photography*. New Haven: Leete's Island Books.

10 Fayruz, the Rahbani Brothers, Jerusalem, and the Leba-stinian song

Christopher Stone

Jerusalem, as the other essays in this book make clear, represents so much to so many. For Arabs and Palestinians it has become, particularly since 1948, and more so since 1967, a symbol for loss: the loss of land and home, the loss of hope for a unified Arab world, the loss of honor. It will surprise no one that many Arab poets, famous and unknown alike, have both written about this loss and expressed hope of recovery. Many of these poems have taken the form of popular song. It would be difficult to find an Arab singer who has not sung for Palestine generally or Jerusalem specifically. It is arguable that no one's songs for Jerusalem and Palestine have been more listened to than those of the Lebanese diva Fayruz. She is undoubtedly the most famous living Arab singer and one of the best known in the last century. She and her artistic team of her husband Assi Rahbani and her brother-in-law Mansur Rahbani have collaborated on hundreds of songs, both singles and those sung as part of musical films and plays. Though Fayruz and the Rahbanis are most famous in the wider Arab world for their songs for Palestine, most of their work focused on Lebanon in general and the Christian mountain village in particular. If there is a unifying theme to their work, it is nostalgia. Singing for Palestine and Jerusalem, then, was a natural fit. This essay examines several paradoxes in some of Fayruz's most famous works for Palestine and Jerusalem, paradoxes that speak both to the nature of nostalgia and to the nature of imagined spaces.

One scene in a recent documentary on the impact of Fayruz on her listeners takes the viewer to the Shatila Palestinian refugee camp in the south of Beirut (Janssen 2003). We first witness an interview with a father and his middle-aged son, longtime residents of the camp. As we hear the son expressing some of the difficulties of life in Lebanon for Palestinians, we are shown a variety of shots meant to convey the tough conditions of the camp. In the background we hear, faintly at first, Fayruz singing her 1967 "The Flower of the Cities" (*Zahrat al-Mada'in*), perhaps the most famous of all of her ten or so songs written explicitly for Palestine. The city referred to is, of course, Jerusalem. The song acts as a bridge between this and the next scene. From the living room of father and son we move to a rooftop in the camp where younger refugees sit around listening to this song while chatting and smoking the water pipe (*argile*). The youth speak about the importance of Fayruz to them generally, and specifically about the significance of this song. By way of example, they describe a trip to the south of Lebanon before the Israeli withdrawal in 2000 to demonstrate against the occupation. The demonstrators clashed with Israeli troops and one of them was killed. Back on the bus, the mood already heavy, someone played "The Flower of the Cities," and everyone burst into tears like children.

In these scenes lies a paradox that will be the focus of this article. Fayruz is best known throughout the Arab world for her songs for Palestine. The Palestinian poet Mahmud Darwish has said that Fayruz and her artistic partners the Rahbani Brothers did more for Palestine artistically than anyone (quoted in Tarabulsi 1998, 203). A Palestinian musician has been quoted as saying that "Fayruz is more Palestinian than the Palestinians" (quoted in Habib 2005, 214). How can Fayruz be considered a champion of and a unifying force for the Palestinian cause and a siren for Jerusalem, even by Palestinians inside of Lebanon, when her early work, as I argue elsewhere, helped to forge an elite Lebanese Christian nationalism that pitted itself against the Palestinians and other "Others" inside of Lebanon during the series of Lebanese civil wars that ran from 1975 to 1990? (Stone 2003–4). I will attempt to explain the paradox by discussing a few of Fayruz's songs for Palestine. As the key to this paradox lies in the description of place, I will focus on her songs for Jerusalem, arguably the epicenter of the Palestinian resistance song and poem in general and the only specific space that makes multiple appearances in Fayruz's Palestinian works. In addition to "The Flower of the Cities," I will also look at her "Old Jerusalem" (*al-'Ids al-'ati'a*, 1966). Further evidence of the association of Fayruz with Jerusalem and perhaps of Jerusalem for all of Palestine is the fact of Fayruz's receipt of the Jerusalem Award in 1997, described by Mahmud Darwish on that occasion as being given to "a distinguished Palestinian or Arab artist who defended Jerusalem and kept it alive in our hearts" (quoted in Habib 2005, 212). In the daily Lebanese *al-Nahar* newspaper on the day after the award was announced there is a cartoon of Fayruz's head coming up out of the ground of Jerusalem with the caption "Fayruz of Old Jerusalem," with "Old Jerusalem" being a reference to the song of that name to be discussed below.

Elsewhere I have argued that one of the lenses through which we can view the career of Fayruz and the Rahbani Brothers is that of Lebanese nationalism and identity formation. I argue that in their songs, films, and musical theatrical productions they participated in an elite national project that spoke primarily to the Christian minority of Lebanon, the same minority that would pit itself against Lebanon's largely Muslim Palestinian refugee population, among others, at the start of the civil war (Stone 2003–4). The Rahbanis completed their rise to fame in Lebanon when they began contributing folkloric musical theatrical works on an almost annual basis to the International Ba'labakk Festival starting in 1957, just two years after the festival's founding, when the committee in charge of its composition, at the behest of President Camille Chamoum's wife Zulfa, agreed to add a folkloric section to the festival's mélange of international and avant-garde acts. Through decreasingly folkloric and increasingly spectacular plays such as *The Moon's Bridge* (*Jisr al-'amar*, 1962), *The Days of Fakhr al-Din* (*Ayyam Fakhr al-Din*, 1966), and *Mountains of Granite* (*Jibal al-Sawwan*, 1969) at Ba'labakk and other venues in Lebanon and the region, in addition to their musical concerts, television shows, movies, and albums up through and even beyond the start of the civil war in 1975, the Rahbanis participated in the propagation of the myth of Lebanon as primarily a Christian country modeled on a fantasy of the Christian Mt. Lebanon village, where conflict is always caused by an outsider and is inevitably solved by a combination of love and miracle almost always administered by the character played by Fayruz. These musical theatrical works evidence a nostalgia for the Lebanon of al-Mutasarafiyya (self-rule on Mt. Lebanon), that period between the violence of the 1860s and the re-imposition of Ottoman rule during World War I. They portray a fantasy Lebanon absent of sectarian tensions, a Lebanon of one accent, of one *dabke* (national folkloric dance), of many miracles. The miracles dried up, of course, if not in the Rahbani theater, in Lebanon itself in 1975 when the civil war broke out.[1]

It is important to state that though Christian, Fayruz and the Rahbani brothers never consciously or publicly associated with Lebanon's right-wing Christian nationalists and in fact saw themselves as forces of unity and inclusion in a country where the majority Muslim population has been ruled by the minority Christian population since the formation of Lebanon as a modern state after World War I. This fact, however, does not preclude their artistic output from aiding that cause. Given that their works for Lebanon have become synonymous with a narrow Lebanese Christian nationalism, how can Fayruz and the Rahbani Brothers have become a symbol for the Palestinian resistance movement through their songs for Palestine? I will begin searching for an answer by looking at some of Fayruz's songs for Palestine and particularly her songs for Jerusalem. I will begin with the most famous of these, "The Flower of the Cities."

It would be difficult to overstate the impact the events of the 1967 Six-Day War had on the people of the Arab world, for they had been led to believe, even as the Arab armies were being crushed, that victory was imminent. Thus 1967, along with 1948, has to be seen not only as one of the most important political but also cultural dates in the modern Arab world. The effect of this event is noticeable in popular and high culture throughout the region.[2] One of the quickest responses to this devastating loss came from popular song, of which Fayruz and the Rahbani Brothers' "The Flower of the Cities" can be seen as a prominent if not pre-eminent example, as what Joseph Massad sees as "the most popular song of the period" (Massad 2003, 26).

Late in the summer of 1967, just two months after the events of the Six-Day War, a music festival was arranged at the famous cedar forest in the north of Lebanon. It is here that Fayruz first sang "The Flower of the Cities." This song would eventually be released on Fayruz's second album of songs for Palestine, the 1972 *Jerusalem in my Heart*. It first gained wide-spread exposure, however, through the two most powerful media of the day: cinema and radio.

A few months after the 1967 war, Fayruz and the Rahbani Brothers released a musical film called *Exile* (*Safar Barlak*). As with the other two musical films in which she starred, this one was shown widely in Lebanon, even at high-end theaters in the West Beirut neighborhood of Hamra that normally only showed western or Egyptian films.[3] It was also shown extensively in other Arab countries, a relatively rare occurrence for an Arabic-language film not made in the Egyptian dialect. The Rahbanis prefaced the film, which is about the Ottoman re-occupation of Mount Lebanon during World War I, with a clip of Fayruz singing "The Flower of the Cities" at the Cedars. Many radio stations throughout the Arab world played the song incessantly (Abi Samra 1985, 37).[4] It is easy to forget the impact of radio, but at that time, when tele-vision was still young and not as adept at crossing borders as it is now, radio was the satellite television of its day. It was this song, in fact, that marked the moment when many young non-Christian or leftist literati in Lebanon and other places in the Arab world began listening seriously to Fayruz.[5] It was also for this song that Fayruz and the Rahbanis were presented with the key to the city of Jerusalem made out of olive wood by exiled residents of Jerusalem and presented by Jerusalem's two prewar representatives in the Jordanian Parlia-ment in a 1968 Beirut ceremony (Aliksan 1989, 30). Another example of the impact of "The Flower of the Cities" is that in 1968, during a visit to Syria, Fayruz was presented with a poem written for her by the official poet of the Syrian Ba'th party, Sulayman al-'Aysa, as a gift for having performed the song (Abi Samra 1985, 38–39).[6]

Before looking more closely at the song itself, it is important to mention that Fayruz and the Rahbanis did not, of course, have a monopoly on the Jerusalem poem or song. In modern times, some examples from poetry are Khalil Mutran's "Salute to Exalted Jerusalem" (*Tahiyya li-l-Quds al-sharif*), 'Ali Mahmud Taha's "Anthem of Jihad for Palestine Day" (*Unshudat al-jihad fi yawm Filastin*, which was sung by Muhammad 'Abd al-Wahhab), Ibrahim Tuqan's "Jerusalem" (*al-Quds*), Nizar Qabbani's "Jerusalem" (*al-Quds*), and of course Mahmud Darwish's collection of poems entitled *Under the Old Windows* (*Taht al-shababik al-'atiqa*), some of which were put to music and sung by Marcel Khalife. Songs for Palestine were also performed by 'Abd al-Halim Hafiz, Umm Kulthum, Warda al-Jaza'iriyya and, more recently, by singers like 'Amr Diyab, Hani Shakir, and Kazim al-Sahir.[7]

Juliane Hammer, in an article on 1948 and Palestinian memory, mentions how often Jerusalem itself is featured in poems about Palestine (Hammer 2001, 458). Muwasi, in his monograph on Jerusalem in modern Palestinian poetry, mentions that Fayruz's "The Flower of the Cities" was one of the first to deal with the city in any detail (Muwasi 2004). Let us take a closer look at this song to see what kind of detail he might have had in mind.

This eight-minute song opens with the violins that by the mid-sixties had become a key ingredient of the Rahbani sound. The melodious strings are joined by martial-sounding brass, the combination of the two comprising a trademark of the Rahbanis' works for Palestine dating back to their 1957 "We Are Returning" (*Raji'un*).[8] Before even hearing the song's lyrics, the listener gets a hint of treatment of space from the title, which uses the relatively rare plural of city, *mada'in*, instead of *mudun*. On the one hand, it is clear that this was a choice made out of poetic expediency—*mada'in* has the same rhyme (*wazn*) as the word *masakin* (places of living) in the same line. I would argue, however, that the word, for its rareness of use, also lends an abstractness to the description from the very beginning, an impression not undermined by the martial and anthem-like ninety-second musical prelude to the song. And though from the start the narrator addresses the city in the second person, there is never much of a Jerusalem to hold on to:

> For you, city of prayer, I pray
> For you beautiful city, flower of cities
> Jerusalem, Jerusalem, city of prayer, I pray
> Our eyes travel to you every day
> Moving about the hallways of the temples
> Embracing the old churches
> Wiping sadness from the mosques
> Night of the isra', path of he who ascended heavenward
> Our eyes travel to you every day, and I pray
> The child and his mother Maryam in the cave, two crying faces.[9]

This beginning also offers its own explanation for the vagueness, as it quickly becomes clear that Jerusalem is being described from afar, being remembered. The reason for the distance, in case anyone listening to the song would need to be reminded, comes in the middle of the song:

> For those made homeless
> For the children without houses
> For those who defended at the gates and were martyred
> Peace itself was martyred in the nation of peace
> and Justice fell at the gates
> When the city of Jerusalem toppled
> Love retreated and in the hearts of the world war settled
> The child and his mother Maryam in the cave, two crying faces.

The last part of the song is dedicated to inspiring the listener to efface the distance so evident in the rest of the song. There is no question that this is a powerful resistance song aimed at inspiring steadfastness, as can be seen in the song's last lines:

> The blinding anger is coming and I am full of faith
> The blinding anger is coming and I'll bypass the sadness
> From every road it is coming, with the awesome steeds it is coming
> As the omnipresent face of God it is coming, coming, coming
> The gate to our city will not close, for I am going to pray
> I'll knock on the gates, I'll open the gates
> And you Jordan River will wash my face with sacred water
> And you Jordan River will erase the traces of the barbaric feet
> The blinding anger is coming, awesome steeds it is coming
> It will defeat the face of oppression
> The house is ours, Jerusalem is ours
> And with our hands we are going to return the city to its splendor
> With our hands peace is coming to Jerusalem.

Just before reaching this conclusion to the song, there is a melodious sadness, as Fayruz and the female members of the chorus sing about the crying of Jesus and Mary. Then we get a blast of horns, after which the male members of the chorus sing twice that the "blinding anger is coming." Fayruz picks it up from there, occasionally echoed by the chorus, singing with a resolve matched by the increased tempo and volume. A rousing end to a song that also conveys the sadness of the Palestinian predicament, no doubt, but where is Jerusalem in all of this?

One feature that distinguishes "The Flower of the Cities" from most of Fayruz and the Rahbanis' songs about Lebanon and also perhaps adds to its lack of specificity is that it is in Classical Arabic, as are most of their songs about non-Lebanese places: Damascus, Mecca, Kuwait, and so forth. These non-Lebanese songs, most of them written by Sa'id 'Aql, the Lebanese poet and mentor of Fayruz's husband and brother-in-law, are equally vague in their descriptions of space.[10] It is possibly more than mere coincidence, for example, that a bootleg compact disc of Fayruz's songs for Palestine that I purchased in Damascus also contains Fayruz's song for Mecca, which was written, as it turns out, in the same year as "The Flower of the Cities." The formality of the language of "The Flower of the Cities" also gives it an epic quality, epic in the sense of timeless, and this impression is augmented by the mention of Jesus, by the reference to the "awesome steeds" which could be meant to make us think of Saladin's recapture of Jerusalem from the Crusaders in 1187. And though the song is one of the few resistance songs for Palestine that mentions the places of worship of all three main monotheistic faiths,[11] this is about as specific as the descriptions get.

Let us see if this lack of specificity holds for Fayruz's other song written specifically for Jerusalem, "Old Jerusalem" (*al-'Ids al-'ati'a*). The Lebanese novelist Ilyas Khuri cites "Old Jerusalem" as an example of how Fayruz's works about the Palestinian cause are more detailed than her songs about Lebanon (quoted in Abi Samra 1985, 103 [in supplement]). The comparison to Fayruz and the Rahbanis' Lebanon songs is apt at least insofar as "Old Jerusalem" is also in a dialect of spoken Lebanese Arabic.

Like "The Flower of the Cities," this song can also be found on the 1972 record *al-Quds fi 'l-bal* (literally "Jerusalem on My Mind" but translated on the album itself as "Jerusalem in My Heart"). It turns out, however, that "Old Jerusalem" is not a post-1967 song, as many fans think because of its presence on this 1972 album, but rather was first performed in 1966.[12] Just as its being sung in spoken Arabic gives it an earthier quality than the ethereal "The Flower of the Cities," so do its details or perhaps more precisely the proximity of the narrator to the scene being described. We can see this in the opening lines:

> I walked the streets ... the streets of old Jerusalem
> In front of the stores ... from what is left of Palestine
> We talked about the news together and they gave me a vase
> They said to me that this is a gift from the people who are waiting
> And I walked the streets ... the streets of old Jerusalem
> I stopped at one of the doors and made friends.

If this song seems to have more detail than "The Flower of the Cities," it may be because parts of it are based on Fayruz's actual and only visit to Jerusalem, in 1964. It is purported that she and the Rahbanis went there for inspiration. The story goes that she was so moved by her visit to the Old City, under Jordanian control at that time, that she began to weep and that an old woman gave her the vase mentioned in the song to make her feel better (Mansur 2003, 8–9). The fact of the visit and its pre-1967 timing helps to explain some of the differences between this and "The Flower of the Cities." Instead of our eyes moving about the city every day, here the narrator of the song herself is able to be present, walking through the streets of the city.

The most fruitful place to look for the significance of similarities and differences between these two songs, however, is not in the effect that events of 1967 had on songs for Palestine in general, but rather in a shift in the Rahbanis' works for Lebanon that cannot wholly be explained by the ruptures caused by those events. Pre-1967 is the period in which Fayruz and the Rahbani Brothers were rising to fame in Lebanon primarily on the strength of folkloric musical theatrical plays and sketches very clearly set in the Lebanese mountain village, plays like *The Moon's Bridge* and *The Ring Seller*. While this may have been an idealized village, it was a specifically described place: the town square, the village spring, the red-roofed houses, the unkempt boulder-filled meadows on the outskirts of town.

"Old Jerusalem" is not a village song, but in a sense there is nothing particularly urban about it: its streets, windows, doors, and shops are ubiquitous in the early village songs and plays of the Rahbanis. Muhammad Abi Samra has commented that even when the Rahbanis are talking about the city, they are really writing about the village (Abi Samra 1985, 33).[13] This is true of most of their works for Palestine, including their first, the somewhat overlooked "We Are Returning."

In 1955, just as Fayruz and the Rahbanis were becoming known in Lebanon and Syria, they were invited to Egypt by Cairo Radio and asked to write some songs for Palestine. What they came up with was "We Are Returning" (*Raji'un*), a semidramatic work in which Fayruz's voice is in dialogue with a chorus of male and female voices. It is said that the chorus represents the Palestinians and Fayruz's voice their collective conscience (Weinrich 2001, 4).

If you look at the album as a whole, which is how it is meant to be heard, it quickly becomes apparent that the vocabulary of these songs for Palestine is precisely the vocabulary of the subsequent early songs and plays about the Lebanese mountain village. The title track, "We Are Returning," for example, has the breezes, nights, flowers, fields, hills, suns, soils, dreams, dawns, springs, squares, winds, rains, and insomniacs of their early Lebanese plays.

Over time, the Rahbanis' plays for Lebanon became less folkloric and more epic in scale and scope. In works like *The Days of Fakhr al-Din*, *Petra*, and *Mountains of Granite*, the specificity of place began to be replaced by vague, grand, and ethereal descriptions. It is in this sense that the mistiness of place in 1967's "The Flower of the Cities" can be seen as the natural outgrowth of a trend that can be traced in their Lebanese works of this time.

Throughout the years the Rahbanis/Fayruz song may have become less specific, but in important ways, whether for Lebanon or Palestine, it remained the same. The Rahbani works about the Lebanese village were written in the context of mass migration both abroad and to Lebanon's urban centers, particularly Beirut. One of the reasons they struck such a chord with their local listeners is that they are infused with nostalgia, not only for the left-behind village, but also for the simpler days that are the context for the memory of life in those villages.

This nostalgia is often accompanied by its counterpart *ghurba* (alienation, homesickness, life outside of homeland). The songs for Palestine, whether or not these exact words are always used, share these elements. Upon receiving the key to Jerusalem in 1968, Fayruz's brother-in-law Mansur said: "We sing for those of you who resist inside and our wounds mesh with your wounds and we sing for the children who were born outside of their homeland [*fi'l-ghurba*], so that they always remember that they are traveling" (Abi Samra 1985, 37)—that they are, in other words, just waiting to return home.

In "Old Jerusalem" of 1966, the narrator seems to move back and forth between pre- and post-1948 Jerusalem. After the relative detail and proximity as seen above, there is sadness, punctuated by a lugubrious violin phrase after the line

And their sad eyes, from the window of the city
take me with suffering's alienation [*ghurba*].

After that, however, the violins almost disappear completely, replaced by an up-tempo synthesizer phrase accompanied by happy pre-1948 memories of a nation being built:

There was land and there were two hands building under the sun, under the wind
And then there were houses and windows gleaming and children, with books in their hands.

The mood changes quickly again with the return of the violin:

And in the dark of night hatred spread to the shadows of the houses
And the black hands tore off the doors and the houses became uninhabited
And between them and between their houses are thorns, fire and the black hands
I'm screaming in the streets, the streets of old Jerusalem.

These images, obviously a reference to the expulsion of thousands of Palestinians in the 1948 Arab–Israeli war, explain the living outside the homeland, the *ghurba*, mentioned mid-way through the song. After the tone of terror and despair comes the same resoluteness heard in the post-1967 "The Flower of the Cities," despite an absence of martial horns.

Let the song become a raging storm
May my voice remain aloft, a hurricane in these consciences
Let them know what is happening, perhaps their consciences will awaken.

The two songs are similar too in the use of *hanin* and *ghurba*, even if neither word is used specifically in "The Flower of the Cities." Instead, we get the mind's eye roving the streets, implying distance and exile, and the narrator of "The Flower of the Cities" prays for those made homeless in general and specifically for the children without houses.

All of this nostalgia and alienation—again whether in works for Palestine or for the "ideal" Lebanese village—are accompanied, of course, by the idea of return. Most of the plays and songs for Lebanon are staged in the village, so the idea of return is implied in the sense that the mostly urban audience is meant to imagine a return to the simpler time and place represented by the village on the stage. In the songs for Palestine, in the songs for those whose land is occupied, the idea of return becomes not only explicit but is also foregrounded in the very titles, such as the album and song title "We Are Returning" from 1955.

There are other examples of the idea of return being made explicit in the songs for Palestine. In the few years before the Six-Day War of 1967, Fayruz sang songs like "The Bells of Return" (*Ajras al-'awda*) and "We Shall Return One Day" (*sa-Narji'u yawman*). In "The Bells of Return," written in 1966 and considered a battle anthem for Arab armies fighting in 1967, Fayruz sings: "Today, today and not tomorrow, let the bells of return be struck."[14] We know that the song "We Shall Return One Day" was written for Palestine, but there is actually nothing specific about it. In fact, according to Weinrich, after the start of the civil war in 1975, many who had to leave Lebanon understood the song as being sung for them (Weinrich 2001, 16). And it is this song perhaps more than any other that Fayruz includes in her concerts outside of the Arab world where her audience is largely made up of expatriate Lebanese.

Fayruz seems to pick when and where to sing her other Palestinian songs with equal care. In looking at reviews of some of her concerts throughout the years, it becomes clear that Fayruz, or those responsible for song selection, always knows her audience quite well. When she sings in Jordan or the Gulf, for example, where most of her audience is Palestinian, she brings out the favorite Palestinian songs, and the reviews always mention the absolute hysteria these songs cause.[15] Likewise, when Fayruz sang in Las Vegas in May of 1999, she sang a number of songs for Palestine. When she toured other cities in the United States in 2003, however, it appears that she did not sing for Palestine—a fact that was noted on at least one Palestinian website that surmised critically that in the post-September 11 atmosphere, Fayruz was concerned about controversy (*ghabat al-Quds hatta 'an Fayruz*, 2003). Similarly, Fayruz's February 2005 concert in Montreal only contained one song "for" Palestine, "We Shall Return One Day," and it wasn't clear if the homesick audience was responding to it as a Palestinian song or one of general longing for the motherland.[16]

This is part of the real genius of the whole Fayruz project, for who in this day and age does not feel a kind of alienation, a longing for return, if not home, then to a simpler time? Fawwaz Tarabulsi conjectures that many of Fayruz and the Rahbanis' works for Lebanon can be read as having been written for Palestine and vice versa (Tarabulsi 1998, 204).[17] But the assumption seems to be that the Rahbanis' songs for Palestine developed out of their Lebanon mountain village aesthetic. It is important to remember, however, that before the Rahbanis and Fayruz became famous for their Lebanese song of longing and nostalgia for Mt. Lebanon they wrote "We Are Returning" (*Raji'un*) for Palestine in 1955. So instead of looking for the seeds of their Palestinian songs in works for Lebanon, I am suggesting that the Rahbanis' whole Lebanon project, as divisive as it was, can just as easily be seen as having been informed by their heartfelt work for Palestine, not the other way around.

We started with what appeared to be a paradox: how did Fayruz become an icon for the Palestinian cause when her artistic roots are in narrow

Christian Lebanese nationalism? Before trying to explain that paradox I offer another: How is it that their divisive narrow Lebanese nationalism grew out of their early work in support of the Palestinian cause, work which would continue in the years leading up to 1967 and beyond? Perhaps the solution to both of these paradoxes lies in the descriptions of Jerusalem in "The Flower of the Cities" and "Old Jerusalem," or, more precisely, the absence of Jerusalem. In the fuzzy and foggy *hanin*/nostalgia of the Rahbanis, home becomes, simply, both wherever and whenever you are not. I end with some lines from "We Shall Return One Day," the song written for Palestine but often understood by the Lebanese to have been written for them:

> We shall return one day to our neighborhood and drown in the warmth of its hope,
> We shall return, no matter how much time passes or how large the distances between us.

This is not specifically a song about Lebanon or Mt. Lebanon, but it could be; it is not specifically a song about Jerusalem, but it could be—for is this not exactly what Jerusalem is to many of the Jews, Christians, and Muslims who consider it to be holy? Is it not a kind of unreachable heaven on earth that both *although* unreachable and *because* it is unreachable appears destined to be a site of conflict for some time to come? Let us hope that the same cannot be said of Lebanon, though one can argue that Fayruz and the Rahbanis' idealized descriptions of it from the 1950s, 1960s, and 1970s remain powerful conduits if not producers of nostalgia today. Just like their Jerusalem, however, their idealized Lebanon not only does not exist, but never existed.

Notes

1 Despite the start of the civil war in 1975 the Rahbanis continued to perform musical theatrical works, with Fayruz in the starring role, that portray Lebanon as a land of miracles. Such a work is *Petra* (1978). For an account of the deteriorating situation in Lebanon leading up to the war, see Salibi 1976 and Petran 1987.
2 For an account of this response, see Mina and al-'Attar 1976.
3 Hamra was the pre-Lebanese-civil-war center for highbrow culture in Beirut. *Exile* (*Safar Barlak*) was recently shown on an outdoor screen in Martyrs' Square in central Beirut as part of a unity celebration in the context of the current tensions in Lebanon.
4 More recently the song became an anthem of the Palestinian uprisings in the West Bank and the Gaza Strip (Bibawy 2002).
5 The Lebanese novelists Hasan Dawud and Ilyas Khuri mention this song specifically in this regard, as does the Egyptian writer Yusuf al-Qa'id (quoted in Abi Samra 1985, 78, 86, and 97 [all in supplement]).
6 In the context of world events today, it is perhaps worth mentioning that from the start of her career Fayruz was as popular in Syria as she was in Lebanon, and in fact, Fayruz has performed as often in Damascus as she has in Beirut. So just as the focus of this essay is to explore this Palestine paradox in the work of

Fayruz, one could also comment on the irony of the fact that the young Lebanese gathered recently in Martyrs' Square in Beirut protesting the Syrian presence in Lebanon and Syrians in Damascus demonstrating in support of their country's Lebanon policy were all blasting Fayruz songs.

7 For a survey of popular resistance songs for Palestine, see Massad 2003.

8 Massad points out that the Palestinian resistance song has, from its origins, been a mélange of Arab-music quarter-tone scales and western march music, noting that this mix has scarcely raised an eyebrow in debates over authenticity, as the focus has been on the songs' content. He credits Muhammad 'Abd al-Wahhab for starting this trend (Massad 2003, 23). In fact, the music of songs such as "The Flower of the Cities" has as much in common with the Rahbanis' own 1957 "We Are Returning" than with 'Abd al-Wahhab's musical experimentations in this period. Of course, one can find such musical combinations even earlier, such as in Sayyid Darwish's resistance songs.

9 All translations are my own.

10 There is a double irony in the fact that most of these songs for non-Lebanese places were penned by Sa'id 'Aql, for not only was he known to be a staunch supporter of the brand of Lebanese nationalism that believes the Lebanese to be Phoenicians and not Arabs, but he was and remains to this day perhaps the most vociferous advocate of making the Lebanese dialect—written in a Latin-based alphabet—the national language of Lebanon. For more on the relationship between the Rahbanis and Fayruz, see Abi Samra 1992.

11 For exceptions, see Muwasi 2004.

12 So common is this error that even Massad seems to infer mistakenly that "Old Jerusalem" is a post-1967 song (Massad 2003, 28).

13 He calls this *al-madina al-mutarayyifa* (the countrified city) and *al-rif al-mutamaddin* (the citified country).

14 I mention as an aside that though very much an iconic figure, when it came to the shock of the 1967 defeat even Fayruz was fair game for sarcasm. The poet 'Abd al-Mutallib al-Amin wrote a poem in response to this song after the defeat: "Pardon me Fayruz and with apologies, but the bells of return were not struck, rather it was our bottoms that were struck, from Sharm al-Shaykh all the way to [the Palestinian village] Sa'sa' (quoted in Tarabulsi 1998, 212n4).

15 See, for example, Bibawy 2002 and Shams 2002.

16 From personal observation at the concert.

17 This article by Tarabulsi is an insightful study of the Rahbanis' 1969 play *Mountains of Granite* as a parable for Palestine. My focus here is on Fayruz and the Rahbanis' songs for Palestine rather than their musical theater; for further reading on that topic see Stone 2002 and Tarabulsi 2006.

References

Abi Samra, Muhammad. 1985. "Zahirat al-akhawayn Rahbani: 'Fayruz'." Master's thesis, Lebanese University.

——. 1992. "Fayruz wa-l-akhawan Rahbani: mithal bana Lubnan Sa'id 'Aql bi-hijara min nujum." *Mulhaq Jaridat al-Nahar*, May 9, 14.

Aliksan, Jan. 1989. "Al-Rahbaniyyun wa-Fayruz, al-juz' al-khamis: mahatta asasiyya bayn Lubnan wa-l-'alam." *Majallat Alhan*, May 27, 27.

Bibawy, Amir. 2002. "I Loved You in the Summer: Fairouz Moves Paris Audience to Tears." *The Daily Star*, June 19, electronic edition. http://dailystar.com.

"Fayruzat al-Quds al-'atiqa." 1997. Caption of unattributed drawing in *al-Nahar*, October 16, 20.

"Ghabat al-Quds hatta 'an Fayruz." 2003. *Al Watan Arab American Newspaper*, 20 October, electronic edition. http://www.watan.com/print.php?sid = 602.

Habib, Ken. 2005. "The Superstar Singer Fairouz and the Ingenious Rahbani Composers: Lebanon Sounding." Ph.D. diss., University of California, Santa Barbara.

Hammer, Juliane. 2001. "Homeland Palestine: Lost in the Catastrophe of 1948 and Recreated in Memories and Art." In *Crisis and Memory in Islamic Societies*, ed. Angelica Neuwirth and Andreas Pflitsch, 453–482. Beirut: Ergon Verlag Wurzburg in Kimmission.

Janssen, Jack, director. 2003. *We Loved Each Other So Much*. Prod. Pieter Van Huystee. New York: First Run/Icarus Films.

Mansur, M. 2003. "Filastin fi al-ughniyya al-Rahbaniyya." *al-Funun* 33 (September): 6–10.

Massad, Joseph. 2003. "Liberating Songs: Palestine Put to Music." *Journal of Palestine Studies* 32.3: 21–38.

Mina, Hanna, and Najah al-'Attar. 1976. *Adab al-harb*. Damascus: Manshurat Wizarat al-Thaqafa.

Muwasi, Faruq. 2004. "Al-Quds fi al-shi'r al-Filastini al-hadith." *Oufouq.com*, 1 September, electronic edition. http://www.ofouq.com/today/modules.php?name = News&file = article&sid = 1510. Also in Faruq Muwasi, *al-Quds fi 'l-shi'r al-Filastini 'l-hadith*. Nazareth: Mu'assasat al-Mawakib, 1996.

Petran, Tabitha. 1987. *The Struggle over Lebanon*. New York: Monthly Review Press.

Salibi, Kamal. 1976. *Crossroads to Civil War: Lebanon, 1958–1976*. New York: Caravan Books.

Shams, Duha. 2002. "Ism Filastin ya'rifuhu sawt Fayruz fi jami'at Dubayy al-Amirikiya." *Al-Safir*, May 1, 24.

Stone, Christopher. 2002. "The Rahbani Nation: Musical Theater and Nationalism in Contemporary Lebanon." Ph.D. diss., Princeton University.

———. 2003–4. "The Ba'labakk Festival and the Rahbanis: Folklore, Ancient History, Musical Theater and Nationalism in Lebanon." *Arab Studies Journal* 11–12.1–2: 10–40.

Tarabulsi, Fawwaz. 1998. "Jibal al-sawwan: Filastin fi fann Fayruz wa'l-Rahabina." *Al-Karmil* 57 (Autumn): 203–213.

———. 2006. *Fayruz wa-al-Rahabina: masrah al-gharib wa'l-kanz wa'l-a'juba*. Beirut: Riad El-Rayyes Books.

Weinrich, Ines. 2001. "Notes on Salvation and Joy: Reflections on the Repertory of Fayruz and the Rahbani-Brothers." In *Crisis and Memory in Islamic Societies*, ed. Angelika Neuwirth and Andreas Pflitsch, 483–499. Wurzberg: Ergon.

11 Jerusalem in the visual propaganda of post-revolutionary Iran[1]

Christiane J. Gruber

Introduction

As the hub of hagiographic events in all three Abrahamic faiths and the contested ground for the establishment of religio-political authority in the Middle East, the city of Jerusalem has maintained a prominent symbolic position in Islamic history from the time of Muhammad until today. Before it was revealed to the Prophet to change the direction of prayer (*qibla*) to Mecca, the early Muslim community, according to the Islamic tradition, faced Jerusalem in the consecrated act of communal worship. Even though Mecca replaced Jerusalem as the most revered location on earth, Jerusalem nevertheless preserved its sanctity in Muslim thought and practice throughout the centuries.[2]

The Dome of the Rock (*Qubbat al-Sakhra*), the prototypical architectural project evocative of Islamic political and religious ascendancy in the Holy City of Jerusalem from the Umayyad period (661–750) forward,[3] has been depicted in the visual arts of Islam in a variety of ways. Examples include twelfth-century pilgrimage certificates (Roxburgh, forthcoming; Aksoy and Milstein 2000), Ilkhanid and Timurid *Mi'rajnamas*, which are illustrated books on Muhammad's ascension (Gruber 2005), and Ottoman pictorial guides to Mecca and Medina (Milstein 1994).[4] Illustrations of the Dome of the Rock during the pre-modern period in this manner served as visual reminders of pilgrimage rites and pictorial affirmations of Muhammad's night journey (*isra'*) to Jerusalem and his subsequent ascension (*mi'raj*) to Heaven.[5] These pre-modern images also stress Jerusalem's religious merits, as well as its eschatological potential in providing a specific locus for otherworldly events such as the raising of the scales of justice and the weighing of souls on the Day of Judgment.[6]

It was not until the last quarter of the twentieth century, however, that images of the Dome of the Rock became pervasive. During the Khomeini and post-Khomeini years in Iran, images of Jerusalem became truly omnipresent in the visual arts of Islam and, more notably, entered the public sphere of a particular Islamic culture. At this time, murals, paintings, maquettes, stamps, coins, posters, and other ephemera depicting the Dome of the Rock came together to generate the rhetorical media for political mobilization and the visual metaphors for freedom from tyranny. Shedding references to a shared Abrahamic past, popular practices of pilgrimage, and the prophetic ascension, representations of the Dome of the Rock came to play a central role in Iranian public propaganda campaigns aimed at promoting Islamic solidarity across state borders and endorsing a universal rising up against global oppression.

As can be gathered from a wide array of visual evidence, the "idea" of Jerusalem in revolutionary and post-revolutionary Iran (1979–present) has been cultivated fastidiously by various individuals and organizations in order to fashion Iranian public opinion in favor of the Palestinian cause and to (attempt to) create a united Muslim front within the rather muddled arena of international politics. Chief protagonists in these efforts include the supreme religious leaders of Iran, Khomeini and Khamenei, and their immediate entourage. Other powerful institutions, most notably the Organization of the Martyrs of the Islamic Revolution (*Bunyad-i Shahid-i Inqilab-i Islami*) and other organizations, actively promoted, and continue to promote, a specific vision of Iran's responsibility toward the city of Jerusalem and the occupied Palestinian territories.

From his years of exile under the monarchical rule of Reza Shah Pahlavi (d. 1980) to his return to Iran in 1979 to spearhead the new Islamic Republic, Khomeini (1901–89) cultivated the notion that Israel constituted the fiercest "enemy of Islam." He systematically argued that the occupation of Palestine and Jerusalem had to be remedied by all Muslim countries, inspired and guided by Iran's own revolutionary successes (Khomeini 1982, 35). Khomeini and his followers strongly believed that Iran was at the vanguard of worldwide Islamic activism and the fighting for freedom from subjugation and imperialism, two concepts subsumed under the general rubric of "international Zionism" (Khomeini 1982). As the political father-figure, Khomeini envisioned himself as the protector of occupied lands and oppressed people in the face of international theft and military attack as embodied by the Israeli "regime."[7]

In the midst of grappling with the sweeping changes brought about by the Islamic Revolution, Iran had to face yet another large-scale trauma: the Iran–Iraq War (1980–88). The sheer brutality of trench warfare, not seen since World War I, the Iraqi use of chemical weapons, and the self-sacrificial raids of Iran's boy soldiers across the Iran–Iraq border shocked the world (Davis 2003). Saddam Hussein, by and large considered a secular and genocidal ruler by Iranians, and his military aims were likened to Israel's own imperialist efforts further west. By elaborating Iraq's qualitative connection to Israel as a belligerent entity, Iranian politicians and military leaders extended the margins of their political rhetoric. What resulted in connection with these efforts was a burst of images in Iran comparing the freeing of Jerusalem from Israeli hands to the liberation of the shrines of Karbala and Najaf, the most significant Shi'i holy sites, from the grip of Saddam Hussein. As the ultimate goal of salvation from coercion and cruelty, the Dome of the Rock began to symbolize the long quest for Iranian religious and political triumph during the Islamic Revolution and the Iran–Iraq War.

At the close of the Iran–Iraq war in 1988 and the death of Khomeini in 1989, the 1990s inaugurated a new series of images linked to Jerusalem under the stewardship of Khamenei, today's supreme religious leader of Iran, and the various governmental organizations under his authority. Most impressive among all current art forms are the many large-scale murals scattered throughout Tehran and other major cities in Iran. These murals include a number of slogans that endorse the liberation of Palestine and glorify martyrs of the cause. They utilize the visual mechanisms of advertising to promote a highly visible "culture of martyrdom" in contemporary Iran.[8] Their iconographic vocabulary is just as unabashed as their accompanying slogans, which stress repeatedly the Muslim world's obligation to rally to the Palestinian cause under the charitable dispensation and watchful supervision of the Islamic Republic of Iran.

The study of visual materials representing Jerusalem in the public art of post-revolutionary Iran presents several methodological problems. First and foremost, the data are transient or subject to change: architectural maquettes are discarded after having been used for a specific occasion, and many old murals are replaced by newer compositions. Other ephemera such as posters and stamps also are discardable, so it is difficult to judge their diachronic impact on Iranian culture. Secondly, although these works of art circulate in the public domain, their influence is impossible to gauge without conducting extensive interviews and long-term ethnographic work. Although the main audience tends to consist of local Iranians, a number of works incorporating bilingual Persian–Arabic or Persian–English slogans[9] also appear to target Muslims and non-Muslims living outside of Iran. Here too, determining the impact, if any, of these murals on a more international audience must await further investigation. Although it is clear who or what entities are at the center of creating a new authoritative and normative system of visual information in the Islamic world, it is still difficult to get a sense of its public (Eickelman and Anderson 2003).

Despite the challenges posed by the numerous ways in which these materials were, and continue to be, received at both the domestic and the global levels, they have certainly left imprints, whether subliminal or not, in the minds of casual observers. They also have come to define the visual landscape of urban centers throughout Iran, especially its capital city, Tehran. By mixing political propaganda with dramatic pictorial forms, representations of Jerusalem combine the tools of marketing, the immediacy of photo-realism, and the idioms of popular graffiti to broadcast several forceful messages. These include Iran as trustworthy doyen of the global Islamic community's welfare, its championing of the Palestinian cause, and its duty in liberating the city of Jerusalem, itself the ubiquitous symbol of the "imperialist" occupation and subjugation of Muslims worldwide.

"The road to Jerusalem goes through Karbala"

Although the concern with liberating the Dome of the Rock from Israeli occupation was historically relevant during the 1980s, the allegorical meanings embodied in the structure fluctuated widely depending on time and circumstance. During the trying events of the Iran–Iraq War, the edifice came to represent a symbol of freedom in Iran's "holy defense"[10] against Saddam's invasion across the Shatt al-'Arab and into the western Iranian provinces of Khuzistan and Ilam. Saddam leveled a number of cities and villages along the Iran–Iraq border, including Khorramshahr and the ethnically Kurdish city of Kermanshah.

A number of posters, billboards, and murals painted in the provinces of Khuzistan and Ilam during the war, a great many of which no longer exist today, suggest that Iran's struggle against Saddam's regime was imagined as a total liberation of Islamic lands from the grip of war criminals. Khomeini, his buttressing ministries, and those supporting war efforts saw the liberation of the Shi'i shrines of Najaf and Karbala in Iraq as closely connected to the release of the Dome of the Rock from Israeli hands. In fact, one constituted a seamless extension of the other. Addressing both soldiers heading to the front and a local populace suffering through the ravages of war, the surviving visual materials make use of the image of a floating Jerusalem to convey the profound emotions of hope and deliverance. Adopting the dream imagery of Surrealist art,[11] designers, muralists, and painters depicted an attainable and heavenly Jerusalem as a way to promote war efforts in Iranian provinces on the Iraqi frontier.

A transportable billboard in Mehran, a city located on the western plain of the Zagros mountain range in the province of Ilam, represents an Iranian soldier striding forward with a rifle on his back and ammunition wrapped around his shoulder and waist (Figure 11.1).[12] He carries a large green banner inscribed with the profession of faith (*shahada*): "There is no God but God, and Muhammad is the Prophet of God." He marches vigorously, his body inclined on his right leg, toward the high portal of the Shrine of Imam Husayn in Karbala, topped by a gold dome and two flanking minarets. Beyond the opening and into the incandescent distance emerges a spectral simulacrum of the Dome of the Rock, immediately recognizable by its octagonal walls decorated by sets of arcades. The visual conflation of the Karbala shrine and the Dome of the Rock intimates a continuous passageway through both time and space, while it also illustrates the ultimate goal of the Iranian campaign into Iraq: first to free Shi'i shrines and then to liberate the first *qibla* of all Muslims, Jerusalem.

At the top of the panel runs Khomeini's famous wartime saying that "the road to Jerusalem goes through Karbala," while, in the lower right corner, the statement concludes with the added specification that "the road to Karbala goes through Mehran." The poster localizes events of the Iran–Iraq War and places Mehran at the center of liberation efforts. This strategically placed city certainly played a central role at this time: Iraqi forces occupied it for a month in 1986 before Iranian forces recaptured it. As a jumping point for incursions into Iraq, Mehran achieved a special status in the quest toward Iraq and, by extension, Israel. The poster's inscription records Mehran's contribution and pays tribute to the soldiers who passed through this strategic way-station.

In the bottom right corner of the poster appears the rifle logo of the Iranian Revolutionary Guard Corps (IRGC or *Pasdaran-i Inqilab-i Islami*),

Figure 11.1 "The Road to Jerusalem Goes through Karbala," billboard, Mehran, c. 1983.

established by Khomeini in 1979 to promote the revolution and to implement Islamic codes. A force consisting of battalion-size units, the IRGC carries on military operations both domestically and abroad. It was active in the Iran–Iraq War, having provided a number of volunteer fighters sent to the front line, and still today includes a smaller and mysterious group called the Jerusalem (*al-Quds*) Force. The Jerusalem Force is responsible for extraterritorial operations and, because of its focus on liberating Muslim lands and Jerusalem in particular, it retains strong ties to Hizbollah, Hamas, and Islamic Jihad.[13] Within this highly charged military context, it is not surprising to find a link between the IRGC, the Iran–Iraq War, and its final objective (Jerusalem) in the Mehran billboard.

In the bottom left corner appears another emblem comprising a circle inscribed with the words "Construction Jihad" (*Jihad-i Sazandegi*). Construction Jihad is an Iranian ministry with a focus on engineering research for defense and the sponsoring of other applied sciences; it roughly resembles the U.S. Army Corps of Engineers (Cordesman 1999, 237). It was created by Khomeini and the Islamic Consultative Parliament in 1983 to curb rural poverty and promote agricultural self-sufficiency. (Since 2000, Construction Jihad has been merged with the Ministry of Agriculture to form the Ministry of Agricultural Jihad.) Its duties expanded during the Iran–Iraq War because of its close affiliation with the IRGC. While the IRGC carried out operations through sheer manpower, the engineers of Construction Jihad provided much needed logistical support by constructing bridges and freeways for armored vehicles. Moreover, at the height of the Iran–Iraq War, in 1982, Construction Jihad's public-relations section played an active role in promulgating the Islamic Revolution and Khomeini's vision of the Iran–Iraq War by publishing two works on the subject.[14]

The billboard of a young soldier heading to war, as well as advancing on the geographic corridor toward the liberation of Najaf and Jerusalem, creates a compelling product of the joint efforts of the IRGC and Construction Jihad at the peak of the Iran–Iraq War. In this particular case, the Iranian army has collaborated with a national ministry to promote the war in visual form, purposefully selecting the city of Mehran as its dramatic backdrop. Like Construction Jihad's publications of the time, the poster provides a compelling mechanism of public relations in pictorial form. This image—as part and parcel of the panoply of war tactics—promises the liberation of Iraqi lands and, by extension, the attainment of the Promised Land. The Dome of the Rock, the leading symbol of the war's objective, looms large in the distance, glowing like a luminescent gem suspended in the seventh heaven.

Graphic materials such as the Mehran billboard not only promoted Iranian incursions into Iraqi soil but also reflected Iranian military parades and popular demonstrations that took place during the Iran–Iraq War. Contemporaneous photographs reveal how military operations were carefully "staged" in order to reify the symbolic goals of a war that, more often than not, felt futile, unending, and directionless. For example, a photograph (Figure 11.2) included in the journal *Shahid* (No. 133, 21 May 1987), the mouthpiece of the Martyrs' Organization, records a military procession that occurred in Kermanshah in 1987, that is, toward the end of the war. Soldiers bearing a variety of weapons, holding up banners inscribed with the *shahada*, and carrying photographs of Khomeini strapped to their backs march under Iranian flags toward a surprisingly accurate replica of the Dome of the Rock. This enactment of a triumphant procession provides a tangible recollection of the billboard's composition and affords the allegorical locus for the fulfillment of the war's otherwise thwarted aspirations.

Below the photograph of the Kermanshah military procession, a poem in Persian addresses Jerusalem in the vocative case (Oh Jerusalem!/ *Ya Quds!*). It describes the city as the first *qibla* of Islam and "light of the torch of revelation." Its soil is tinted by "the sanguine color of the lovebird's blood," that is, by the expiration of the old man, the young boy, and even the child. Despite the deep sorrow in Jerusalem's chest, the poet nonetheless promises the city that

Figure 11.2 Military procession in Kermanshah, 1366/1987.

the Islamic community will strive until it and the entirety of Palestine are free. The poem complements the photograph by stressing the kinship of all Muslims, remembering their collective sacrifice, and advocating Jerusalem as the ultimate reward for those who endure unspeakable hardship.

In a similar way, the architectonic facsimile of the Dome of the Rock functions as a physical node around which Iranian soldiers can perform a celebratory circuit. Despite the war's stalemate and its inglorious cessation by U.N. Resolution 479, the Iranian illusion of conquest is maintained here by a surrogate shrine erected on the fictionalized landscape of the Holy Land. The mirage of Jerusalem solidifies into a visible form and provides a ritual space for the staging of war pageantry and the carrying out of conquest, both bittersweet and illusory acts disguising the otherwise horrid failures of the Iran–Iraq War.

Although the model of the Dome of the Rock provides a substitute for the real thing, it must have been used to draw upon particularly Shi'i commemorative events and rituals. Through overt references to Karbala—such as the recurring combat adage exclaiming that "the road to Jerusalem goes through Karbala"—Iranians elaborated upon the emotive similarities between the Iran–Iraq War and the Umayyad forces' ambush of Imam Husayn on the plain of Karbala in 680 CE. For both Iranians and Iraqis, the war was cast in anachronistic terms, because its dramatis personae historicized the figures of the Umayyad caliph Yazid into Saddam, and that of Husayn into Khomeini.[15] Iranians deemed Saddam a Sunni despot attempting to annihilate the Shi'i community and to desecrate its holiest shrines in Najaf and Karbala, while the vast numbers of Iranian soldiers who died in the war were seen as modern-day martyrs of Karbala fighting against injustice and for the Shi'i cause. The Iran–Iraq War was transformed into the neoteric channel for Iranians to rectify Shi'i grievances more than 1,300 years old. For these reasons, Iranians assimilated military processions to 'Ashura ceremonies and even passion plays (*ta'ziya*) during the Iran–Iraq War.[16] These mourning rites, which were held to commemorate the killing of Husayn, were sponsored and revived at this time by Khomeini, who believed that

> maintaining the 'Ashura alive is a very important politico-devotional matter. 'Ashura is the day of general mourning by the oppressed nation. It is the epic day, the rebirth of Islam and Muslims. And, in this, the blood of our martyrs is a continuation of the pure blood of the martyrs of Karbala.

> (Khomeini 1994, 47)

For Khomeini, sponsoring popular forms of Shi'i rituals such as 'Ashura provided the foundations for mustering support for the Iran–Iraq War. At the same time, these ceremonies constructed an almost genetic bond between the blood of contemporary Iranian martyrs and those who perished in Karbala for the sake of Husayn's cause.

Traffic's inner sanctum: the Dome of the Rock models

In official observances of 'Ashura and the Iran–Iraq War, maquettes representing Najaf, Karbala, and the Dome of the Rock were carried around cities such as Kermanshah (Mahmudi and Sulaymani 1985, 76) (Figure 11.3). Traffic roundabouts in particular provided theatrical spaces for the re-enactment of ritual circumambulation so closely linked with pilgrimage rituals both at the Ka'ba in Mecca and, at least during the pre-modern period, the Dome of the Rock in Jerusalem.[17] Maquettes of the Dome of the Rock, such as the one in Figure 11.3, provided visual recollections of the Holy City and needed not to be entirely accurate in their architectural details. For example, the dome of this maquette has been extended upwards rather than shaped as a semi-hemisphere. The walls of the maquette also tend toward white hues rather than the blue tones found in the tiles revetting the actual building's exterior.[18]

The proliferation of Dome of the Rock maquettes in Iran offers an intriguing modern foil to the medieval European practice of building churches and baptisteries roughly in the shape of the Holy Sepulcher (Krautheimer 1942), whose centrally-planned, domed Anastasis Rotunda not only provided an architectural prototype for the Dome of the Rock but whose purpose also revolved around marking the locus of a prophetic ascent into the heavens. In both cases, the multiplication of a holy shrine is intended to serve a variety of local ritual purposes activated through a community's collective memoirs of a distant Holy Land. In the case of Iran, however, the proliferation

Figure 11.3 Maquette of the Dome of the Rock, Kermanshah, c. 1980.

of three-dimensional mock-ups of the Dome of the Rock suggests a meta-phorical taking-over, transplantation, and naturalization of one of Islam's holiest shrines to its new Iranian setting. The fact that this phenomenon reached its peak during the 1980s in Iran does not seem coincidental what-soever, since the liberation of Jerusalem was a mainstay of official rhetoric concerned with exporting the Islamic Revolution abroad.

Eventually portable maquettes of the Dome of the Rock utilized in war parades and in Shi'i ceremonies materialized into fixed, permanent struc-tures dotting the urban landscapes of cities like Kermanshah, Tehran, and Mashhad. For example, the miniature model in Kermanshah eventually became a full-fledged structure replicating the Dome of the Rock (Figure 11.4). The structure is now located on a platform surrounded by a pool placed in the center of the main roundabout in Kermanshah, called Free-dom Square (*Maidan-i Azadi*). The name evokes the city's liberation from the Iraqi assault. After all, Kermanshah, located in the ethnically Kurdish province of Kermanshah (also known as Bakhtaran), was badly damaged by Iraqi air strikes and land raids. The name also suggests a link to its central building, that is, a freeing of Jerusalem and its holy monument, the Dome of the Rock. The square's imprecise name and its reference to the processes of liberation and rebuilding engender a suggestive elision between the cities of Kermanshah and Jerusalem.

Figure 11.4 Model of the Dome of the Rock, *Maidan-i Azadi* (Freedom Square), Kermanshah, 2005.

The octagonal building topped by a golden dome is intended as a creative facsimile of the Dome of the Rock, even though it departs from the forms of the historical shrine in several notable ways. Unlike the blue-tiled exterior of the Dome of the Rock, the Kermanshah building includes eight sides decorated with alternating arches painted in yellow and blue above a white dado. Furthermore, the drum is painted in green and includes brown registers inscribed with sayings in white paint. The inscriptions are not Qur'anic and thus do not reproduce the textual excerpts on the actual façade and in the interior mosaics of the Dome of the Rock. Rather, the registers contain a number of Shi'i maxims about prayer and its benefits. For example, one panel quotes the sixth Shi'i imam Ja'far al-Sadiq (d. 765), who warns that "anyone who counts prayer lightly will be deprived of our (the imams') intercession."[19] Another saying attributed to 'Ali (d. 661) exhorts that "prayer is the antidote to conceit."[20]

These Shi'i aphorisms inscribed on the Kermanshah replication of the Dome of the Rock add an overt and unmistakable religious twist to the monument.[21] By quoting Shi'i religious authorities such as 'Ali and Ja'far al-Sadiq, the building becomes clad in a new sectarian skin. In this way, the building's Shi'i eschatological inflection demarcates Kermanshah as the geographic setting for the cosmic battle between good (Iran) and evil (Iraq, Israel, and the West). The maquette of the Dome of the Rock punctuates its focal point and signifies the restitution of war-torn zones to the Iranian polity. Although this architectural centerpiece also provided the node for the carrying out of a sacred pilgrimage imagined through armed conflict, it has been dwarfed by commercial clutter and the hustle and bustle of today's metropolis.

Permanent copies of the Dome of the Rock, some more accurately representing the historical building than others, began to sprout all over Iran during the 1990s as part of the larger post-war effort to keep the city of Jerusalem alive in domestic and global Muslim consciousness. No longer limited to mobile maquettes or structural props accompanying religious festivals and military parades, models of the Dome of the Rock have been absorbed into urban life and architectural complexes in Iran. A number of these models are imbued with new concerns via the (re)location and (re)deployment of the structure.

In one case, a maquette has been incorporated into the ever-expanding plan of the *sanctum sanctorum*, the Shrine of Imam Reza in Mashhad.[22] A recently added courtyard named "the Jerusalem Courtyard" includes a fairly accurate rendition of the Dome of the Rock, whose size is exactly one-eighth of the original structure's dimensions (Figure 11.5).[23] Here, a miniature Dome of the Rock serves as a public drinking-place in the center of a 2,500-meter courtyard bound on its sides by twenty-eight chambers and a tall portal. The portal's name is *Qibla*, an appropriate appellation for Jerusalem as the first direction of prayer.

The recent inclusion of a Dome of the Rock fountain in the Shrine of Imam Reza carries some intriguing symbolic implications for the Shi'i community and the crowds of foreign pilgrims, both Sunni and Shi'i, it attracts. It harks back to the commonly held view that the Rock upon which the historical monument stands provides the starting point for earthly and heavenly rivers (see Chapter 6 by Suleiman A. Mourad in this volume). This cosmological allusion is certainly not lost upon visitors to the Shrine, transforming it into the primordial and universal source of sustenance. Its

Figure 11.5 Dome of the Rock Fountain, *Sahn-i Quds* (Jerusalem Courtyard), Shrine of Imam Reza, Mashhad, 2005.

power to conjure up the celestial waters provides just one instance of the maquette's "fluidity" of meaning.

The other, perhaps more significant, implication of the Dome of the Rock replica revolves around its placement in a Shi'i shrine complex, a sacred precinct amenable to international pilgrim traffic. The minimized Dome of the Rock falls under the benevolent guardianship of the Astan-i Quds Foundation. As Khomeini reiterated time and again: "Jerusalem is the first *qibla* of the Muslims and it belongs to them" (Khomeini 1994, 126), and this architectural reconstruction of Jerusalem's most famous Islamic shrine assures that the monument—or at least its functional carbon copy—is placed under Islamic management. The harmonization of the Dome of the Rock to the Astan-i Quds architectural complex provides just one of the many ways Iranians have attempted to forcibly reclaim and effectively protect Jerusalem.

A number of other Dome of the Rock maquettes are (or were) used in traffic roundabouts in the capital city of Tehran. For instance, one permanent elevated model is included in the Jerusalem three-street junction in the northeastern section of Tehran called Niavaran (Figure 11.6). Although seemingly temporary, this maquette has remained in this area of town for many years, and the three-street junction's name (*Serah-i Quds*, or the three-

Figure 11.6 Dome of the Rock Maquette, *Serah-i Quds* (Jerusalem three-street junction), Niavaran, Tehran, 2001.

street Jerusalem junction) assures that a visual reference to the Holy City will continue to be maintained. The model is fairly faithful to its original, as it decorates the octagonal façades with blue and yellow tile-work and places the gold dome on a high drum.

The inscriptions in the upper frieze make use of the structure to glorify the many names and epithets of God. It calls out to God in the vocative (*O!/ya!*) with a litany of His soubriquets: "Best of Forgivers," "Best of Providers," "Best of Creators," "Guide to those who go astray," and "Light of the Heavens and Earth." The structure thus serves as a traffic centerpiece, a homage to Jerusalem, and an extended tribute to God.

Another Dome of the Rock maquette used to be located in the center of Palestine Square, a busy roundabout on south Palestine Street toward Revolution Street, the area of Tehran University's main campus (Chelkowski and Dabashi 1999, 204, Figure 12.13) (Figure 11.7). The model includes the yellow and blue tiles typical of the monument in Jerusalem but places the dome on two tiers of pierced arcades, creating a sort of architectural veranda. The gold dome is topped by a large green banner reminiscent of the war banners carried into battlefield during the Iran–Iraq War (Figure 11.1). Around the base of the maquette runs an inscription in Persian, initiated by the hexagram Star of David, the standard symbol of the Jews as well as the state of Israel. The writing in white that follows reads: "Israel is a usurper and it must exit Palestine immediately."[24] The call for Israel's withdrawal from Palestinian territory is typical of slogans and graffiti found on walls throughout Tehran, which oftentimes read "Death to Israel"[25] or "Israel must be wiped out."[26]

Jerusalem, the martyred soul

The Dome of the Rock maquette in Palestine Square was eventually taken down and replaced by an iconographic ensemble combining sculpture and mural work related to the Palestinian cause (Figure 11.8).[27] Palestine Square provides the most complete multi-media amalgam of images related to Jerusalem. These include a large bronze sculpture depicting a fissured map of Israel, a young mother holding her dead child in her lap, and a Palestinian fighter striding forward with his right fist upraised. Two murals frame the square as well: one seven stories high depicting a political figure, a fighter, and the Dome of the Rock (Figure 11.9), and the other the ensnaring of Islamic holy sites (Figure 11.10).

The vertical mural represents a Palestinian throwing a rock through a cracked Star of David, with the Dome of the Rock crystallizing from a ghostly haze in the background (Figure 11.9). The inscriptions flanking the Dome of the Rock specify that the bearded man at the top of the composition is the martyr 'Abbas al-Musawi, the secretary-general of the Lebanese Hizbollah, who, along with his wife and six-year-old son, was killed by an Israeli gunship attack; as the inscription further specifies, "he was murdered at the hands of the occupying, criminal Zionist forces in southern Lebanon in 1992."

Above the specters of his veiled wife and son appears another inscription quoting Iran's supreme religious leader, Khamenei, as stating that "the mercy of God is upon this learned, religious, brave, devoted, and conscientious man, and the curse of God is remaining a slave to all criminal Zionists." The inscription transcribes verbatim Khamenei's speech on the occasion of Musawi's death, lending the mural a photo-journalistic feel. The

Figure 11.7 Dome of the Rock Model, *Maidan-i Filistin* (Jerusalem Square), Tehran, c. 1990.

transcription also records the martyr's noble qualities and calls upon the destruction of Israel at the same time as it trumpets its support of Hizbollah, Hamas, and Islamic Jihad.

This mural vividly supports and praises liberation movements and martyrizing individuals for the greater sake of Islamic political determination, drawing most explicitly on the Palestinian and Lebanese paradigms. It also promotes martyrdom as the ultimate sacrifice of self for the greater good of society. This is not so surprising when we take into consideration that the mural's program and iconography were developed and underwritten by the Martyrs' Organization, whose official logo appears in the mural's upper-left corner. The Martyrs' Organization's emblem shows a white dove drinking liquid out of an open red tulip, symbolizing that martyrdom provides the lifeblood of existence. The organization's name appears on the side of the logo, and below the tulip is its foundation date, 1979–80.

The Martyrs' Organization was established during the Islamic Revolution by Khomeini to supervise the affairs of martyrs' families and incapacitated veterans. At present, the foundation is an extensive and solid organization that provides education and welfare facilities to martyrs' families and their children (Khomeini 1994, 51n1). It is one of several agencies not accountable to any branch of the state and overseen directly by Khamenei through his representatives.[28] It is financed by the state, receives donations, and generally benefits from tax-exemption status.

Figure 11.8 View of *Maidan-i Filistin* (Palestine Square), Tehran, 2005.

The Martyrs' Organization owns about three hundred companies in various commercial and economic sectors, and as a consequence is one of the most affluent and influential organizations in Iran. It publishes extensively on the subject of martyrdom, as its main duty consists in handling the affairs and moneys of the families of the deceased or veterans of the Revolution and the Iran–Iraq War. In its 1985 publication *Ashna-i ba Bunyad-i Shahid-i Inqilab-i Islami* (*An Introduction to the Martyrs' Organization*), the Martyrs' Organization presents its charter, its structure, and its various responsibilities and activities. One of its most active divisions is its department of culture, which oversees the sections on teaching, propaganda, public relations, and art. The art section comprises several divisions as well: film, theater, photography, poetry, painting, calligraphy, design, and handicrafts. The photography section is responsible for publishing photos of martyrs and working together with other sections (*Ashna-i ba Bunyad* 1985, 48), while the painting section carries out a variety of activities, including creating paintings of martyrs' faces and working collaboratively with other foundations and organizations to promote the representation of martyrs and place them on walls (*Ashna-i*

Figure 11.9 Mural of Sayyid 'Abbas Musawi, *Maidan-i Filistin* (Palestine Square), Tehran, 2005.

ba Bunyad 1985, 60). By delineating carefully its division of labor, the Martyrs' Organization has effectively produced the largest and most widespread program of public art in Iran, whose goal revolves primarily around the promotion of martyrs fighting for Islam.

Images of martyrs like Musawi extol martyrdom as a "good deed," a sacred duty in the way of God, and a voluntary, conscious, and selfless action. It is precisely through the afflatus and promulgation of self-sacrifice that Iran finds its closest pictorial muse and political cohort in Palestinian and Lebanese martyrs, motivated at its source by a deep and emotional yearning to liberate consecrated sites. In other words, the sufferer for a cause has for his ultimate cause Jerusalem.

The connection between individual martyrdom—the ultimate act of political self-determination and the breaking loose from the shackles of deprivation—finds a parallel in the liberation of Islam's holiest shrines, which appear in another mural bordering Palestine Square (Figure 11.10). Here, a united Muslim military force attempts to bring down a colossal eagle (the United States) embracing the "Zionist" grip on the Dome of the Rock in Jerusalem, Saddam's occupation of the Shrine of Imam Husayn in Karbala, and Saudi Wahhabi control of the Ka'ba in Mecca. The mural vehemently condemns Islamic puppet regimes entrapped in the malignancy of U.S. foreign policy, as well as their desecration of Islamic holy sites. Furthermore, it

Figure 11.10 The Ensnaring of Holy Sites, *Maidan-i Filistin* (Palestine Square), Tehran, 2005.

also encourages military action, spurred by Iranian zeal, against these forces of evil—such exploits bring the fruits of martyrdom, so clearly endorsed in the mural of Musawi immediately above.

Palestine Square provides the home turf for the enactment of the visionary emancipation and symbolic invasion of Jerusalem, as echoed in Khomeini's declaration: "It is a duty of the proud nation of Iran to harness the interests of America and Israel in Iran and invade them" (Khomeini 1994, 130). The murals certainly offer a visual counter-offensive, a local invasion of sorts, through allowing a deluge of graphic images to enter into a continuous discourse with contemporary events. The inclusion of the Dome of the Rock in both murals transforms the building from a commemorative structure into the essential landmark of global tyranny and subjugation, remedied in due course through collective military action and personal altruism.

A mural north of Palestine Square on Modarres Highway echoes these same themes (Figure 11.11). It depicts a youth screaming in agony upon the death of his friend or family member, who is wrapped in a white burial shroud below which red tulips take root and spring to life, a motif evocative of the Martyrs' Organization logo. This motif of the life-giving blood of the martyr is summarized vividly in the conviction of the time, best described in Motahheri's words:

Figure 11.11 Mural of a Palestinian Martyr and the Dome of the Rock, Modarres Highway, Tehran, 2005.

At no time is the blood of a martyr wasted. It does not flow into the ground. Every drop of it is turned into hundreds of thousands of drops, nay into tons of blood, and is transfused into the body of his society. Martyrdom means the transfusion of blood into a society, especially into a society suffering from anemia. It is the martyr who infuses fresh blood into the veins of society.

(Motahheri 1986, 136)[29]

This lifeblood is not just the corollary of a selfless act, but the creation of sustained, collective fervor and unremitting commitment to a cause greater than physical existence.

On the left-hand side of the mural, Khamenei preaches with his finger raised upwards as an angelic Khomeini observes the scene from an opening in the sky. In the middle ground, an accurate representation of the Dome of the Rock evokes Palestine. At the top, a sentence ascribed to Khamenei proclaims in Persian and in English translation: "The Islamic Community will always stand by the side of Palestinians and against their enemies."

The Persian inscription does not correspond entirely to the English. The Persian expression "community of Imam Khomeini" has been abstracted into the "Islamic Community" in the English translation. For the international audience, Khomeini's name has been omitted in favor of a sort of pan-Islamism, although the Persian-speaking community would understand that here Khomeini's community is synonymous with the Muslim world at large. The expression "Islamic Community" appeals to those Muslims outside of Iran's borders who would object to the overtly Shi'i message of the mural and Khomeini's claims of being the principal leader of the global Islamic cause. The use of several languages attempts to put Khomeini's assertion that "we shall export our revolution to the whole world" into full effect (Khan 2004, 154).

This intentional slip in translation probably reveals a compromise between the mural's two sponsoring organizations, the Martyrs' Organization and the Palestinian Solidarity Organization. Their two logos appear on the mural: on the right, the Martyrs' Organization's and on the left, and slightly hidden in the batch of red tulips, the Palestinian Solidarity Organization's, whose emblem includes an abstract representation of the Dome of the Rock and its title in both Arabic and Persian (Figure 11.12). To my knowledge, this is the only mural in Tehran that was commissioned as a joint effort, and this fact reveals why certain rhetorical concessions were in order.

The mural also speaks to two different audiences, the domestic and the international, through the use of Persian and English. However, one message which remains unambiguous in the verbal and iconographic make-up of the mural is that the supreme religious guides of Iran (Khomeini and his successor Khamenei) must serve as the inspired leaders of Muslims worldwide—who, like the besieged Palestinians, must strive to free themselves from the imperialist occupation of world powers. In less flattering terms, as Behrouz Souresrafil states in his book *Khomeini and Israel*, the Ayatollah wanted to cultivate Islamic solidarity at the same time as he called for the obliteration of the State of Israel:

> Khomeini and his followers have used the slogan of the annihilation of Israel as a means to benefit from the religious feelings of the Iranian masses and to cash in on so-called "Islamic Solidarity." In this respect, they have surpassed and outdone most of the Arab countries, neighbors of Israel, and even Palestinian organizations.
>
> (Souresrafil 1988, 127)

In this contest for rousing Islamic sentiment, the Dome of the Rock becomes the contemporary marker of the aspired unity of the Muslims.

Another mural that makes use of the Dome of the Rock and the figure of Khomeini appears on a tall building on 'Abbas Abad Street in southern Tehran (Figure 11.13). It represents him as a physical appendage growing almost organically out of the masses present at the Holy Sanctuary of Jerusalem. Emerging like a giant and connected by his clothing to those below him, he waves victoriously to the crowds. The colors blue, black, and yellow,

Figure 11.12 Logo of the Palestinian Solidarity Organization, Modarres Highway, Tehran, 2005.

which serve almost as short-hand abstractions of the hues of the Dome of the Rock, dominate the painting and lend it a journalistic feel.

Turning to a 1987 publication entitled *Téhéran: Capitale Bicentennaire* (Adle and Hourcade 1992, 128), we can imagine what the mural looked like more than seventeen years ago (Figure 11.14). The book's illustration is revealing in several ways: first and foremost, the original composition included the *takbir* ("Allahu Akbar" or God is Great) in the now empty area taken over by the sky, brushed with serrated blue strokes. The second small detail barely catches our eye, but might suggest some interesting dynamics between the many Tehran organizations that vie for infomural space in the capital city. In the original painting, the remaining word *mustad'afin* (Arabic) or *mustaz'afin* (Persian) is visible in the lower-left corner. The word means "oppressed people," and the title of the illustration supports the identification of this work as a commercial for the Foundation of the Oppressed People.

This organization is the *Bunyad-i Mostaz'afan va Janbazan* (Foundation of the Oppressed and Disabled People), founded in 1979 with the Shah's

Figure 11.13 Ayatollah Khomeini and the Dome of the Rock, 'Abbas Abad Street, Tehran, 2005.

confiscated property and monies. By 1989, it took over the responsibility of managing the welfare of persons disabled by the Iran–Iraq War. Today, it pursues charitable works, establishes institutions catering to those in need, and, just like the Martyrs' Organization, is a real economic force in Iran. It has a yearly budget of more than $10 billion (that is, 10 percent of the Iranian governmental budget) and has 200,000 employees in many business areas.[30] Over the past few years, however, it has begun consolidating its holdings and diminishing its size by selling shares of some of its companies and real-estate.

The mural of Khomeini at the Dome of the Rock, initially commissioned by the Foundation of the Oppressed People, may well have been painted on one of the Foundation's buildings that was either sold or donated to the Institute for the Compilation and Publication of Imam Khomeini's works (*Mu'asasa-yi Tanzim va Nashr-i Asar-i Hazrat-i Imam Khomeini*), thus showing that the new owner saw it fit to alter the mural according to its own objectives.

The choice of Khomeini emerging as the quasi-biological leader of all oppressed people and occupied lands essentially symbolized by the Palestinians

Figure 11.14 Ayatollah Khomeini and the Dome of the Rock, 'Abbas Abad Street, Tehran, c.1992.

and the Dome of the Rock seems a natural choice for both foundations' visual propaganda. The Foundation of the Oppressed People may have used this mural to suggest that all the "tyrannized and downtrodden people of the world" (Khomeini 1994, 17) must rise up against despots, much like the triumphant Ayatollah and his Islamic Revolution. It also implies that all Muslims must choose their own destiny, with the Iranians at the forefront of rallying the Muslims to defend Islam's sacred land. This kind of populist message and imagery directed to the downtrodden masses and deprived classes was Khomeini's way of promising that whoever fights oppression will indeed "inherit the world" (Abrahamian 1993, 52–53).[31]

For the Institute as well, the mural communicates in a visual manner the Ayatollah's thoughts and writings on Palestine. Khomeini made it clear until the day of his death that all Muslims must unite and combat western imperialism; his last will, published by the Institute itself, calling on them to unite: "Oh you oppressed masses of the world, you Muslim countries and Muslims, rise to your feet and get your dues with your teeth and claws, defying the noisy propaganda of the superpowers" (Abrahamian 1993, 62). The mural, like Khomeini's many writings, constitutes a form of galvanization through visual counter-propaganda that uses the recyclable imagery of the Dome of the Rock.

Conclusion

There are many other murals in Tehran that depict the Dome of the Rock with Khomeini and/or Khamenei or in combination with a Palestinian, Lebanese, or Iranian martyr. These murals all draw on the religious correlation between martyrdom and freedom from oppression. Whether the martyr perished in the Islamic Revolution, the Iran–Iraq War, or in an uprising against Israel, he typically is experienced as "a ritual of purification that leads to perfection" (Butel 2002, 305). He becomes the embodiment of deliverance from iniquity and a symbol of generosity to humankind, as well as the ultimate and irrevocable refutation of repression. The Iranian concept of *shahadat-talabi*, that is, the seeking of martyrdom or the facing of great obstacles, embraces both aspects of this belief.

Martyrdom is a poignant act of liberation from the chains of depravity. During the Republican period in Iran, it became intimately connected with its closest architectonic equivalent, the Dome of the Rock. In posters,[32] billboards, maquettes, murals, and other materials, the monument provided an evocative pictogram of a society's aborted hopes. In paintings as well, such as in Iraj Iskandari's *Starless Night* (*Shab bi-Sitara*), the monument becomes synonymous with the community's martyred soul (Figure 11.15).[33] The Islamic body, its hand fettered by barbed wire, can only survive through the pumping of lifeblood to its beating heart. The blood of martyrdom feeds that nucleus, just as it nourishes hope and marshals unison to free the Dome of the Rock. Khomeini, his followers, and Iranian institutions played a

Figure 11.15 Starless Night (Shab bi-Sitara) by Iraj Iskandari, c. 1980.

major role in bringing Jerusalem back into the hearts of Muslims all over the world.

Khomeini and Iranian government institutions like the IRGC, the Construction Jihad, the Martyrs' Organization, the Institute, and the Foundation of the Oppressed People did so by several mechanisms, most especially by mediating the linguistic with the visual. By using visual materials available in the public realm, formal bodies of government and high-ranking leaders in Iran employ demagogic art forms to promote Iran's official and universalist vision of Islam. As Khomeini himself noted, murals and public art in general are just like ritual ceremonies or pilgrimages in that they are intended to "cement brotherhood among Muslims" (Khomeini 1994, 41).

According to Iranian leaders and the murals they sponsored, the Dome of the Rock was the strongest adhesive for a collective Islamic identity, a symbol that could break through sectarian lines. It became the irreplaceable "core value" for the entirety of the Muslim world (Khan 2004, 103). As the emblem of the victory of the underprivileged and the freedom of the Islamic World, Iranian murals that included the Dome of the Rock became a kind of jihad for martyrdom, political authority, reconstruction, urban beautification, and popular mobilization—that is, a selling of ideology in pictorial form both at home and overseas. These many constructs and uses of Jerusalem in the public art of modern Iran arose through calculated and collaborative efforts between painters, mural artists, politicians, and foundations, working together to define the symbolic role(s) of the Islamic Holy City in Iranian domestic and international politics.

Notes

1 This study forms a part of the author's ongoing book project *The Art of Martyrdom in Modern Iran*.

2 For a discussion of Jerusalem's position in Islamic history, see Chapter 6 by Suleiman Ali Mourad.

3 For studies on the Dome of the Rock, see Rabat 1989, Raby 1992, Grabar 1996, and Grabar and Nuseibeh 1996.

4 See, for example, Muhyi Lari's *Futuh al-Haramayn*, which includes representations of Jerusalem after a number of paintings of Mecca, Medina, and various sites associated with pilgrimage rituals. For an example see New York Public Library, Turk ms. 2, in Schmitz 1992, 42–46 (a copy of Lari's *Futuh*, c. 1558, probably executed in Mecca).

5 According to some Muslim legends, the Rock preserves the mark of Muhammad's footprint when he stepped on it to rise to the celestial spheres. Although there is no evidence that the Dome was built to commemorate the ascension or any other episode in Muhammad's career, the relationship between the building and the Prophet became indissociable in later centuries (Rabat 1989).

6 For a discussion of the merits (*fada'il*) of Jerusalem literature, see Chapter 6 by Suleiman Ali Mourad.

7 The terms "state" and "country" are never used in official Iranian discourse about Israel. Instead, the terms "occupational forces," "Zionist regime," and "enemy of Islam" are used widely in order to de-legitimize Israel's claims to political sovereignty.

8 On this prevalent concept, see Najafabadi 1983.
9 For a catalogue of Persian slogans chanted during the Islamic Revolution, a number of which appear in murals and posters as well, see *Farhang-i Shi'arha-yi Inqilab-i Islami* 2000.
10 In Iranian parlance, the Iran–Iraq War was never described as a bilateral conflict. Iranians considered the fighting an "imposed war" and their response a "holy defense." By coining idioms laden with symbolic overtones and appealing to enduring revolutionary fervor, official rhetoric transformed the war into an effective ideological vehicle for popular mobilization and recruitment: see Seif-zadeh 1997, 90–97.
11 Many of the "Surrealist" paintings of Jerusalem produced during the Iran–Iraq War appear to derive inspiration from paintings executed by Salvador Dalí (d. 1989), the most notorious champion of the Surrealist cause.
12 Mahmudi and Sulaymani 1985, 67. This publication provides a number of images of murals and posters produced during the Iran–Iraq War in Iranian provinces bordering Iraq. One of these posters (p. 166) shows an Iranian soldier breaking through the emblems of global domination—that is, the Iraqi, Israeli, American, and Soviet flags—toward the twin symbols of his own sovereignty and salvation, Najaf and Jerusalem. The poster includes Khomeini's saying, "the road to Jerusalem goes through Karbala."
13 The Jerusalem Force remains a very secretive constituent branch of the IRGC. It is believed that Iran's Ministry of Foreign Affairs (*vizarat-i khariji*) typically provides diplomatic cover, material support, and logistical assistance to members of the Jerusalem Force: see Khan 2004, 160–161; and Cordesman 2005.
14 Muhajiri 1982a and 1982b.
15 For the Iraqi artistic response, see Khalil 1991, 10–15.
16 On the *ta'ziya*, see Chelkowski 1979, 1–11.
17 Various pilgrimage (*ziyarat*) guides describe the ambulatory of the Dome of the Rock and the various stations of worship in Jerusalem: see Meri 2004, 72–74.
18 The Ottoman sultan Süleyman ordered the damaged mosaic work on the building's façade to be replaced with tiles c. 1555–56. These tiles were restored later by exact replicas made in Italy during the 1960s.
19 Persian: *har ka namaz sabuk shumarad az shafa'at-i ma mahrum ast.*
20 Persian: *namaz daru-yi takabbur ast.*
21 At the time that this article was being written, the structure was undergoing renovations, so its current form is unknown.
22 The shrine complex built over the imam's grave was most extensively developed first during the Timurid and Safavid periods (fifteenth to seventeenth centuries). Since the Revolution, it has been going through a process of unprecedented expansion, with the addition of a number of courtyards such as the Khomeini Courtyard, the Revolution Courtyard, and the Jerusalem Courtyard.
23 I wish to thank the staff at the Astan-i Quds Foundation for providing me with photographs and information on the Jerusalem Courtyard during my visit in 2005.
24 Persian: *Isra'il ghasib ast va har cha zudtar bayad Filistin-ra tark kunad.*
25 This graffito is usually coupled with slogans "Death to America" or "Death to Imperialism": see *Farhang-i Shi'arha-yi Inqilab-i Islami* 2000, 323–335.
26 *Isra'il bayad az bayn baravad.* It also appears on a poster in the Bihisht-i Zahra' Cemetery in southern Tehran, where scores of Iranian soldiers are buried.
27 Select murals are briefly discussed in Grigor 2002, 37.
28 The Martyrs' Organization has recently posted its history and its mission on its official website, http://www.shahid.ir.
29 Motahheri was assassinated in 1979, the year of the Revolution. He was one of the most versatile and prolific members of the Iranian religious establishment,

having written a number of works on holy war (*jihad*), jurisprudence (*fiqh*), sexual ethics, and women's rights.

30 For an economic analysis of the Foundation of the Oppressed People, see "For the Oppressed," *Economist* 328/7830 (September 25, 1993), which criticizes the Foundation and other Iranian organizations for not being accountable to the public, since they fall directly under the leadership of the supreme religious leader.

31 Abrahamian shows that Khomeini did not consider the "oppressed" people as those necessarily from the lower classes, but rather those who strive against domination. Khomeini derived this notion from *Qur'an* 30.39. For a further discussion of populist politics, see Bayat 1997.

32 For a discussion of posters from the time of the Revolution and the Iran–Iraq War, see Hanaway 1985; Cordesman 1989; Fischer and Abedi 1989; and Ram 2002.

33 Goordazi 1989, 23. Iskandari was born in 1956 and graduated from the College of Decorative Arts in Tehran. A number of his paintings were transformed into murals in Tehran.

References

Abrahamian, Ervand. 1993. *Khomeinism: Essays on the Islamic Republic*. Berkeley and Los Angeles: University of California Press.

Adle, Chahryar, and Bernard Hourcade, eds. 1992. *Téhéran: Capitale Bicentennaire*. Paris and Tehran: Institut Français de Recherches en Iran.

Aksoy, Şule and Rachel Milstein. 2000. "A Collection of Thirteenth-Century Illustrated *Hajj* Certificates." In *M. Uğur Derman: 65 Yil Armağani,* ed. Irvin Cemil Schick, 101–134. Istanbul: Sabanci Üniversitesi.

Ashna-i ba Bunyad-i Shahid-i Inqilab-i Islami. 1985. Tehran: Bunyad-i Shahid-i Inqilab-i Islami.

Bayat, Asef. 1997. *Street Politics: Poor People's Movements in Iran*. New York: Columbia University Press.

Butel, Eric. 2002. "Martyre et sainteté dans la littérature de guerre Irak–Iran." In *Saints et Héros du Moyen-Orient contemporain: actes du colloque des 11 et 12 décembre 2000 à l'Institut Universitaire de France,* ed. Catherine Mayeur-Jaouen, 301–317. Paris: Maisonneuve et Larose.

Chelkowski, Peter. 1979. "Ta'ziyeh: Indigenous Avant-Garde Theatre of Iran." In *Ta'ziyeh: Ritual and Drama in Iran,* 1–11. New York: New York University Press.

Chelkowski, Peter, and Hamid Dabashi. 1999. *Staging a Revolution: the Art of Persuasion in the Islamic Republic of Iran*. New York: New York University Press.

Cordesman, Anthony. 1989. "The Image and the Transformation of Iranian Culture." *Views* 10.3: 7–11.

———. 1999. *Iran's Military Forces in Transition: Conventional Threats and Weapons of Mass Destruction*. Westport: Praeger.

———. 2005. *Iran's Developing Military Capabilities*. Washington: CSIS Press.

Davis, Joyce. 2003. *Martyrs: Innocence, Vengeance, and Despair in the Middle East*. New York: Palgrave MacMillan.

Eickelman, Dale, and Jon Anderson. 2003. "Redefining Muslim Publics." In *New Media in the Muslim World: The Emerging Public Sphere,* 1–18. Bloomington and Indianapolis: Indiana University Press.

Farhang-i Shi'arha-yi Inqilab-i Islami. 2000. Tehran: Intisharat-i Markaz-i Asnad-i Inqilab-i Islami.

Fischer, Michael, and Mehdi Abedi. 1989. "Revolutionary Posters and Cultural Signs." *Middle East Report*: 29–32.

Goordazi, Mustafa. 1989. *A Decade with Painters of the Islamic Revolution, 1979–1989.* Tehran: Office of Culture and Art, Islamic Propagation Organization.

Grabar, Oleg. 1996. *The Shape of the Holy: Early Islamic Jerusalem.* Princeton: Princeton University Press.

Grabar, Oleg, and Said Nuseibeh. 1996. *The Dome of the Rock.* New York: Rizzoli.

Grigor, Talinn. 2002. "(Re)Claiming Space: the Use/Misuse of Propaganda Murals in Republican Tehran." *The International Institute for Asian Studies* 28: 37.

Gruber, Christiane. 2005. "The Prophet Muhammad's Ascension (*Mi'raj*) in Islamic Art and Literature, ca. 1300–1600." Ph.D. diss., University of Pennsylvania.

Hanaway, William. 1985. "The Symbolism of Persian Revolutionary Posters." In *Iran Since the Revolution: Internal Dynamics, Regional Conflict, and the Superpowers,* ed. Barry Rosen, 31–50. New York: Columbia University Press.

Khalil, Samir. 1991. *The Monument: Art, Vulgarity, and Responsibility in Iraq.* Berkeley: University of California Press.

Khan, M. A. Muqtedar. 2004. *Jihad for Jerusalem: Identity and Strategy in International Relations.* Westport: Praeger.

Khomeini, Imam Ruhollah. 1982. *Imam dar barabar-i Sahyunism: Majmu'a-yi Didgaha va Sukhanan-i Imam darbara-yi Razhim-i Ishghalgar-i Quds.* Tehran: Daftar-i Siyasi-yi Sipah-i Pasdaran-i Inqilab-i Islami.

———. 1994. *Pithy Aphorisms, Wise Sayings and Counsels.* Tehran: International Affairs Division of the Institute for the Compilation and Publication of Imam Khomeini's Works.

Krautheimer, Richard. 1942. "Iconography of Mediaeval Architecture." *Journal of the Warburg and Courtauld Institutes* 5: 1–33.

Mahmudi, Hasan, and Ibrahim Sulaymani. 1985. *Jilva-yi az Hunar-i Inqilab: Majmu'a-yi Yakum-i Mantiq-i Jangi: Kurdistan, Bakhtaran, Ilam, Khuzistan/Profiles of the Revolutionary Art.* Tehran: Culture and Art Center of the Ministry of Islamic Propagation.

Meri, Josef. 2004. *A Lonely Wayfarer's Guide to Pilgrimage: 'Ali ibn Abi Bakr al-Harawi's Kitab al-Isharat ila Ma'rifat al-Ziyarat.* Princeton: Darwin Press.

Milstein, Rachel. 1994. "Drawings of the Haram of Jerusalem in Ottoman Manuscripts." In *Aspects of Ottoman History,* ed. Amy Singer and Amnon Cohen (*Scripta Hierosolymitana* 35), 62–69. Jerusalem: The Magnes Press.

Motahheri, Morteza. 1986. "Shahid." In *Jihad and Shahadat: Struggle and Martyrdom in Islam,* ed. Mehdi Abedi and Gary Legenhausen, 125–152. Houston: Institute for Research and Islamic Studies.

Muhajiri, Masih. 1982a. *Islamic Revolution: Future Path of the Nations.* Tehran: Jihad-i Sazandegi.

———. 1982b. *Light of the Path: Selected Messages of Imam Khomeini.* Tehran: Jihad-i Sazandegi.

Najafabadi, Reza Hashimi. 1983. *Farhang-i Shahadat.* Tehran: Bunyad-i Shahid-i Inqilab-i Islami.

Rabat, Nasser. 1989. "The Meaning of the Umayyad Dome of the Rock." *Muqarnas* 6: 12–21.

Raby, Julian, ed. 1992. *Bayt al-Maqdis: 'Abd al-Malik's Jerusalem.* Oxford and New York: Oxford University Press.

Ram, Haggai. 2002. "Multiple Iconographies: Political Posters in the Iranian Revolution." In *Picturing Iran: Art, Society and Revolution*, ed. Shiva Balaghi and Lynn Gumpert, 90–101. London and New York: I. B. Tauris.

Roxburgh, David. Forthcoming. "Pilgrimage City: Representations of Mecca, Medina, and Jerusalem." In *The City in the Islamic World*, ed. Renata Holod et al. Leiden: Brill.

Schmitz, Barbara. 1992. *Islamic Manuscripts in the New York Public Library*. New York: Oxford University Press.

Seifzadeh, Hossein. 1997. "Revolution, Ideology, and the War." In *Iranian Perspectives on the Iran–Iraq War*, ed. Farhang Rajaee, 90–97. Gainesville: University Press of Florida.

Souresrafil, Behrouz. 1988. *Khomeini and Israel*. England: I Researchers Inc.

12 Negotiating the city

A perspective of a Jerusalemite

Sari Nusseibeh

I carry a Jordanian passport, and an Israeli travel document. I have them in my pocket actually—a Jordanian passport and an Israeli pass; so when asked what my citizenship is, and what my residence is, my answers to those questions have nothing to do with who I really am. I am not a Jordanian or an Israeli. I am a Palestinian. And clearly it is hard for a person in my position to try to describe this complex situation even to myself, let alone to other people (such as to passport-controllers at airports). So that is why I often tell myself we are living a life in Jerusalem—at least in East Jerusalem—which is maybe a little bit like the one described in the *Wizard of Oz*, or, perhaps more aptly, like the one described in *Alice in Wonderland*—that is, where everything is upside down.

I was reminded of the upside-down-ness of our situation when I traveled in 2004 to Catalonia to receive, along with Amos Oz, the sixteenth Catalonia International Prize. Oz gave me a copy of the autobiography he had just published. He is ten years older than me, but when he was growing up he lived just on the other side of the divide from where I was raised in Jerusalem. And so, although I describe my feelings growing up in Jerusalem, and put together my recollections and memories, with the sense that mine was *the* authentic story of the city and its people, he astonished me with totally "foreign" stories. His book is actually a beautiful rendering of *his* authentic version. It is full of his own emotions and aspirations and feelings and memories and those of people like him, who were growing up on the other side of the divide, just hundreds of meters away. And it was amazing for me to see how totally different these two worlds were from one another, how totally different the experiences were, though we were hardly two kilometers apart; he on that side, I on this side. Yet it seems we built our two worlds on a common platform, so to speak.

I should perhaps mention one other personal note, which is that I was born in Damascus because my mother, like many other Palestinians, had left the country during the 1948 fighting, when her family moved to Damascus. When I was two or three years old, we moved to Egypt. My father, who was a lawyer, was involved in the 1947–48 fighting (he actually lost his leg), and he had to move to Cairo to join the first Palestinian government that was established there after the declaration of the State of Israel. It was called the "All Palestine Government." My mother joined him there, and that is where I went after Damascus, and only after living in Damascus and Cairo was I able to finally come back to Jerusalem, a place where my family claims to be able to trace its history back many hundreds of years. The very first ancestor we have in Jerusalem, according to our narrative, is buried near St. Stephen's Gate, and he is from the time of the caliph 'Umar. He was one of the Prophet's companions from Medina, and he was appointed as the first Muslim high judge of the city; since then, family members have often assumed similar posts, either in schools or in the religious courts. So we have been there since those times. I mention this because I feel that it is important to add a personal touch to the discussion about Jerusalem.

In the Mamluk cemetery in western Jerusalem I can go and visit ancestors of mine who were buried there in the fourteenth and fifteenth centuries. Their names are still inscribed on the tombstones. And I am not alone in this. Just imagine, therefore, the weight that is on our shoulders as modern Jerusalem Palestinians, that immense history, as we consider our predicament in the city, as we look across to the other side and see ourselves facing the Israelis, as we try to think about our present and our future. It is an immense weight and it is a weight that I believe will continue regardless of what happens today or tomorrow or in ten years' time, because I feel that whatever happens in the political arena, or whether we have a solution in ten or twenty or thirty years or never, the fact is that people will remain there. Whether we are Arabs or Israelis, Jews or Christians or Muslims, we will have somehow to bear that weight together. I mention this because I want to add another dimension, namely that Jerusalem is not just religion, and it is not just walls, and it is not just God, although God is important and people are important, too. But it is also specific people, specific families, and specific demographic collectivities, as it were, that have generation after generation regenerated themselves and lived there. As in my case, although I was born in Damascus, I very much belong to Jerusalem. As in the case of my passports, I am not sure how it is that I belong, but I feel that my belonging there is as a Jerusalemite; it is really very basic and very essential and very much part of my history and identity.

I was telling somebody the other day that I feel I get reborn every generation. They told me, "What are you talking about?" I said, "You know I feel, somehow—I do not know how it goes or how it works—that I am not just living in the year 2007, but I have lived also ten years ago, twenty years, one hundred years, and two hundred years ago." I really do feel that. The reason is simply that I belong to a line that is very connected to this place, even though Palestinian nationalism came about only recently. I do not know who invented it or why, but it was invented only in the last century or two. When the grandfather or great ancestor of mine who ruled in Jerusalem, two or three thousand years ago, or four hundred years ago, or who was a high judge, or an architect, or taught at school was asked, "What are you?" "Who do you see yourself as?" he certainly would not have said about himself that he was Palestinian. He would have said that he was a Jerusalemite. And I think one has to say that people of Jerusalem, and especially the old families of Jerusalem—Arab families and certainly some of the Jewish families as well—belong to the city far more than they belong either to an Israeli nation or a Palestinian nation. These are people who belong to the actual city and for whom it is extremely difficult to exist without thinking of themselves as belonging to Jerusalem.

Having said this, I have to come back to address the question of how one looks at the future and how one sees it evolving. There's certainly some room for optimism about a resolution. But let me say that as far as the Jerusalemites—Arabs or Palestinians, Arabs or Muslims—are concerned, a solution that is comprehensive and conclusive and final between the Palestinians and the Israelis must be based upon an agreement over Jerusalem. In other words, in my opinion there is no way that anybody can conceive of a solution, a settlement, between the Israelis and the Palestinians that would somehow exclude Jerusalem. It was said, for example, that as far as Arafat was concerned when he was alive, the one thing he had on his mind, the one dream he wanted to bring about in order to be able to finally sign an agreement with Israel, was the dream of coming to Jerusalem and especially to the Haram al-Sharif (Temple Mount). Now it seems not only that this is on the minds of people like Arafat, but that it is something in fact impossible for *anyone* to forget as they engage in finding a solution. So what happened at Camp David, and why did the two parties fail to achieve a solution?

I heard from Saeb Erekat (the Palestinian head negotiator), who was with Arafat, that on the last day—on the day Arafat would be upset—it was the minute Ehud Barak raised the question of Jewish claims to the Haram al-Sharif area that Arafat knew that Barak was not going to give him what he considered the major concession he needed from the Israeli side. At that moment, Erekat said, Arafat's hands began to shake and he started to get up from the table where everyone was seated; Erekat said he had to grab Arafat by the arm in order to keep him seated at the table. He was loath to see Arafat's emotions get the better of him on this sensitive occasion. But Erekat says that it is because of this—the primacy of the Jerusalem issue—that Arafat finally pulled out of negotiations that might otherwise have reached a positive conclusion.

Why did Arafat want Jerusalem? Again, there is an explanation. Perhaps what Arafat wanted to do was to be able to go back to the Palestinian people and to tell them, especially the refugees, "Look, I have got you back this, I have got you back Jerusalem. This is a treasure for the entire nation. This is something therefore that you, as refugees, have to accept as compensation—psychological, national, political compensation for the painful fact that you cannot, in the context of the solution, return to your homes in Mandatory Palestine."

Arafat and the Palestinian leadership had been promising refugees since 1948 that they could return to pre-1967 Israel. This promise has never been withdrawn. Indeed, even in the meeting that took place between Palestinian factions in March 2005 in Cairo, to discuss a cease-fire, the parties only agreed on a *tahdi'a*, or a "quieting down" of the situation. When they came together to discuss quieting down as opposed to a formal cease-fire, the Egyptians presented a draft of a possible joint declaration, the preamble to which contained a general clause referring to the refugees and their rights. But it wasn't specific enough, and Hamas demanded that it be replaced with the well-known Palestinian formula about returning refugees to their original homes and properties. I should perhaps explain that we are talking about former homes and properties like those, for example, that my mother had before 1948, properties and homes to which the Palestinians will not be able to return (in my mother's case, simply because the house in question is no longer on the face of the earth). But in insisting on including this phrase Hamas was not acting out of line with general Palestinian sentiment. This is the major issue for the Palestinians, and at Camp David Arafat had this on his mind. The reason he insisted on settling the issue of Jerusalem in a negotiation deal with Israel was probably in order to be able to make the deal possible, and to raise as much support for it as possible among Palestinians. The only way to get Palestinians to agree to forgoing the implementation of the right to return to pre-1967 Israel was to view this as being in exchange for the return of Jerusalem to the Palestinians and for control over the Haram in particular. By Jerusalem I mean East Jerusalem.

This is how I expect things to evolve. When Oslo was signed, various important issues, including Jerusalem, were postponed until the final talks. The idea was that people would be able to get together to agree on some issues, over which there was very little disagreement, and in the meantime, over the years, build up trust and confidence between the two sides. When enough trust had been built, later down the road the two sides would be able to sit down and discuss the really hot issues, which include Jerusalem, the refugee question, and the settlements. Water was a problem, is a problem, but it is one that can always be resolved more easily because it is not psychological. But Jerusalem, refugees, and settlements are issues that, in addition to being observable and physical, are also psychological, for both sides. So these are the issues that have really been problematic, and they were postponed. But what happened in the years since 1994 is that instead of trust being built up between the two sides, the opposite happened. In other words, had we gone, in 1994, directly to a final agreement between the Israelis and the Palestinians, which might have included all of those issues, it is quite plausible that in fact a final agreement could have been reached then and there. Why? Because the Palestinians at the time were undergoing a major political transformation, accompanied by the euphoric expectation that peace and the end of occupation were round the corner. They really did think that this was the final agreement between themselves and the Israelis, and they were psychologically prepared to pay the price for it.

In reality, this did not happen, and trust broke down for different reasons we need not go into. The question now is, as we look at the prospects for renewed negotiations today, and as some people once again see positive signs (for example, in the Israeli government's disengagement from Gaza and the support that the Israeli public and the Knesset gave to disengagement, as well as the death of Arafat which some people see as a positive sign in the process toward a possible agreement)—the question now is: will the opportunity that might present itself be missed once again, as we missed it before? Are the steps that are unfolding now before our eyes going in fact to lead, one step after another, away from a solution rather than toward one?

Well, the future is open. Everything is possible. I do not think anybody can tell us what will, in fact, unfold. However, it is quite possible, for example, that the Israeli government might be aiming toward (and implementing step by step) the establishment of—let us call it "a security regime"—not an unstable security regime, but a very stable one. A regime that will safeguard the security and the long-term interests of the state of Israel; until such a time, conceivably, maybe ten, fifteen or even twenty years down the road, the Palestinians are more ready to accept terms for a settlement that they are not prepared to accept today.

Today we see the line-contours of the Wall looking as though they are very much contiguous with the 1967 lines. But nobody really knows how the wall will in fact end up looking. Nobody really knows exactly how much land the Wall will in fact be expropriating, and not only from the western side, which is the side we saw drawn, but also from the eastern side. According to some of the plans, the Wall will surround Palestinians on both west and east, and according to some calculations, Israel is thinking of retaining as much as perhaps 40, 50, 60 percent of the West Bank territory—territory that will of course be totally unavailable to the Palestinians, but will be used by Israel as an area from which to maintain general security control over the rest of the territories. Let us thus suppose that the following is what the Israeli government is doing in a series of planned steps: disengaging from Gaza, setting up a security belt around it, withdrawing from some population centers in the West Bank (40 percent of the population centers), allowing Palestinians to rule themselves in those centers, building tunnels and bridges for the Palestinians to move more easily from one population center to another, and in the meantime continuing to build in and around Jerusalem where the Jewish population is something like 200,000 people.

So let us suppose the Israeli government succeeds in implementing these steps, or in carrying out its plan to establish an overall, stable security regime (instead of a peace agreement with the other side). It augments the Jewish population in the East Jerusalem area, it strengthens its chosen settlements in the West Bank, and succeeds in imposing its overall security regime, thus managing to postpone a final settlement until a so-called more favorable time from the Israeli perspective. What, in these circumstances, are the Palestinians likely to be doing in the meantime? They are likely to be doing the same kind of thing: President Abbas first tries to bring onboard the rejection front factions, especially Hamas. But in exchange for joining ranks with him, those factions will most likely ask him not to go the full length of signing a conclusive and final settlement with Israel. They will do this because it would not be in their interest (not consistent with their declared ideology) to get a Palestinian government in which they share in signing such a final agreement with the Israelis—one which will involve the recognition of Israel and the giving up of various rights that they will want to remain up for the asking. In other words, we will have, or we already have, forces within the Palestinian political leadership community that will be putting on the brakes in order to prevent the possibility of getting to a final settlement. Likewise, as we hypothesized, we will have people on the Israeli side, in the leadership, let us say like the Likud Party, but also a leadership clique, which will also want to put the brakes on a final settlement, going only for an interim solution, or an interim security regime. So here we have an unblessed collusion of forces and interests. That is, while at the popular level the readiness to go for a final solution between the Israelis and the Palestinians, based on more or less knowable lines, may exist, the leaderships on both sides seem on the contrary to be compelled by their own calculations to head in the opposite direction. Now this, if true, is a major problem, even a tragedy. The question is whether this time the people on both sides can or will actually do anything about this or whether they will simply allow themselves, once again, to be made by their respective leaderships to miss the opportunity of a real peace between them.

Let me make one last point about the envisioned solution for peace. I think that all kinds of possibilities are open for people with the will and the imagination. For example, those who want an open Jerusalem can actually work to have an open city. If there are going to be two states divided by borders, it is possible to maintain an open city nonetheless, and have borders around the whole city. In such an arrangement, both Palestinians and Israelis could come into the city, then only Palestinians could go back into Palestine, and Israelis into Israel, unless of course they have permits to go into the other country. Things are possible. It is possible to imagine a united municipality, a municipality which will in fact adjust itself to specific functions that are not necessarily political, whether it is garbage, tourist issues, police, sanitation, and so forth. We could have, at the same time, two associated municipalities, each one of which would be centered on the cultural and national needs of one of the two states, and their citizens. In any case, whatever one does, if people want to take this seriously it is best, I think, if they try to look fairly far into the future, and try to imagine a Jerusalem which in fact will reflect their best dreams: what their loved city should have and look like. A Jerusalem that is beautiful, aesthetically pleasing, with institutions that reflect the people's needs in both societies. Working backwards, then, one can design a roadmap to achieve that dream.

I do not think any one who knows Jerusalem today can say that Jerusalem is a beautiful city. It is actually a very ugly city in very many parts of it. And the reason it is ugly is us, is the people, the Israelis and the Palestinians. One of the major reasons for the ugliness of the city is the competition between the Israelis and the Palestinians to build as much as possible in and around Jerusalem. The Israelis put as many Jews there as possible, and prevent the Palestinians from having permits to build. And the Palestinians build without permits, in as ugly a fashion as the Israelis. And so the whole city is actually developing into a very ugly place.

If one wants to negotiate Jerusalem, I think planners from both sides should sit together, they should look forty or fifty years into the future, imagine what kind of city would be ideal for both the Palestinians and the Israelis. What institutions, what zones, what demographic balances, what simple general layout, what centers of learning, Jewish, Islamic, Christian— for example, joint centers of learning, joint libraries—would make the city livable? Things have to be done, worked out together. In my opinion, to divide up Jerusalem and to create another situation like the one in which Amos Oz and I lived in separate worlds, is actually not doing the city or its citizens any good. I think the only healthy thing to do is, in fact, to somehow make sure that Jerusalem is united and united for the good of the people on both sides.

13 Jerusalem in the late Ottoman period
Historical writing and the native voice

Issam Nassar

According to archaeological remains, the history of the place now called Jerusalem, one of the ancient cities of Canaan, goes back some five thousand years (Franken 1989, 11–41). Located in a land at a crossroads, in the center of Afro-Eurasia, Jerusalem fell to the rule of most of the ancient empires that emerged in the region. Like the rest of the Syrian region, it was ruled at times by ancient Egypt, Assyria, Persia, Macedonia, Rome, Byzantium, and the various Muslim caliphates. In more recent history, it was at the center of several conflicts between European Christendom and the Islamic world (in the Middle Ages), of European colonial aspirations (in the nineteenth century), and of Arab–Israeli and Palestinian–Israeli conflicts (in the twentieth century).

Not surprisingly, this rather small town has generated an amount of literature comparable to that generated by some of the greatest cities in the world. In the nineteenth century alone, more than two thousand books about Jerusalem were published in Europe (Rohricht 1989). Needless to say, the writing of the history of Jerusalem became an important "frontier" where competing claims would be shaped into self-serving historical narratives. Different narratives do not reflect just different styles of scholarship, but often different visions of the present politics surrounding the control over the city. That the writing of the history of the city has become such a powerful tool at the service of political and/or religious interests warrants some reconsideration of how we think about the discipline of history itself. This essay will partially do that, but more importantly, it will tackle the more critical issue of the agency of the natives. Because the dominant historical discourse on the city, both in Israel and the West, views the modern period largely as the product of the encounter of the Europeans, or the Zionists, with the city, the native population is never seriously considered as an agent of change, if considered at all. Biblical imagination was heavily employed in this discourse, and in its accompanying visual representations, such as in photographs. I will offer a critique of this narrative, and at the same time suggest ways in which the agency of the native can be considered. By suggesting alternative sources for the study of the modern period, I attempt to place the natives at the center of the city's history in the age of modernity.

Writing history

Historical writing is generally thought of as concerned with events of the human past. Historians study documents, texts, art works, and other objects, subject them to analysis, theorize about their causes and connec- tions to other events/objects, and assign them meanings. The result is the construction of historical narratives that have an aura of authority and objectivity. In this process, few—if any—would announce that their projects of studying the past are connected to issues in the present. Instead, histor- ians insist on seeing themselves as truth seekers who examine facts and reveal their interconnectedness. That historians typically study documents and other textual sources, rather than real events, is rarely ever questioned. Similarly, that the accounts historians produce bear some weight on present events—at least in the sense that their narratives construct frames of refer- ence to current events—but are rarely examined in the context of current politics. Instead, the idea that *History*—as if it had nothing to do with the work of the historian—has an impact on the present seems to be universally accepted. While I have no quarrel with the idea that historical events do influence present events, I believe it is the narratives of the historians about past events that exercise the most influence. Consider the very simple fact that by highlighting certain historical events over others, historians create a sense of hierarchy in terms of the significance of those historical events in the mind of the public. In such a case, the line between history and collec- tive memory is often blurred, granting the latter the aura of objectivity that is often assumed to be an element of the former. By "collective memory" I am referring to the memory carried by a specific group, limited in space and time, which reflects a subjective experience of the group, or of a large number of its members, and is of immense importance in maintaining their sense of unity and cohesion (Halbwachs 1992; Confino 1997). In con- structing this memory, reality and myth are often intertwined. History, on the other hand, is thought of as a narrative constructed by the historian that, presumably, deals with factual past events.

The problem we face when we study most historical accounts of Jerusalem is that they are heavily based on religious myths turned into collective memories (i.e., communal memories and religious tales, which are largely produced, disseminated, and interpreted in the same manner in which myths are usually transmitted). Generations of Jews, Christians, and Muslims first learn about Jerusalem through the tales of their elders, stories they learn in religious (or Sunday) schools, and from reading the holy books (the Old and New Testaments and the Qur'an). The knowledge they acquire through these methods—which invariably focuses on a small fraction of the general history of the city—becomes, in their minds, the history of the city. Not only are they consistently presented with narratives that span thousands of years and have a strong sense of linearity (with a beginning, middle, and end) but, most importantly, they are presented with narratives that connect the city to their

communities alone. But each of these competing histories only holds together when seen in isolation from the history of the city itself. They necessarily exist in the realm of historical fiction, rather than of history. For only in
fiction and myth does it become possible for distant events to be causally
connected to one another. How else can we explain the example of the
modern Jew who immigrated to Jerusalem to settle down after two thousand
years of wandering? As one author has suggested, it is only "within myth
[that] the passage of time takes the form of predetermination" (Buck-Morris
1995, 78). The mere possibility of a history of Jerusalem that would include
all major historical events in a period—or that would, at least, cut aggres-
sively across the boundaries of the various communities' narratives—would
result in the collapse of all narratives currently considered authoritative.
Cornerstone events that stand in a relationship of causality to each other in
the narrative would be revealed as distant and unrelated. The very possibility
of a narrative that connects Israel's 1967 occupation of Jerusalem to King
David's conquest of the city three thousand years earlier, Britain's conquest
of Jerusalem to the life of Jesus, or Salah al-Din's defeating the Crusades to
modern Arab nationalism, would seem unfounded, to say the least. As
Michel de Certeau pointed out, by "combining the power to keep the
past ... with that of indefinitely conquering distance ... writing produces
history" (de Certeau 1988, 215). The written history of Jerusalem presents,
indeed, an excellent example of myths becoming history by way of writing
and transmission of memory—two necessary acts for the formation of historical imagination.

In this context, it follows that the written histories of Jerusalem ought to
be read critically. The discriminating reader must question the "ways in
which the production of [these] historical narratives involves the uneven
contribution of competing [modern] groups and individuals who have
unequal access to the means of such production" (Trouillot 1995, xix). The
power of such competing groups functions on more than one level. Prominent among them are the grand historical narrative, the sources used in its
production, and the historiographical method employed. The first level can
be seen directly in relation to grand narrative, its players, and the bulk of
the sources used. To translate this into an example regarding Jerusalem, the
narrative line might focus on one modern national group while downplaying
another, thus privileging the favored group's particular current political
claim. A narrative that chooses to start with Jewish history underplays the
long intervening periods of Islamic or Arab rule, and ends with the Israeli
annexation of the city after the 1967 war reflects—intentionally or unintentionally—the political interests of the Zionist movement and Israel, at
the expense of those of the Palestinians.

The second level in which the power of competing groups functions is
more indirect and relates to the sources that historians use. In his study of
women in Jerusalem in the seventeenth century, Ze'evi (1995) contrasted the
traveling ethnographies with *shari'a* courts' *sijills* [records] as sources for the

study of women's lives in the city. Although the fact that the *sijills* are local sources and the travel accounts are foreign is in itself significant, Ze'evi argued that the difference between them lies in "the relative degree of whatever shreds of reality each historical source contains" (Ze'evi 1995, 169). Both sources are biased, he argued, "but those local sources written for immediate, practical purposes, lacking a continuous narrative thread, seem to be a truer reflection of that dim distant reality" (169). This is a funda-mental point that often goes unnoticed. In the work of Yehoshua Ben-Arieh—an often celebrated historian of nineteenth-century Jerusalem—we find just the opposite, more common, trend. In his effort to prove that nineteenth-century Jerusalem was largely a Jewish city—and perhaps as jus-tification for the city's current political status—he uses statistics provided by a European travel writer from that period. Perhaps aware of the irony involved in granting more weight to visitors' accounts than to the Ottoman census, he argued that "the travel account of European tourists who came to visit the country and the Orient" in the first half of the nineteenth century constitutes "one of the most important sources for discovering facts about the settlements of Eretz Israel and Jerusalem" (Ben-Arieh 1989, 16). There is no doubt that the thousands of narratives written about Palestine in the nineteenth century constitute an important source of study. But the impli-cation that they should be used for information regarding the census of population, to the exclusion of the Ottoman records, is simply absurd. In fact, visitors' accounts are as informative in what they describe as they are in what they omit. And this has a direct bearing again on the question of accessibility to power in the writing of history.

The third level in which power functions in historical writing relates to the question of historiography. Trained historians frequently fall into the trap of Eurocentric historiography. Assumptions regarding the process of historical development are often central to the work of the historian. In the case of the Middle East, Palestine, and Jerusalem, many studies are groun-ded in what might be called "the modernization narrative" (Doumani 1992, 6). Based on the European experience between the sixteenth and the nine-teenth centuries, the assumption is often made that civilizations in "decline" eventually modernize and catch up—and that this would only happen under European influence, and in its terms. Proponents of this view see, in their narratives, the modernization process in Palestine as a process whose pre-history is to be found in the French occupation of Egypt in 1798 and its modernizing effect on Egypt. They also locate its beginning in the 1831 conquest of Syria and Palestine by (now modernized) Egypt:

> At the beginning of the nineteenth century, under the rule of the Otto-man pashas in Palestine (1799–1830), Jerusalem was a small, *traditional Middle Eastern town* ... But significant changes soon occurred in many facets of life. In the wake of [the Pasha of Egypt] Muhammad 'Ali's revolt against his Ottoman suzerain, Jerusalem fell without resistance to

the Egyptians in 1831 ... For the first time in centuries, order and public security were enforced in the city.

(Kark and Oren-Nordheim 2001, 26–27; italics added)

The authors then explain the changes that took place during the decade of Egyptian rule in Jerusalem, strongly implying that they constituted a milestone in the process of modernization and revival of the city. Their sentiment echoes that of another historian who stated, unequivocally, that "Egyptian rule brought a modernizing spirit to the administration of the country" (Wasserstein 2002, 27).

The modern history of Palestine in general and Jerusalem in particular starts, for other scholars, in 1882, that is, with the arrival of the first wave of Zionist Jews. This view—typically advocated by Zionist historians—has even been incorporated in the narrative of several Palestinian historians (Kayyali 1978). In all such cases, the agency is given to outside forces, the Europeans or their allies. The city's society, *traditional* and *Middle Eastern* as it was, was not considered capable of developing from within; it needed the good efforts of the Europeans.

In addition to relying heavily on Western agency and sources, many historical works on Jerusalem remain confined to, and conditioned by, a conception of the city as holy. Books on the history of the city abound in such phrases as Holy City, Holy Land, Bible Land, Endless Crusade, the hand of God, the City Jesus Knew, and the City of David. And just as nineteenth-century literature in English focused on Jerusalem's Christian history, more recent English-language historical studies—those written since around the 1970s—focus largely on the city's Jewish history. More important, however, is the fact that even studies that do not focus exclusively on Jewish history are likely to adopt—uncritically—the narratives and the periodization employed in the work of Zionist historians. A clear example of this is the use of the term "second temple period" to refer to the Roman period or the times of Jesus.[1]

Is it possible to write a history of modern Jerusalem without falling into the traps of religious, national, or sectarian histories? Is it possible to write a history of the city in modern times without having to rely extensively on Western travelogues, diplomatic documents, and the like? Is it possible to produce a history that is not grounded in the grandiose modernization narrative? And is it possible, in this day and age, to write a narrative that does not fall into the teleological trap that takes legitimization of one of the sides in the Israeli–Palestinian conflict as its ultimate goal?

There are no easy answers to these questions. But the point could be made that, to borrow Chakrabarty's words, such a project "refers to a history that does not yet exist." Henceforth, the task at hand is to be more concerned with the writing "into the history of modernity the ambivalences, contradictions, the use of force and tragedies and ironies that attended to it" (Chakrabarty 2000, 42–43). In the same line of thought, then, the task should not be to do away with all the histories that have been written so far, but to subvert them and to point to their historicity in order to write a history that gives agency to the natives. The people of Jerusalem are the city; they need to be taken into account in the study of the history of their city. Without them there would not have been a city, but perhaps a mere archaeological site. It does not necessarily follow that other voices and actors could not be incorporated into such history. It means, rather, that the agency of the natives as active subjects must become a part of any narrative produced—a narrative which would then be grounded in a multiplicity of overlapping modernities that shaped and reshaped the ways in which Jerusalemites lived and had their lives transformed. In the next section, I will examine the history of Jerusalem in the period of early modernization, utilizing sources from the margins in order to place the Jerusalemites at the center of the history of their city.

Memoirs are an important source for the study from the margins of the modern history of Jerusalem, and one that has been underutilized. Quite a few memoirs written by Jerusalemites from the late Ottoman and British Mandate periods have come to light only in the last decade or so. They include memoirs by a musician (Wasif Jawhariyeh), a member of the communist party (Najati Sidqi), an educator (Khalil Sakakini), an Ottoman conscript (Ihasn Turjman), and a lawyer (Salih al-Barghouthi), among others. Unlike the diaries and travelogues of European visitors, these records abound in descriptions of the transformations that were taking place in the city.

Another important but neglected source for the study of the history of Jerusalem from the margins is photography. As a powerful medium of representation, the photography of Jerusalem illustrates—through both its products and its own history—significant changes that were taking place in the city from the second half of the nineteenth century on. Early photography of Jerusalem—which was almost exclusively European and American—presented the city as a holy biblical location. Early photographers were not interested in photographing the people of the city and their lives, nor were they expected to. To their customers abroad Jerusalem was the city of Jesus, and it needed to appear that way in the photographs. Yet it did not take long for photography to establish roots in the city and become a local trade. From the Armenian Convent of St. James an entire generation of photographers would emerge who would eventually leave their mark on the city and its image. They were the students of Patriarch Yessai Garabadian, who, since the late 1850s, had been laying the foundations for a photography school within the confines of the convent. One of his students would be the first to open a commercial photography establishment in the city (1885). Grabed Krikorian, Jerusalem's first native photographer, was soon followed by a few others, such as his apprentice, Khalil Ra'd, and his own son Johannes. By the end of the Ottoman rule in Palestine in 1917/1918, Jerusalem had a number of photography establishments that functioned within, or just outside of, the Old City's walls (Nassar 2005). With photography came albums of family pictures. And with albums came a variety of visual biographies, structured narratives that tell about life in the city and about the subjects' own ideas of their lives.

In the next section, I will use memoirs, photographs, and personal albums to illustrate how such sources can enrich the historical narrative by adding important elements of the social history of the city, elements in which the natives play a significant and active role. Furthermore, these accounts from local sources within the city can illustrate how the process of modernity was sometimes internally instigated and how it transformed the city's social life.

Modernizing Jerusalem: the city in the late Ottoman period

Jerusalem entered the modern age as part of the Ottoman Empire. Despite its religious significance, the city did not occupy an important place within the Ottoman body politic, at least not until the nineteenth century. The Ottoman administration incorporated Jerusalem into the larger province of Damascus. Although the development of the Syrian province was never high on the list of priorities of the Ottoman rulers, Jerusalem received some special attention from the authorities during the sixteenth century. At the time, it had a population of around 16,000 people (according to 1553 estimates): a majority of Muslim Arabs—with a small number of non-Arab Muslims—and two large minorities of Christians and Jews (Cohen 1984, 16). Most Christians were Arabic-speaking Greek Orthodox, but there were also smaller numbers of Armenians, Copts, Abyssinians, Serbs, Greeks, and Syrians. Most Jews were members of the Sephardic community whose roots were in Muslim Spain, although native Arabic-speaking Jerusalemite Jews also lived in the city. Ottoman Turkish was the main language of government in the Sultanate, Arabic being the lingua franca in all Arab regions.

Despite its relatively small population, Jerusalem served as the central city for a large number of surrounding villages. With meat and spice markets, and a modest production of soap and olive oil, the city's markets catered primarily to the local population. The city had several professional guilds—about forty of them in the sixteenth century—including a bakers' and a millers' guild. It exported soap and grains to Egypt while importing textiles from it (Armstrong 1996, 325). With the decline in prestige and power of the Ottoman Sultanate, however, Jerusalem began to lose its special status. Far from the center of power in the empire and lacking economic significance, the city experienced a decline in living standards. Still, Jerusalem's economic life remained vibrant in comparison to that of other nearby cities and towns. The seventeenth-century Turkish visitor Elia Shalabi (Evliya Tshelebi) described Jerusalem as "a prosperous province" with some sixteen hundred villages (Tshelebi 1980, 61). Similarly, the account given by the Armenian clergyman Zvar Jiyerji, who arrived in Jerusalem from Istanbul in 1721, shows that the city's economic vigor did not wane in the eighteenth century. Describing the scene just outside of the Church of the Holy Sepulcher, Jiyeji wrote:

> As you emerge from the narrow door and out of the tumult, on the left is a cloth merchant's shop, belonging to a Greek man called Hanna. Next to him is the house of Sheikh Mustapha, then a barbers' shop, and then a sweetmakers' shop. Then there is a slipper shop, underneath a goldsmith where women sit without ever getting tired of waiting.
>
> (Hintlian 2001, 42)

He goes on to list the businesses he saw in the city, which included "shops of glass-vendors, locksmiths, barbers, and a coffeehouse" (Hintlian 2001, 42). By the turn of the nineteenth century, however, Jerusalem's population would shrink to a mere 8,000—a fact that suggests a more general decline in all aspects of life.

A dramatic transformation took place during the nineteenth century. The city grew outside the walls of the Old City and witnessed a substantial increase in population, as well as economic growth. It also saw law and order restored, which in turn made traveling to and from the city safer than ever before. These changes were the result of a combination of factors, the most important of which was the changing nature of Ottoman administration itself. As Jerusalem entered its fourth century under the rule of the Ottomans, a number of unsuccessful attempts by foreign powers to gain a foothold in the city began to leave their marks (Scholch 1993, 47–75). In 1826, the local Jerusalem notables led a revolt, which was suppressed by authorities in Damascus and Istanbul (Gerber 1985, 8). In 1831, Palestine and Syria fell under the control of Muhammad Ali, the Pasha of Egypt. During this period a number of significant changes in the administration of Jerusalem as a district were put into place. The Egyptian rule in Syria implemented a series of reforms similar to those already implemented in Egypt itself (Gerber 1985, 8). Changes in residency and property rights of non-Ottomans were introduced. European missionary groups and diplomatic representations were allowed to establish themselves in Palestine (Nassar 2006, 75). Britain established the first consulate in 1838 and was soon followed by most European countries (Verete 1970, 316, and Mana' 2005, 70). The Egyptian administration was forced to leave in 1840, and Jerusalem, as part of Syria, fell back under the sultan's rule. However, the new Reform (*Tanzimat*) policies of 1839 were in place by then. The Ottoman government upgraded the administrative status of the district of Jerusalem into that of an enlarged *Sanjak* (district) (1841) and subsequently into that of a *Mutasariflik*—a semiautonomous district within the empire (1874) (Mana' 2005, 70). The change in status translated into further enlarging of, and greater prestige for, the district (Scholch 1993, 241). Jerusalem became the second city, after Istanbul, to have a municipal council. Along with the establishment of the municipality came the establishment of courthouses. And in 1877 the city sent the first of two representatives, Yusuf Dia' al-Khalidi and Sa'id al-Husseini, to the newly established, and short-lived, Ottoman Parliament (*majlis al-mab'outhan*) in Istanbul (Scholch 1993, 245).

Obviously, these events reflect important changes in the city that are well known to many historians. Interestingly enough, however, this knowledge rarely affects historical narratives of the city, perhaps because it does very little to qualify the dominant historical imaginations and collective memories.

The city reached a population of over 50,000 by the end of the century (estimate based on Scholch 1993, 38). This growth was part of the general growth in the population of Palestine, and it included an increase in the non-Muslim population of the city. New Christian and Jewish religious institutions in the city also matched this increase. In the first half of the century, an Anglican bishopric (at first Anglo-Prussian) was established, and the Latin Patriarchate was re-established in the city (Greaves 1949, 328). In 1842, Protestant missionaries began to build the Church of the Messiah opposite the citadel. Shortly after, construction began on a Catholic church, the Church of the Flagellation, on the traditional site of the Second Station of the Cross, on the via dolorosa, in the Muslim quarter of the Old City. Similarly, with the growing influence of the Russian Empire, the Russian Orthodox Church established itself and built two major churches and a hospice for pilgrims. In 1898, Lutherans inaugurated the Church of the Redeemer at *al-Dabagha* market, close to the Holy Sepulcher. The German emperor Wilhelm II came to Jerusalem especially for this occasion. In the 1830s, Ashkenazi Jews began to arrive in the city and to establish a number of synagogues (Armstrong 1996, 350–351).

The nineteenth century witnessed the arrival of masses of tourists and pilgrims. Tourist agencies, such as Thomas Cook, were readily available to host and organize tours for the flood of tourists. Local translators (*dragomen* or *turjuman*s) were also easy to find. Increased security made traveling in Palestine safer than ever before, and the inauguration of the railroad service between Jerusalem and Jaffa, toward the end of the century, made it easier to move around. By the last decade of the nineteenth century, the city also had a branch of the Ottoman Bank.

The increase in safety, population, and tourism translated into economic development, a rise in prices, and the emergence of new crafts and trades. Artisans now produced mother-of-pearl and olive-wood religious artifacts. Pottery, engraved brass, and painted icons were among the many other products available in the tourist market. The printing industry also flourished during this period and saw the production of religious and tour guidebooks, most notably by the Franciscan press (Davis 2002, 12). As was mentioned earlier, in the early 1860s a workshop to teach photography was established by the Armenian patriarch, inside the compound of the Armenian St. James Church in the southwestern part of the Old City. By the mid-1880s, the city would have its first local photography shop, which would be followed shortly by a considerable number of competing studios in the area of Jaffa Gate. That area would also see a significant increase in the number of new shops inside and outside the wall, built by the Greek Orthodox Patriarchate and by private Palestinian Jerusalemite entrepreneurs.

By the middle of the nineteenth century, the growth of population resulted in the city's expanding outside the walls. New neighborhoods were established to the west, south, and north of Jerusalem. The first to move beyond the walls were members of the Jewish community. With donations from wealthy European Jewish philanthropists, such as Sir Moses Montefiore (the Sheriff of London) and Baron Edmond de Rothschild, two new areas, *Mea Sha'rim* and *Yemin Moshe*, were established west and northwest of the city. Wealthy Arab, Greek, and Armenian Christians also started to build new neighborhoods, such as *al-Talbiyeh* and *al-Baqa'a*. Muslim notables also moved outside of the walls, and neighborhoods such as *Sheikh Jarrah* were established north, west, and south of the city. Similarly, the German Templars—a millenarian Christian group—built their own neighborhood west of the city, still known to this day as the German Colony (Davis 2002, 25–33). The religious composition of the new neighborhoods was mixed, in terms of both belief and denomination, except for the newly-built Jewish areas. Similarly, the period between 1850 and 1860 saw several new buildings arise just outside the wall—the Protestant School on Mount Zion, the Russian Compound, and the Schneller Orphanage complex, among others (Kark and Oren-Nordheim 2001, 74). By the turn of the twentieth century Jerusalem was the most populated city in Palestine, with a population of over 60,000 on the eve of World War I (Ben-Arieh 1975, 262).

Once again, these details of the history of Jerusalem are well known to historians of the city, who do take the information seriously. The irony, however, is in the way such information is usually used. Population statistics and the expansion of the city are often taken as evidence of certain claims over the city in the present, rather than as source materials to study the history of everyday life of the city.

Toward the end of the first decade of the twentieth century, people in the city were already feeling the tide of the new technical age, with the introduction of gaslight and electricity. In the words of Wasif Jawhariyeh:

> The Notre Dame de France in Jerusalem [just outside of the New Gate] was the first to bring an electric generator into the city . . . we used to pass this building and see the electric lights coming out of the main entrance and windows. Luckily, the first time I was out with my father and brother Tawfiq spending the evening with Hussein effendi [al-Husseini, mayor of Jerusalem] and as we were on our way back, Tawfiq and I walking next to our father who rode his white donkey, we passed by the Notre Dame. As it turned out, my father knew the guard . . . and he asked him to show us how the electric light works . . . To our surprise and astonishment, the guard turned on a button that was there on the

wall, and immediately the light went off; and in no time, as he turned the button on once again, the light came back.

We kept telling the story to our mother and to friends for a long time, enjoying their astonished reaction. It did not take too long before this invention was spread to many other buildings in the city.

(Jawhariyeh 2004, 50; my translation)

We also learn from Jawhariyeh about the arrival of the first automobile—or "horseless carriage," as he called it—in 1912. The car belonged to some friends visiting a Mr. Vester at the American Colony in Jerusalem (Jawhariyeh 2004, 169). As in many other places, the arrival of the automobile caused a transformation of the city. Streets were paved and widened, and distances that had seemed great only a few years before became considerably shorter. Jawhariyeh gives us a glimpse of the drastic changes in modes of transportation when he explains that his father, Jirgis, had used a donkey to go to his work during the first decade of the century (Tamari 2000a, 8). In the various photographs of the city available to us from the first two decades of the century, we can see easily the transformation of the square outside of Jaffa Gate from a parking stand for horse carriages into a bus stop. Similarly, photographs from the World War I period show how streets inside the Old City were being paved with the use of hand-pushed street rollers. In 1914, the people of the city patiently awaited the landing of the first plane ever to come to the city. Jawhariyeh described that day:

I recall that in the summer of 1914, right after the Ottoman state entered the war, news spread in Jerusalem that a plane would land for the first time near the *Kazakhaneh* in upper Baqaʻa [to the south of the Old City] on the road to Bethlehem near where Talpiot is located nowadays. Everybody in the city was there on the appointed day, including government officials and the army. It was a very hot day, and water sellers must have made a good profit that afternoon.

(Jawhariyeh 2004, 169; my translation)

Khalil Sakakini also described that same day:

On the occasion of the arrival of the Ottoman pilots today we shut down the school ... The weather was very pleasant and tens of thousands of people gathered at al-*Baq'aa* neighborhood of Jerusalem looking to the north horizon from where they expected the plane to arrive.

(Sakakini 2004, 64; my translation)

Unfortunately, the plane did not arrive; it crashed on the way, near *Samakh* in the north of the country. But, according to Jawhariyeh, another one arrived a short time later in the same area.

Signs of the coming of the modern age were to be seen throughout the city: photography studios, printing houses, newspapers, libraries, and hospitals. Photographs from the period show a clock tower placed on top of Jaffa Gate. This tower, placed there on the occasion of the jubilee of Sultan Abdul Hamid in 1906, is an indication of the arrival of standardized time— an important sign of the age of modernity. Other signs of the advent of the modern period, or what Walter Benjamin described as "the new in connection with that which has always already been there" (cited in Buck-Morris 1995, 108), included the presence of new institutions such as municipal authorities, postal services, public space (parks), modern schools, and financial institutions. The diaries of Khalil Sakakini, like the Jawhariyeh memoirs, provide us with plenty of information about such institutions. While Jawhariyeh listed the various postal services that operated in Jerusalem in the prewar period, Sakakini used them in his correspondence with his friends and family during his yearlong stay in the United States (1907–8). In addition to the Ottoman postal service, five other countries, Russia, France, Germany, Austria, and Italy, established and operated their own postal services in the city (Jawhariyeh 2004, 165). With the emergence of Palestine as a separate entity under the British Mandate, the Department of Post and Telegraph run by the government would also be established. While working for the department, Najati Sidqi encountered Jewish workers who introduced him to communist ideas. He soon joined the Palestine communist party and set out for Moscow, in 1921, to study at the KUTV (Communist University of Toilers of the Orient) (Tamari 2000b, 51). Sidqi's experience is a good indicator of the arrival in the city of new ideologies that were internationally popular. It also tells us about the relations between the native population of Jerusalem and the new Jewish immigrants in the city. Describing his experience, Sidqi wrote:

> In the department we used to associate with Jewish immigrants either as work mates or through socializing. Many of us patronized a small café behind the building where Barclays Bank is located today. A Russian Jew of robust build, who always wore white trousers with a black shirt on top, with its buttons opened on the left shoulder, owned it. He used to shave his head with a razor to keep his head cool during the summer, and had a trimmed beard and huge moustache curled in the Russian manner. The waitress was a blonde and attractive Polish woman with reddish cheeks and blue eyes.
>
> (Sidqi, cited in Tamari 2000b, 53)

Najati Sidqi further elaborates about the role this café played in his intellectual and political life:

> In this café my mates and I would congregate in the evening, and socialize with its foreign customers. I recall from those days a Tsarist

captain with a white beard, who claimed that the Bolsheviks seized his ship in Odessa; and a young municipal employee whose father was Russian, and his mother was Arab; an immigrant painter who used to sketch the customers for a few piasters; an elegant lady who always dwelled about her lost real estate in the Ukraine, and scores of immigrant youth who would buy soda water to dampen their thirst in the summer.

(Sidqi, cited in Tamari 2000b, 53–54)

The coffeehouse as a space of literary and politically subversive activism is a theme we also find in the diaries of Sakakini. Salim Tamari discussed the rise of the literary coffeehouses, which, he argued, were places of social interaction and pleasure. Men from various social backgrounds would meet there to socialize, play cards, smoke the *narjile*, and listen to storytellers narrate Arab folk tales (Tamari 2003, 28). During World War I, reading newspapers aloud to an audience also became a common practice in these places. Wasif Jawhariyeh lists several coffeehouses that emerged in Jerusalem, in the period following the Ottoman reinstitution of the constitution, in 1908. One of those was *al-mukhtar* coffeehouse, just outside of Jaffa Gate. Khalil Sakakini was one of the patrons of this café, and there he and other patrons launched the nihilistic movement they called the Vagabond Party. As a result, this coffeehouse became known as "The Vagabond Café" (Tamari 2003, 29).

The coffeehouse scene appears to have had a significant influence on the cultural and artistic landscape of the city. The Jawhariyeh Café, owned and run by Khalil, Wasif's brother, in the new part of the city, near the Russian compound, served Lebanese-style *mesa*. We also know that it was the first to serve the traditional *Arak* with ice. The coffeehouse also featured a number of artists who sang and played music.

Diaries and memoirs demonstrate the multiplicity of connections that existed between the various religious and denominational communities in the city in everyday life. Jews, Christians, and Muslims lived side by side in the various quarters of the Old City, forming a larger community and regularly participating in each other's religious festivities, as described in the memoirs of the Christian Jawhariyeh. Of course, such a sense of one community rather than many is rarely to be found in the works of prominent historians such as Ben-Arieh, Armstrong, and Wasserstein, who see the different religious and denominational communities as being always in conflict rather than working in cohesion with one another. Describing the Ramadan night festivities in Jerusalem during his childhood period, around the turn of the twentieth century, Jawhariyeh wrote:

Often, my brothers and I would participate in the Zikr celebrations in the shrine of Sheikh Rihan—in the Sa'diyeh quarter of the Old City— next to our house, and we would participate in the chanting with the amateurs and the professionals. Then late at night, we would visit our neighbors, Sheikh Muhammad al-Saleh among them, ... and others, and spend the nights enchanted by music, particularly when I would take my musical instrument (*al-Tanbourah*) and would sing accompanied by my brother Tawfik. We would eat, drink, and enjoy the sweets and would be very happy.

(Jawhariyeh 2004, 77; my translation)

Similarly, he described the annual Jewish picnic (*shat'ha*) in the city in which "the Christian and Muslim Jerusalemite Arabs used to participate." The picnic took place in the Sheikh Jarrah area north of the Old City and constituted a visitation to what Jews believe to be the tomb of Simon the Just.

Twice a year they used to visit the tombs and spend the entire day in the shade of the olive trees. Most were Eastern (Mizrahi) Jews who kept their traditions, in particular, those among them who were Palestinian Jews. Musical string groups and choirs were always present. I remember Haim, the *Oud* player, and Zaki from Aleppo who used to play the *Daffy* (tambourine) and sing on a high pitch the *Mowashahat of Andalusia* ... with the Jewish public in the celebrations.

(Jawhariyeh 2004, 74; my translation)

The fluidity that existed between these communities was reflected in the new local educational practices in the city, such as the *Dusturiyeh* (Constitutional) school that was set up by Sakakini along with 'Ali Jarallah, Aftim Mushabbek, and Jamil al-Khalidi in the aftermath of the Ottoman constitutional revolution of 1908. The school offered an education that was free of the corporal punishment commonly practiced in the missionary schools in the city at the time. In an entry recorded on Sunday, January 1, 1911, Sakakini wrote:

A year and a half had passed since my new school was established ... The *Dusturiyeh School* is distinguished by several traits:
1) It brought together students from different religious and denominational background ...
2) The school functions on the principle that the pupils are honorable and not subservient, are in need of support to grow in pride not the opposite, and in need of emotional growth and freedom to be creative.

(Sakakini 2003, 347; my translation)

Jawhariyeh and his brother Tawfiq attended the *Dusturiyeh* school after their father took them out of the German Lutheran school (*al-Dabagha*), following a violent assault on Wasif by one of the teachers. Jawhariyeh described the education he received in his new school, listing the topics that he had to study. They included "grammar, literature, mathematics, English, French, Turkish, physical education, and *Qur'anic* studies for Christians" (Gelvin 2005, 103).

The entry of the Ottoman Sultanate into World War I in 1914 had a great impact on Jerusalem (and Syria in general). Diplomatic missions and missionary schools affiliated with the British, French, and Russian enemies were closed down and tourism and pilgrimage fell to a record low. Economic recession was only beginning. Things got even worse over the following years. Photographs from the period show the hangings of a few young Arab nationalist men who were not in favor of the war and of locals who avoided conscription. The unpublished diaries of Ihasn al-Turjman, a young Jerusalemite soldier who served in the military administration of the city during the war, illustrate the sense of solidarity that the people of Jerusalem had with their Ottoman rulers (Turjman 2007). A widespread famine during the war resulted in severe food shortages affecting the population of the city.

Close to a year before the official end of the war, the city surrendered to British forces. The surrender note, delivered to the British by the mayor of Jerusalem, Hussein al-Husseini, stated their desire to prevent the destruction of the city's holy sites that would have taken place, had the Ottomans opted to defend the city. General Allenby's entry into Jerusalem on December 11, 1917 marked the end of four centuries of Ottoman rule.

Photographs: a source from the margins

Memoirs and photographs from the time show Ottoman Jerusalem as a city open to all and accessible to anybody within the Ottoman world and beyond. They illustrate how modernity and change affected everyday life. They also speak to the way Jerusalemites related to each other and to their city. Far from suggesting a future of contestation and division, they depict a city of three faiths, a city of its entire people—regardless of communal affiliations. They also show the transformation of the city and its life as a byproduct of local events and developments, that is, as the result of administrative and socioeconomic changes in the city and in the Ottoman Empire at large.

Because these changes did not always bear fruit immediately, they were, and continued to be, mistakenly ignored by subsequent rulers. Thus, one finds British, Jordanian, and Israeli rulers taking turns as self-proclaimed agents of modernization in the city. Tracing the roots of change and development back to the Ottoman period and to people and events within the city enables us to reconsider the issue of agency in the process of modernization the city.

I would like to end by looking into history through a photograph. Figure 13.1 shows a photograph of the surrender of Jerusalem to the British, a rather famous image. It is one of the pictures in the albums of Wasif

Figure 13.1 The surrender of Jerusalem to British officers, December 9, 1917.

Jawhariyeh, and it was taken by one of the photographers of the American Colony in Jerusalem on December 9, 1917. It appears in a number of books about World War I, with captions that invariably refer to the surrender and name the two British officers depicted. A fortuitous example of simultaneous, nonintersecting histories—which effortlessly brings home the point I have been trying to make, if from the opposite direction. The photograph in question appears in Jawhariyeh's album with a list of the names and positions of everyone in the picture—everyone, that is, except for the two British officers. He writes about being with his brother and mother at his older sister's house near the YMCA, and he lists the names of those who were with them that day, many of them soldiers who had abandoned their positions. Then, continuing his relation of daily events, he talks about the surrender and the accompanying picture. His narrative and comment on the photograph is a striking and unintentional counterpart to the prevailing narrative in the West, and it reminds us of the city's people and of their lives during that historic moment. It provides us with a precious opportunity to bridge nonintersecting histories and incorporate the voice of Jerusalemite life into history.

Note

1 See, for instance, the works of popular historians like Martin Gilbert and Karen Armstrong.

References

Armstrong, Karen. 1996. *Jerusalem: One City, Three Faiths*. New York: Alfred A. Knopf.

Asali, K. J., ed. 1989. *Jerusalem in History*. England: Scorpion Publishing.

Al-Barghouti, Omar Saleh. 2001. *Al Marahel*. Ed. Rafif al-Barghouti. Beirut and Amman: al Mu'assasah al Arabiyya LilDirasat wal Nashr.

Ben-Arieh, Yehoshua. 1989. *Jerusalem in the Nineteenth Century*. Tel-Aviv: MOD Books.

Buck-Morris, Susan. 1995. *The Dialectics of Seeing: Walter Benjamin and the Arcades Project*. Cambridge, MA: MIT Press.

Chakrabarty, Dipesh. 2000. *Provincializing Europe: Postcolonial Thought and Historical Difference*. Princeton and Oxford: Princeton University Press.

Cohen, Amnon. 1984. *Jewish Life Under Islam: Jerusalem in the Sixteenth Century*. Cambridge, MA: Harvard University Press.

Confino, Alon. 1997. "Collective Memory and Cultural History: Problems of Method." *American Historical Review* 102.5: 1386–1403.

Davis, Rochelle. 2002. "Ottoman Jerusalem: The Growth of the City Outside the Walls." In *Jerusalem 1948: The Arab Neighbourhoods and their Fate in the War*, ed. Salim Tamari, 10–29. Jerusalem: Institute of Jerusalem Studies.

de Certeau, Michel. 1988. *The Writing of History*. Trans. Tom Conley. New York: Columbia University Press.

Doumani, Beshara B. 1992. "Rediscovering Ottoman Palestine: Writing Palestinians into History." *Journal of Palestine Studies* 21.2: 5–28.

Franken, H. J. 1989. "Jerusalem in the Bronze Age: 3000–1000 BC." In Asali 1989, 11–41. Essex: Scorpion Publishing.

Gelvin, James. 2005. *The Modern Middle East: A History.* New York and Oxford: Oxford University Press.

Gerber, Haim. 1985. *Ottoman Rule in Jerusalem, 1890–1914.* Berlin: Klaus Schwarz Verlag.

Greaves, R. W. 1949. "The Jerusalem Bishopric, 1841." *English Historical Review* 64: 328–352.

Halbwachs, Maurice. 1992. *On Collective Memory.* Trans. and ed. Lewis Coster. Chicago: University of Chicago Press.

Hintlian, George. 2001. "Mapping a Pilgrimage: The Accounts of an Armenian's Travels to the Holy Land." *Jerusalem Quarterly File* 14 (Autumn): 37–48.

Jawhariyeh, Wasif. 2004. *Ottoman Jerusalem in the Jawhariyeh Memoirs.* Ed. Salim Tamari and Nassar Issam. Beirut: Institute for Palestine Studies. (In Arabic.)

——. 2005. *British Mandate Jerusalem in the Jawhariyeh Memoirs, 1918–1948.* Ed. Issam Nassar and Salim Tamari. Jerusalem: Institute of Jerusalem Studies. (In Arabic.)

Kark, Ruth, and Michal Oren-Nordheim. 2001. *Jerusalem and Its Environs: Quarters, Neighborhoods, Villages, 1800–1948.* Israel Studies in Historical Geography. Detroit: Wayne State University Press.

Kayyali, ʿAbd al-Wahhab. 1978. *Palestine: A Modern History.* London: Croom Helm.

Manaʿ, Adel. 2005. "Was Jerusalem the Capital of Late Ottoman Palestine?" In *Pilgrims, Lepers & Stuffed Cabbage: Essays on Jerusalem's Cultural History,* ed. Issam Nassar and Salim Tamari, 62–78. Jerusalem: Institute of Jerusalem Studies.

Miron, Dan. 1996. "Depictions in Modern Hebrew Literature." In *The City of the Great King,* ed. N. Rosovsky, 241–288. Cambridge: Harvard University Press.

Nassar, Issam. 2005. *Snapshots: Early Local Photography in Palestine, 1850–1948.* Beirut: Kutub.

——. 2006. *European Portrayals of Jerusalem: Religious Fascinations and Colonialist Imaginations.* Lewiston: Edwin Mellen.

Rohricht, Reinhold. 1989. *Bibliotheca Geographica Palestinae.* London: John Trotter Reprints.

Sakakini, Khalil. 2003. *The Diaries of Khalil Sakakini, Book One: New York, Sultana and Jerusalem, 1907–1912.* Ed. Akram Musalam. Ramallah: Khalil Sakakini Center and Institute of Jerusalem Studies. (In Arabic.)

——. 2004. *The Diaries of Khalil Sakakini, Book Two: The Orthodox Rebellion, the Great War and the Damascene Exile.* Ed. Akram Musalam. Ramallah: Khalil Sakakini Center and Institute of Jerusalem Studies. (In Arabic.)

Scholch, Alexander. 1993. *Palestine in Transformation (1856–1882): Studies in Social, Economic and Political Development.* Trans. William C. Young and Michael C. Gerrity. Washington, D.C.: Institute for Palestine Studies.

Sidqi, Najati. 2001. *Memoirs of Najati Sidqi (1905–1979).* Ed. Hana Abu Hana. Beirut: Institute for Palestine Studies.

Tamari, Salim. 2000a. "Jerusalem's Ottoman Modernity: The Times and Lives of Wasif Jawhariyyeh." *Jerusalem Quarterly File* 9 (Summer 2000): 5–27.

——. 2000b. "The Enigmatic Jerusalem Bolshevik: The Memoirs of Najati Sidqi." *Jerusalem Quarterly File* 14 (Autumn 2000): 49–55.

——. 2003. "The Vagabond Café and Jerusalem's Prince of Idleness." *Jerusalem Quarterly File* 19 (October 2003): 23–36.

Trouillot, Michel-Rolph. 1995. *Silencing the Past: Power and the Production of History*. Boston: Beacon Press.

Tshelebi, Evilya. 1980. *Travels in Palestine (1648–1650)*. Trans. H. Stephan. Jerusalem: Ariel Publishing House.

Turjman, Ihasn. 2007. *Memoirs of an Ottoman Soldier in Jerusalem*. Ed. Salim Tamari. Jerusalem: Institute of Jerusalem Studies.

Verete, M. 1970. "Why Was a British Consulate Established in Jerusalem?" *English Historical Review* 85 (April): 316–345.

Wasserstein, Bernard. 2002. *Divided Jerusalem: The Struggle for the Holy City*. New Haven and London: Yale University Press.

Ze'evi, Dror. 1995. "Women in Seventeenth-Century Jerusalem: Western and Indigenous Perspectives." *International Journal of Middle East Studies* 27:157–173.

14 Jerusalem in and out of focus

The city in Zionist ideology[1]

Tamar Mayer

The symbolic importance of Jerusalem cannot be underestimated; for almost two millennia it has been the focus of the yearning of Diaspora Jews. This longing for Judaism's spiritual center has found expression in the Jewish liturgy and in poetry, where Jerusalem and the biblical land of Zion are often synonymous. Given this intense spiritual connection, we might have expected that Jerusalem would be crucial to the Zionist project. We might also have anticipated that this city, so rich in national and religious symbolism, would be the perfect choice for the capital. But the Jewish relationship to Jerusalem has a complicated and nuanced history. Only many years after the advent of Zionism did the city become the object of Zionist interests, the capital of the Jewish nation, and, finally, the capital of the state of Israel.[2] Not until 1967, in fact, did a united Jerusalem begin to be transformed from a sleepy, peripheral town to a more cosmopolitan city, suitable for the capital of a modern state.

The long history of debate about the centrality of Jerusalem to the Zionist project—and later to the state of Israel—reflects conflicting sentiments about what the city represents. So, too, discussions about making Jerusalem the capital city echo changes in Jewish nationalism and reflect pragmatic political choices that Jewish leaders have made since the late nineteenth century. In this chapter I will examine the shifting interests in Jerusalem and suggest that Jerusalem, like other Jewish national symbols, became important to the Zionist project when religious discourse entered the national debate, and that the history of this debate reflects a shift to the right in Jewish nationalism in Israel.

Zionism and Jerusalem

Zionism emerged in the later part of the nineteenth century as a reaction to the exclusion of Jews from the emerging national movements in Europe. A revolutionary and utopian movement, it sought to create a new national subject—the *New Jew*—as well as a new culture anchored in the Jewish homeland, a new language, and a new psychology in which Jews were no longer victims or national subjects of other countries. The *New Jews* would be the antithesis of the urban Jewish intellectual: they would be fighters, settlers, and farmers who would engage in productive work and govern themselves in the new homeland.[3] This hegemonic Zionist vision and ideology, associated with Labor and Socialist Zionism and ultimately with the Labor Party, was later credited with envisioning and implementing the Zionist dream for the homeland. Other elements—such as the Revisionists (later associated with the Likud Party) and Ha-Mizrachi (later associated with the National Religious Party)—had very little voice.

The early Zionists were consciously undertaking a modern project, and they had little interest in anything associated with the Old World. Although Jerusalem was an important symbol of the glorious Jewish religious past and enjoyed a unique status as the object of love, longing, and admiration among Jews, it represented the Old World and reminded the Zionists of the Diaspora Jew who needed to be transformed. Jerusalem's Jewish community (at the time, the largest in Palestine) was divided, ultra-Orthodox, and economically unproductive.[4] Its members (particularly those of European descent) lived off handouts from European Jews and vehemently attacked Zionism for spearheading the secularization of the Jewish community (Goldstein 1989). Zionist leaders, on the other hand, tended to ignore the city; very few mentioned it in their writings, and those who did were dismissive.[5] Even the Hebrew national poet, H. N. Bialik, avoided the theme of Jerusalem (Miron 1996, 243), and Ben-Gurion spent three years in the new land before he paid a visit to the city (Ben-Gurion 1925, 1971).

Jerusalem's physical and political geographies contributed to its marginalization in the Zionist agenda. In the mountains, far from where new immigrants landed, Jerusalem was not easily accessible, and its location limited opportunities for productive employment. In the 1920s and 1930s new immigrants were directed to the more desirable coastal region and even to lower Galilee rather than to Jerusalem. So, too, the Zionist leadership carefully calculated the possible ramifications of a Zionist presence in Jerusalem. Because the city was important to Islam during the Ottoman period and had been ruled by Muslims for more than 1,200 years, the early Zionist leaders, especially those in Russia, were careful not to have (and certainly not to voice) political plans for Jerusalem, at least until the first decade of the twentieth century (Goldstein 1989). Such plans, they feared, might spoil the real Zionist plan of settling the homeland and precipitate the collapse of the national agenda altogether. As a result, they came to Palestine with no real plan for building and developing Jerusalem (Aaronsohn 1989), and in fact they paid very little attention to it.

The city's sizeable Arab population was yet another factor in its marginalization.[6] Like all national projects, the Zionist goal of constructing a new home for the Jewish people focused solely on members of the Jewish nation. Any plan that involved Arabs, at least in the eyes of some segments of the Jewish national movement, would directly contradict Zionist ideology. Over the years several suggestions were made about how to deal with the Arabs of Jerusalem; for example, Ben-Gurion, in the early 1920s, thought that the fairest solution was to have two separate municipalities—one Jewish and one Arab—and a mutual committee to handle all shared business that could not be divided between the two (Ben-Gurion 1928, 1971, 340). In reality, however, Arabs were integral to the city and so, in the Zionists' view, an obstacle to an exclusively Jewish project.

The first few Zionist conferences failed to generate any policy regarding Jerusalem or, for that matter, any other urban center. In the first part of the twentieth century, urbanization directly conflicted with the ideology of Labor Zionism. The focus of this movement was on reclaiming the land through establishing, in the spirit of socialism, Hebrew (Jewish) communities, many of which were agricultural collectives. Although this ideology gradually changed, and Zionists eventually settled in cities, Jerusalem remained marginal to their program.

Zionist interest in Jerusalem began to grow at the beginning of the twentieth century, perhaps after some members of the movement recognized the paradox of claiming Palestine, but not Jerusalem, as a home. To that end, a special Zionist commission traveled to Palestine to survey land in the city for possible acquisition by Jews (Harel 1989; Katz 1989). A bank known as the Anglo-Palestine Company opened a branch in Jerusalem in 1904 and financed important educational institutions, such as Bezalel Art School. In 1917 the Zionist Commission to Palestine (headed by Chaim Weizmann) established its offices in the city. International interest in Jerusalem increased after World War I, particularly once Britain was granted the Palestine Mandate by the League of Nations.

The year 1917, writes Michael Hudson, "was fateful for the inhabitants of Jerusalem—both Arab and Jewish" (1990, 249). As the Muslims lost their almost 1,200-year control over Jerusalem and as Britain fulfilled its mandate, the city slowly lost its Arab character and became more European. The Arabs' loss was the Jews' gain. The Jews cheered the British conquest of the city on December 17 (an official holiday during the mandate period), which came only six weeks after the Balfour Declaration. They believed that the British control over Palestine and Jerusalem signaled that a Jewish state was indeed possible (Gross 1992).

The Mandate brought two important changes. First, Britain both claimed Jerusalem as the capital, from which it would implement its mandate (Roman 1989), and designated itself as the protector of the city's holy places. For the first time in hundreds of years Christians controlled the Old City and its religious sites; hence Jerusalem became the only city in Palestine that the British really cared about (Shavit 1998). Second, in the spirit of the Balfour Declaration, Britain's policies permitted, even encouraged, Jewish immigration into Palestine and therefore into the city. This policy brought about a dramatic change in Jerusalem's Jewish/Arab balance and set the city's Jews and Arabs, who for generations had lived amicably, on the road to collision.

The Jerusalem of the early part of the twentieth century was poor. Its supply lines were severed during World War I, it had no economic base, and its Jewish and Arab residents suffered severely from hunger and disease. Britain cleaned and paved the streets, restored the railway system to the coastal plain as well as from Gaza to Syria, repaired and updated the electrical and sewage systems, planted trees, and constructed public parks throughout the city. It also restored some of the old buildings and used them to house the police, courts, and hospitals (Shavit 1998).

The international attention focused on Jerusalem led to significant investments in its infrastructure: public buildings, educational institutions, and the transportation system. These developments, the Zionist leaders thought, would modernize the more backward *Old Yishuv* and the Arabs, potentially bringing them together. Both populations, however, resisted the change (Shilo 1989); they were suspicious of the Zionists' motives and feared the possible consequences. Despite a few Zionist achievements such as the construction of the Hebrew University on Mt. Scopus and the national library in Jerusalem—two very important projects that showcased Hebrew culture and its newness in Palestine—the city remained of relatively little interest to the Zionist community as a whole. Some Zionist organizations bought land in Jerusalem (Katz 1989; Roman 1989) and built new Jewish neighborhoods, particularly in the western part of the city, but they were not able to transform the *Old Yishuv*. The old and new Jewish communities remained segregated.

What interest there was in Jerusalem focused on specific sites. The Western Wall, for example, the most important historical relic in the city, had been a site for Jewish prayer since the Middle Ages and represented the pinnacle of Jewish history. In itself, the Wall had become the focus of Jewish yearnings for a homeland—and thus strongly associated with the Old World. In an attempt to connect the past with the present and to make the territorial homeland—specifically Jerusalem—relevant to the Jewish national movement, the head of the Zionist Commission to Palestine, Chaim Weizmann, tried to buy the Western Wall from its Muslim owners for £1,000. Jewish ownership of such a central historical site, he thought, would strengthen the Zionist movement vis-à-vis the *Old Yishuv*, the Jews of the Diaspora, the Arabs, and even the British (Segev 1999, 247). His attempt failed because the Wall was in the heart of the Old City and the Maghrebi neighborhood would have to be razed in order to allow access to it. Not for another fifty years would Israel conquer East Jerusalem and gain control of the Wall along with it (Lavsky 1989b).

Most Zionist activities and interests in Jerusalem, however, were limited to the western part of town, what would become known as "Hebrew Jerusalem" or simply the "New Jerusalem" (Paz 1994, 113). In the early 1930s, Chaim Arlosoroff, the head of the Department of State in the Jewish Agency, proposed to divide Jerusalem into an Arab and a Jewish section, each with its own council (Wasserstein 2001). The Arab section in his plan would include the Old City with its religious sites and the predominantly Arab East Jerusalem, while the Jewish section would include the western part of the city—Hebrew Jerusalem—along with Mt. Scopus and the Hebrew University, and the Hadassah hospital—all parts of the Zionist project. In other words, Arlosoroff's plan assigned the new parts of Jerusalem to the Jews and the old to the Arabs. In response to this and to the next several proposals for the partition of Jerusalem, most of which were based on the initial 1932 Zionist plan,[7] the leadership of the *Yishuv* expressed their willingness to let go of Old Jerusalem with its religious sites and its Jewish Quarter.

As the pace of immigration into Palestine intensified, however, it threatened the delicate social fabric in Palestine, particularly in Jerusalem. Although Arabs controlled the city, they feared that they would lose their political power, and in response to what they perceived as Britain's lax immigration policies for the Jews, they struck back. They mounted a general strike in Palestine and later incited what would become known as the Arab Revolt (1936–39). To try to relax the growing tensions between Jews and Arabs, and between both parties and themselves, in 1937 the British sent the Peel Commission to Palestine to study how to divide Palestine between Jews and Arabs. Their proposal, designed in the spirit of Arlosoroff's early plan, recommended a clear geographical division between Jewish and Arab areas, a kind of cantonization of Palestine. The Commission, however, also offered something new, namely, to remove Jerusalem itself from the control of both Jews and Arabs. It recommended that Jerusalem, Jaffa, and a corridor between be put under Mandatory British control,[8] an arrangement designed to protect the Christian holy sites in the city.

After much debate, Arabs and Jews alike rejected the proposal. Jews embraced the idea of a separate Jewish state, even if the price was the loss of Jerusalem and its Jewish population.[9] Indeed, this was the first time in the history of the modern Jewish nation that its leaders had taken an explicit stand toward Jerusalem (Golani 1998, 268). They could not, however, accept the small size of the proposed Jewish province, which would undermine the success of the Zionist project,[10] or the exclusion from the Jewish state of the New Jerusalem, with all its Zionist accomplishments. Jews were willing to compromise, but they would not give up their new neighborhoods, their commercial district, and the national institutions at Mt. Scopus, which by then had become symbols of Zionist modernization. As Ben-Gurion, later Israel's first prime minister, noted in his memoirs: "[I]f England wants an honorable solution ... it ought to give Jerusalem to us, *part* of Jerusalem" (1937, 1974, 238–39; my translation; emphasis added).

The Peel Commission's proposal also had an unexpected result. It forced the executives of the Jewish Agency to decide which parts of the homeland they might be willing to give up. Suddenly Jerusalem became dearer to the Zionist leaders. The most profound changes of heart, especially among public figures, were those of Moshe Shertok (later Sharett) and David

Ben-Gurion. For Ben-Gurion, Jerusalem had had no practical importance since it did not serve two of the most important Zionist goals of Jewish immigration and expansion of borders. In response to pressure from friends and colleagues (Golani 1998, 269), however, he changed his mind, at least publicly. As he presented the Peel Commission's recommendation to the Zionist Workers' Union in Zurich in July of 1937, Ben-Gurion noted publicly, possibly for the first time, that Jerusalem was far more than a modern city, that its past actually was as important as its present, and that the Jewish nation's past was indeed anchored in Jerusalem:

> The place of this city is in our distant past ... [A]s a political and spiritual center of our people and as a symbol of its unique and historical destiny; the precious relics of [our] glorious past are present in this city; the carving of the holy and admirable name of Jerusalem in the heart of the nation ... and the oath of allegiance to our holy city have been repeated by every generation ... over the rivers of Babylon ... until today, over all the rivers in the world; the repeated attempts throughout the days of Diaspora to return to this city despite the hardships and difficulties ... since the Roman conquest; the old Jewish presence has been rooted in this city for generations; the value of new Jerusalem [is] that [it] has become once again mostly a Hebrew city and contains sixth of the Jews in the land; the central national institutions have been established in this city—the Hebrew University, the Jewish Agency building, the National Library, etc. ... [And] all these make Jerusalem the focus of love, longing, aspirations, and hopes of the Hebrew people.
>
> (Ben-Gurion 1937, 1974, 358–359; my translation)

His change of heart marked a new pragmatic attitude toward Jerusalem on the part of the Zionist leadership,[11] which led them to offer an amendment to the Peel Commission's plan. In it they proposed that the Commission leave the holy sites in the hands of the British, but annex the new Jewish neighborhoods in the city (and Mt. Scopus) to the Jewish state. So despite Ben-Gurion's emphatic speech in Zurich in 1937, once again Zionist leadership indicated that the religious sites, the heart of the Jewish nation, could be bartered for a future Jewish state. The opinion of the Jewish community, of course, was not monolithic. Nonetheless, the hegemony of Labor Zionism—executives of the Jewish Agency—defined the Zionist project, and for their ideologues Old Jerusalem was still a liability. As was true of many other proposals, the Peel Commission's plan was never carried out, in this case because Britain entered World War II. For the duration of the war, the Partition Plans for Palestine and Jerusalem would remain on a back burner.

For twenty-five years Jerusalem served as the capital of the British Mandate over Palestine. During this period the Jewish population of the city increased by more than 160 percent (Amiran 1986, 24) and Jewish neighborhoods expanded. In addition to the massive housing projects that sprang up throughout the western part of the city, several new commercial centers appeared in the new parts of the capital. Despite this remarkable urban development, however, most of the important Zionist institutions continued to be located in Tel Aviv.

Future proposals regarding Palestine were modeled on the Peel Commission's proposed partition and internationalization of Jerusalem. As the international community offered alternative partition plans throughout the 1930s and 1940s, the Zionist leadership regularly voiced concerns about the fate of the Jewish population of (new) Jerusalem. It appeared that they claimed that it was not *place* that was important, but *people*. While this was an important concern, in the 1930s the Zionist leadership had already made clear its willingness to accept a two-state solution and to give up control of the historic remains of the Jewish past. Responses to all the proposals put forward until Jerusalem became the official capital of Israel in 1950 indicated the leadership's continued support for such a plan.

Concern for the Jewish people would be voiced even more loudly after the passage of the November 1947 United Nations General Assembly Resolution 181, which called for the partition of Palestine into a Jewish and Arab state, while leaving Jerusalem a *corpus separatum*. In reality, however, the Zionist leadership was much more concerned with the fate of the Negev and other parts of Mandatory Palestine than it was with Jerusalem. In fact, the Jewish community in Palestine and abroad, as well as the Zionist leadership in Palestine, wholeheartedly endorsed Resolution 181. Historical and religious sites connecting the present to the past would not be part of the Jewish state; neither would the almost one hundred thousand Jewish Jerusalemites placed under international rule.

Zionist leaders' support of this plan is curious, especially given that they (principally David Ben-Gurion) had declared emphatically the spiritual and religious importance of Jerusalem and that they liked the idea that (at least, by November 1947) all major Jewish national institutions were to be located in the city. Why, then, were they willing to sacrifice the city? Were its Jewish inhabitants, its religious sites, and its modern markers of Zionism suddenly unimportant? Answers to these questions are complicated, involving personalities, pragmatism, and ideology.

Ben-Gurion was a pragmatist: when he thought it possible to secure Jerusalem as part of the Jewish state, he emphatically favored its inclusion; when he thought it was not possible, he abandoned his commitment to the city (Lorch 1989, 384). Other politicians were equally pragmatic. They felt that the fate of the 1947 Partition Plan and the possibility of having a separate state for the Jews depended on their willingness to give up Jerusalem and agree to its internationalization (Bialer 1984; Golani 1994). In their view, the time was right for creating a Jewish state: this was the first time in history that the international community had recognized the special concerns of the Jews and their need for a separate Jewish state; politicians must seize the opportunity or lose it, even if the price was Jerusalem. Of course, ideology is likely to have played some part as well. If Jerusalem had always been a focal point of the Zionist project, as were Galilee and the Coastal Plain, Zionist leadership most likely would have been reluctant to give it up.

While Ben-Gurion favored Jerusalem's internationalization, Moshe Shertok, his second-in-command and later Israel's first foreign minister, preferred to partition the city between Jews and Arabs. In an effort to have both worlds, a Jewish Agency delegation to the United Nation, headed by Shertok, tried to influence the U.N General Assembly's Subcommittee on Borders before the completion of the final draft of Resolution 181. In the Agency's plan, Jerusalem would be divided into three parts—Arab, Jewish, and international (Golani 1994, 36)—appeasing all three constituencies. The Jewish area, however, would include the western parts of the city and Mt. Scopus, leaving the Old City to international governance.

In the months after the passage of the U.N.'s Resolution, the real war for Jerusalem began. Arabs rioted against the U.N. decision and attacked several Jewish communities. Almost as soon as the riots began, most Zionist leaders, including Ben-Gurion, left Jerusalem for Tel Aviv. From there they launched the battle for the city (Golani 1994, 38). Seeing that United Nation forces could not control the chaos in the city and that they did not intervene on behalf of Jewish Jerusalemites attacked by the Arabs, Ben-Gurion worried that this was a harbinger of how Jews would fare in an international Jerusalem. So he changed his mind once again: he abandoned his support for Jerusalem's internationalization and called for its partition. His proposal followed the demographic line of the city with the inclusion of Mt. Scopus in the east (see Figure 14.1). The map that emerged in 1948 was identical to the plan that the Jewish Agency proposed for Jerusalem in 1937.

In the war over Jerusalem, Arabs attacked the Jewish quarter of the Old City, blockaded Mt. Scopus, and tried to cut off Jerusalem's only road to the west. Discourse, however, focused not on concern for historic and religious sites, but on the capabilities of the *Yishuv* to protect the Jewish population of Jerusalem and secure New Jerusalem. As Arabs intensified their attack on the Old City, the Jewish leadership decided to abandon the Jewish Quarter. It soon fell, and it would remain in Jordanian hands for the next nineteen years. To be fair, the decision to sacrifice East Jerusalem might have been strategic (Lapidot 1997), but it also happened to mesh perfectly with the Zionist agenda at the time. Ben-Gurion's commitment to a divided city sealed the fate of any possible Jewish control of or access to the Western Wall and the old Jewish Quarter. Thereafter, discussion about Jewish Jerusalem referred only to West Jerusalem.

By 1948, Zionists had successfully established a sovereign Jewish state in Israel. The full Zionist agenda, however, could not be fully achieved as long as anti-Jewish sentiments around the world remained high and until the

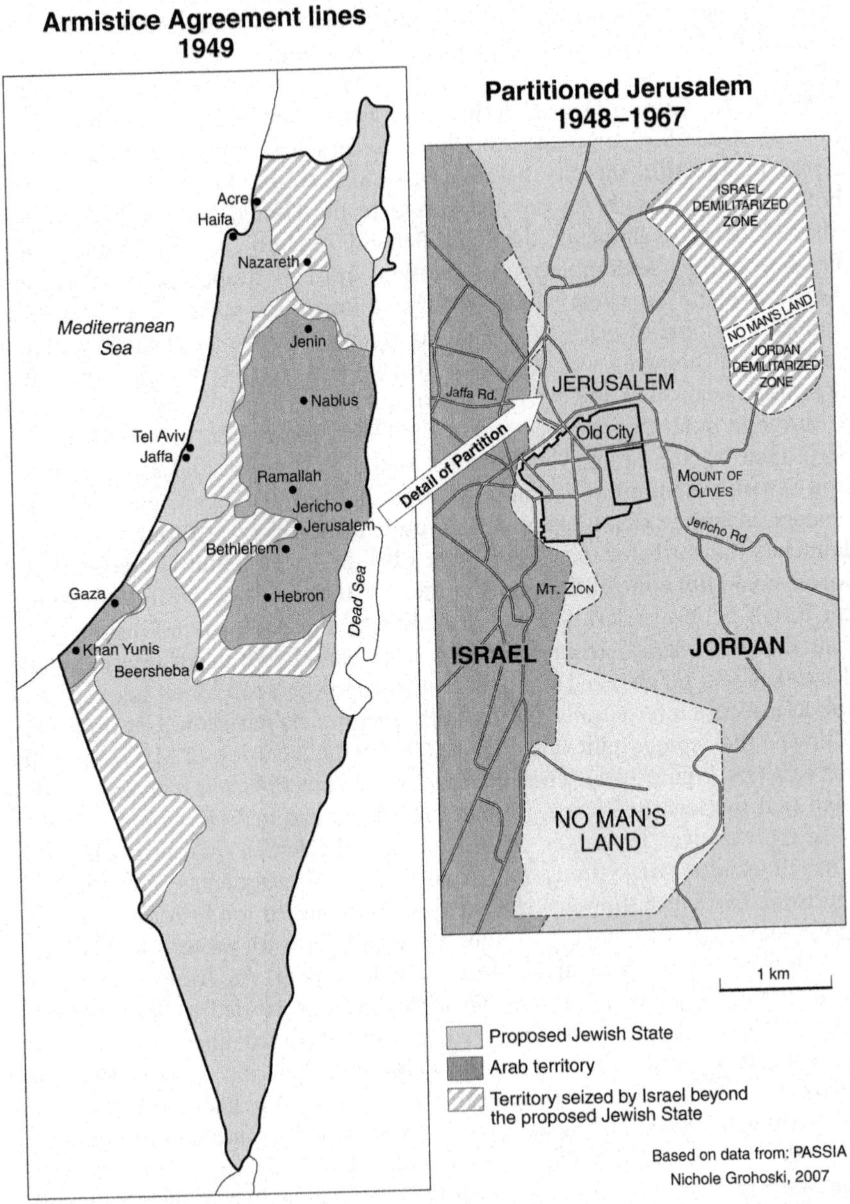

Armistice Agreement lines 1949

Acre
Haifa
Nazareth
Mediterranean Sea
Jenin
Nablus
Tel Aviv
Jaffa
Ramallah
Jericho
Jerusalem
Bethlehem
Gaza
Hebron
Khan Yunis
Beersheba
Dead Sea

Partitioned Jerusalem 1948–1967

ISRAEL DEMILITARIZED ZONE
NO MAN'S LAND
JORDAN DEMILITARIZED ZONE
Jaffa Rd.
JERUSALEM
Detail of Partition
Old City
MOUNT OF OLIVES
Jericho Rd
MT. ZION
ISRAEL
JORDAN
NO MAN'S LAND

1 km

Proposed Jewish State
Arab territory
Territory seized by Israel beyond the proposed Jewish State

Based on data from: PASSIA
Nichole Grohoski, 2007

Figure 14.1 Partitioned Jerusalem.

state's borders were secure and all Diaspora Jews had returned to their homeland. In the meantime Zionist ideology would adapt to new circumstances. But because the pre-statehood Zionist leadership had assumed leadership of the new state, the Zionist agenda remained virtually unchanged. There was, however, one change: the voices of once marginalized elements in Zionism—the religious Zionist movement Ha-Mizrachi and the Revisionist Movement (the precursor of Likud)—began to grow louder.

Jerusalem after 1948

Although in 1948 Israel was established as a state[12] and it secured territorial contiguity throughout the land and to West Jerusalem, UN Resolution 181 remained in effect. In fact, the international community did not recognize the new arrangement in Jerusalem and pressured Israel (which now controlled the western part of the city) and Jordan (in control of the eastern part) to abide by the Resolution and move toward the internationalization of the city. From Israel's point of view, the territorial gains of the war were some of the most significant achievements of Zionism and had changed the map drawn by the U.N. Partition Plan. Consequently, there was no reason to cede West Jerusalem to international control. More specifically, internationalizing Jerusalem might be taken to mean that they accepted the Partition Plan as a whole, undermining Zionist achievements (Breecher 1981). Of course, had the Resolution been accepted, Israel not only would have had to give up its newly acquired territory, but would also have had to allow hundreds of thousands of Palestinian refugees to return to their homes.

Even as international pressures mounted, the Zionist leadership, now in political control of the state, became ever more committed to Jerusalem. In June 1948, with Israel in the midst of its battle over Jerusalem, Ben-Gurion spelled out his and the government's commitment to both the Old City and the new:

> Jerusalem is under the jurisdiction of the Jewish government (at the moment, regretfully without the old city) just like Tel Aviv, and there is no distinction between Jerusalem and Tel Aviv, between Haifa and Hanita ... they are all under the jurisdiction of the Jewish government.
> (Quoted in Breecher 1981, 388; my translation)

This was the first time that the Zionist leadership had openly declared that it was interested in the Old City—which was, in their view, only temporarily out of Jewish hands. Moreover, Ben-Gurion actually elevated Jerusalem in the Zionist consciousness to the same level of importance as Tel Aviv, the first Hebrew city. His public commitment to secure control of both sides of the city would remain alive in the consciousness of the Jewish nation.

In December of 1948, seven months after Israel declared its independence and just as Israel was trying to become a member of the United Nations, there was another attempt to internationalize Jerusalem. In December 1949, even after Israel had become a member (May 1949), and more than a year and a half after Israel had gained its independence, the U.N. would vote yet a third time on the Resolution. In both cases, the leadership of the State was confronted with two difficult scenarios. They could abide by Resolution 181 and lose access to Jewish religious sites in the Old City and to the Jewish residents of West Jerusalem, or they could reject it, annex West Jerusalem (still without access to the Old City), and risk being either denied membership in the U.N. (1948) or expelled from it (1949). In fact, before the 1949 vote Ben-Gurion told his foreign minister, Moshe Sharett, "[I]f we had the choice to get out of Jerusalem or the UN, we would choose to leave the UN" (quoted in Bialer 1984, 184). At this same time, the Knesset passed a resolution making Jerusalem inseparable from Israel, although it stopped short of designating it as Israel's capital.

During this time Israel and Jordan were secretly negotiating to partition the city into distinct Jewish and Arab sections. Their assumption was that their bilateral action would help avoid the city's internationalization (Golani 1999). They were right. According to their agreement Jordan would control the eastern part of the city and Israel would hold on to Mt. Scopus and to the parts of the city where Jews lived. Mt. Scopus, in other words, would become an Israeli enclave within Jordan. The map that emerged from these negotiations was almost identical to one drawn by the Jewish Agency in 1937. As in the past, that is, in accordance with the Zionist ideology, the loss of the religious sites was a price they were willing to pay for retaining the Zionist achievements in the city, in particular, the Hebrew University and Hadassah Hospital.

Jerusalem the capital

In the early days of statehood, Israel would repeatedly debate Jerusalem's future, in large part because of pressure from the international community. Although in all of these debates the historic importance of Jerusalem to the Jewish people was underscored, most Knesset members did not take a clear stand on the issue—this despite Israel's annexation of the western part of the city and Ben-Gurion's proclamation that Jerusalem was an integral part of the state of Israel. As a result, Menachem Begin, the leader of the opposition, proposed legislation for the immediate designation of the entire city of Jerusalem (including the parts that were now in Jordanian hands) as the capital city of Israel. No one, not even the prime minister, went along with him. They may have thought that Begin's goal was to appropriate for Israel all of "Greater Jerusalem," that is, both its Jordanian and Israeli sectors. More likely, most Knesset members thought that such legislation was redundant given the city's high symbolic value.

In response, for example, to mounting international opposition, K. M. Pinhas Sapir (of MAPAI),[13] emphatically declared that "Jerusalem as the capital of [the nation of] Israel and of the State [of Israel] is not a problem ... but a fact ... In our opinion [Jerusalem] is not only a political object or a territorial concept but rather a symbol of both the nation and the state, the symbol and the essence of its existence." In his view "neither the nation nor the state could survive without this symbol, with all its meaning in the past, to the present and to the future of the nation" (*Knesset Chronicles* 1950, 223; my translation). Such statements on the floor of the Knesset etched the importance of Jerusalem to the Jewish people even deeper in the minds of the Jewish community in Israel—and of the international community as a whole. They therefore smoothed the way for declaring the city Israel's modern capital.

Even before this, Ben-Gurion had made several bold moves to establish Jerusalem as the capital. First, in September 1948 he had the highest court built in Jerusalem. Then, in a defiant step taken in response to the third U.N. vote (December, 1949), Ben-Gurion instructed the government to move its seat from Tel Aviv to west Jerusalem. In this way, the major city believed to be Israel's least developed—socially, culturally, and economically—and considered a frontier city (besieged on three sides) became *de facto*, if not *de jure*, the capital of Israel. Although purely symbolic, the move of government offices and later of the Knesset to Jerusalem (Katz and Paz 2004) marked the beginning of the long process through which Jerusalem was reborn as Israel's state capital.

It would take decades, however, before Jerusalem would grow into a true capital city. Efforts to make it the central seat of power in Israel were hindered by the city's location and by the long ideological resistance on the part of the Zionist leadership to Jerusalem and what it represented. Although by 1951 almost all government offices (except for the defense and foreign ministries) had moved to Jerusalem, they nonetheless retained Tel Aviv offices as well. This, along with the fact that most Knesset members, the prime minister, and the first president continued to reside anywhere but in Jerusalem, made the city a capital for weekdays only.[14] Leaders spent far more energy declaring that Jerusalem was its capital than actually treating it as such. At the same time, to signal their opposition to Israel's having designated Jerusalem as its capital, almost all foreign governments established their main embassies in Tel Aviv. For decades to come Jerusalem would remain a marginal site, the poorest city in Israel, and a handicapped capital. As recently as 2005 the Jerusalem Economic Forum and the Jerusalem Chamber of Commerce said they "condemn the successive Israeli governments for failing to give Jerusalem the status that a capital city deserves" (Cashman 2005).

Nor did any Israeli government do much to improve the physical appearance of the city. In heated debates throughout the 1950s and into the 1980s, Knesset members, especially those from the (right-of-center) religious and opposition parties, called on the prime minister and the Knesset to invest in Jerusalem's urban development. "[B]uilding in Jerusalem," said Eri Jabotinsky (August 1, 1950), "is not a local thing, it is not something that is of interest only to Jerusalem and its municipality; [rather] this is something of interest to the entire country" (*Knesset Chronicles* 1955, 2391). Other Knesset members asked the government to help change the image of the "village called Jerusalem." They wanted it to develop the city, move more official functions there, reduce its taxes in order to attract a more varied population and businesses, build a better infrastructure, and direct funds for construction to the city, as it had to new towns such as Beer Sheba (*Knesset Chronicles* 1956, 421–422, and 1957, 821–823). Religious and right-wing politicians, critical of what they perceived to be the Coalition Government's lack of accomplishments in Jerusalem repeatedly voiced such concerns.

Despite tensions between the Coalition and its Opposition, the Israeli government finally began to transform Jerusalem into more of a capital city. Its efforts concentrated on constructing national symbols, such as the national monument and public parks in the western part of Jerusalem. In the pre-state years, Zionist ideologues and practitioners had constructed only a few national monuments in the city, such as the Hebrew University and the Hadassah Hospital, which after statehood were in an enclave in Jordanian territory. But as early as April 1949, even before the fate of the city was decided, the young government of Israel designated land for and planned the construction of a national memorial site (Golani 1998) to capture the story of the Jewish nation in the twentieth century.

This national memorial, the Mountain of Remembering (*Har Hazikaron*), is where Israel has buried the remains of Theodor Herzl, the father of Zionism, as well as its prime ministers, presidents, and ministers, and located its Central Military Cemetery. On the other side of the same mountain, opposite where those who envisioned, led, and fought for the Jewish homeland are buried, is the Holocaust museum, *Yad Vashem* (Azaryahu 1994). Together the cemeteries and museum tell the story of the modern Jewish nation's vision, near-destruction, and revival, *Hazon, Sho'a, U' Tekuma.* Consequently, the mountain has become "a kind of alternative pilgrimage site in the Western City" (Golani 1999, 590).

Two other monumental projects would soon follow. Education Hill became the home of the Hebrew University's campus at Giv'at Ram and later the site of the Israel Museum. On Government Hill were located government offices and later the Knesset. And as the city expanded westward, Israel constructed a wide avenue connecting two of these sites, Mount Herzl with Giva't Ram. The new avenue became the main axis of West Jerusalem: the site for military parades (1955, 1958, and 1961), memorial processions, and funerals of national importance (Azaryahu 1995). Indeed, such markers are necessary elements of a capital city, although they usually appear gradually in the landscape. The speed with which Israel's new national landscape took shape suggests that the Israeli government was under considerable pressure to construct Jerusalem as quickly and as efficiently as possible—even before it was officially designated the capital. In doing so it integrated West Jerusalem into the new story of the nation.

Neither the construction of monuments nor pleas from Knesset members, however, were enough to make Jerusalem the legal capital of Israel. With the *Jerusalem the Capital Law* members of the Opposition, who were strongly committed to legalizing Jerusalem's status, proposed making Greater Jerusalem the legal capital of Israel. Initially the legislation failed. Reintroduced twice, it finally became law in 1980. Its success was due to the change in the political climate in Israel: the end of the hegemony of the Labor Party with its Labor Zionist ideology and the empowerment of the right-wing Likud Party, headed by the long-time Opposition leader, Menachem Begin.

Jerusalem after 1967

On the eve of the Six-Day War, however, West Jerusalem was still only Israel's *de facto* capital. So removed was the Old City from Israeli consciousness that even when Israel entered the 1967 war, it had no clear plans to conquer Jerusalem or reunite it.[15] The results of the 1967 war are well known. In less than seven days Israel more than quadrupled its size by conquering the Golan Heights, the Sinai, the Gaza Strip and the West Bank. Of all its territorial gains, the conquest and reunification of Jerusalem on the third day was particularly important and subsequently has been celebrated as a national holiday.[16] The euphoria felt that day by all Israelis, regardless of political affiliation, and by Jews around the world, opened a dam of intense emotions. In fact, "life for the Jewish state without Jerusalem became difficult to imagine" (Wasserstein 2001, 208). From this moment on, the Wall, so marginal to the early Zionist narrative, would become a focal point of the city, occupying a central place in the discourse regarding Jerusalem. Furthermore, the bloody battle for the Old City and the territory surrounding Jerusalem, as well as Israel's efforts to settle and rebuild it, were no longer in conflict with the Zionist program, but would become part of the story of modern Israel.

Although there were no clear plans for Jerusalem before the 1967 war, it took Israel less than two weeks to initiate radical physical and equally radical political change in the city. As soon as the war ended Israel extended its jurisdiction to East Jerusalem. Then, on June 28, it passed the *Law of Jerusalem's Unity*, which in Israelis' eyes legalized their sovereignty over East Jerusalem and the land around the city and set up the administrative structure for both parts of the city. It thus defined which neighborhoods would now be included in the new municipality.

This unilateral action was perceived by many Israelis as "a continuation of the Zionist enterprise and the completion of a process that had begun in 1948" (Klein 2001, 64). In addition to increasing the size of the city from 38 to 108 sq. km (Asaf-Shapira 2007), within days of the end of the war Israel flattened the Maghrebi neighborhood in front of the Wall, after evicting all its Arab residents. By erasing the entire neighborhood, an act conceived of five decades earlier by the Zionist leadership but never carried out, Israeli leadership thought it could unite the Old Jewish Quarter with the Wall and make it visible to anyone coming through the Dung Gate and through either the Jewish or Muslim Quarters. In place of the twenty-five Arab homes that constituted the Maghrebi neighborhood, there now stands the Wall's plaza, intended to mediate between religious and national activities taking place in the area. The quintessential symbol of the past was about to become a central symbol of the modern state of Israel.

Indeed, the paratroopers' victory in Jerusalem helped to incorporate this ancient religious symbol into the Zionist narrative, and it once again became inseparable from the celebration and observation of all Jewish holidays, thus restoring its religious importance. Now the Wall embodied not only the remnants of the Old World but also the story of the Israeli soldiers who had heroically fought and died for it and freed it from the hands of the Arabs, just as the Zionists had freed the homeland. Soon after the Plaza was created the Wall became the backdrop against which many secular national ceremonies took place. It was here, for example, that military units pledged allegiance to the army and the state. Carefully sited and minimally reconstructed after the demolition of Maghrebi, the Plaza helped transmit the critically important national message that the past and the present were connected. Every soldier's duty was to defend the Wall: as the heart of both the nation and the state, it should never again be torn from Israel's hands. Using this religious symbol as a background in military ceremonies helped to naturalize the Wall, that is, to give it secular as well as religious meaning. But above all this site had become important to the now right-leaning Zionist ideology.

The newly conquered territories in and around Jerusalem also played a role in the Zionist program. Israel enacted a settlement policy whose sole purpose was the consolidation of Israeli control over all of the Palestinian territories around Jerusalem. By constructing houses and establishing new Jewish neighborhoods, it was believed, Israel could establish a Jewish presence in Arab areas and so would prevent any future re-division of the city (Dumper 1992) or the return of areas to the Arabs. From a geographic perspective, the new borders of Jerusalem, which now included several Arab villages, lacked urban logic (Efrat 2001). Nevertheless, the newly acquired Arab territories provided the stage on which the old Zionist ideology of settlement and defense could be played out. The massive build-up in and around Jerusalem, which began soon after the 1967 war and accelerated after 1977, represents the changing commitment of Israel to Greater Jerusalem and reflects a move to the right in Jewish nationalism.

Conquering Jerusalem was a foundational event in the life of the Jewish nation. A united Jerusalem was now the capital of Israel. But as long as the Labor Party (represented by both Labor and Socialist Zionism) was in power, there was no push to make the city look more like a capital. The *Knesset Chronicles* of that period suggest that, despite changes in governments, attitudes toward

Jerusalem had remained the same. During the 1970s, just as in previous decades, Knesset members bemoaned the fact that Jerusalem still did not look or function like a capital city and that the government had no strategic and comprehensive plan for its development (*Knesset Chronicles* 1976, December 15). In fact, massive build-up of new Jewish neighborhoods in the conquered Arab areas, the rebuilding of the old Jewish Quarter, and attempts by the municipality of Jerusalem to extend its services to the Arab parts of the city had favored the periphery over the center. The result was a weakening of the western part of the city.

Israel's attitude toward Jerusalem changed drastically during the 1970s as the Settlers', Movement gained momentum. In 1977, when the Likud Party came to power and Menachem Begin became Israel's prime minister, interest in Jerusalem and the Occupied Territories grew. Massive settlement projects were undertaken in these territories, and the *Basic Law: Jerusalem the Capital*, proposed first by Begin in 1961 and again by his political ally Shmuel Tamir in 1971, was finally passed in 1980. Once Israel's polity became identified with the political right, the annexation of Jerusalem and its surrounding areas was finally complete.[17]

With the support of the Likud government, Jews settled not only in the Old Jewish Quarter, a process which had begun shortly after the 1967 war, but in parts of the Muslim Quarter, which meant the eviction of its Palestinian residents (Dumper 2002, 60). This process intensified in 1993 when the Likud candidate, Ehud Olmert, defeated his Labor opponent, Mayor Teddy Kollek. Rather than continue the policy of a "quiet and creeping annexation of East Jerusalem and its surroundings, Olmert believed that the annexation should proceed openly and dramatically" (Klein 2001, 255). He wanted to change the character of East Jerusalem, settle as many Jews in Arab neighborhoods as possible, and build new neighborhoods. His broader goal was to promote the religious Zionist program of settling Judaea and Samaria (West Bank), and specifically settling Jerusalem and it environs. Such a development would prevent the linking of the Arab neighborhoods of East, North, and South Jerusalem, and so would obstruct any attempt to form a Palestinian state (Klein 2001, 261). The build-up of new Jewish neighborhoods effectively blocked the possible expansion of most Arab villages. It also underscored the repeated declarations by most Israeli governments since 1977 that Jewish sovereignty in Greater Jerusalem was indeed Israel's most important goal.[18] This was a complete reversal of the old Zionist ideology held by Ben-Gurion and other Labor Zionists: they favored having a Jewish majority in all areas of Israel, however small, over creating a large territory populated exclusively by Arabs (Segev 2001, 74). Now Jewish nationalism was wed to religious ideology. *Place* had become more important than *people*.

Despite Israel's having "legalized" the reunification of Jerusalem and having authorized the creation of settlement blocs to create contiguous Jewish areas in the vicinity of the city, the reality is that Jerusalem was, and still is, divided. Moreover, the international community has yet to accept Jerusalem as Israel's official capital; very few embassies have ever been located there. In an effort to secure Jerusalem's position, both nationally and internationally, the government of Israel appointed a Ministerial Committee for Jerusalem's Affairs. Its purview is the city of Jerusalem at large, but most of its work has focused specifically on the Wall, now a symbol of Jewish identity. The magnificent secular Zionist accomplishments of Jerusalem—Education and Government Hills—have become secondary.

Conclusion

Changes in Jewish attitudes toward Jerusalem in the last century have reflected the changing currents in Jewish nationalism. As formerly marginal groups became more powerful in the Israeli polity, as the Settlers' Movement became the quintessential "new Zionists," and as Jewish nationalism moved increasingly toward the religious right, Jerusalem moved into full focus in the Zionist ideology. Now, even the Wall, once a religious site, has been made accessible to secular Jews. It has become the cornerstone of the connection between the people and their nation, the people and their religion, and the people and their state.

So important has the Wall become to the Jewish nation that it is the place where soldiers, whether Jewish or not, pledge allegiance to the state and the army, and presidents and prime ministers, regardless of their political affiliation, visit the Wall on special occasions. Even Shimon Peres, Ben-Gurion's protégé and now the politician with the strongest ties to the traditional Labor Party, visited the Wall on the day of his induction as Israel's ninth president (July 15, 2007). Did he want to appease the growing religious Jewish population of Israel? Or did he visit the Wall because Jerusalem's Jewish religious sites have now become national sites, and it is no longer possible to separate religion and nationalism? Perhaps both.

Indeed, as Jewish nationalism has become more religious and religion has become more nationalistic, Jerusalem has become a symbol of this change. The inauguration speech of President Peres clearly exemplifies this trend. "Jerusalem," Peres proclaimed, "is yearning for momentum and is thirsty for renewal. To be the city promised to us and holy to all believers. To be the spiritual and political center of the Jewish people and a center of prayer for seekers of peace of all beliefs" (Peres 2007). Indeed, in 2007, after more than 100 years of Zionism, Jerusalem once again has become the promised city, the spiritual center, and a place of prayer—all characteristics that made the city initially marginal in the Zionist agenda.

Notes

1 Earlier versions of this chapter were presented at the departments of geography at Syracuse University and at the University of Connecticut, Storrs. I benefited also from discussions with Orna Blumen of Haifa University in Israel.

2 I distinguish between a state and a nation. While the former is a political unit, a subdivision of the globe, the latter is a glorified ethnic group whose members share a number of objective and subjective characteristics, and who believe in a shared past and yearn for a shared destiny. Perhaps the most important attribute of every nation is the connection to a territory that the nation calls its homeland, where it believes the nation was born.

3 On early Zionism and the construction of the *New Jew*, see Mayer 2007 and Mayer 2000.

4 As early as the Second Zionist Congress, in 1898, the Jews of Jerusalem were referred to as *different*, and more like the Old Jew. "[Their] troubles robbed them of courage; silently they carry the ridicule and disgrace inflicted upon them by others... Happily they carry their diasporic yoke" (Orlan 1997, 91; my translation).

5 Moshe Leib Lilenblum, one of the leaders of the Zionist movement at the time, wrote in 1882, "[W]e have no need for Jerusalem's walls, for Jerusalem itself, the city that is not central ... we need the land of Israel, we need a real center" (quoted in Aaronsohn 1989, 53). In a letter from Chaim Weizmann to his wife, Vera, dated April 18, 1918, he describes the situation in Jerusalem:

> It is sad, very sad in Jerusalem ... There are few young Jews there, and the old ones make a dreadful impression. They are all broken-off splinters, dusty, feeble, soft, covered with age-old mould. The Jewish quarters in Jerusalem are nothing but filth and infection. The indescribable poverty, stubborn, ignorance and fanaticism – the heart aches when one looks at it all!
>
> (Weizmann 1977, 132–133, letter 163)

In letter 165 to Nahum Sokolov, written on the next day, he comments that "the community here is split up into factions and cliques, which are working against each other ... The result is a tremendous disorganization both vis-à-vis the Jewish Community and the British Authority" (Weizmann 1977, 143; April 18, 1918, letter 165). To Louis Brandeis he writes: "In speaking of the position of the Jewish population one has to make a clear distinction between Jerusalem and the rest of the population. The situation in Jerusalem is very sad ... The misery, dirt and squalor of the Jewish quarters is above description ... " (Weizmann 1977, 162; April 25, 1918, letter 175). On another trip to Jerusalem he writes to his wife Vera about his impressions of those in Jerusalem surviving on the charity of Europeans:

> There is nothing more *humiliant* than "our" Jerusalem. Anything that could be done to desecrate and defile the sacred has been done. It is impossible to imagine so much falsehood, blasphemy, greed, so many lies, and when one realizes that Jewry is spending 4 million francs a year on Jerusalem, and all that goes to maintain a system of complete moral corruption, one feels ashamed and frightened.
>
> (Weizmann 1977, 218; July 1, 1918, letter 219, italics in the original)

6 In 1873 Arabs comprised 73 percent of Jerusalem's population, and the percentage declined as new Jewish immigrants arrived in Jerusalem. By 1922, 44 percent of the population was Arab; by 1944, about 40 percent (Hudson 1990, 249).

7 Arlosoroff proposed a division of Jerusalem into two sections, Jewish and Arab. The Jewish section would include the new parts of the city, Hebrew Jerusalem (including the Hebrew University and the hospital on Mt. Scopus), and the Arab section would include the Old City as well as the eastern parts of Jerusalem.

8 Ben-Gurion, in the fourth volume of his memoirs, which includes the events and discussions that took place in 1937, spends a great deal of time recounting the interactions between himself and other leaders of the Zionist movement and

members of the Peel Commission. His discussions of the canton system proposed for Mandatory Palestine and the separation of Jews from Arabs are highly detailed. See particularly the first half of the volume.

9 Although this proposal was seen by many Zionists as a real victory, the debate was not only about what lands, resources, and Zionist projects would be given up but also what Jewish self-governance would mean. In fact, David Ben-Gurion feared that "the Jews [were] not ready for self governance" and that instead of building their land they might engage in brotherly war (1937, 1974, 64).

10 Chaim Weizmann, for example, worried, and expressed it during the 20th Zionist Congress, that the proposed small state might not be big enough to absorb the annual immigration flow of fifty to sixty thousand Jews over the following twenty to twenty-five years. These concerns were expressed, of course, before World War II and before the Jewish Holocaust even began.

11 For all practical purposes, the Zionist leadership is identical to the leadership of the Jewish Agency, which served during the years of the British Mandate as the de facto government of the soon-to-be state. The Agency's task was to serve the administrative needs of the Jewish community in Palestine, the *Yishuv*.

12 The leadership of the *Yishuv* was not in unanimous agreement about whether to declare statehood or to agree first to a cease-fire proposed by the United States. Even the Zionist leadership and their dominant political party were divided on this question, and indeed some of the high-ranking members voted against declaring independence at the time (Naor 2006).

13 MAPAI was the first incarnation of the Labor Party, whose members were members of the Jewish Agency.

14 For more than three decades, Jerusalem was the capital during the first part of the week and Tel Aviv (unofficially) during the latter part of the week. Most government offices and the headquarters of all political parties continued to be in Tel Aviv. It would not be until 1971 that the Knesset would vote to eliminate Tel Aviv as Israel's capital on Thursdays and Fridays, and at least another decade before the Wednesday-night exodus of government officials to Tel Aviv had stopped altogether. The vote to eliminate Tel Aviv as the unofficial capital was very close: 24 for, 22 against, and 5 abstaining (*Knesset Chronicles* 1971, 866–867, and 1971/2, 349). Still, the practice of government officials did not match this vote.

15 In the late 1950s, during the Sinai Crisis, when Israel feared Jordanian involvement, it devised a plan to secure the road to Mt. Scopus if Jordan attacked the road and cut access to this Israeli enclave. It also had a contingency plan to seize the West Bank and East Jerusalem if a coup against the Hashemite regime were to materialize in the early days of the Hashemite Kingdom (Wasserstein 2001). Despite the opportunities, Israel chose not to carry out these plans; they became the "dress rehearsal" for what would happen in 1967 (Golani 1999, 254).

16 The day the city of Jerusalem was reunited, the 28th of the Hebrew month of Iyar, has been proclaimed by the Israeli government as a national holiday, Jerusalem Day. It is marked with national ceremonies, parades through the city, special religious and memorial services for the soldiers who died in the fight for Jerusalem.

17 The law was introduced in 1980 by Geula Cohen of *Hatchiyah* (The Revival) Party. It aimed at fixing the status of united Jerusalem as Israel's capital and assuring that its border would not deviate from the one established by the 1967 war, and it called once again for naming Jerusalem the permanent seat of the government, the Knesset, and the High Court, as well as the Rabbinate and the Zionist Federation.

18 The efforts to increase the proportion of Jews in Jerusalem's population have largely succeeded. By the end of 2007, 424,300 people lived in the areas annexed by Israel in the 1967 war, and they constituted 59 percent of Jerusalem's residents.

Of these, 184,300, or 43.4 percent, were Jewish, and they comprised 39 percent of the Jewish population in the city (Asaf-Shapira 2007).

References

Aaronsohn, Ran. 1989. "Jerusalem in the Eyes of Members of the First *Aliyah*." In Lavsky 1989a, 47–66. (In Hebrew.)

Amiran, David. 1986. "The Geographical Development of Jerusalem, 1860–1985." *Ariel* 43: 9–45. (In Hebrew.)

Asaf-Shapira, Yair. 2007. "The City in Numbers, 2007." In *Statistical Data*. Jerusalem: Jerusalem Institute of the Study of Israel.

Azaryahu, Maoz. 1994. "The Mountain, the Wall, and the Narrative of the Third Temple: Jewish-Israeli Symbolic Geography of Jerusalem." *COMPAR(A)ISON* 2:109–26.

——. 1995. *State Cults: Celebrating Independence and Commemorating the Fallen in Israel, 1948–1956*. Beersheva: Ben-Gurion University of the Negev Press. (In Hebrew.)

Ben-Gurion, David. 1928, 1971. *Memoirs*. Vol. 1. Tel Aviv: Am Oved Publishers. (In Hebrew.)

——. 1937, 1974. *Memoirs*. Vol. 4. Tel Aviv: Am Oved Publishers. (In Hebrew.)

Bialer, Uri. 1984. "The Road to the Capital—Making Jerusalem the Official Seat of Israel's Government in 1949." *Cathedra* 35: 163–191. (In Hebrew.)

Breecher, Michael. 1981. "The Political Struggle over Jerusalem." In *Jerusalem in the Modern Period: Yaacov Herzog Memorial Volume*, ed. Eli Shaltiel, 384–417. Jerusalem: Yad Izhak Ben-Zvi and Ministry of Defence Publications. (In Hebrew.)

Cashman, Greer. 2005. "Government Criticized for Failure to Support Jerusalem." *Jerusalem Post*, March 15, 17. Accessed on Lexis-Nexis March 21, 2005.

Dumper, Michael. 1992. "Israeli Settlement in the Old City of Jerusalem." *Journal of Palestine Studies* 21.4: 32–53.

——. 2002. *The Politics of Sacred Space: The Old City of Jerusalem in the Middle East Conflict*. Boulder and London: Lynn Reinner.

Efrat, Elisha. 2001. "Seek Peace for Jerusalem." *Mifneh*, January, 12–18. (In Hebrew.)

Golani, Motti. 1994. "Zionism without Zion? The Attitude of the Leadership of the Yishuv and the State of Israel on the Question of Jerusalem." In *Divided Jerusalem, 1948–1967*, ed. Avi Bareli, 30–52. Jerusalem: Yad Ben Zvi Publisher. (In Hebrew.)

——. 1998. "Yearnings and Actions Apart: Israel's Policy on the Jerusalem Question 1948–67." In *Independence: The First Fifty Years*, ed. Anita Shapira, 267–296. Jerusalem: Zalman Shazar Center. (In Hebrew.)

——. 1999. "Jerusalem's Hope Lies Only in Partition: Israeli Policy on the Jerusalem Question, 1948–67." *International Journal of Middle East Studies* 31: 577–604.

Goldstein, Joseph. 1989. "Jerusalem in the Ideology of Russian Zionists." In Lavsky 1989a, 67–74. (In Hebrew.)

Gross, Yaakov. 1992. "Jerusalem's Conquest Day—The Biggest Holidays of All, Chanukah, December 1917." *Ariel* 88: 71–72. (In Hebrew.)

Harel, Chaya. 1989. "Herzl's Attitude to Jerusalem." In Lavsky 1989a, 75–90. (In Hebrew.)

Hudson, Michael. 1990. "The Transformation of Jerusalem, 1917–87 AD." In *Jerusalem in History*, ed. K. J. Asali, 249–278. New York: Olive Branch Press.

Katz, Yossi. 1989. "The Change in Attitude of Ussishkin and the *Hovevi Zion* to the Development of Jerusalem and the Founding of the Hebrew University Prior to the First World War." In Lavsky 1989a, 107–136. (In Hebrew.)

Katz, Yossi, and Yair Paz. 2004. "The Transfer of Government Ministries to Jerusalem, 1948–49: Continuity or Change in the Zionist Attitude to Jerusalem?" *Journal of Israeli History* 23.2: 232–259.

Klein, Meachem. 2001. *Jerusalem: The Contested City*. New York: New York University Press

Knesset Chronicles. 1950. Vol. 3. Jerusalem: Knesset.

Knesset Chronicles. 1955. Vol. 6. Jerusalem: Knesset.

Knesset Chronicles. 1956. Vol. 19. Jerusalem: Knesset.

Knesset Chronicles. 1957. Vol. 23. Jerusalem: Knesset.

Knesset Chronicles. 1971. Vol. 59. Jerusalem: Knesset.

Knesset Chronicles. 1971/2. Vol. 62. Jerusalem: Knesset.

Knesset Chronicles. 1976. Vol. 76. Jerusalem: Knesset.

Lapidot, Yehuda. 1997. "The Division of Jerusalem in 1948: A Military Weakness or a Policy?" *Nativ: A Journal for Political Thought* 58.5: 48–53. (In Hebrew.)

Lavsky, Hagit, ed. 1989a. *Jerusalem in Zionist Vision and Realization: Collected Essays*. Jerusalem: The Zalman Shazar Center for Jewish History.

——. 1989b. "The Zionist Commission to Palestine in Jerusalem." In Lavsky 1989a, 167–182.

Lorch, Netanel. 1989. "Ben-Gurion and Jerusalem as Israel's Capital." In Lavsky 1989a, 377–406. (In Hebrew.)

Mayer, Tamar. 2000. "From Zero to Hero: Masculinity in Jewish Nationalism." In *Gender Ironies of Nationalism: Sexing the Nation*, ed. Tamar Mayer, 283–308. London: Routledge.

——. 2007. "Nation and Gender in Jewish Israel." In *War, Citizenship, Territory*, ed. Deborah Cowen and Emily Gilbert, 327–344. New York and London: Routledge.

Miron, Dan. 1996. "Depictions in Modern Hebrew Literature." In *City of the King: Jerusalem from David to the Present*, ed. Nitza Rosovsky, 241–287. Cambridge, MA: Harvard University Press.

Naor, Mordechai. 2006. "Big Wednesday." *Haaretz*, 2 May, B 2–3. (In Hebrew.)

Orlan, Hayim, ed. and trans. 1997. *The Protocols of the Second Zionist Congress, August 28–31, 1898*. Jerusalem: R. Mas.

Paz, Yair. 1994. "A Zionist Partition Plan for Jerusalem." *Cathedra* 72: 113–134. (In Hebrew.)

Peres, Shimon. 2007. Address at the Presidential Induction Ceremony. *Jerusalem Post*, Online Edition, July 15.

Roman, Michael. 1989. "The Shift of the Demographic and Economic Center from Jerusalem to Tel Aviv during the Mandate." In Lavsky 1989a, 217–234.

Segev, Tom. 1999. *Palestine under the British*. Jerusalem: Keter. (In Hebrew.)

——. 2001. *The New Zionists*. Jerusalem: Keter. (In Hebrew.)

Shavit, Yaakov. 1998. *Jerusalem: Biography*. Tel Aviv: Am Oved Publishing, Zlaman Shazar Center. (In Hebrew.)

Shilo, Margalit. 1989. "From Jaffa to Jerusalem: The Attitude of the Zionist Organization to Jerusalem during the Second *Aliyah*." In Lavsky 1989a, 91–106. (In Hebrew.)

Wasserstein, Bernard. 2001. *Divided Jerusalem: The Struggle for the Holy Land*. New Haven: Yale University Press.

Weizmann, Chaim. 1977. *Letters and Papers*, series A, vol. 8: *November 1917–October 1918*. Ed. Meyer Weisgal. New Brunswick: Transaction Books, Rutgers University Press; Jerusalem: Israel University Press.

15 Administering Jordanian Jerusalem

Constructing national identity[1]

Kimberly Katz

Jordan's governmental policies toward Jerusalem just prior to King Abdullah's death in 1951 and during the period of King Hussein's rule over Jerusalem (1953–67) aimed to increase political and national authority in the Holy City. Although the kingdom's records are limited, Jordanian efforts to change the status of the city clearly succeeded, as foreign consular officials, particularly the British, consistently recorded Jordan's political, administrative, and symbolic actions in Jerusalem. While many within and without Jordan continued to dispute the kingdom's control of Jerusalem, the fact that local and foreign figures and officials responded to the kingdom's activities through administrative and diplomatic channels indicates that they took seriously, and felt threatened by, Jordanian assertions of control in the Holy City.

Filastin, one of the first Palestinian newspapers established in the late Ottoman period (1908) and during the period under review a Jordanian daily, reported in February 1950 that Abdullah made frequent visits to Jerusalem to attend the Friday prayer in the Aqsa mosque (*Filastin*, February 17, 1950). As part of his effort to preserve Jerusalem's Islamic and Arab character after 1948, and thus strengthen his political control over the city, Abdullah refused outside requests that threatened the nature and character of the city or that challenged his control of it. He resisted British and American pressure to implement the scheme for Jerusalem's internationalization called for in the 1947 UN Partition Plan for Palestine (Resolution 181) and in UN General Assembly (UNGA) Resolution 194 of 1948, on which the Vatican also insisted.[2] The king also refused to allow a passage for Jews to pray at the Western Wall, contrary to the Armistice Agreement of 1949 with Jordan and to UNGA 194, as he tied visits to the holy places by Israeli Jews to Israel's implementation of the article in UNGA 194 that called for the repatriation of (Palestinian) refugees to their home. Neither scenario occurred. Some Jews from other countries, however, traveled to Jordan's holy places in Jerusalem during this period, as Jordan did not ban all Jews, but just Israeli Jews, owing to the state of war between the two countries. Arab Christians living under Israeli rule from 1948 to 1967 also gained passage to Jordan to visit the holy places, but only under special circumstances. As a final affirmation of his intention to maintain the kingdom's link to the city of Jerusalem after the Palestine War, Abdullah rejected the Arab League's suggestion in 1949 that Jordan withdraw from Jerusalem in favor of internationalization. Abdullah, in an interview at the end of 1950, established, unequivocally, his view of the city's religious and political value when he is reported to have said, "There are 1000 Damascuses, 1000 Beiruts and 1000 Baghdads, but only one Jerusalem" (Nashashibi 1980, 63–67).

Jordan's recognized position in Jerusalem

Despite signed treaties and agreements over borders and military cooperation, the kingdom held no internationally recognized legal position from which to administer Jerusalem's holy places after they came under Jordan's control in 1948. The earliest legal document in the twentieth century claiming control over the holy places, the British mandate for Palestine and Transjordan, specified in Articles 13 and 14 that during the mandate period, responsibility for the administration and control of—in fact, the rights and claims to—the holy places rested with the mandatory authority (Hurewitz 1987, 106–111). Article 25 of the mandate specifically exempted the "territories lying between the Jordan [River] and the eastern boundary of Palestine" from the provisions of the mandate. While this measure was taken in large part to prevent Jewish immigration to Transjordan (limiting it only to Palestine), it had the added effect of separating the administration of Transjordanian territory from Palestinian territory, a fact that influenced how officials would consider Jordan when it sought to exert its control over Jerusalem after 1948. While Article 8 of the Treaty of Alliance (1946) between Great Britain and Transjordan accorded that "all obligations and responsibilities devolving on His Majesty the King [of England] in respect of Transjordan in respect of any international instrument which is not legally terminated should devolve on His Highness the Amir of Transjordan," the document did not specifically mention "obligations and responsibilities" for the holy places, as they were not at issue at that time.[3] The 1948 Treaty of Alliance that superseded the 1946 treaty, which was never ratified, specified no provision for "obligations and responsibilities" of holy places. At the signing of the treaty in March 1948, Jordan's Prime Minister added a letter to the treaty stating that, despite the omission of Article 8, Transjordan would not deviate from the principles outlined in the first treaty.[4] Still, March 1948 was nearly two months before the end of the British mandate, and the prospect that Jerusalem's holy places would fall under Jordanian control did not yet exist. Finally, the 1949 armistice agreement with Israel merely delineated the Jordanian–Israeli borders after the war. It did not accord international recognition to either Jordan's or Israel's claims to sovereignty over Jerusalem.

A 1954 British Foreign Office report noted that Jordan's leaders had been developing a new strategy to incorporate the Holy City into the kingdom, despite the unacceptability of such a prospect to the international community.[5] Britain's Foreign Office concluded that although the mandate had clearly prevented Transjordan from assuming "any Treaty obligations in that respect," the 1948 war changed the situation on the ground. The report suggested that "with the incorporation of parts of former Palestine in Transjordan it can be held that the [Jordanian] Prime Minister's statement [in the above-mentioned letter] concerning Article 8 of the 1946 Treaty applied there also." In other words, now that Jordan had annexed the West Bank and Jerusalem, the British might be willing to hear a Jordanian argument for taking control of the Holy City in the absence of the mandate authority. This 1954 British report indicates that British officials considered a legal *justification*, if not a legal *right*, for Jordanian actions in Jerusalem. Though the policy was not recognized internationally, it was clear to the British that, by 1954, the Jordanians "regard[ed] themselves as hereditary guardians of the holy sites and shrines."[6]

For the Jordanians, the policy had taken shape several years earlier. King Abdullah had conveyed clearly his country's position in a newspaper interview in 1949, saying in part, "With regard to the sanctity of the Holy Places, Transjordan is conscious of its responsibilities."[7] This statement helped pave the way for Jordan's leaders to fully incorporate Jerusalem into the kingdom, beginning with the ministerial/ceremonial position King Abdullah would create in 1950 for the supervision of Jerusalem's holy places.

After the 1948 war, both Jordan and Israel took measures to secure their respective political and administrative positions in the parts of the Holy City that each controlled. Almost immediately after signing the armistice agreement, Israel moved all but its Defense Ministry to Jerusalem, and began constructing a parliament, among other buildings, to solidify its position in the western part of the city. Jordan took legal measures, including annexation, to solidify its rule over Jerusalem, and appointed an official, a custodian, to manage the holy places. Additionally, Jordan altered Jerusalem's administrative status in the kingdom to match that of the capital city of Amman; those two cities were the only ones to be designated administratively as *amana* (a high-ranking municipal district). Jordan did not, however, consider Jerusalem a capital city, as it did Amman. While Britain resolved to grant only de facto recognition to Jordan's rule in Jerusalem, it was one of two countries to accord de jure recognition to Jordan's rule in the rest of the absorbed area of Palestine, the area that became known as the West Bank.[8] Most other countries also dealt with Jordan's position in Jerusalem on a de facto basis, as they did with Israel's position in the western part of the city.

Appointing a custodian of the holy places

Abdullah's efforts to exert his authority over Jerusalem after 1948 culminated in his decision to formalize his sovereignty over the Holy City and the holy places. He needed to take action in a way that would signify both Jordan's political and symbolic authority with regard to Jerusalem. He decided, at the end of December 1950, to appoint Ragheb Nashashibi as "Custodian of the Holy Places and Protector of the *Haram al-Sharif*" (Nashashibi 1980, 67).[9] Within a week of the Royal Decree establishing the appointment, Abdullah ordered a ceremony in Jerusalem for Ragheb Nashashibi to celebrate the new position, which carried the title of Minister.[10]

The written sources recording the position of the "Custodian of the Holy Places" are few, but what does exist gives some indication of how Abdullah expressed political power over Jerusalem by engineering the incorporation of the Holy City into the Hashemite Kingdom of Jordan, and how he perceived the political consequences. Nasser Eddin Nashashibi was a Jerusalemite Palestinian, and served as a close advisor to King Abdullah in the few years leading up to the latter's assassination in 1951.[11] His book *Man qatala al-malik 'Abd Allah?* (*Who Killed King Abdullah?*) offers a semi-personal/semi-historical analysis of the events leading up to the king's death, written to exonerate the Palestinians in the matter of Abdullah's assassination. It provides few references to historical sources, but the information has been corroborated here by other sources when possible.

News of the appointment and ceremony sent warning signals rippling through Jerusalem's diplomatic and religious communities, according to Nasser Eddin Nashashibi.[12] He states that the Christian leaders wondered if there was a hidden agenda behind this Royal Decree, while the French consul consulted with his government as to the official French response to the appointment. Israel, Nashashibi adds, expressed its indignation by saying that any independent Arab measures in the appointment of a Custodian, who was not under international supervision, were completely illegitimate. The British Ambassador, meanwhile, questioned whether the king thought he would rule Jerusalem along the path of the "Rightly Guided Caliphs," and the Italian ambassador spoke vehemently against mixing religion and politics.[13] The latter added that Jerusalem was for the entire world, not solely for Jordan. Clearly, based on reading Nashashibi's account, the world community understood this measure as Abdullah had intended it: it was a move to strengthen Jordan's presence in, and control over, Jerusalem and its holy places.

For some of the guests attending the ceremony, their presence offered only tacit recognition of Abdullah's political claim to the city. Others, Nashashibi notes, went in full support of the king, the appointment, and the new link between Jordan and Jerusalem. The Shaykhs of the *Haram al-Sharif* and the Arab elites of Jerusalem and the West Bank attended the event, and likely they fell into both of these groups. Diplomats from America, France, Italy, and the Vatican chose to boycott the celebration (Nashashibi 1980, 67–68). For these countries to accept the appointment of Jordan's new minister would imply recognition of Jordanian sovereignty over the Jordan-held sector of Jerusalem. As members of the United

Nations and thus bound by the UN partition plan for Palestine, these countries were not ready to accord recognition that might pre-empt the implementation of an international solution for Jerusalem.

One wonders why Abdullah, after taking decisive action to express his sovereignty over Jerusalem, chose not to attend the installation of his appointed custodian. Nasser Eddin Nashashibi, who was Abdullah's representative at the ceremony in 1951, has explained that Abdullah listened to the broadcast of the event on the radio, awaiting a report from Nashashibi upon his return to Amman after the ceremony (Nashashibi 1980, 67–68). From Amman, Abdullah privately savored the moment in which the whole world—even if they disputed it—understood that he held the power to appoint the individual who would control Jerusalem's holy places—a feat the international powers had failed to accomplish in recent history, let alone during the preceding several centuries.

Ragheb Nashashibi's appointment to the post fulfilled the need to have someone from a legitimate, elite Jerusalemite Palestinian family in the new position. Ragheb Nashashibi had been involved in building up the city during the years when Jerusalem was part of the British mandate for Palestine. That he had served as mayor of Jerusalem for nearly 15 years added legitimacy to the post; the new "Custodian" would not be new to the city's affairs.[14] In an interview in 1999 in Jerusalem, Ragheb's nephew Nasser Eddin Nashashibi claimed that this new position was supposed to make Jerusalemites, the Muslim world, and the Christian world feel that the king was giving Jerusalem its due respect.[15] Perhaps this response was true for those loyal to the king, as the Nashashibi family had long been, but the Christian world strongly rejected such a notion. It remained committed to an international solution to the Jerusalem problem and opposed the appointment of the Custodian.

Ragheb Nashashibi's written reply to the appointment was a resounding affirmation of his close, personal relationship with Abdullah. Always loyal to Abdullah, his reply clearly displayed that loyalty, of which Ragheb was particularly proud. He wrote to Abdullah, "Thank God that I was chosen to be one of your chosen soldiers ... thank God who made my life beautiful with my connection to you ... I have become liberated by my loyalty to you" (King Abdullah of Jordan 1978; Nashashibi 1980, 68–69). Not long after his appointment Ragheb became ill, and he died in the spring of the same year.

King Abdullah had not planned to create such a prestigious post. In *Man qatala al-malik 'Abd Allah*, written in 1980, Nasser Eddin Nashashibi tells the story of an interview with an American journalist, who pressured the king about his views toward Jerusalem (1980, 63–67). At the end of the interview, which Nasser Eddin attended, the king placed a telephone call and then told Nasser Eddin that within one week's time there would be a ceremony in Jerusalem for Ragheb Nashashibi, to celebrate his appointment to the new position of "Custodian of the Holy Places in Jerusalem."[16]

In his 1990 biography of Ragheb Nashashibi, Nasser Eddin Nashashibi tells the story of Ragheb's appointment differently (Nashashibi 1990, 212–226). After Jerusalem and the West Bank fell under Jordan's control in 1948, King Abdullah first appointed Ragheb Governor General of the West Bank. As Governor General, Ragheb had consistent political interference from then Prime Minister Tawfiq Abu al-Huda, who, Nasir comments, "was known for his pro-Mufti tendencies" and anti-Palestinian sentiments, a seeming inconsistency (Nashashibi 1990, 219). Unable to perform his duties, Ragheb conveyed his dissatisfaction to the king. As compensation for losing the post of Governor, Abdullah then appointed Ragheb Custodian of the Holy Places and Minister of the Haram al-Sharif (Nashashibi 1990, 219).[17] In this later account, it is domestic Jordanian political in-fighting that led to the creation of the position, rather than Abdullah's desire to glorify the Holy City.

Ragheb considered the appointment, contrary to what Nasser Eddin (Nashashibi 1980) suggested, a demotion. In his later book, Nasser Eddin has provided a more realistic account of his and Ragheb's response: "We both knew in our hearts that a leader of the Arabs of Palestine, a former mayor of Jerusalem, had, at the end of a distinguished career, been reduced to a local personality, a player on the periphery—a Jordanian administrator in a dusty corner of Jerusalem." Despite their upbeat appearance at the Jerusalem celebration, both were unhappy with the current situation, as Nasir says, "We both wore the smiles the occasion demanded but we mourned in our hearts. For we knew that possessing the old Arab quarter of Jerusalem was simply no compensation for the loss of the rest of the great city to the Zionists" (Nashashibi 1990, 219–220). The western part of Jerusalem had many Arab quarters that the Jordanian army did not save from Israeli takeover in 1948. Yet, at the time, the fact that Jordan's Arab Legion saved the Old City and the holy places from falling under Israeli control had carried weight in the Arab world, despite the fact that they later came to differ as to how Jerusalem should be ruled. The Arab neighborhoods in West Jerusalem boasted prominent families living in large houses. The Nashashibi family lived in Shaykh Jarrah, just north of the Old City, which Jordan controlled after the war. It seems unlikely that if forced to choose between West Jerusalem and the holy places, one would choose even wealthy neighborhoods to Islam's third holiest site as well as one of Christianity's holiest sites. Nasser Eddin does not specify in his book what attributes to his change in thinking although a brief historical analysis may shed some light on this question.

The 1990 story is inconsistent both with Nasser Eddin's previous account and with the argument maintained in this chapter. The issue of control of Jerusalem for Nasser Eddin in his later book no longer is one of international political posturing. It is likely that, by 1990, he was grappling with the fact that Israel had controlled the *entire* city since 1967. His historical memory, his recollection in 1990 of the events in Jerusalem from 1948 to

1967, may have been influenced by his having lived for 25 years in Jerusalem under Israeli occupation (Swedenburg 1995). One can speculate at the reason for the change of heart by Nasser Eddin, living in Jerusalem for the long period following Jordan's loss of Jerusalem after the 1967 war. The political tides were changing in the years leading up to the publication of the second account. The Palestinian *Intifada* had begun in late 1987, resulting in the convening of the Madrid Conference in 1991 following the Gulf War. With the prospect of Palestinian, rather than Hashemite, rule over Jerusalem in the near future, Nasser Eddin perhaps thought it best to dissociate himself, and perhaps his family, from the decades-long Nashashibi-Hashemite relationship, in order to secure a respectable position for the family in contemporary politics.[18] In the years following the 1967 war, serious tensions arose between Palestinians and the Hashemites and led to a civil war from 1970 to 1971, resulting in the Hashemite monarchy's exiling of the Palestine Liberation Organization (PLO) that had resided within its shrunken borders after 1967. Although Jordanian–PLO relations fluctuated over the decades, the possibility that the PLO would come to rule over Jerusalem existed, and perhaps for Nasser Eddin it was better to distance his family a bit from its decades of loyalty to the Hashemite regime.

In 1999, Nasser Eddin Nashashibi, when asked about the circumstances of Ragheb's appointment as Custodian nearly 50 years after the event, explained that for Abdullah being King of Jordan was not enough; he needed to be King of Jerusalem as well, because "whoever rules Jerusalem, rules the Middle East."[19] He disregarded his 1990 statement—that the appointment was political appeasement to calm a tense situation among Jordanian governmental officials—and reclaimed his 1980 position—that Abdullah's appointment of Ragheb Nashashibi was a spontaneous reaction to the newspaper interview—adding that it demonstrated Abdullah's respect for the Holy City. As to why Ragheb Nashashibi was chosen, again it was part of the respect the King had for the city. If Abdullah was going to make such a bold move as to appoint someone to serve as Custodian of the Holy Places in the face of opposition from many elements of the world community, then it would have to be from a notable Jerusalem family, which would lend credibility and legitimacy to the appointee, Ragheb, and to the appointer, Abdullah. Appointing someone who was not from a Jerusalem family would have added to the uncertainty the Hashemites had as rulers of the city, as they were not accepted by all Jerusalemites, or by all Palestinians (nor by all Transjordanians). Additionally, it does not seem that this post was entirely new in Jerusalem, nor was it new to the Nashashibi family. A gravestone dated from the 900s CE, currently located in the garden of the Nashashibi family home in Jerusalem, shows that the post of *nazir al-Haram al-Sharif*, the Custodian of the Holy Places, was occupied by a member of the same family during the tenth century.[20] The Nashashibi family had a strong connection with the Hashemite Monarchy throughout the period; thus, Ragheb was a logical choice. For Abdullah, appointing a member of the Nashashibi family also served to block Husseini family involvement in Jordanian Jerusalem's religious affairs, as that family was not loyal to Abdullah.[21]

Contrary to what Jerusalem's consular corps had hoped, the Custodian's position continued after Ragheb Nashashibi's death in 1951, although the budget for the position was allocated at a reduced level. Dr. Hussein Fakhri al-Khalidi succeeded Ragheb Nashashibi and remained in the post for a year—one filled with difficulties. British consular officials saw the continuance of this position likely as Jordanian officials had intended: "bound up with a new drive by Jordan to secure international recognition for its control of part of Jerusalem."[22]

The Custodian position, however, was not just the result of Abdullah's drive to assert control over Jerusalem; underlying political considerations also shaped the king's decisions. The Nashashibi family had supported Abdullah since the 1930s during the mandate period. Abdullah chose his first Custodian as a means to shore up support among a long-time ally's supporters. The appointment of Dr. Hussein Fakhri al-Khalidi, also from a prominent Jerusalem family, after Ragheb Nashashibi, further complicated the situation. At one time, the Khalidi and Nashashibi families had been allies, but their alliance dissolved over political matters and the Khalidi family broke away from the Nashashibi-led opposition during the mandate. Dr. al-Khalidi challenged Ragheb Nashashibi for the mayoralty of Jerusalem in 1934. The latter had served as mayor for nearly 14 years, following his appointment by the British to replace Musa Kazim al-Husseini. Hussein Fakhri al-Khalidi, now a Husseini supporter, won the election and received British backing for the position in 1934.[23]

King Abdullah likely chose Dr. al-Khalidi to succeed Ragheb Nashashibi as Custodian in 1951 because, as an ally of the Husseini faction with strong support among Palestinians in the kingdom, he appealed to a broad segment of Jordan's population. The selection of Dr. al-Khalidi coincided with the waning public appeal of the Nashashibi family—evident by their absence from the Jericho Congress in 1948 (Nevo 1996, 160). Abdullah may also have chosen him as a gesture of accommodation with Israel, as the Jewish Agency in mandatory Palestine had supported Dr. al-Khalidi over Ragheb Nashashibi in the 1934 contest for mayor (Porath 1977, 62–64, and Halabi 1993, 9–10).

The Office of the Custodian of the *Haram al-Sharif* and the Holy Places did not last much longer. By the summer of 1952, an incident arose that challenged the authority of the Custodian's position. Dr. al-Khalidi ruled on a dispute between the Greek Orthodox, who replaced the oil lamps on a star in the Church of the Nativity in Bethlehem with electric lamps, and the Latins and Armenian Orthodox, who opposed the change.[24] Al-Khalidi ruled against the Greek Orthodox as their action challenged the status quo that had been passed down from the Ottoman period and upheld by the British. After al-Khalidi's decision, the Greek Orthodox appealed the decision to the Ministry of the Interior in Amman (Dearden 1958, 189–191). By reversing the ruling, the Ministry, in effect, undermined the Custodian's authority, and Dr. al-Khalidi resigned his post. Though sustaining Amman's sovereignty over holy places, the Ministry contradicted the status quo that Jordan's government claimed it intended to uphold. The Governor (*mutasarrif*) of Jerusalem then took charge of the holy places and assumed the other responsibilities of the Custodian.[25] Dr. al-Khalidi would later serve as the Jordanian Minister for Foreign Affairs, thereby regaining much of his personal authority in Jordanian politics. The British reported three months later, in November 1952, that the Jordanians had decided to use the salary of the vacant Custodian's post to pay a Vice-Minister of Interior who would live in Jerusalem and have primary responsibility for the West Bank.[26] By the time King Hussein took the throne in 1953, the Custodian position no longer existed. Nevertheless, the precedent set by Abdullah—appointing a Jordanian political official solely to oversee the holy places in Jerusalem—would facilitate Hussein's administrative changes in the Holy City during the middle part of the 1950s.

Sovereignty without taxation?

Less than a year after King Abdullah's death, the new Jordanian government changed the customs policy for Jerusalem's consular corps. The consular corps, a recognized institution in the city from the middle of the nineteenth century, "embodied the Christian interest in the Holy Places" and, according to Evan Wilson, an American Foreign Service officer in Jerusalem from 1964 to 1967, "maintained close contacts with ecclesiastical leaders in the city" (Wilson 1970, 43).[27] During the Ottoman period, the Sultan had allowed members of the corps to import items without paying duty. In late 1951, the Jordanian government's decision to change that policy and exact customs from the consular corps set off a wave of diplomatic opposition.

The imposition of taxation on the consular corps was an effort to elicit their acceptance of Jordanian sovereignty over Jerusalem. Had the corps agreed to pay the taxes, they would have validated Jordan's rule over Jerusalem (Franck 1990, 96ff.). Recognition by one authority—the consular corps—of the act of another—the Jordanian government—reinforces the authority of the latter, something the corps was unwilling to do with regard to control of Jerusalem by Jordan.

In January 1952, the French consul general, the doyen of the consular corps, addressed the matter in correspondence with the Governor of Jerusalem. By contacting the local official in Jerusalem, rather than a governmental minister in Amman, France's government, in effect, refused to acknowledge Jordan's national sovereignty over the Holy City.[28] After referring the matter to the Council of Ministers in Amman, the Governor of Jerusalem responded that changes would, in fact, take place with regard to the new customs duties.[29] The Council of Ministers decided, ultimately, that diplomats could only be granted exemption from customs duties after "they have presented to the Jordan Government their letters of appointment and received exequaturs [written permission from the Jordanian government], as is required by international law."[30] Like the payment of taxes, exequaturs would also offer the Jordanians a symbolic "cue" to validate their rule of the Holy City.[31] Acceptance by foreign governments of either notion would, in effect, imply recognition of Jordan's sovereignty over Jerusalem.

The consular corps was not prepared to recognize Jordan's sovereignty over Jerusalem. After discussing the issue among its members, the corps suggested several ways to deal with the matter, including: (1) having consular officials present their credentials to the Jordanian Governor of Jerusalem, thereby recognizing local, rather than national, rule in Jerusalem; and (2) separating the territorial areas of the West Bank and Jerusalem when requesting a diplomat's exequatur. The corps noted a number of problems that recognizing Jordan's sovereignty in Jerusalem would raise: it would obviously contrast with the international position toward Jerusalem's status, and any recognition of Jordan's sovereignty in Jerusalem would likely stir Israel's government to take similar actions to force international recognition of Israeli sovereignty over the western part of the city, an issue that would, in fact, arise two years later.[32]

Jordan's efforts to force recognition of its sovereignty over Jerusalem by withholding exequaturs did not bring the desired result. Foreign diplomats refused to recognize Jordan's sovereignty in Jerusalem. Legal records in the British Foreign Office state that "on strictly legal interpretation the act of seeking and obtaining exequatur would not necessarily imply recognition of Jordan sovereignty ... [although] it would be bound to be viewed in that light and should therefore be avoided."[33] British diplomats debated the matter of exequaturs for several months and, although the Foreign Office documents do not reveal the outcome, it is unlikely that consular (including British) officials presented their credentials to the Jordanian government seeking exequaturs.

Administrative control through re-districting

In the early 1950s, some Palestinians in the kingdom, including parliamentarian Kamil Erekat, suggested moving Jordan's capital to Jerusalem, thus bringing to the fore the competition over geo-national space between West Bankers and East Bankers, between Palestinians and Jordanians.[34] Jerusalem was a source of contention for many Palestinians, who claimed that the Holy City was being discriminated against, while Amman, the capital city, received a disproportionate share of political, economic, and infrastructural attention (Sofer 1976, 84–86). Israeli historian Naim Sofer argues, however, that Jerusalem remained a political, cultural, and religious center under the Jordanians (Sofer 1976, 79–80). He lists a range of factors from which one can discern the maintenance of Jerusalem's status under

Jordanian control: the presence of many opposition groups loyal to the Mufti, the high number of newspaper headquarters located there, as well as it being the center for many of the Christian churches and the location for the weekly pilgrimage to the Aqsa mosque (Sofer 1976, 78–79).

Some Palestinians argued that Jordan had the legal authority to make Jerusalem the capital since the kingdom's constitution permitted changing the capital under special juridical circumstances.[35] Amman, however, had served as the capital city of Transjordan during the period of the British mandate, and any move to change that after Jordan took control of Jerusalem after 1948 would have had grave consequences. Such a move would have required relocating the center of government to the geographic heart of Palestinian political and cultural life, which might have led to a kind of "Palestinianization" of the kingdom and instability for the Hashemite regime. More importantly, it would have implied that the sense of communal identification with East Bank national sites that Abdullah had created for Transjordanians during the Amirate period was now discredited in the face of a rival city (Katz 2005, 16–40). Finally, a Jordanian decision to move the capital to Jerusalem would have generated intense criticism from the international community, which favored internationalization of the Holy City, and from Israel, which also claimed Jerusalem as its capital.[36]

The prospect of making Jerusalem the Jordanian capital had repercussions on the status of the city, as the government changed its title, or status, several times during the mid-1950s. It is difficult to derive a direct causal relationship between the two issues—the call for Jerusalem to become a capital and the changing administrative status of the city. Both subjects, however, appeared concurrently in public discourse, particularly in the Jordanian press, and both equally agitated the consular corps in Jerusalem, which opposed any changes in Jerusalem in lieu of an internationally sanctioned solution.

The discussions concerning the administration of Jerusalem that occurred after King Hussein's ascension to the throne reflect, in fact, a kind of continuation of the policy that King Abdullah began when he established the Custodianship of the Holy Places. The position did not endure, but the duties of the Custodian became part of the city's administration under a deputy in the Jordanian Ministry of the Interior with a title of *mutasarrif*, or governor.[37] At the end of November 1954, approximately the same time as the issue of Jerusalem as a capital city aired publicly, Ibrahim al-Shanti, founder of *al-Difa'* newspaper in 1934 under the British mandate, wrote that Jerusalem could not be only a *mutasarrifiya* (district), "rather it was natural that it should be a *muhafiza mumtaza*" (*Al-Difa'*, November 25, 1954). Both were administrative districts, but the latter was apparently a more respected title suitable for a holy city, as the adjective *mumtaza* indicated a privileged or superior status. Al-Shanti envisioned it having an administrator with the rank of minister, perhaps similar to the earlier "Custodian of the Holy Places" position. Less than two weeks after al-Shanti's comments, *Filastin* reported that the deputy minister's position in Jerusalem would be abolished and that the government intended to replace it with the position of *muhafiz mumtaz*, although not with the rank of minister (*Filastin*, December 1954). In addition to the duties of the *mutasarrif*, the new *muhafiz*, Hasan al-Katib (who was the *mutasarrif* at the time), would have control over the holy places, thereby acknowledging, in al-Shanti's words, "their importance from an international and historical perspective" (*Al-Difa'*, November 25, 1954). Indeed, Jordan's leaders were aware that any change in the status of the city would incite the international community, but throughout the decade they would alter the status of Jerusalem to fit Jordan's political and national goals.

Just as Abdullah's actions with regard to Jerusalem had alarmed the Western powers, so too did Hussein's efforts to reconfigure the role of Jerusalem in the kingdom. In the spring of 1955, King Hussein issued a Royal Decree that split the position of *mutasarrif* into two positions—*mutasarrif* and *muhafiz*—although the differentiation between the two positions was never entirely clear.[38] The pre-1955 *mutasarrif* governed the city of Jerusalem, but the title made no mention of sovereignty over holy places. Because it made no mention of the holy places, the title was not contested by the city's consular corps as de facto Jordanian rule in the city had been widely accepted by that time. The office of "*muhafiz* of Jerusalem and the Holy Places," however, became a point of contention. British official F. A. Vallat remarked that such a change "indicates an intention to strengthen the Jordanian claim to the part of Jerusalem over which they have control."[39] After the re-division of powers in the city, the *mutasarrif* governed the wider district of Jerusalem, including Bethlehem, Bayt Jala, and other towns, while the *muhafiz* ruled over the city of Jerusalem and the holy places.[40] The "*muhafiz* of Jerusalem and the Holy Places" made the title of *mutasarrif* appear, retroactively, less threatening to the international community, as the introduction of the new position simultaneously reinforced Jordanian rule over Jerusalem and the holy places and Jordan's rejection of the possibility of international rule over the Holy City as outlined in the 1947 Partition Plan.

The Jordanians offered a few explanations for the creation of the new position. In 1955, the British inquired into the difference between the *mutasarrif* and the *muhafiz*, which elicited the explanation that there was far too much work in the Jerusalem district for one man. By splitting the position of *mutasarrif* into two positions, the work could be distributed.

> The *Mohafez* will be responsible for Jerusalem town and for the Holy Places, whether inside or outside Jerusalem, whereas the *Mutassaref* . . . will be responsible for the remainder of the Jerusalem district. The *Mutassaref* will depend directly on the Ministry of the Interior, although he will probably consult the *Mohafez* on the more important questions. The situation in Jerusalem will thus correspond roughly to

that in Amman where there is a *Mohafez*, who deals with the town, and a *Mutassaref* who is responsible for Amman district.[41]

The British Consul General in Jerusalem offered details relating to the new position. The incumbent *mutassarif*, Hasan al-Katib, apparently conveyed to British Consul General Wikeley that the split occurred because a member of the Jordanian government decided to find a job for one of his relatives, an explanation the Consul General had already suspected.[42] Then, on June 22, 1955, the Jordanian Minister of the Interior defined the differences between the two positions somewhat differently:

> The *Mutassarref* was not directly under the *Mohafez*, although he took orders from him in certain matters. In addition to being Governor of Jerusalem, the *Mohafez* was also the representative of the Minister of the Interior for dealing with the Holy Places and settling disputes between the different sects ... This was a continuation of the practice under the Mandate, since responsibility for the Holy Places, which had been vested in the Mandatory Government, now lay with the Ministry of the Interior of the Jordan Government. The intention of the Jordan Government was to maintain the *status quo* and to make no change of any kind. They did not wish to transfer responsibility for the Holy Places outside the Jerusalem Municipality away from the *Mohafez*, with whom the foreign Consuls in Jerusalem, some of whom were preoccupied with the *status quo*, would continue to deal.[43]

The Minister's comments confirmed "that the post of *mohafez* had been created in order to show the importance which the Jordan Government gave to Jerusalem."[44] Almost one year earlier, the British, in their report on "The Holy Places of Palestine," mentioned above, had acknowledged a possible legal justification for Jordan's assumption of control over Jerusalem and the holy places.[45] They never actually sanctioned Jordanian sovereignty of the Holy City, and although some future memos came down more harshly on the Jordanians and their efforts to legitimize their rule over Jerusalem, others expressed ambivalence.

Response to the administrative change was almost immediate, although restrained. The French were suspicious of Jordanian intent "to encroach upon the sovereignty of Jerusalem."[46] The American and British legations in Jerusalem viewed the move as constituting "an unwarranted assumption of authority."[47] The British insisted that "the Jordan Government ... did not have a free hand in Jerusalem," yet British diplomats hesitated to chastise the Jordanian government for its actions.[48] Israel, "having broken all the canons of law relating to sovereignty over Jerusalem,"[49] the British reported, had already "gone as far as, if not further than, Jordan in asserting sovereignty over it," though holy places located in Israel's part of Jerusalem were considered less important.[50] For the sake of proper diplomacy, addressing one would necessarily involve addressing the other.[51]

From the resulting diplomatic concerns, it is clear that Jordanian officials succeeded in promoting Jerusalem, administratively, as an integral part of Jordan. For all of their diplomatic rhetoric about non-recognition of Jordanian sovereignty over the Holy City, the British were well aware that "the Jordanians regard[ed] themselves as ... sovereign over Jerusalem."[52] The British and the rest of the consular corps in Jerusalem were now resigned to the fact that they would have to deal with these Jordanian officials in Jerusalem as the need arose no matter who they were, what their titles were, or whether the policy of their appointments followed the status quo.[53]

Jerusalem: a capital city in Jordan?

Public discussion of Jerusalem as a capital city, both in Jordan and other Arab states, arose in response to Israeli actions in the western part of the city. The discussion was complicated and contradictory, whether it took place in newspapers, on the radio, or in the Jordanian parliament. In 1954, the British and American ambassadors presented their credentials to the Israeli president *in Jerusalem*. In response, the Jordanian daily, *al-Difa'*, published a short piece by Yusuf Hanna titled "The Status of Jerusalem." Hanna wrote that Israel had made Jerusalem the capital of its state, but as for Jordan, "we reduced Jerusalem from a position of preeminence to its current place that does not rise above the rank of village" (*Al-Difa'*, November 5, 1954). The Palestinian-turned-Jordanian newspaper gave voice to Palestinian criticisms of Jordan's policies toward Jerusalem. This excoriation led not to a change in policy, but at least to some public debate. The debate quickly revealed gaps in Jordan's efforts to co-opt Palestinians into the nation-building project, particularly around the issue of Jerusalem. Seven years since Jordan took control of Jerusalem, and five years since its annexation by the Jordanian parliament, the kingdom had not sufficiently absorbed Palestinians and made them feel equal to Transjordanians; Palestinians continued to criticize Jordan's rule in varying degrees.

Less than a week after Hanna's article appeared in *al-Difa'*, Cairo Radio (Voice of the Arabs) reported that "The Old City of Jerusalem is to become the capital of Jordan. With the transfer of the Jordan Ministry of Foreign Affairs to Jerusalem, western ambassadors will have to present their letters of credence there. The Arabs will thus forestall any Israeli claim to both the new and old cities of Jerusalem."[54] The broadcast clearly referred to "the Arabs" and not "the Jordanians" as responsible for preventing further Israeli action in the Holy City. The broadcast had originated in Cairo, and reflected the Pan-Arab policy of Egyptian president Nasser, rather than the Pan-Arab policy of the Hashemites. With Israel staking physical and diplomatic claim to Jerusalem, the Arabs worried less about Jordan claiming authority there. The Voice of the Arabs had reported on the matter even before it came up in the Jordanian parliament.

On November 12, 1954, *Filastin* reported that Kamil Erekat, a Palestinian representative in the Jordanian parliament, proposed in the House of Representatives that Jerusalem become the second capital of Jordan (*Filastin*, November 12, 1954). Four days later, Jordan's radio station in Ramallah reported that Jerusalem was being considered for a new status as the second capital of Jordan.[55] Jordan's Minister of Foreign Affairs is reported to have said that any decision to move Jordan's capital to Jerusalem could only be taken in consultation and agreement with the other Arab states.[56] Monitoring a Beirut broadcast, the BBC reported on December 10, 1954 that while the Arab League Political Committee had not yet concluded discussions on the issue of giving Jerusalem "capital" status in Jordan, the plan to move the foreign ministry there was very likely, but would again need the Arab states' agreement. Jordan's government never moved the foreign ministry to Jerusalem, as rhetoric prevailed over action by Jordan and by the Arab states, which first raised the idea publicly.[57] The idea circulated for several years but fell prey to the hostile inter-Arab politics of the 1950s.

The public discourse on Jerusalem as a Jordanian capital was part of Jordan's efforts to deal with two difficult loci of opposition: externally, Nasser and his socialist vision of Arab nationalism threatened Jordan's leadership; internally, Palestinians in the kingdom loyal to Nasser challenged regime stability. By debating the issue of Jerusalem, the Jordanian government aimed to placate the opposition in the country, many of whom were Palestinian. The kingdom appeared to be giving Jerusalem its due as a Muslim and Christian holy city. It was hoped that throwing "Jerusalem" into the inter-Arab political arena would help counter Nasser's efforts to dominate the Arab world: the city tugged at religious sensitivities from which the Jordanians hoped to gain support for the Hashemite brand of Arab nationalism. The issue, however, remained pure rhetoric: Jerusalem did not become the capital city of Jordan, the government did not succeed in its efforts to placate Palestinians, and the Hashemite monarchy never won the Arab masses away from Nasser.

The 1950s was a whirlwind for local politics in Jordanian Jerusalem. The period began with uncertainty over the composition and function of Jerusalem's Municipal Committee that carried over from the British mandate period. All other functions aside, the Committee concerned itself, according to Daniel Rubenstein, with a "prolonged campaign to prevent the transfer of government offices and other public institutions from Jerusalem" (Rubenstein 1980, 89). Despite rhetoric to the contrary, the government decided to re-locate central ministries left from the mandate period, and their officials, to Amman at the expense of Jerusalem. In a memo to the Prime Minister, Anwar Nusseibeh, Member of Parliament for the Jerusalem region, complained of discrimination toward the city at a time when Israel was fortifying its position in the western part of the city (Rubenstein 1980, 89).

Just prior to the 1959 municipal elections in Jerusalem, the Jordanian government made several political and symbolic gestures toward the city of Jerusalem. A governmental meeting convened in Jerusalem in 1959 announced the decision to upgrade the status of the city from a *baladiyya* (municipality) to an *amana* (district). It was now the only city in the king-dom other than Amman to have that distinction. At the same time, the government decided to build a royal palace in Jerusalem, the unofficial second capital of the kingdom (Halabi 1993, 19). These decisions, published in the *Official Gazette* on September 1, 1959, followed discussions on the subject between Ruhi al-Khatib, the new *amin* (District Governor) of the *amana*, and Jordan's Minister of the Interior, to whom the new *amin* now reported. The pending municipal elections in the Holy City likely encour-aged these decisions, as the Jordanian government sought to promote the city's position within the kingdom.

Some contemporary figures considered these decisions a positive change in the Jordanian government's policy toward the Holy City, although some scholars have offered a competing theory for the basis of these changes, which must be considered (Rubenstein 1980, 98). One Israeli scholar claims that the gesture by the Jordanian government amounted to nothing more than a propaganda ploy to convince the Jerusalemites not to rebel during a politically unstable period for inter-Arab politics. At the time, Jordan was isolated from the United Arab Republic (UAR), the new Arab union between Egypt and Syria, and was weakened following the demise of the Jordan–Iraq union after a successful coup d'état in Iraq (Rubenstein 1980, 93). It is difficult to tell what Jordanian popular reaction to these decisions was. The idea of Jerusalem as a political capital of Jordan, however, con-tinued to circulate in rumors and rhetoric, remaining symbolically and politically as well as nationally charged. Jordan's parliament convened in Jerusalem the following year, adding further political and symbolic weight to Jerusalem's status in Jordan. In his speech to the parliament in Jer-usalem, the king reiterated the change in the Holy City's position within the kingdom, and in the kingdom itself, welcoming, on January 19, 1960, the members of Parliament to "the Holy Land" (*al-balad al-muqaddas*) and "to the second capital of the Hashemite Kingdom of Jordan" (King Hussein, n.d.).

The idea of Jerusalem as the "spiritual capital of Jordan" took root early on, although it did not carry much legislative backing. King Hussein often referred to Jerusalem as the kingdom's "spiritual capital" in his official speeches, and only infrequently used the appellation "Second Capital of the Hashemite Kingdom of Jordan," as he did in his address to the Parliament in Jerusalem in 1960. On October 6, 1954, in an interview with an American journalist, the king explained his government's position regarding the Holy City: "The position of my government regarding internationalization of Jerusalem has not changed as stated on a number of occasions. Jerusalem is the spiritual capital of our country, it is the cradle of our heritage and our glory" (Abu 'Alba and al-Khummash 1998, 17).

The use of the term "spiritual capital" was not promoted for foreign consumption alone. The king often added it when speaking to the Jordanian public on national or religious holidays. For example, King Hussein, in his speech on *Yawm al-maydan* (Battle Day) on June 3, 1956, greeted the youth of the country "from the noble Jerusalem, the Jordanian spiritual capital, cradle of the prophets and messengers" (Abu 'Alba and al-Khummash 1998). The king took the same message abroad when he spoke, on August 25, 1963, to Arab students at the 12th Arab Student Congress in the United States, reminding them that they "must not forget our centers in the city of Jerusalem, the spiritual capital of the kingdom" (Abu 'Alba and al-Khummash 1998). He also used the expression to welcome a conference of Arab Physicians to Jerusalem on July 28, 1964, saying, "It pleases me that your honored gathering and conference is convening in the spiritual capital of the Hashemite Kingdom of Jordan, near the Aqsa mosque which has been blessed by God and near the cradle of the Christian prophet, may peace be upon him" (Abu 'Alba and al-Khummash 1998, 46).

In contrast, the king rarely spoke of the Holy City as the capital, without referring to it as either the spiritual or second capital of Jordan. On February 26, 1957, Hussein commemorated the Islamic holiday of the Night Journey and Ascension of the Prophet by praising the Aqsa mosque while also making reference to the Christian attachment to the Holy City. He said, "*Bayt al-Maqdis* (Jerusalem), our capital, and the city of Islam remains the site for pilgrimage for Arabs and Muslims, and the dwelling place of the hearts of Christians" (Abu 'Alba and al-Khummash 1998, 22). This official mention of Jerusalem as a capital, *not* a spiritual capital, may be the only time that the king mentioned Jerusalem in this context during a religious Muslim holiday.[58] Coming as it did during the turbulent time of the Nabulsi government in which Prime Minister Nabulsi was ultimately forced to resign, the statement is somewhat over-determined. Mentioning Jerusalem in this manner at this particularly sensitive political juncture suggests that the king might have invoked the sanctity of Jerusalem and its place in the kingdom as a means to re-affirm his authority during a period of domestic political instability. This was not a change in policy, but rather reflected the monarch's effort to give Jerusalem a prominent position in the Hashemite Kingdom of Jordan and to provide a cover of Islamic legitimacy. Jerusalem appeared in other speeches for the variety of occasions mentioned here, but the "national" embodiment of the city seems rare in official discourse during Islamic holidays.

Notes

1 This chapter is based on Chapter 3 of my book *Jordanian Jerusalem: Holy Places and National Spaces* (Gainesville: University Press of Florida, 2005), and is reprinted with permission of the University Press of Florida.
2 UN General Assembly Resolution 181, November 29, 1947; UN General Assembly Resolution 194, December 11, 1948.

3 *Treaty of Alliance between His Majesty in respect of the United Kingdom and His Highness the Amir of Trans-Jordan* (with annex and exchange of notes), London, March 22, 1946. This clause from the 1946 Treaty of Alliance between Great Britain and Transjordan can also be found in a British Consular report on Jordan's Constitutional Position. FO 371 110854, n.d., as well as in FO 371 121443 VE 1781/21 CH/4/54, September 26, 1954.

4 *Treaty of Alliance between His Majesty in respect of the United Kingdom of Great Britain and Northern Ireland and His Majesty the King of the Hashimite Kingdom of Transjordan* (with exchanges of letters), Amman, March 15, 1948. The full text of the 1948 Treaty of Alliance: Britain and Transjordan, without the letters, can be found in Hurewitz 1987, 296–299.

5 FO 371 121443 VE 1781/21 CH/4/54, September 26, 1954.

6 These three quotes are found in FO 371 121443 VE 1781/21 CH/4/54, September 26, 1954.

7 King Abdullah's quote is also found in FO 371 121443 VE 1781/21 CH/4/54, September 26, 1954. See also *The Times*, February 22, 1949.

8 Pakistan was the other. British Consular report on Jordan's Constitutional Position. FO 371 110854, n.d.

9 The Royal Decree was published in the *Official Gazette* on January 16, 1951, issue 1053, p. 718. Confirmation for the appointment by the Prime Minister and the King and correspondence between the Prime Minister and the Royal Court Chief appears in the following documents: From the Prime Minister to the Royal Court Chief (no document number), December 30, 1950 (p. 364); From the Prime Minister to the King (no document number), December 30, 1950 (p. 365); From the Royal Court Chief to the Prime Minister, document number 781–81/8, January 2, 1951 (p. 366). These documents are found in al-Bakhit et al., *al-Watha'iq al-hashimiya*, 364–366. (These will be cited hereafter as *Hashemite Archives*.)

10 *Hashemite Archives*: From the Prime Minister to the King (no document number), December 30, 1950 (p. 365); From the Royal Court Chief to the Prime Minister, document number 781–781/8, January 2, 1951 (p. 366).

11 It should be remembered that the Nashashibi family allied itself with Abdullah and the Hashemites already during the Amirate/Mandate period, specifically in opposition to the Mufti (Katz 2005, 52).

12 Nashashibi offers no documentation for these foreign reactions to Abdullah's creation of the position. Based on the political-historical context, they are most likely accurate. The remainder of this chapter addresses foreign opposition to Jordan's assumption of authority in Jerusalem, so it is likely that al-Nashashibi's comments are correct, even if they are undocumented.

13 It is unclear what the British official might have meant by this, as the "Rightly Guided Caliphs" ruled from Medina, with the exception of the last of them, 'Ali, who ruled from Kufa, in today's Iraq. Perhaps the official thought that the king was relying on his Hashemite origins, from the family of the Prophet Muhammad, to legitimize his rule, or perhaps he saw Abdullah as ruling over a Holy City from his "imperial" capital a distance away, in this case Amman on the East bank, as the Umayyad and Abbasid Caliphs did from Damascus and Baghdad.

14 Ragheb Nashashibi was mayor of Jerusalem from 1920 to 1934 (Halabi 1993, 66).

15 Author's interview with Nasser Eddin Nashashibi, May 6, 1999.

16 al-Nashashibi, *Man qatala*; see also *Hashemite Archives*: From the Prime Minister to the King (no document number), December 30, 1950 (p. 365); From the Royal Court Chief to the Prime Minister, document number 781–781/8, January 2, 1951 (p. 366).

17 Nasser Eddin has translated the title in *Jerusalem's Other Voice* to "Servant of the Aqsa Mosque, Custodian of the Holy Places in the city and Superintendent of the Haram al-Sharif."

18 This is purely circumspection by the author in an effort to make some sense of the difference in Nasser Eddin Nashashibi's accounts in 1980 and 1990 of the creation of the position of Custodian of the Holy Places in Jerusalem in 1950.

19 Interview with Nasser Eddin Nashashibi in Jerusalem on May 6, 1999.

20 I saw the tombstone during a 1999 interview with Nasser Eddin Nashashibi.

21 Interview with Nasser Eddin Nashashibi in Jerusalem, May 6, 1999.

22 April 5, 1952, FO 371 98488 1782/2/52.

23 Dr. Hussein Fakhri al-Khalidi won the election, but according to Palestine law under the mandate, the Government (i.e., the British) had the right to appoint whomever they wanted as mayor from among those elected to the municipal council (Porath 1977, 63).

24 Little is available in the way of historical documentation regarding this position of "Custodian of the Holy Places" and what is available has generally focused on Ragheb, not on Hussein Fakhri al-Khalidi. What is presented here is found in reports from the British Consulate General in Jerusalem to the Eastern Department of the Foreign Office in London. FO 371 98503, June 11, 1952 (1782/4/52); August 20, 1952 (1782/11/52), as well as in Dearden 1958.

25 August 20, 1952, FO 371 98503 (1782/11/52).

26 November 28, 1952, FO 371 98503 (1810/12). I believe this was the *mutasarrif* position, and that it first appeared during 1952. Immediately after the war, Jerusalem had a Military Commander, who appointed the mayors of Jerusalem. Change, it seems, came after the introduction of the position of the Custodian of the Holy Places.

27 According to Wilson, the basis of the Consular Corps was the consulates that had been established in the mid-nineteenth century when there were no Arab states. The Arab states joined Jerusalem's Consular Corps when they began to send diplomatic representatives to Jerusalem. They did not always agree with the positions of their western counterparts and they are barely mentioned in the British consular reports reviewed here.

28 A copy of this memorandum was also sent to the British Consulate General in Jerusalem. The French memo, dated January 16, 1952, can be found in FO 371 98488. The French memo refers to this Jordanian official as "*le Directeur général,*" rendered in English by British officials as Governor. Again, here I believe this Governor of Jerusalem to be the *mutasarrif*, a position that raised controversy in mid-1950s Jerusalem among the diplomatic corps and is discussed later in this chapter.

29 The details are found in a memo from the British Consulate General in Jerusalem to the Eastern Department, Foreign Office in London. FO 371 98488 (1923/3/52) dated March 12, 1952.

30 Memo from the British Consulate General in Jerusalem to the Eastern Department, Foreign Office in London. FO 371 98488 (1923/3/52) dated March 12, 1952. This quote is attributed to the Jordanian Governor of Jerusalem in the memo.

31 For more on how an exequatur can be used as a symbolic "cue" used to invoke authority see Franck 1990, 96ff.

32 Memo from the British Consulate General in Jerusalem to the Eastern Department, Foreign Office in London. FO 371 98488 (1923/3/52) dated March 12, 1952. The 1954 issue referred to in Israeli Jerusalem is addressed below.

33 FO 371 98488 minutes in response to FO 371 98488 (1923/3/52) March 12, 1952 and Departmental Distribution memo from Foreign Office to Jerusalem, No. 46, April 4, 1952.

34 Kamil Erekat stated in the Jordanian parliament that the constitution permitted a change of the capital city (*al-Difa'*, February 22, 1956).

35 Both the 1946 and 1952 Constitutions include a clause proclaiming the capital of the kingdom to be Amman, "but it may be changed to another locality by a

special law." An English translation of the Constitution may be found in Khalil 1962, 43 and 55 for the quoted clause. See also Sofer 1976, 84–86.

36 Most of the literature on this subject suggests that Jerusalem was almost completely neglected by the Hashemites and the Jordanian government during the 1948–67 period. I do not dispute this entirely, but instead offer evidence here that Jordan invested in the Holy City for national purposes, i.e., identity building.

37 The Consular Corps rendered *mutasarrif* in English as Governor (I have retained the original transliteration in quotations, but have used a more acceptable transliteration in my own text). The British Consul General in Jerusalem at that time had the following to say about the position:

> *Mutassaref* was the title given under the Turks to the man in charge of Jerusalem (though he was usually known as the Pasha), and the title denoted an official one degree lower than *Wali* or Governor General (who resided at Damascus); it would, therefore, seem quite normal to translate it as "Governor."
>
> Wikeley (British Consulate General) to Brewis (Levant Department),
> April 15, 1955, FO 371 115663

38 FO 371 115663, memoranda from April 15, 1955 to May 18, 1955 (1020/6 April 15, 1955, 1020/11 May 12, 1955, 1020/14 May 18, 1955, 1018/9/55 May 18, 1955) and *al-Difa'*, No. 5853, May 13, 1955, with excerpt found in FO 371 115663 (1020/14) on May 18, 1955.

39 FO 371 115663, letter by Vallat dated April 14, 1955.

40 Jordanian officials expanded the municipal boundaries of Jerusalem in 1952 (Halabi 1993, 18). British Consul General Wikeley mentions that the wider boundaries include these towns, although he does not say when the boundaries were re-drawn to include them.

41 FO 371 115663 1018/9/55 May 18, 1955. The transliteration here adheres to the original British document, and thus is inconsistent with my transliterations.

42 FO 371 115663 1020/15G May 19, 1955.

43 FO 371 115663 1018/17/55 June 24, 1955.

44 Ibid.

45 For the report on "The Holy Places of Palestine," see FO 371 121443 VE 1781/21 CH/4/54, September 26, 1954.

46 FO 371 115663 1781/39/55 May 3, 1955, Confidential memo from the British Embassy in Tel Aviv to the Levant Department, Foreign Office in London.

47 Ibid.

48 Ibid.

49 Ibid.

50 FO 371/115663, Registry No. VJ1082/13, June 1955, Confidential Draft Memo from Mr. Rose (likely in London) to Mr. Duke, at Britain's embassy in Amman.

51 Ibid.

52 FO 371 115663, No. 1018/9/55, Registry 26/5/55, Dated May 18, 1955, letter from Chancery in Amman to the Levant Department, Foreign Office in London. "Authority in Jordan Jerusalem" in FO 371 115663, May 23, 1955 and May 25, 1955.

53 FO 371 115663 1018/9/55 May 18, 1955.

54 November 11, 1954, Cairo Radio (Voice of the Arabs) found in FO 371 110880.

55 November 16, 1954, Jordan Radio (Ramallah) found in FO 371 110880.

56 "Possibility of Jordan Seat of Government Being Transferred to Jerusalem," December 21, 1954, found in FO 371 110880.

57 Ibid.

58 I have located King Hussein's speeches for the *'Id al-isra' wa-l-mi'raj* holiday for five out of the nineteen years that Jerusalem was part of Jordan (1957, 1958, 1960, 1961, and 1962). For more on this holiday and its role in Jordan's nation-building practices see Katz 2005, 111–117.

References

Abu 'Alba, Muhammad, and Nibal Taysir al-Khummash, eds. 1998. *Hawl shu'un al-Quds al-sharif wa-al-muqaddasat, al-nutq al-sami, 1952–1998.* Amman: Ibrahim Zahran.

Abu 'Odeh, 'Adnan. 1999. *Jordanians, Palestinians, and the Hashemite Kingdom in the Middle East Peace Process.* Washington, D.C.: United States Institute for Peace.

Aruri, Naseer. 1972. *Jordan: A Study in Political Development, 1921–1965.* The Hague: Nijhoff.

Al-Bakhit, Muhammad 'Adnan et al. 1995. *Al-Watha'iq al-hashimiyya, awraq al-malik 'Abd Allah bin al-Husayn: al-idara al-Urduniyya fi Filastin, 1948–1951.* Vol. 6. Amman: Jami'at Al al-Bayt.

Dearden, Ann. 1958. *Jordan.* London: Robert Hale.

Franck, Thomas. 1990. *The Power of Legitimacy among Nations.* New York: Oxford University Press.

Halabi, Usama. 1993. *Baladiyyat al-Quds al-arabiyya.* Jerusalem: PASSIA. (In Arabic.)

Hurewitz, J. C. 1987. *Diplomacy in the Near and Middle East.* Princeton: Van Nostrand.

Katz, Kimberly. 2005. *Jordanian Jerusalem: Holy Places and National Spaces.* Gainesville: University Press of Florida.

Khalil, Muhammad. 1962. *The Arab States and the Arab League.* Beirut: Khayyat.

King Abdullah of Jordan. 1978. *My Memoirs Completed.* Trans. Harold Glidden. London: Longman.

King Hussein of Jordan. 1962. *Uneasy Lies the Head: The Autobiography of His Majesty King Hussein I of the Hashemite Kingdom of Jordan.* London: Heinemann.

———. n.d. *Khams wa-'ishrun 'amman min al-tarikh: majmu'at khutab jalalat al-malik al-Hussein bin Talal al-mu'adhdham, 1952–1977.* Vol. 2. London.

Nashashibi, Nasser Eddin. 1980. *Man qatala al-malik 'Abd Allah?* Amman: Dar al-Aruba. (In Arabic.)

———. 1990. *Jerusalem's Other Voice: Ragheb Nashashibi and Moderation in Palestinian Politics, 1920–1948.* Exeter: Ithaca Press.

Nevo, Joseph. 1996. *King Abdallah and Palestine: A Territorial Ambition.* New York: St. Martin's Press.

Porath, Yehoshua. 1977. *The Palestinian Arab National Movement, 1929–1939.* London: Frank Cass.

Rubenstein, Daniel. 1980. "The Jerusalem Municipality under the Ottomans, British, and Jordanians." In *Jerusalem: Problems and Prospects,* ed. Joel Kraemer, 72–99. New York: Praeger.

Sofer, Naim. 1976. "The Political Status of Jerusalem in the Hashemite Kingdom of Jordan, 1948–67." *Middle Eastern Studies* 12 (January): 73–94.

Swedenburg, Ted. 1995. *Memories of Revolt: The 1936–1939 Rebellion and the Palestinian National Past.* Minneapolis: University of Minnesota Press.

Wilson, Evan M. 1970. *Jerusalem: Key to Peace.* Washington: The Middle East Institute.

16 The Palestinian political leadership in East Jerusalem after 1967

Elie Rekhess

Introduction

The Six-Day War of June 1967 between Israel and Egypt, Syria, and Jordan represented a major watershed in the Israeli–Arab confrontation and heralded the 'Palestinization' of the conflict. After the war, attention focused on the Israeli occupation of the Palestinian territories in the West Bank and the Gaza Strip, and on the Palestinian struggle for liberation. It was only natural to expect that the opposition to Israeli rule of the territories would be led by the Arab leadership in Jerusalem, the historical capital of Palestine, whose residents had traditionally played a major role in the social, cultural, historical, and above all religious history of the region.

Under British rule (1917–48), Jerusalem enjoyed a brief period as the political and administrative capital of Palestine. When East Jerusalem came under Jordanian rule (1948–67) it lost much of its political glory. Even after the elimination of direct Jordanian control over East Jerusalem following the Six-Day War and the unification of both sections of Jerusalem under Israeli rule, the East Jerusalem leadership failed to establish itself as a major national-political center of Arab-Palestinian activism. Their political impotence was, to some extent, due to a lack of internal cohesion, a longstanding characteristic of the Palestinian society in general and Palestinian society in Jerusalem in particular.[1] However, even more important than local disunity, the emergence of an effective East Jerusalem leadership was undermined by the incessant interference of three external political entities, Israel, Jordan, and the Palestinian Liberation Organization (PLO), which shared an interest in curtailing the development of an autonomous local leadership.

This chapter traces the motives and *modi operandi* of the three actors since the Six-Day War, and the shifting balance of power between Jordan, Israel, and the Palestinian Authority in East Jerusalem over time. Two examples are presented in detail, attempts to control the Muslim Council and attempts by the Palestinian authorities to reestablish a foothold in the city after 1994, in order to highlight how each worked to undermine the influence of the others. Jointly and independently, Israel, Jordan, and the PLO ultimately crippled the local political leadership of Jerusalem, preventing the emergence of local leadership that could have a direct and profound impact on the Palestinian arena as a whole.

Jordanian attempts at incorporation, 1948–67

Jordan's ties to Jerusalem, the third holiest city in Islam, are deep-rooted (see Chapter 6 by Suleiman Ali Mourad and Chapter 15 by Kimberly Katz). Jerusalem was a living symbol of the noble status of the Hashemites, descendants of the Prophet Muhammad and traditional guardians of the Temple Mount. The city was also an important source of legitimacy for their dynastic rule of Jordan and their claim to leadership status in the Arab world. Hence, Jordan considered Jerusalem an extremely important political asset (Merhav and Giladi 1999), although it had no direct involvement in the management of Jerusalem's religious affairs and institutions during the British Mandate period.

After formally annexing the West Bank in 1950, Jordan's strategy was to preserve the region's dependence and counter any aspiring Palestinian challenge from local power bases, including East Jerusalem. In this process, which came to be known as the "Jordanization" of the West Bank, Jordan stripped Jerusalem of the trappings of status that it had enjoyed during the British Mandate period.[2] Notwithstanding these efforts to incorporate the West Bank and Jerusalem under Jordanian control, the city became the site of one of several political nuclei that opposed the unification of the East and West Banks of the Jordan. In response, the Hashemite regime blocked the economic development of the city, and reallocated resources to reflect Amman's privileged status as the sole capital of the Kingdom. Another measure used to weaken the city's independent political base was the appointment of non-Jerusalemites to key positions in the city's administration (Stendel 1974, 493; Benvenisti 1973, 53).

Jordan's campaign to divest Jerusalem of all remnants of its former prestige targeted the great family matrix of Jerusalem notables (the Nashashibis, the Dajanis, and, above all, the Husseinis). When King Abd Allah of Jordan was assassinated by a Palestinian resident of Jerusalem while visiting the Aqsa mosque in Jerusalem on July 20, 1951,[3] the confession of one of the chief conspirators, Dr. Musa 'Abd Allah al-Husseini, a member of the Jerusalem elite, was sufficient reason to curtail his family's power and influence. Thus, the political significance of Jerusalem and its leading figures declined considerably under Jordanian rule, while its dependency on the Jordanian government increased.

The post-1967 era

On June 28, 1967, the Israeli Minister of the Interior issued an administrative order expanding the area of the (Israeli) Jerusalem municipality, effectively applying Israeli law, jurisdiction, municipal ordinances, and administration to the Arab part of the city. This order established the legal framework for what became known in Israel as the "Reunification of Jerusalem," and in non-Israeli sources as the annexation of Jerusalem (*Jerusalem Post*, June 27–28, 1967, cited in Dishon 1967, 290). Imposition of Israeli law over East Jerusalem, following the city's unification, replaced Jordanian law, which continued to be valid and implemented in other towns in the West Bank. After the unification of Jerusalem in late June 1967, Israel applied the most stringent measures to abort the activity of any Arab political body which might threaten its rule over the city or undermine the city's unification. Any indication of emergent Palestinian sovereignty was interpreted by Israel as anathema to the historical Jewish bond to Jerusalem and the sovereignty of the State of Israel over the city.

While elsewhere in the West Bank, municipalities and mayors were recognized by Israel as the local foci of power (e.g., Shaykh Muhammad 'Ali al-Ja'bari in Hebron), Israel recognized only one Jerusalem municipality, headed by a Jewish mayor. The East Jerusalem municipality was dissolved on June 29, 1967, the pro-Jordanian Arab mayor, Ruhi al-Khatib, was dismissed (and deported to Jordan in 1968; see below), and the Arab municipality ceased to exist as a separate polity shortly thereafter. The new, enlarged municipality established a special Liaison Office in East Jerusalem (Dishon 1967, 29), but since the councilors of the East Jerusalem municipality refused to join the new City Council, the population of East Jerusalem lacked appropriate representation in the city's Council (Dishon 1967, 29; Benvenisti 1973, 195; Benziman 1973, 62–64).

In this period, Israel also acted decisively to eradicate any residual Jordanian influence, and specifically targeted two major pro-Jordanian religious and political foci of power, the Muslim Council (al-Hay'a al-Islamiyya) and the Higher Committee for National Guidance (al-Lajna al-Ulya lil-Tawjih al-Watani). These organizations, founded in East Jerusalem shortly after the war, constituted a first attempt by local leaders at organizing the opposition to the Israeli occupation and filling the lacuna in leadership created by the elimination of the Jordanian rule in the city. As a result of Israeli actions, leading figures of the Committee and Council were first exiled to Jewish towns inside Israel and then deported to Jordan. (See below for a detailed discussion of the structure and activities of the two organizations, and the background to Israel's policy.)

The firm action by the Israelis weakened the remaining local leadership, and the limited power they wielded was not translated into concrete results. In 1968 and 1969, civil unrest in protest of the Israeli occupation evolved in Jerusalem, initiated by the Muslim Council and the Guidance Committee. It included commercial strikes, closure of schools, demonstrations, and occasional violent confrontations with the Israeli security forces. The harsh Israeli response effectively extinguished the civil protest. As Farhi noted, in 1969 the local leadership understood that more than strikes and demonstrations were needed to abolish Israeli rule (Farhi 1971, 16).

Local leadership was also weakened by Jordanian efforts to bolster its presence in response to the Israeli occupation. Jordan used its network of loyalists, including Anwar Nusseibeh (the former Ambassador to London and the Minister of Defense), Anwar al-Khatib (the governor of Jerusalem), Ruhi al-Khatib (mayor of Jerusalem), Kamal Dajani (former minister in the Jordanian Government), and Dr. Dawud al-Husseini (a member of the Jordanian Parliament).

The extent of the local leadership's debilitation was highlighted by the events surrounding the 1969 Jerusalem City Council elections. To express opposition to Israeli rule, both pro-Jordanian leaders and local leaders who supported the Palestinian organizations called strongly on the Jerusalemites to boycott the election. Exerting counter-pressure, the Israeli authorities demanded that city residents vote. This pressure was productive, and 7,500 of the city's 35,000 eligible voters (21 percent) cast their ballot.[4] Notwithstanding the fact that many city residents feared that their refusal to vote would lead to repercussions by Israeli authorities, the relatively high turnout of Arab voters, against expectations and in opposition to leaders' instructions, reflected the residents' acceptance of the new situation (Benvenisti 1973, 197; Stendel 1992, 337) and the local leadership's enervation. Although the terror attempts or violent demonstrations never ceased completely, the local Arab leadership in Jerusalem adopted a policy of "opposition through adjustment" (Stendel 1992, 337), generally seeking to maintain the status quo with Israeli authorities.

The policy of opposition through adjustment was effectively fed by a combination of factors. Israel's firm actions, the re-emergence of Jordanian influence, and the growing economic prosperity in East Jerusalem diminished the local leadership's motivation for rebellion and opposition to the annexation of East Jerusalem. Israel implemented a firm security policy that effectively curbed any attempt to establish a center of local opposition in East Jerusalem. However, in light of the marked rise in pro-PLO sentiments in the West Bank and the Gaza Strip, Israel became more open to accept Jordan's role as a potential partner in resolving the West Bank issue as the lesser of the two evils. This change in policy (which became known as "the Jordanian Option") was expressed, for example, in Israel's tacit agreement to the transfer of salaries from Jordan to East Jerusalem government employees and particularly Waqf officials. The considerable sums transferred through the Jordan Bridges preserved the employees' dependence on Amman. Finally, East Jerusalem enjoyed economic prosperity because of its role linking Israel and the territories in commercial transactions (Stendel 1992, 344–346; Zilberman 1994, 177), and its role in creating an active market for the large number of Israelis who declared their support for a unified Jerusalem by flooding the eastern section of the city as visitors and consumers. Israel also became an important source of employment for East Jerusalemites, who were also employed in massive construction projects in the city.

Political developments in the West Bank in the 1970s and 1980s also detracted from the centrality of the East Jerusalem leadership. The PLO's growing authority and influence following the Rabbat Summit of 1974[5] was reflected in the emergence of a new class of Palestinian leaders who viewed the PLO as their sole legitimate representative. Many of these leaders were elected in the 1976 municipal elections in West Bank cities, marking the corresponding decline in the impact of the traditional leadership on West Bank affairs.[6]

Growing support for the PLO played against both Jordanian and Israeli efforts to influence East Jerusalem politics. The newly elected West Bank city mayors stepped up their support for the PLO when the Likud won the Knesset elections in 1977, and in expression of the general vigorous Palestinian opposition to the 1978 Camp David Agreements and the subsequent 1979 peace treaty between Israel and Egypt. Motivated by the Camp David Agreement clause calling for the establishment of a Palestinian autonomy in the West Bank and Gaza Strip within five years, West Bank (and not East Jerusalem) political leadership established a new organization, "The National Guidance Committee for National Guidance" (unrelated to the organization of the same name that had been created in East Jerusalem immediately after the 1967 War) in 1978. The new committee, which operated until it was outlawed in 1982, unconditionally supported the PLO's position and evolved as the most authentic national representative of the region's residents since 1967 (Qra'im 1982, 24). Its growing force further undermined the power of the pro-Jordanian and traditional leaders in the West Bank in general, and specifically in East Jerusalem. Following the outbreak of the *Intifada*, the popular uprising against the Israeli occupation, in the territories in December 1987, support for Jordan was depleted even further due to reinforced Palestinian national sentiment and identification with the PLO. In 1988, King Hussein of Jordan declared Jordan's official detachment from the West Bank.

PLO interests in Jerusalem were more complex than those of Israel and Jordan. Since the beginning of the Israeli occupation in 1967, relations between Palestinian leaders "inside" the territories (*al-Dakhil*), and those who were "outside" (*al-Kharij*), had been tense. "Outside" PLO leadership exerted its utmost efforts to undermine any local autonomous leadership that could threaten Arafat's position as the uncontested leader of the Palestinian national movement. Anticipating resolute Israeli actions against any PLO organization efforts in East Jerusalem, and recognizing that Israel and Jordan had, in any case, all but quelled its opponents in the city, the PLO strove to strengthen its position in the territories by establishing professional associations and unions, universities (Bir Zayt near Ramallah, Al-Najah in Nablus), and charitable organizations that were typically located outside Jerusalem. The "National Guidance Committee" established in 1978 focused mainly on West Bank affairs and maintained hardly any connection to Jerusalem, other than the fact that the charter meeting took place in Bayt Hanina, on the outskirts of Jerusalem.

The only exception to the PLO's lack of political activism in East Jerusalem involved the East Jerusalem press, which became a major center of power and the capital of the Arab Palestinian press. Unlike the West Bank, where military government regulations prevented the publication of free press, East Jerusalemites under Israeli law were free to publish daily newspapers and other periodicals. The first daily to appear was the pro-Hashemite *al-Quds* in 1968, followed by the pro-PLO *al-Fajr* and *al-Sha'b*.

The East Jerusalem press undoubtedly played a major role in molding public opinion in the West Bank and Gaza, and senior editors such as Mahmud Abu Zuluf and Hana Siniora were considered key national figures. However, whenever Israeli authorities felt that the Palestinian press crossed the "red lines," that is, published news and viewpoints that they considered inflammatory anti-Israeli materials, action was taken and closure orders were issued.

The power struggle between these three powers, Jordan, Israel, and the PLO, over control of East Jerusalem and its effect on the local East Jerusalem leadership is illustrated in the following case study.

The Muslim religious establishment after 1967

The Muslim Council (Al-Hay'a al-Islamiyya), was established on July 24, 1967 by a group of 22 political and religious Muslim leaders.[7] Despite the similarity in names (the Supreme Muslim Council, dissolved in 1948, was the highest religious institution in charge of Muslim community affairs under the British Mandate in Palestine), there was no statutory continuity between the two Councils (see Kupferschmidt 1978, 260).

Israeli authorities were taken by surprise by the move. They had assumed that the religious establishment of East Jerusalem, under the impact of humiliating defeat in the war and occupation, would accommodate itself to the new circumstances and, while expressing protest, would be willing to cooperate with the Israeli Ministry of Religious Affairs. Israel opposed the new organization, which it considered a center of anti-Israeli opposition, from the time of its inception, and it withheld formal recognition of the Council.

The Council was a self-appointed body of 22 members, representing a wide spectrum of the local leadership. Charter members included members of the city's longstanding elite families, senior government officials, former ministers, members of the Jordanian parliament, senior Muslim religious authorities, educators, lawyers and physicians, and members of Arab nationalist parties such as *al-Ba'th* and *al-Qawmiyyun al-Arab*.[8] Religious figures included Shaykh 'Abd al-Hamid al-Sa'ih (President of the Shari'a [Muslim Law] Court of Appeals), Shaykh Hilmi al-Muhtasib (a member of the court), Sa'd al-Din al-'Alami (Mufti of Jerusalem), and Hasan Tahbub (Director of the Awqaf [religious endowments] in Jerusalem). Among the Council's secular members were Anwar al-Khatib, Kamal Dajani, 'Aref al-'Aref, a known historian, 'Abd al-Muhsin Abu Maizer, attorney and a leftist Ba'thist, Dr. Dawud al-Husseini, a former member of the Jordanian Parliament, Ruhi al-Khatib, Ibrahim Bakr, attorney and Member of Jordanian Parliament, and 'Ali Taziz, Head of the Chamber of Commerce, a central institution in the city's economic life.[9]

The Council focused its activities on the religious sphere. In its charter meeting, the Council declared itself "the Muslim body in charge of the Muslim affairs on the West Bank, including Jerusalem" (Dishon 1967, 293), and Shaykh Abd al-Hamid al-Sa'ih was appointed Chairman of the Council and Chief Justice (*Qadi al-Qudah*) of the Muslim Shari'a courts. However, the meeting quickly turned into one of political protest: a memorandum was issued protesting the interference by the Israeli Ministry of Religious Affairs in the administration of the Muslim community and its Waqf property, and the Council declared that they "did not recognize the annexation of Jerusalem" and would continue to regard the city as occupied territory and part of the West Bank and Jordan (Dishon 1967, 293).

Despite its original religious focus, the Muslim Council became a leading factor behind the protest movement in Jerusalem against the Israeli occupation of the West Bank and the Gaza Strip in general, and of Jerusalem in particular. The Council issued numerous statements decrying Israeli policies concerning the Muslim holy places in Jerusalem; it vehemently opposed Israeli archaeological excavations near the Wailing Wall and repeatedly called for mass prayers on the Temple Mount and general protest strikes (Stendel 1992, 261).

Once Israel realized that the new Council was operating as a center of agitation against its rule in the city, it acted swiftly against it. On July 31, 1967, four Arab notables, all signatories to the July 24 declaration, were banished from Jerusalem to Jewish cities within Israel for three months to prevent their continued "agitation for non-cooperation with Israel."[10]

Shortly afterwards, Shaykh al-Sa'ih founded a new political body, the Supreme National Guidance Committee. Despite its predominantly secular character, the new Committee was closely associated with the Muslim Council, an impression strengthened by the fact that al-Sa'ih headed both organizations. The Committee conducted widespread actions of resistance against the Israeli military government, including incessant publication of petitions and the organization of strikes and demonstrations (Benvenisti 1973, 263; Benziman 1973, 75; Shemesh 1984, 294; Shargai 1995, 270, 324).

Israel also took firm measures against the Supreme National Guidance Committee and its leader. On September 23, 1967, Shaykh al-Sa'ih was deported to Jordan for having "engaged in incitement to carry out hostile acts in Jerusalem and the West Bank." After his deportation, al-Sa'ih was immediately appointed Awqaf Minister in the Jordanian government and later served as Chairman of the Palestinian National Council.[11]

Ruhi al-Khatib, former mayor of East Jerusalem until June 1967, replaced al-Sa'ih as head of the Supreme National Guidance Committee, and was similarly deported to Jordan on March 7, 1968, for "hostile activities against the authorities and instigation to insurgence."[12] Six months later, the Israelis deported an additional three leading activists from East Jerusalem to Jordan: Kamal Dajani, who had assumed the position of Committee Chairman following al-Khatib, Dr. Dawud al-Husseini, and Mrs. Zalikha al-Shihabi, head of the city's Arab Women's Union.[13]

The Israeli policy of deportation and the accompanying countermeasures applied by the Israeli security forces, including temporary seizure of shops that closed down during commercial strikes, proved successful. From 1969 on, the influence of the Supreme National Guidance Committee gradually diminished.

In the late 1960s, the Supreme Muslim Council under the chairmanship of Shaykh Hilmi al-Muhtasib, who replaced al-Sa'ih, had adopted a much more moderate policy in an attempt to avoid direct confrontation with the Israeli authorities and deportation. A status quo was achieved between the Council and Israel: although the Council was not officially recognized by Israel, it was not declared an illegal organization. As long as the Council maintained a low-key profile and avoided instigating widespread resistance, Israel tacitly accepted the Council's activities. Jordan, for its part, strengthened its grip over the Council, through the main means at its disposal—the payment of salaries to hundreds of Waqf employees and other Islamic functionaries, which was permitted by the Israeli authorities.

The Council's influence was further curtailed by opposition from other centers of political power in the West Bank. One staunch opponent of the Council was Shaykh Muhammad 'Ali Ja'abri, the mayor of Hebron, who refused to defer to the Council, even on religious matters, believing himself to be the supreme political authority. Another opponent was Hikmat al-Masri of Nablus, former Speaker of the Jordanian House of Representatives, who questioned the representative nature of the Council and its base of legitimacy. The external opposition was the outcome of regional conflicts characteristics of West Bank political life. Since the beginning of the twentieth century, Hebron and Nablus had traditionally competed with Jerusalem. Personal rivalries between political figures from different parts of the West Bank helped entrench the political and ideological differences that continued to exist under Israeli occupation.

In summary, in the period immediately following the 1967 War (1967–69), the Muslim Council and its offshoot, the Supreme National Guidance Committee, influenced the religious establishment in Jerusalem and the West Bank, and played a central role in organizing civilian protest against the Israeli occupation. Nevertheless, the Council's political influence outside Jerusalem and its immediate environs remained limited, and it never attained the status and prestige enjoyed by the Supreme Muslim Council of Jerusalem during the Mandatory period.

By the end of the 1980s, Israel recognized the rising power of the PLO and Jordan's significant decline in prestige in the territories. In response,

Israel's policy of control over East Jerusalem shifted from the political activities of pro-Jordanian East Jerusalem activists, and became more seriously concerned with the city's pro-PLO Palestinian elements, which had meanwhile expanded their foothold in the city.

Palestinian Authority efforts to gain a foothold in Jerusalem in the post-Oslo era

Following the Oslo Accords signed by Israel and the PLO in 1993, direct Palestinian control was established in parts of the West Bank and the Gaza Strip. The Palestinian Authority (PA), established in 1994, became a legitimate, independent authority in territories transferred on the basis of the Oslo Accords. On January 20, 1996, the Palestinian Legislative Council was elected, and Arafat was elected President of the PA.

The signing of the Oslo Accords in 1993, the establishment of the Palestinian Authority in 1994, and the Israeli–Jordanian peace treaty signed the same year signaled the beginning of a new era and highlighted the shifting political weights of these three players in their power struggle over East Jerusalem. As Jordan eventually removed itself from the scene of Jerusalem politics, events increasingly reflected the diverging interests of Israel and the Palestinian Authority. The PLO held fast to its view of Jerusalem as the future capital of an independent Palestinian state, and Palestinian officials intensified their efforts to consolidate and legitimize this claim.

One area where the new balance of power was evident was the issue of control over the East Jerusalem religious Muslim establishment. After almost three decades of negligible involvement in Jerusalem politics due to the simultaneous efforts by the Israelis and the Jordanians to limit the PLO's influence in the city, one of the PLO's preliminary targets was to tighten its grip over the Muslim religious institution in East Jerusalem.

The new PLO-controlled "political paradigm" gave the religious establishment a key role in its two-pronged effort: replacement of pro-Jordanian religious establishment employees by PLO loyalists, and defining the Temple Mount as the focus of the PLO's national-political struggle against Israel.[14]

Following the establishment of the Palestinian Authority in 1994, the PLO established an Awqaf ministry to oversee Islamic sites in an effort to replace the Jordanian-controlled Waqf administration and deprive Jordan of an important source of its influence (Maddy-Weitzman 1996, 166). Hasan Tahbub, a staunch PLO supporter, was awarded responsibility for the Awqaf portfolio. He was also elected to head the Muslim Council, with Faysal al-Husseini as his deputy.

For the PLO, the death of the mufti of Jerusalem, Shaykh Sulayman al-Ja'bari, in October 1994 was yet another opportunity to further undermine Jordan's influence. As the new mufti, Jordan appointed Shaykh 'Abd al-Qadir 'Abdin, who had served as acting chief qadi in the West Bank, but shortly afterwards, Arafat appointed Shaykh 'Akrama Sabri as the mufti of

Jerusalem and of "all Palestine." Popular support for the PLO, combined with the team of security guards posted around Shaykh 'Abdin's office to discourage access to the new mufti, convinced most Palestinians of Shaykh Sabri's authority. In 1998, following Shaykh 'Abdin's retirement, Shaykh Sabri completed his takeover and firmly established his position as the sole Jerusalem mufti (Amirav 1994, 243).

In the power struggle between Israel and the Palestinian Authority, Israel ultimately foiled Palestinian actions designed to demonstrate the PA's sovereignty over East Jerusalem.[15] One of the main strategic goals of the PA was to establish a strong power base in East Jerusalem comprising ministerial offices as well as security and propaganda agencies functioning as arms of the new Palestinian government. Although East Jerusalem remained under the direct and exclusive control of Israel, the establishment of the PA had a strong impact on the pro-PLO political leaders in the city.

The most serious and, to some extent, most successful attempt to establish political Palestinian presence in the city occurred soon after the establishment of the PA in 1994, when the Palestinian Authority lent assistance and support to efforts to establish new Palestinian "national institutions" that would pave the way for a resurgence of local leadership in East Jerusalem under PLO control and supervision.

Although the interim agreement signed between Israel and the PA in September 1995 included a clause limiting the establishment of PA institutions to areas under direct Palestinian rule, the PA continued to implement a systematic comprehensive plan to assume control of all spheres of life in Jerusalem, by establishing a network of administration offices. Saeb Erekat, PA Minister for Local Government and one of the PLO's chief negotiators with the Israelis in the post-Oslo Accords period, argued that the Palestinians were obliged to do their utmost to establish facts in the field and ensure Jerusalem's Arab character.

The PLO managed to establish a wide network of political, social, economic, religious, security, cultural, scientific, media, and professional institutions and organizations, which all began to leave their mark on the city.

Orient House, where PLO headquarters was located, was undisputedly the most important of the new PLO-affiliated organizations. Since late 1992, Orient House became known as the "Palestinian Government House" and effectively functioned as the "Palestinian Foreign Ministry" under the directorship of Faysal al-Husseini, who hosted visits by 47 official delegates representing 17 countries, including the prime ministers of Denmark and Turkey, the U.S. Secretary of State, and the Foreign Ministers of Great Britain, France, Russia, Egypt, Canada, and Greece, between 1993 and 1995 (Berkovits 2000, 134; Maddy-Weitzman 1997, 372). Orient House, whose official letterhead indicated "The State of Palestine," also housed the offices of the Palestinian delegation to the peace talks, the offices of Saeb Erekat (Minister for Local Government), the Palestinian Bureau for Information and Press, and other offices.

Faysal al-Husseini was the most prominent political figure to emerge in Jerusalem in the 1980s and 1990s, and a leading *Fath*[16] activist in the West Bank. In 1980, he established and directed the Arab Studies Institute, which soon became a central platform for pro-PLO intellectuals, writers, and media personalities, including Sari Nusseibeh and Hanna Siniora. Al-Husseini's status was based on his respected lineage (his father was 'Abd al-Qadir al-Husseini, the legendary military commander of the Jerusalem area in the 1948 War) and his extensive public and military service in support of the PLO, for which he served several prison terms in Israel. As a member of the PLO Executive Committee and PA Minister without Portfolio in charge of Jerusalem (after 1994), he was considered the highest ranking Palestinian official in the city.

An outspoken advocate of the notion that East Jerusalem belonged to the Palestinians, al-Husseini firmly urged Israel to begin immediate negotiations on Jerusalem in 1995. He referred not only to Palestinian land in pre-1967 Eastern Jerusalem, but claimed that 70–80 percent of Western Jerusalem belonged to the Palestinians as well. He believed that Jerusalem should be the united city and capital of both Palestine and Israel, and supported internationalizing the city. Al-Husseini stressed that Jerusalem was the essence of the Palestinian question and would be a decisive factor in determining future peace (Maddy-Weitzman 1997, 138).

Other institutions established by the PA included the Palestinian Center of Statistics and the Palestinian Economic Council for Development and Reconstruction (PECDAR).[17] The Jerusalem District, established by the PA in May 1996 under the governance of Jamil 'Uthman Nasir, was sharply criticized by Israel, which claimed that the PLO openly violated its commitment to refrain from operating within boundaries of East Jerusalem (Maddy-Weitzman 1996, 155). Nasir, who established his headquarters in Abu Dis, a village neighboring Jerusalem, officially stated that he would operate outside the scope of Jerusalem (the district included 44 villages and neighborhoods which, as part of the West Bank, remained under Israeli occupation, in contrast to East Jerusalem, which was unified with its western part in 1967). However, it soon became clear that he regularly met with East Jerusalem municipal employees and reportedly instructed them how to undermine the influence of the Jerusalem municipality in the eastern part of the city (Maddy-Weitzman 1996, 155). In fact, Nasir's appointment was seen by the Palestinians as "an important step forward [in] reasserting Palestinian control over their sector of the city." Moreover, in May 1996 the Palestinian Ministry of Local Government announced that the Palestinian District of Jerusalem officially included the Old City, most of the Arab neighborhoods in East Jerusalem and its surrounding villages. Although this statement had no practical effect, since these localities continued to remain under Israeli jurisdiction, it was yet another declaration of intentions (Berkovits 2000, 150–151). Another example of al-Husseini's leadership efforts to entrench Palestinian local leadership was the 1996 campaign to gather legal documents affirming Palestinian ownership of property in East Jerusalem and in Jewish-inhabited West Jerusalem.[18]

Several institutions relating to health, social welfare, and education were established. In 1996, the PA assumed control of the Al-Maqasid Hospital on the Mount of Olives. Dr. Fathi Arafat, the Chairman's brother, was appointed Director General. The Palestinian Tourism Council and al-Quds University, headed by Professor Sari Nusseibeh, financed by the PA Authority for Higher Learning. Furthermore, the Ministry of Youth and Sports (headed by Talal Sidr), the Ministry of Education (headed by Yasir 'Amru), and the Ministry of Finance (headed by Muhammad Zuhdi al-Nashashibi) opened offices in Jerusalem or its surrounding neighborhoods.

The Palestinian security services played a major role in the power struggle between the Israeli and Palestinian authorities over control and influence in East Jerusalem. The official security organizations included Amin al-Hindi's General Intelligence, Musa Arafat's Military Intelligence, "Force 17" headed by Faysal Abu Sharakh, and the Palestinian Police, headed by Ghazi al-Jibali.[19] Particularly noteworthy was Jibril Rajjub's Preventive Security Service (PSS), a vigilante-type body whose semi-clandestine agents operated in the city, settling local disputes, preventing East Jerusalemites from selling land to Jews,[20] enforcing general strikes, punishing drug dealers, imposing censorship on PA critics, and silencing political rivals. Not least through its aggressive methods, which included intimidation, coercive interrogations at the PSS headquarters in Jericho, and even kidnapping, the PSS succeeded in establishing itself as a powerful authority in the West Bank and East Jerusalem. The PSS also received the tacit approval of Israel, despite the latter's concerns over its intimidating methods, perhaps because of the close cooperation between Israel and the PSS in curbing Palestinian terrorist activity.

Israel was determined to act firmly against these new centers of power and curb their activity wherever possible (Diker 2004). For example, the 1995 attempt to establish an Arab Municipality headed by Dr. Amin al-Majjaj was immediately thwarted (Maddy-Weitzman 1997, 372; Berkovits 2000). The Israeli Government and the Jerusalem Municipality repeatedly issued closure orders against many of the institutions mentioned above.

Israel became occupied with Orient House more than any other institution or agency, although here Israeli government policy changed several times between 1991 and 2001. Under Rabin, Israel adopted a more cautious approach, due to the symbolic importance of Orient House. Israel feared that overly drastic actions against the Palestinian institutions in East Jerusalem would undermine negotiations with the PLO and the PA in general, and specifically the talks on the implementation of the Oslo Accords. Netanyahu, elected prime minister in 1996 on a more hawkish ballot (including, inter alia, criticism of the Oslo Accords), had no such qualms and adopted a stricter policy of opposing PA attempts to reinforce its position in East Jerusalem. This policy was expressed primarily in bringing pressure to bear on foreign representatives and persuading them to refrain from official contact with Orient House officials. During the Barak administration (1999–2000), Israel reverted to its former stance and acquiesced to PA activities at Orient House while Barak conducted negotiations with the Palestinians on a settlement that included the issue of Jerusalem. During the entire decade, however, no Israeli government employed the extreme sanction of closing Orient House, until 2001, when Sharon's government, at the peak of the Second *Intifada*, finally shut down Orient House and put an end to one of the most important centers of Palestinian power in the city.

Israel's policy was not, however, the sole cause of the decline of Orient House. Arafat was also interested in undermining Faysal al-Husseini's authority and power. Arafat disliked the wide-ranging diplomatic activities and international connections of al-Husseini, whom he began to consider as a political threat (Berkovits 2000). Arafat and al-Husseini deeply disagreed on the method of funding for developing a Palestinian Authority presence and improving social services in East Jerusalem; Arafat wanted all donations to be channeled through him personally, whereas al-Husseini preferred to operate independently from Orient House, the unofficial base of the Palestinian Authority in East Jerusalem. Al-Husseini applied to the Arab states to channel funds for this purpose directly through him, claiming that Arafat's dictatorial personal and political style was weakening the Palestinian Authority's newly-established administrative offices and preventing them from doing their jobs. During a visit to Kuwait for this purpose in late May 2001, he died unexpectedly at the age of 61. His premature death undoubtedly eliminated the only serious bud of genuine Jerusalemite leadership to emerge in recent times.

Although the PLO managed to establish a wide network of political, social, economic, religious, security, cultural, scientific, media, and professional institutions and organizations, which all began to leave their mark on the city, Israel ultimately foiled Palestinian actions designed to demonstrate the PA's sovereignty over East Jerusalem.[21] The fierce Israeli opposition resulted in the almost complete elimination of official Palestinian presence in the city, and the neutralization of any pro-PLO hubs that attempted to gain a foothold in East Jerusalem.

Conclusion

Since Israel's administration of East Jerusalem beginning in 1967, no authentic local leadership developed in the city, either in the opposition to the Israeli occupation or in attempts to negotiate with Israel. The absence of a core of leadership in Jerusalem is all the more glaring in view of the city's traditional role as a center of religious significance and political power for Islam, and the alleged designation of the future capital of the Palestinian Authority.

Despite Jordan's attempts to maintain its status as "custodian of the holy places" following the 1967 War, pro-Hashemite supporters in East Jerusalem were significantly weakened by the political developments of the next two decades, specifically Israel's fluctuating support of the Jordanian Option, the growing power of the PLO, and the outbreak of the *Intifada*.

Israel was resolute in attributing supreme status to its interests in Jerusalem, and viewed the re-unification of the city as an irreversible historic event. As a result, Israel conducted a relentless policy to uproot any emerging locus of power in the city that could undermine its authority and control. The Oslo Accords and the establishment of the Palestinian Authority in 1994 created a unique opportunity for the PLO to gain a dominant hold over East Jerusalem. Despite their extensive efforts, Israel would not yield and forcefully prevented the realization of this plan.

The three major players had competing interests and motives, yet occasionally two sides of the triangle tacitly joined forces to undermine the aspirations of the third. While Jerusalem retained and even reinforced its position in Palestinian and Muslim consciousness as a center of religion, the efforts of Israel, Jordan, and the PA prevented East Jerusalem from developing as a center of political leadership.

In 2000, as a result of the deadlock reached in negotiations between Israel and the Palestinians, on one hand, and the growing Palestinian terror on the other, Israel initiated the construction of the "Security Fence," which, in a single stroke, created a physical barrier effectively isolating the Arab leadership in Jerusalem from its potential constituency, the West Bank and Gaza, further reducing any chance for the emergence of a local, authentic, and autonomous Arab leadership in the city in the near future. Today, as it becomes clear that the future of Jerusalem depends on the outcome of future negotiations between all interested parties, the voice of local Arab leadership in Jerusalem remains silent.

Notes

1 Political divisions in Jerusalem can be traced to the 1920s. During the British Mandate period, the local political scene was divided between the Husseini and Nashashibi clans and their supporters. The Husseinis' exalted status stemmed from traditions that regarded them as descendants of Husayn, the son of the Prophet Muhammad's cousin 'Ali Ibn Abu Talib. Members of the family traditionally held senior religious and political positions in the Arab community in Jerusalem. The Nashashibis, its rival prominent family, represented the opposition within the Palestinian national movement. The Nashashibi clan controlled the mayoralty of Jerusalem and represented a relatively moderate line in Palestinian politics. See appendix of the Jerusalem families in Shimoni 1947, 211–223; Stendel 1974, 490–491; Rubinstein 2001.

2 For the political activity in the West Bank and Jerusalem under Jordan, see Cohen 1982.

3 'Abd Allah Bin Husayn was successively Emir of Trans-Jordan (1921–46) under the British Mandate, then King of Transjordan (1946–49) and finally King of the Hashemite Kingdom of Jordan (1949–51).

4 For a detailed discussion of the elections see Benziman 1973, 234–237.
5 The Rabbat Summit was an Arab summit meeting held in Morocco, which called for the return of any Palestinian territory occupied by Israel to the Palestinian people under the leadership of the PLO.
6 On these developments see Ma'oz 1984.
7 The discussion on the Muslim Council is largely based on Farhi 1979. See also Reiter 1977, 7–9.
8 On the establishment of the Council, its structure and activities, see Radio Amman, July 25, 1967; BBC, July 27, 1967; *Haaretz*, July 27, 1967; al-Ahram (Cairo), July 30, 1967—all quoted in Dishon 1967, 293; Benvenisti 1973, 235–236; Benziman 1973, 69–74; *Al-Jarida* (Beirut), August 1, 1967; Sahliyeh 1988, 22; Shargai 1995, 261–263.
9 Only a minority of the 22 founding members were of genuine Jerusalem origin, such as Mufti al-'Alami. The remaining religious dignitaries were non-Jerusalemites (al-Muhtasib, Barakat, and Tahbub were Hebronites, while al-Sa'ih was from Nablus). The strong Hebronite presence in the city can be traced to the influx of Hebron residents to Jerusalem during the British Mandate period and a subsequent steady decline in the original Jerusalemite population. The Hebronite presence in the Council demonstrated Jerusalem's changing social-political composition under the Jordanian rule. As mentioned above, after 1948 Jordan strove to diminish the political influence of the veteran Jerusalemite families such as the Husseinis, the Nashashibis, the Khalidis, and the Alamis. Members of these families were stripped of their former Jerusalem-based governmental positions and many were co-opted into the Jordanian establishment in the East Bank. They were replaced by leading figures of Hebronite descent; even though most Hebronites tended to prefer commerce, business, and finance and were much less inclined to be involved in politics. See Farhi 1971, 14; Benvenisti 1973, 89–90; Stendel 1974, 496–500; Zilberman 1992. The author wishes to thank Dr. Menachem Klein for his remarks on this issue.
10 Anwar Khatib was banished to Safed, Abd al-Muhsin Abu Maizer to Tiberias, Dr. Dawud al-Husseini to Hadera, and Ibrahim Bakr to Jericho. See *Jerusalem Post*, August 1, 1967; Dishon 1967, 293; *Al-Jarida* (Beirut), August 1, 1967; Benvenisti 1973, 67; Shargai 1995, 267.
11 *Haaretz*, al-Difa' (Amman), September 24, 1967; Dishon 1967, 294.
12 *Haaretz*, March 7, 1967; Dishon 1968, 565.
13 Dishon 1968, 565; *Al-Jarida* (Beirut), September 7, 1968; Benvenisti 1973, 263–264; Benziman 1973, 75–81.
14 The transition to the new paradigm, and the collaboration between the PLO and the local Jerusalem leadership, were already apparent at the onset of the *Intifada*, when Shaykh Sa'd al-Din al-'Alami, head of the Muslim Council, expressed his warm support for the uprising, staunchly condemning the IDF's conduct in quelling the riots. See Amirav 1994, 241–242; Shargai 1995, 335–337.
15 Maddy-Weitzman 1997, 138. For a detailed discussion of the PLO's efforts, see Berkovits 2000, 133–161; Klein 1997, 211; Klein 1999.
16 *Fath* (also spelled *Fatah*), a reverse acronym from the Arabic name *Harakat al-Tahrir al-Watani al-Filastini* (The Palestinian National Liberation Movement) is the largest Palestinian secular political and military organization. It is the largest party in the PLO and is considered center-left of the spectrum.
17 Maddy-Weitzman 1996, 144. See also Torpstein 1994; Roni Shaked, "The Husayni Government in East Jerusalem," *Yediot Aharonot*, June 10, 1994, cited in Berkovits 2000, 468.
18 Simultaneously, the Jerusalem-based Land and Water Institute, headed by Khadr Shuqayrat, began registering claims to such properties by means of published notices in the Palestinian press. Maddy-Weitzman 1996, 155.

19 See specifically *Yediot Aharonot*, November 17, 1994; January 17, February 9, 1995; July 22, 1996; Articles by Hillel Cohen in *Kol Ha'ir*, April 20, May 5, 1995, cited in Berkovits 2000, 136–137, 142–143, 149–150.

20 The sale of Arab lands to Jewish developers in East Jerusalem was viewed as a major act of treason, both by Jordan and the PLO, and a symbolic Palestinian surrender to what was considered Zionist colonization efforts.

21 Bruce Maddy-Weitzman 1997, 138. For a detailed discussion of the PLO's efforts, see Berkovits 2000, 133–161; Klein 1997 and 1999.

References

Amirav, Moshe. 1994. "Sanctity and Politics on Temple Mount." In *Islam, Society and Space in Jerusalem—Past and Present*, ed. Luz Nimrod Luz. *Hamizrah Hehadash* 44: 227–252. (In Hebrew.)

Benvenisti, Meron. 1973. *In Front of the Blocked Wall, Jerusalem Divided and Unified*. Jerusalem: Weidenfeld & Nicolson. (In Hebrew.) English translation published as *The Torn City* (Minneapolis: University of Minnesota Press, 1976).

Benziman, Uzi. 1973. *Jerusalem, A City Without Walls*. Tel Aviv: Schocken. (In Hebrew.)

Berkovits, Shmuel. 2000. *The Battle for the Holy Places*. Jerusalem: Hed Arzi. (In Hebrew.)

Cohen, Amnon. 1982. *Political Parties in the West Bank under the Jordanian Regime, 1949–1967*. Ithaca: Cornell University Press.

Diker, Dan. 2004. "The Expulsion of the Palestinian Authority from Jerusalem and the Temple Mount." *Jerusalem Issue Brief* (Jerusalem Center for Public Affairs) 3.31 (August 5): 1–7.

Dishon, Daniel (ed.). 1967. *Middle East Record*, vol. 3. Tel-Aviv University: The Shiloah Center for Middle Eastern and African Studies.

——. 1968. *Middle East Record*, vol. 4. Tel-Aviv University: The Shiloah Center for Middle Eastern and African Studies.

Farhi, David. 1971. "Society and Politics in Judea and Samaria." *Ma'arakhot* 51 (June): 13–19. (In Hebrew.)

——. 1979. "The Muslim Council in East Jerusalem and in Judea and Samaria since the Six-Day War." *Hamizrah Hehadash* 28: 3–31. (In Hebrew.)

Klein, Menachem. 1997. "Quo Vadis? Palestinian Authority Building Dilemmas Since 1993." *Middle Eastern Studies* 33: 383–404.

——. 1999. *Doves in the Skies of Jerusalem*. Jerusalem: The Jerusalem Institute for Israel Studies. (In Hebrew.)

Kupferschmidt, Uri. 1978. *The Supreme Muslim Council: Islam under the British Mandate for Palestine*. Leiden: Brill.

Maddy-Weitzman, Bruce (ed.). 1996. *Middle East Contemporary Survey 18 (1994)*. Westview: Boulder.

——. 1997. *Middle East Contemporary Survey 19 (1995)*. Westview: Boulder.

Ma'oz, Moshe. 1984. *Palestinian Leadership in the West Bank*. London: Frank Cass.

Merhav, Reuven, and Rotem M. Giladi. 1999. *The Role of the Hashemite Kingdom of Jordan in a Future Permanent Status Settlement in Jerusalem: Legal, Political and Practical Aspects*. Jerusalem: The Jerusalem Institute for Israel Studies. (In Hebrew.)

Qra'im, Zadoq. 1982. "The Political Leadership in Judea, Samaria and the Gaza Region vis-à-vis the Camp David Challenge." *Ma'arakhot*, July.

Reiter, Yitzhak. 1977. *Islamic Institutions in Jerusalem*. London: Kluwer Law International.

Rubinstein, Danny. 2001. "The Hebronites' Victory." *Haaretz*, 6 June.

Sahliyeh, Emile. 1988. *In Search of Leadership: West Bank Politics since 1967*. Washington: The Brookings Institution.

Shargai, Nadav. 1995. *The Temple Mount Conflict*. Jerusalem: Keter.

Shemesh, Moshe. 1984. "The West Bank: Rise and Decline of Traditional Leadership, June 1967 to October 1973." *Middle Eastern Studies* 20.3 (July): 290–323.

Shimoni, Yaacov. 1947. *The Arabs of Eretz Yisrael*. Tel Aviv: Am Oved. (In Hebrew.)

Stendel, Ori. 1974. "The Arab Population in East Jerusalem: Leadership and Origin Groups." In *Judea and Samaria*, ed. Avshalom Shmueli, David Grossman, and Rehavam Zeevi, 489–502. Jerusalem: Canaan Publishing. (In Hebrew.)

———.1992. *The Arabs in Israel: Between Hammer and Anvil*. Jerusalem: Academon. (In Hebrew.)

Torpstein, Yossi. 1994. "Palestinian Institutions in East Jerusalem." *Ha'aretz*, 8 June. (In Hebrew.)

Zilberman, Yifrah. 1992. "The Hebronite Migration and the Development of Suburbs in the Metropolitan Area of Jerusalem." *Hamizrah Hehadash* 34: 43–63. (In Hebrew.)

———. 1994. "Palestinian Radical Islam in Jerusalem." In *Jerusalem—Here and Now*, ed. Ora Ahimeir, 174–194. Tel Aviv: Ministry of Defense Publishing House. (In Hebrew.)

17 Yerushalayim, al-Quds, and the Wizard of Oz

The problem of "Jerusalem" after Camp David II and the Aqsa *Intifada*

Ian S. Lustick

In the famous 1939 American movie *The Wizard of Oz*, Dorothy, her three companions, and her dog brave innumerable dangers to petition a wizard—the Wizard of Oz—for his help. But although they have believed with full faith in the Wizard's omniscience and omnipotence, in the movie's climax they learn the truth. Dorothy's dog Toto pulls a curtain away from a booth to reveal an old man working controls and shouting into a microphone. The old man is using smoke and mirrors to create an awesome image of "the great and powerful Oz." He is no wizard, but rather a clever, but weak and desperate man. The truth, that their elaborate beliefs about the wizard are nothing but fantasy, shocks Dorothy and her friends. But once the façade of majesty and mystery has been stripped away, they quickly learn that this ordinary man can actually give them each just exactly what they need—the self-confidence to make practical decisions for themselves and to use the real resources they have to accomplish their goals.

The story of Dorothy and the wizard is the story of reality emerging from behind a sound-and-light show. Considering that nothing has been so emblematic of official Israeli policies toward Yerushalayim as the Hollywood-style sound-and-light show displayed on "King David's Tower"—a tower, next to the Jaffa Gate, which of course was never King David's at all—we can see that the story of Dorothy and the wizard is also very much the story of what has happened to the question of Yerushalayim and al-Quds.[1]

The fetish of Yerushalayim

From 1967 on, but in particular since the Begin government's promulgation of the Basic Law—Jerusalem, Capital of Israel in 1980, almost all Jewish Israeli politicians were constrained to act and speak in accordance with an artfully and seductively contrived fetishization of Yerushalayim and its borders as enlarged in 1967. This project was intended by its wizards to hide the reality of a drastic and bizarre expansion of the city's municipal boundary to include more than 70 square kilometers of land from West Bank Arab villages and to hide as well realities of segregation, discrimination, and occupation. A crucial element of this project included the settlement of 200,000 Jews in massive new neighborhoods in expanded East Jerusalem, choking restrictions on Arab building, expulsion campaigns against Arab residents of al-Quds, and severe inequalities in the delivery of municipal services to Jewish and Arab neighborhoods. Just as important, however, for the fetishization of expanded Yerushalayim in Israeli political discourse was a variety of devices used to implement its psychological, cultural, and political intent. These devices included an anthem (Naomi Shemer's "Jerusalem of Gold"), Jerusalem Day, the Jerusalem Parade, the Jerusalem Covenant, a Jerusalem Ministry, the revival of the cult of the Jerusalem Temple, and the Jerusalem 3000 extravaganza.[2]

A not untypical example of this type of elaborately organized expression of political passion was the invitation issued to American Jews to participate in "The Jerusalem Solidarity Encounter." In a program sponsored by Ateret Cohanim's Jerusalem Reclamation Project, American Jews who could not come to Israel to express their devotion in the actual city on Jerusalem Day could pay $500 per couple for a virtual visit. The elaborate show awaiting those ready to buy these tickets was explained in a press release issued in May 2001:

> The lights dim, a hush settles over the ballroom, giant video screens light up and you are transported to the hubbub and bustle of the El-Al Terminal at JFK airport. "Last call for flight 008 direct to Jerusalem." The El-Al Pilot welcomes his passengers aboard his plane and with a roar of the engines he takes off, leaving the New York City skyline behind. Within seconds the most picturesque sights in Israel come into view, climaxing in an awesome breathtaking view of the ancient walled Old City of Jerusalem.
>
> After landing, you are driven through the streets of Jerusalem and are greeted at the Western Wall by Jerusalem Mayor Ehud Olmert. Enter the quarters of the Old City, and meet authentic Modern Day Maccabees—the men, women and children of Ateret Cohanim including Mattityahu (Mati) HaCohen Dan, Rabbi Shlomo HaCohen Aviner and other unique Jerusalem personalities. Visit Prime Minister Sharon in his Old City home. Thrill to an unprecedented visit behind the scenes to see the new high-tech Old City Security Control Center in action—never before revealed to the American public—including actual police footage of a firebomb attack on Ateret Cohanim's newest home in the Old City.
>
> "It's hard to describe the unique mixture of joy and awe which characterizes the special Yom Yerushalayim [Jerusalem Day] services at Yeshivat Ateret Cohanim," claims Executive Director Yossi Baumol. You will be there yourself—for the intense prayer of thanks, the joyous dancing and the blowing of the Shofar. The camera will then cut to the streets and alleys of the Old City, filled with people singing and dancing. On Jerusalem Day, in the wee hours of the morning, thousands upon

thousands of people, young and old, march down Jaffa Street and enter the Old City through all the gates, converging on the Kotel [Western Wall] to dance and sing for an hour or two before sunrise prayers begin. You too will join the students of Ateret Cohanim dancing at the Kotel, ending with a burst of fireworks over the Old City.[3]

In part the elaborate celebration of manufactured images, epitomized by this particular event, has been meant to compensate for a timid, jerry-built, and unconvincing legal position. In June 1967 the Eshkol government decided not to annex the Jordanian municipality of al-Quds. Under Israeli law this could have been done straightforwardly by using the same statutes employed to annex Western Galilee into the new state after the 1948 war, and then to incorporate the Little Triangle in June 1949. In the immediate aftermath of the fighting then, as in 1967, military governors were appointed to rule areas not seen legally to be part of the State of Israel. Only after the legal annexation of these territories, by application of the Area of Jurisdiction and Powers Ordinance (No. 29 of 5708–1948, *Official Gazette*, September 22, 1948), were these territories considered legally and officially to be part of the sovereign State of Israel. In 1967, however, the government chose not to annex any parts of the occupied West Bank and Gaza Strip. This was true even with regard to Arab Jerusalem. Nor did Israel assert or declare sovereignty over the city or any portion of the territories occupied in the Six-Day War.

There were four primary reasons for this reluctance. First, Israel did not want a confrontation with the world community over this issue. Because of the religious and symbolic importance of the city to Muslims and Christians, because of the historical role played there by many of the great powers, and because Israeli officials had declared, during the war, that Israel entertained no territorial ambitions but sought only peace, it was feared that a confrontation over Israeli annexation of the city would trigger a firestorm of opposition that would deprive Israel of the international goodwill it enjoyed after the war and that it would need in what was hoped would be the post-war bargaining process toward peace. Second, Israel seemed uncomfortable with the international legal implications of annexation. Its subsequent defense of the actions it did take emphasized their conformance with the requirements and expectations of international law, in particular the Hague Regulations of 1907, which did not admit the right of annexation, even following a war of self-defense, unless agreed upon as part of a peace settlement. Third, clear imposition of Israeli sovereignty on part of the Land of Israel occupied during the June war, but not all of it, would have raised ideological and political difficulties with those in Israel who favored imposing Israeli sovereignty on all parts of the Land of Israel under the state's control. Finally, of course, outright annexation of expanded East Jerusalem would have made it impossible, or at least more awkward, to have not also imposed Israeli citizenship on the Arab inhabitants of the portion of the West Bank freshly demarcated as part of "reunited Yerushalayim."[4]

Accordingly, the government adopted a clever but complex ruse. In June 1967 it promulgated a series of amendments to existing legislation and administrative orders. Together they were designed to extend Israel's law and jurisdiction to a greatly expanded area of East Jerusalem and a gerrymandered swath of its hinterland. The trick was to accomplish this without granting Israeli citizenship to the Arab inhabitants of the affected area and without having officially to declare an act of annexation or sovereignty extension. Only by understanding the calculated and complex interaction of the measures I am about to describe can it be appreciated how purposeful and definite was the effort to avoid the actual imposition of Israeli sovereignty. Only on that basis, in turn, can one understand the gap that subsequently opened up between the rhetoric of the mythmakers of "reunited Yerushalayim" and the legal, political, and practical realities of what may be called "occupation through municipal expansion."

Part of avoiding any clear process of annexation or sovereignty extension was the avoidance of any one act that could be held up to symbolic, legal or political scrutiny. Instead the government of Israel enacted or implemented a series of separate measures—two amendments to pre-existing statutes and one administrative declaration. The desired outcome was to be the effect of the interaction of these separate measures. Neither of the two laws as amended even mentioned Jerusalem. Neither of the two laws, nor the administrative declaration, contained the words "annexation" (*sipu'ah*) or "sovereignty" (*ribonut*).

First, on June 27, 1967, the Knesset passed an amendment to the "Law and Administration Ordinance" which had been published in the *Official Gazette* on September 22, 1948. As it stood before this amendment, that Ordinance declared that all laws applying within the State of Israel would apply to "any part of Palestine which the Minister of Defense has defined by proclamation as being held by the Defense Army of Israel." The 1967 amendment to this ordinance reads "In the Law and Administration Ordinance, 1948, the following section shall be inserted after section IIA: 'IIB. The Law, jurisdiction and administration of the state shall apply in any area of *Eretz Yisrael* designated by the government by order'" (*Laws of the State of Israel* 1966/67, 75–76).

Three things are changed here. First, it is not the Minister of Defense who is specifically and solely named as having the power to make the necessary declaration; it is "the government." Second, no specific importance is attached to the Defense Minister's designation of an area as "being held by the Defense Army of Israel." Third, the larger area within which this power is capable of being exercised is within "Eretz Yisrael" rather than "Palestine" (a provision of some semantic but no operative significance). This amendment thereby made it possible for the Minister of Defense to consider some parts of the Land of Israel (Gaza or the larger West Bank, for example) as held by the Israeli army but without Israeli law in force, while other areas (i.e., the 71 square kilometers of expanded East Jerusalem), also held by the army, could be designated, by "government order," as areas wherein Israeli law could be enforced.

A second Knesset action, also taken on June 27, 1967, was to amend the "Municipal Corporations Ordinance" by inserting a paragraph which would add to the powers of the Interior Minister to act, "at his discretion and without holding an inquiry." The power added by this law allowed the Interior Minister to "enlarge, by proclamation, the area of a particular municipal corporation by the inclusion of an area designated by order under section IIB of the Law and Administration Ordinance, 1948" (*Laws of the State of Israel* 1966/67, 75–76, referring to the amendment to that law described above). It is significant that although this law also gave the Interior Ministry the right to appoint municipal councilors from among the inhabitants, there was no mention of whether these inhabitants would need to be Israeli citizens.

The third crucial measure taken was the publication on June 28, 1967, by the Interior Minister, of the following declaration:

> In accordance with my powers under paragraph 8 of the Municipal Corporations Ordinance [i.e., that amendment, passed the day before, and described above] I declare as follows:
>
> 1. The Boundaries of the Jerusalem Municipal Corporation will be the inclusion of the area described in the Annex. [This "Annex" was a three-page list of latitudinal and longitudinal points describing the current, but never pre-existing, municipal border in the North, East, and South.]
>
> 2. This declaration shall be referred to as "The Jerusalem Declaration (extension of the boundaries of the municipal corporation), 1967."[5]

The immediate explanation for these measures offered by the Israeli government emphasized what it characterized as the practical requirements of the inhabitants of the affected area—a rationale directly in keeping with the logic and requirements of "belligerent occupation" as described in the Hague Regulations of 1907, which as a result of subsequent Israeli Supreme Court decisions the Government of Israel came to accept as binding on the manner in which the occupied territories were to be governed.[6] The Hague Regulations permit no change in the permanent status of occupied territory but do permit and require the occupier to assume responsibility for the basic needs of the inhabitants. An official government press release, dated June 28, 1967, read (in part) as follows:

> In order to dispel any possible misunderstanding the Foreign Ministry spokesman declared tonight that the basic purpose of the ordinance concerning the fusion of the Jerusalem municipal areas is to provide full

municipal and social services to all inhabitants of the city. The fusion of the municipal services will ensure that no social inequality and legal differences in respect of services, welfare and education enjoyed by all inhabitants of Jerusalem will exist. From now on all residents will be in a position to receive all the services normally extended by the municipality such as water, electricity, public health, welfare, education, etc.

The purpose and result of the interaction of these measures was to expand the municipal boundaries of Yerushalayim to include al-Quds and a freshly demarcated, oddly shaped swath of the West Bank containing lands from 28 different Arab villages. While the border was mainly intended to exclude as many Palestinian Arabs as possible while including as much land as possible, it was also a compromise between bureaucratic players, some of whom favored much larger and some of whom favored smaller boundaries for the city (Benvenisti 1976, 112–114). In any event these actions, including publication of the three-page list of latitudinal and longitudinal points representing the new municipal boundary across the Green Line, did impose Israeli law and jurisdiction on an area much larger than any that had ever been included within a Jerusalem municipality or had ever been included within Jewish or Israeli emotional, historical, or psychological meanings of "Yerushalayim."[7] Just as important as the historical originality of this boundary line is that its imposition had been accomplished without extending Israeli citizenship to enlarged East Jerusalem's Arab inhabitants, without officially claiming or extending Israeli sovereignty over the area, and without declaring an act of annexation.[8]

But for those in Israel who at the time, or subsequently, have favored reaching a territorial compromise with the Palestinians based on two states for two peoples, this arrangement was too clever by half. Exploiting precedents set by Labor Party governments, right-wing activists came to an important realization about the political potential of this vast expansion of the politically potent category of "Yerushalayim." Secure in the knowledge that no Arab partner would sign a comprehensive peace agreement permitting Israel to maintain exclusive sovereignty over expanded East Jerusalem, right-wing activists avoided explicit efforts to persuade Israelis of the need to stay forever in Nablus and Gaza. It was so much easier simply to persuade Israeli Jews of the need never to leave what they could designate as "Yerushalayim."

Indeed, Israel's annexationists have always known that it would be difficult if not impossible to prevent at least a slim majority of Israelis from supporting a trade of occupied territory for lasting peace. To realize the dream of *Eretz Yisrael ha-shlemah* (the whole Land of Israel) or at least as much of it as possible, they have known that eventually Israel's permanent control of the West Bank and Gaza would have to be established in the consciousness of Israeli Jews as an unquestioned fact of the Jewish state's existence. Hence the compelling political logic of fetishizing "Yerushalayim." If the permanent absorption of a large "united Jerusalem" could be established as a hegemonic (unquestioned) belief, it would constitute an enormous obstacle to progress toward negotiating any type of solution, thereby letting wars and expulsions, as well as settlements and other components of de facto annexation, accomplish their political, cultural, demographic, and psychological objectives.

The political dynamic associated with this cult of Jerusalem was vividly displayed in May 1982 when the Begin government issued an ultimatum that further negotiations with Egypt and the United States over autonomy for Palestinians would be "inconceivable" unless the talks were held in Jerusalem. The demand was refused by the Egyptians as part of their protest against Israel's treatment of expanded East Jerusalem as part of its capital. The negotiations were never resumed. Thus Begin was able to conceal his desire to destroy any real negotiating process toward compromise with the Palestinians behind a publicly unassailable façade of protecting the "unity of Yerushalayim."[9]

The same dynamic was evident more than a decade later in the post-Madrid rounds of Israeli–Palestinian negotiations. Use of the Jerusalem issue to block a general deal with the Palestinians based on land for peace was the purpose of the last Shamir government's encouragement of the media event known as "the Jerusalem Covenant." This parchment document is now on display in an obscure Knesset reception hall. Its rapturous words about "united Jerusalem" are underlined by the signatures of 1,300 Diaspora Jewish leaders flown to Israel to mark the end of "Jerusalem Year," a celebration of 25 years of Israeli rule over the "united city." The spectacle was the one and only accomplishment of the "Ministry for Jerusalem Affairs" established in 1990 by the Shamir government. The ministry, with only six employees and a budget of $1.75 million, was disbanded when the Labor Party took power in 1992, but the Covenant project—a political embarrassment to the new government—could not be scuttled.[10]

From an annexationist perspective, however, events demonstrated the profitability of this kind of political investment. In early 1993 Israel's anti-annexationist government and Palestinian negotiators developed positions on key issues, including security, land, and water, that encouraged many to think an interim agreement might actually be achievable. Right-wing threats of mass mobilization against the "surrenderist" government seemed to fall flat. Demonstrations against the peace process were poorly attended. The spring 1993 closure of the territories, justified as an anti-terror measure, was very popular with most Israelis. Despite the misery it inflicted on the territories' Arab inhabitants, the move was also interpreted positively, as a kind of prelude to the political separation of Israel from the occupied lands.

However, because the Israeli government felt constrained to honor the image of a "united Jerusalem" by barring West Bank Arabs from the eastern sector of the city and its hinterland (inter alia, the ceremonial signing of the "Jerusalem Covenant" was in May 1993), the closure had the unintended consequence of forcing the issue of the fate of expanded East Jerusalem to the center of the negotiations. Privately willing to compromise on various aspects of the issue in the future, but unwilling to say so now because of the public fetish of "united Jerusalem," the Rabin government was stymied in its efforts to find wording on the Jerusalem question that could allow the negotiations to proceed toward an interim agreement—an agreement that Israeli annexationists argued would have led to a two-state solution.[11]

Failure of the fetishization project

Despite the success this fetishization strategy enjoyed as an obstacle to advancing negotiations with the Palestinians on various occasions, the fundamental objective of the project was not attained. As I have documented elsewhere, the image of a greatly enlarged "Yerushalayim," which no Israeli could conceive of ever dividing, was not implanted successfully as a common sense of Israeli psychological or political reality.[12] This was fully apparent by the mid-1990s. Consider the following examples of Israelis regularly acting in accordance with the knowledge and implicit understanding that "al-Quds" was not part of "Yerushalayim." At least since 1988, the Arab neighborhoods, villages, and refugee camps of al-Quds and its environs, including most of the Old City, have been treated as unknown, foreign, "occupied" territories. When not trying hard to recite the official catechism about the city's "reunification," politicians commonly refer to the Arabs of East Jerusalem as Palestinians within the West Bank or Judea and Samaria. The *Statistical Abstract of Israel* places an asterisk next to East Jerusalem to indicate its inclusion within the area of the state as listed. The municipal *eruv*, which runs along the boundary of the city within the Green Line, was constructed carefully in the eastern sector to divide the city, excluding most Arab neighborhoods and villages.[13] Particularly telling was the drumfire of accusations by right-wing parties and politicians that "Rabin," "Peres," or "the Left" were ready *"lehalek et Yerushalayim"* (to divide Yerushalayim), thereby giving the lie to the claim that the city was "indivisible" and its partition "inconceivable" to virtually all Israelis. Early in 1995, Deputy Foreign Minister Yossi Beilin and the PLO Executive Committee Secretary Mahmoud Abbas (Abu Mazen) reached an unofficial, unpublished but widely reported agreement to deal with the Jerusalem issue by establishing a Palestinian capital of al-Quds in East Jerusalem Arab neighborhoods and in the adjacent towns of Abu Dis and Azariyah. Systematic and sophisticated polls of Israeli Jewish attitudes toward the city, which survey researchers in Israel had failed to conduct ever since 1967, were conducted in late 1995. The results showed that even in the absence of favorable discussion of the prospect by leading politicians or government ministers, large pluralities of Israeli Jews were ready to transfer Arab neighborhoods in expanded Jerusalem to Palestinian sovereignty, especially if these were seen to reduce Arab demographic presence in the city and if they were part of an overall peace agreement (Segal et al. 2000, 66).

Against this background it was not surprising to informed observers that no explosion of opposition occurred after the Barak government in late 1999 and early 2000 launched trial balloons with regard to the possibility of treating portions of Arab East Jerusalem as "area B" and, eventually, even recognizing Palestinian sovereignty in those areas.[14] In response to these developments, newspaper editorials and even center and center-right commentators such as Shlomo Gazit and Elisha Efrat began describing Palestinian rule of Arab areas in enlarged "Yerushalayim" as inevitable or even necessary (Efrat 2000; Gazit 2000). Then, at the July summit at Camp David, Prime Minister Ehud Barak built upon the Beilin–Abu Mazen plan by proposing the principle that the municipal boundary for Yerushalayim stipulated in 1967 would not be considered the final boundary of Israel's capital, and that very substantial Arab areas within what had been fetishized as "Yerushalayim" would indeed be treated as "al-Quds." As is well known, that effort collapsed, although subsequent negotiations between Israeli and Palestinian negotiators at Taba closed most of the gaps that had appeared between the Barak government's position and that of the Palestinians regarding the basic nature of the political and territorial solution to the Jerusalem question (Moratinos 2002).

Prior to Barak's treatment of Yerushalayim's municipal boundaries as encompassing areas of al-Quds that would eventually be relinquished to Palestinian rule, perhaps the clearest sign that the fetishization project had failed at the psychological and deep political level was a bill introduced by a Likud Member of Knesset, Yehoshua Matza, in March 2000. This bill proposed an amendment to the Basic Law—Jerusalem, Capital of Israel, that would introduce a legal barrier to the transfer of Arab neighborhoods within expanded East Jerusalem to Palestinian rule. Recognizing that expanded East Jerusalem had not been annexed, or otherwise placed under Israeli sovereignty, Matza's bill proposed that no area within the new municipal boundary established in 1967 could be transferred to any body whose powers did not derive from the State of Israel unless a two-thirds majority of the Knesset (80 MKs) voted to do so. On one level this move was simply another in a long list of attempts by opponents of a Palestinian state to use the putatively sacrosanct issue of "not dividing Yerushalayim" in order to rouse public opinion against efforts to reach a peace agreement with the Palestinians—this time as part of the Oslo negotiations. But much more importantly, this bill signaled the complete failure of the whole fetishization project.

The introduction of the bill was *prima facie* evidence that supporters of a united, enlarged Yerushalayim, as demarcated in 1967, had abandoned even the pretense that dividing the city was politically inconceivable. The perceived need to pass a law to prevent it showed clearly that opponents of dividing Yerushalayim from al-Quds believed that without such a law an elected government in Israel would not only consider the idea but implement it.[15] More than that, Matza's decision to entrench the law as an amendment to the Basic Law—Jerusalem, Capital of Israel, and his inclusion of a requirement that the law could be amended only by a large special majority of the Knesset, suggested that he and his supporters believed that a dangerous possibility existed that not only a government or prime minister, but a plurality or even a majority of members of Knesset were liable to be ready to support Israeli recognition of an al-Quds, comprising sections of the enlarged municipality of Yerushalayim, as the capital of a Palestinian state.

The fear of being tarred with the brush of weakness on the issue of Yerushalayim still dissuaded Labor Party and most other left-of-center politicians from arguing directly against Matza's bill, even though they opposed it. Throughout long debates on the different readings of the bill and on various amendments, the Barak government studiously avoided speaking officially on the matter and sometimes absented itself entirely from the debate. The only government minister to speak at length about the bill was Haim Ramon, whose scathing repartee with the bill's proponents made up in sarcasm what it lacked in substance. His strongest argument was that the bill was actually weakening Israel's chance of maintaining its rule over all of expanded Yerushalayim by telling the world that the Israeli parliament was so afraid of Israeli readiness to compromise on the issue that they had to entrench its provisions behind a two-thirds majority to amend the law. It was partially in response to this type of criticism that Matza agreed to change the terms of the bill so that a simple majority of the Knesset (61), rather than a two-thirds majority, would be necessary to amend it.[16]

Effects of Camp David II and the Aqsa *Intifada*

The Aqsa *Intifada*, named after the mosque in Jerusalem on the Temple Mount/Haram al-Sharif, where Israeli police killed 19 and wounded 140 Palestinians protesting Ariel Sharon's visit to the area, pushed Israelis and Palestinians into an abyss of violence, hatred, distrust, and brutality not experienced since 1948. From late 2000 to early 2004, the virulence of the struggle pushed practical proposals for compromise far away from the centers of political discourse on each side. In Israel, analytic approaches that would parse what actually was offered by the Barak government were drowned out, temporarily at least, by a simplistic but emotionally satisfying belief that the Palestinians were actually offered a viable state and turned it down, embracing instead, as the conventional wisdom goes, the dreams of full refugee return and Israel's demise. The Israeli right, trapped by its own indignation at Palestinian steadfastness and fury at Palestinian violence, was no longer capable of describing a realistic future with which it could be satisfied. It could neither espouse the wholesale transfer options that are the logical implications of its rhetoric nor offer ideas about a negotiated settlement it can even try to defend as capable of satisfying Palestinian aspirations in the long run. Among the Palestinians, rage and dreams of revenge encouraged beliefs in ultimate solutions based on violence or on long periods of time, demographic victories, and South African-style transformations.

Then things started to change. Following Arafat's death, his replacement by Mahmoud Abbas, a drop in levels of terrorism, some adjustments in the route of Israel's "security barrier," and a significant commitment by Prime Minister Sharon to reduce incursions and targeted killings and withdraw from Gaza and a portion of the northern West Bank, levels of Israeli–Palestinian cooperation significantly, if temporarily, improved. As the seemingly never-ending, never-successful, but never-quite-dead "peace process" staggers on, we can try to directly answer the question posed in the title of this essay. How, in the wake of the Camp David debacle and the Aqsa *Intifada*, has the question of the future of Jerusalem been affected?

At the level of political debate, dramatic change is apparent. Previously, delicate and even elaborate techniques of discourse analysis had been necessary to argue that Israeli elites really did *not* believe, expect, or even desire that all of Yerushalayim as established in 1967 would forever remain under Israeli rule. Now such techniques are unnecessary. The negotiating positions of the Barak government at Camp David and at Taba, which focused directly and explicitly on the question of where and how to change the boundaries of Israeli jurisdiction, reinforced now by repeated endorsements of the principle of the two-state solution by Ariel Sharon, will never be forgotten—not by the Palestinians, not by the international community, and not by the Israeli public itself. Whereas previously confidential arrangements were necessary with think-tanks such as the Jerusalem Institute for Israel Studies to lay out possible scenarios for solutions based on the contraction of the putative boundaries of Yerushalayim, now these studies are published openly and have become part of the normal political/policy discourse.[17] Although polls done in the mid-1990s had strongly suggested that the Israeli Jewish public was ready for significant amendments to the official catechism on the future of the city (Segal et al. 2000), after the Camp David/Taba negotiations there is no need to extrapolate from polling results. Indeed, one of the most instructive aspects of the Camp David episode was that fervent and widespread grassroots Israeli opposition to changing Yerushalayim's borders did not materialize.

To be sure, in the absence of active negotiations about the future of the city, the fact–creation struggle continues as it has in the past. On the one hand, under the Sharon government, the Jerusalem municipality has quickened the pace of its demolition of unlicensed houses in Arab neighborhoods while seeking to accelerate construction and settlement in new Jewish neighborhoods (Har Homa and Ras el-Amud). On the other hand, one result of the Aqsa *Intifada* has been to dissuade potential buyers from moving to these neighborhoods. Indeed there has been an exodus of Jewish-owned businesses from the Atarot industrial zone (in the northern tip of expanded East Jerusalem). Evidence indicates that the efforts of sui-cide bombers to target Jaffa Street and Ben-Yehuda Street, in the heart of Yerushalayim, have been assisted by the ease of movement of Palestinians from al-Quds to Yerushalayim under the current arrangement of a formal unity between the two cities. Such evidence led to demands by Jewish resi-dents, not just for a wall between the Yerushalayim municipality and the West Bank, but also for walls to be built separating Jewish and Arab neighborhoods. Indeed work continues on a concrete wall that separates thousands of Palestinians in Arab neighborhoods within the municipality of Yerushalayim from the city. The wall has contributed to a drop in terrorist attacks in the city, but its political and social effects in the area of expanded East Jerusalem are to isolate several villages and Arab neighborhoods, sever ties between the Arab hinterland of the city and the core of al-Quds, and greatly embitter the daily lives of hundreds of thousands of Palestinians. Meanwhile, in the wake of the second *Intifada*, Arab areas of expanded East Jerusalem have become "no-go" zones, or at least "foreign territory," for the overwhelming majority of Israeli Jews.

Despite their overall failure, the discussions at Camp David and at Taba did leave a significant diplomatic legacy with respect to Jerusalem. For example, these deliberations produced a new concept that may prove important in future talks: "the sacred basin." This term, referring to a zone, not coextensive with the Walled City, but surrounding the Temple Mount/Haram al-Sharif and including the Jewish cemetery on the Mount of Olives, is meant to signify an area containing the holy sites of all three religions. In addition, "Arab neighborhoods for Palestinian al-Quds, Jewish neighbor-hoods for Israeli Yerushalayim," as a formula for the future of the city, was given weight by occupying center stage at Camp David and at Taba. The dramatic and explicit formulations of President Clinton regarding Jerusalem effectively inscribed this proposal in the minds of all future negotiators on this issue: "What is Arab should be Palestinian and what is Jewish should be Israeli. This would apply to the Old City as well."[18] Moreover, "Jer-usalem should be the internationally recognized capital of two states, Israel and Palestine" and, on the ground in Jerusalem, "What is Arab should be Palestinian, for why would Israel want to govern in perpetuity the lives of hundreds of thousands of Palestinians?" (Makovsky 2001). In essence, this formula—distinguishing between Jewish Yerushalayim and Palestinian al-Quds—has emerged as a "Schelling point" or a "focal point"—an arrange-ment that all future negotiators will begin by imagining is the world's expectation for a satisfactory outcome.

Oscillating between unprecedentedly forward talk of "Palestine" and of a two-state solution, for example when Arab/Muslim goodwill was required prior to the victory over the Taliban, and a posture of letting the Sharon government handle Palestinian terrorism and resistance according to its own devices, the current Bush administration in Washington has displayed all of the typical characteristics of American foreign policy on Israel–Palestinian matters. On the other hand, both the decision to cancel plans to locate a future U.S. embassy on a plot of mostly Arab refugee-owned land in West Jerusalem and Washington's continued high-profile opposition to the "E-1" or "Eastern Gate" plan for the expansion of the Jerusalem municipality eastward (see below) signaled the Bush administration's intention to avoid doing anything that could be interpreted as moving the U.S. position on this issue closer to Israel's than it has been.

In terms of Israeli legal constraints, it is true, as mentioned above, that an amendment to the Basic Law—Jerusalem, Capital of Israel was passed. But the actual effect of this law as a constraint on future political decisions is less than one might think. The bill was passed on November 27, 2000, with the formal, but coldly silent, support of the government. In its final version the bill declares Yerushalayim "for the purposes of this Basic Law, to include, inter alia, the entire area designated in the appendix to the declaration on the expansion of the area of the municipality of Yerushalayim" in 1967. Article 2, section 6, forbids non-Israeli authority of any kind, whether temporary or permanent, in any part of the municipality of Yerushalayim as defined by its current boundaries. Anticipating that efforts would be made in the future to do just this, section 7 requires a majority of Knesset members (61) in order to override its provisions. The final vote on the bill was 84 in favor, 19 against, with no abstentions and 17 MKs not present.[19]

In a celebratory declaration immediately following the vote, the bill's sponsor, Yehoshua Matza, described the significance of its passage. Matza told the Knesset that his heart was "filled with pride" at the "unity of this house and its support of the Bill." But he immediately blamed the government for turning some of that joy and pride into sadness because of its "continuing negotiations dedicated to transferring neighborhoods in Jerusalem to a foreign element, to Palestinians, and its efforts to turn over the holy of holies, the Temple Mount, to Palestinian sovereignty." In the continuing struggle to block such compromises, the newly amended Basic Law, said Matza, "would correct expectations and destroy illusions entertained by the Palestinians and stave off threats to neighborhoods in Yerushalayim." However, using a full-throated expression of the traditional fetishizing catechism, Matza made clear that the real target of the new amendment was not "foreigners" but Israelis—indeed elected representatives of Israelis:

Henceforth this basic law will stand before every government; this law will stand before every prime minister, and before every minister.

Mr. Prime Minister, for you and for all Prime Ministers after you, there will be no authority to act according to any plan for concessions on Yerushalayim, neither with respect to a permanent or a temporary arrangement. I am referring to such ideas as we have been hearing recently. United Yerushalayim will remain as the capital of Israel, under Israeli sovereignty, forever and ever. If I forget thee O Yerushalayim,

may my right hand forget its cunning. In less flowery language—
Yerushalayim is the essence of our life, the essence of the life of Zionism.[20]

However, Matza's use of his victory celebration to score points against
ongoing efforts by the government to reach an accord with the Palestinians by changing Yerushalayim's boundaries shows just how little, in
fact, had been changed by the law. Indeed the immediate response to
Matza's declaration was an outburst from a One Israel (Labor Party)
MK, Ofir Pines-Paz, that "[the newly amended Basic Law] changes nothing." Indeed, the law had not changed the legal status of the territories
added to the Israeli municipality of Yerushalayim in 1967, but only insured
that attempts by future Israeli leaders to take advantage of the absence of
Israeli sovereignty over those areas for purposes of reaching an agreement
with the Palestinians would require either a majority of 61 MKs or an
amendment to the Basic Law as amended. As is well known, such an
amendment to the provision requiring 61 members of Knesset to make a
change in the Law would itself require only a majority of MKs present and
voting.

The largest impact of the Aqsa *Intifada* on the Jerusalem question is likely
to be felt via Israel's withdrawal from Gaza and a portion of the northern
West Bank. In large measure this plan and the widespread Israeli support it
enjoyed in Israel were the result of the Aqsa *Intifada* (Lustick 2002). Palestinian violence in and from Gaza convinced Israel that holding this coastal
patch, with 1.35 million Palestinian Arabs and 7,500 Jewish settlers, was just
not sensible. The precedent of an unsatisfying unilateral withdrawal from
Palestinian territory along with the routing of the separation barrier through
portions of the expanded municipality of Yerushalayim are both precedents
that could strengthen those who favor rearranging jurisdictional boundaries
between Yerushalayim and al-Quds as a natural and expected part of a process to achieve real peace. If serious negotiations toward a two-state solution
do take place, within the framework of the "Road Map" or some future
diplomatic framework, the importance of the defetishization of expanded
Jerusalem will become even more apparent.

As I have argued here, the project of expanded Yerushalayim has not
achieved hegemonic status in Israel, but it still is a gigantic political fact. By
endorsing withdrawal from parts of the Land of Israel (Gaza and a piece of
the northern West Bank) and by accepting the principle of a two-state
solution, Ariel Sharon's government, based as it was on an alliance of right-
wing parties, dealt a painful and shocking blow to the ultranationalist and
fundamentalist alliance that has held the whip hand in Israeli politics for
more than two decades. Leaders of this movement, including thousands of
deeply committed and politically astute settler activists, suspect that some
kind of peace agreement based on two political entities may be inevitable.
One strategy they will use is to conduct provocative marches and rallies

in the Old City of Jerusalem, focusing specifically on the ultra-sensitive Temple Mount/Haram al-Sharif. Even if the most terrifying threats of the "Rebuild the Temple" groups, to destroy the Muslim shrines there, are thwarted or remain unimplemented, it is not at all unlikely that a repeat of the year 2000 clashes on the Temple Mount, associated with Ariel Sharon's high-profile visit there, which triggered the second *Intifada*, could trigger a third, thereby scuttling some future effort to move toward a genuine two-state solution.

If that technique fails, however, the best hope of Israeli diehards will be to use fetishized Jerusalem to prevent the emergent Palestinian state from being established in a politically viable way. One can thus understand their pressure to implement the "Eastern Gate" plan—expanding the geographical range of the city to include the large settlement of Maale Adumim and all the lands in between. By thus dividing the West Bank, with a massive field of Israeli settlement stretching almost to Jericho, three things could be accomplished. First, it is quite possible that this action alone, including implementation of the government's recently announced plan to build 3,000 housing units for Jewish settlers in this area,[21] could prevent the peace process from being invigorated. Second, if a two-state solution is formally adopted, the implementation of this plan would effectively deprive the Palestinian state of a capital in al-Quds, tar its leadership as having betrayed the Palestinian national cause, and almost surely lead, via unrest, violence, attacks on Israeli targets, and political incapacity, to the statelet's collapse. Third, collapse of the peace arrangements associated with the crippled Palestinian state would, in the eyes of the unreconstructed right in Israel, set the stage for the re-conquest of the Palestinian areas and decisive moves to empty them of Arab inhabitants or otherwise enable their permanent absorption.

Conclusion

Many seekers of peace in Yerushalayim are psychologically afflicted by the same kind of shock and despair suffered by Dorothy and her friends once they discovered the wizard was no wizard, but a product of smoke, mirrors, and their own illusions. But the failure at Camp David, the successes of Taba, and the pain associated with the Aqsa *Intifada* are helping to clear away much of the smoke that for so long obscured the problem of Jerusalem's future. To be sure, neither Palestinians nor Israelis are wearing the kind of magic slippers Dorothy had at the end of the movie to whisk her away from Oz and back to Kansas. On the other hand, as did Dorothy, so do Israelis and Palestinians who want a solution to the conflict over Jerusalem have the design of one readily at hand. The elements of a solution to this important part of the Israeli–Palestinian puzzle are now apparent, even though it will take sacrifices, hard work, and a certain amount of political wizardry to bring it about.

Notes

1 Names are of crucial importance. Maps of the region in the languages of the region do not show "Jerusalem" located in the Middle East, but rather "Yerushalayim" (in Hebrew) and/or "al-Quds" (in Arabic). "Jerusalem" is a Western/ Christian and non-Middle Eastern term, but it implies a united single place that, as we will see, does political injustice to the quite separate and separable communities of Yerushalayim, hallowed by Jews and celebrated as the capital of Israel since 1949, and "al-Quds," cherished and venerated by Arabs and Muslims and regarded, by Palestinians, as the rightful capital of their future state.

2 In June 1993 the Government of Israel announced the following official decision: "The year 1996 (5756–5757) has been declared the 'Trimillennium of Jerusalem, the City of David,' with the city of Jerusalem and the figure of King David at the center of the planned events." http://www.mfa.gov.il/MFA/MFAArchive/1990_1999/ 1993/6/JERUSALEM%203000-%20City%20of%20David%201996.   Concerning the tepid and even critical reception of this extravaganza among some Jews see Landes 1995, 6–7.

3 Baumol 2001, circulated on May 9 as a press release via e-mail from Yossi Baumol, Executive Director of the Jerusalem Reclamation Project—Ateret Cohanim. Ateret Cohanim is one of the most prominent and vigorous of the fundamentalist groups associated with efforts to rebuild the Jewish Temple in Jerusalem. Its efforts to acquire lands and buildings in Arab neighborhoods in East Jerusalem have enjoyed the support and coordination of a number of Israeli governments as part of the policies toward the city I analyze in this chapter.

4 For some details of these considerations see Shlomo Gazit's account of the arguments inside the Israeli Cabinet over exactly what administrative/legal steps to take with respect to East Jerusalem and its environs in the immediate aftermath of the Six-Day War (Gazit 1995, 194–203).

5 *Laws of the State of Israel* 1966/67, 76. This list of latitudinal and longitudinal points can be found in the Appendix below. On June 27, 1967 the Knesset also passed the "Protection of Holy Places Law." Like the other two laws, this law does not mention Jerusalem. Its main purpose was to make desecration of a holy place or interference with free access to a holy place (anywhere where Israeli law was in force) punishable by substantial prison terms. For detailed legal and administrative analysis of the amendments and declarations mentioned, see Lustick 1997.

6 For the evolution of Israeli Supreme Court judgments regarding the applicability of the Hague Regulations to Israeli rule of the occupied West Bank and Gaza Strip, see Lustick 1981. Regarding the applicability of the category of "belligerent occupation" to Israeli rule of those territories, including East Jerusalem, see Dinstein 1971. For a recent reaffirmation, in connection with a judgment regarding the barrier built by Israel in the West Bank, of the Court's view of the binding applicability of the Hague Regulations and Israel's status vis-à-vis the West Bank as that of "belligerent occupation," see Israel High Court of Justice, 2056/04 Beit Sourik Village Council v. The Government of Israel [2004], *Piskei Din* 58.5: 807, 23–24. See HCJ 7957/04, Zahran Yunis Muhammad Mara'abe v. The Prime Minister of Israel [2005] 38(2), 21–22, for the Court's use of the term a "regime of belligerent occupation" to refer to the legal regime within "Judea and Samaria."

7 For a detailed map distinguishing the 1949 Armistice Line in Jerusalem, which was Yerushalayim's municipal boundary until 1967, the Jordanian municipality of al-Quds boundary line between 1949 and 1967, and the 1967 line marking Israel's expansion of Yerushalayim's municipal boundary, see http://www.passia. org/palestine_facts/MAPS/images/jer_maps/Settlements.html.

8 It is often asserted that Israel offered East Jerusalem Arabs the option of becoming Israeli citizens. This assertion is misleading; no special prerogative was

offered. Instead, the opportunity to apply for Israeli citizenship is on offer for East Jerusalem Arabs as it is, in principle, on offer to any non-Jew, including any Palestinian Arab, anywhere in the world. Of course, whether to approve any such application is strictly at the discretion of the Israeli government. The crucial point is that real acts of annexation, such as were promulgated after the 1948 war with respect to Western Galilee and the Little Triangle, entailed the forcible imposition of Israeli citizenship on Arab inhabitants.

9 The ultimatum was delivered by Menachem Begin in a speech before the Knesset on May 3, 1982 and a Cabinet Resolution adopted on May 9, 1982. For exact texts see Foreign Broadcast Information Service (FBIS), May 4, 1982, I1; May 6, 1982, I1; and May 10, 1982, I8. For an analysis of the ulterior motive (to sabotage the negotiations) involved in this sudden emphasis on Jerusalem as a venue for the talks, see Poles, "Camp David: The Second Half," *Ha'aretz*, May 7, 1982. For other examples of the use of this technique in connection with various diplomatic attempts to move the "peace process" forward, see public remarks by National Religious Party Member of Knesset Hayim Druckman, October 10, 1982, IDF Radio Broadcast, transcribed by FBIS, October 12, 1982, I9; Moshe Zak, "A Magic Word Called Federation," *Ma'ariv*, October 13, 1982; reports from *Ma'ariv*, November 5, 1985, and Jerusalem Domestic Service Radio Broadcasts, November 5, 1985, of objections by Ariel Sharon and Gush Emunim (Bloc of the Faithful) settlers against the contradiction between proposals to negotiate with Jordan and the terms of the 1980 "Jerusalem Law," in FBIS, November 5, 1982, I2–3, and remarks by Ariel Sharon to his political associates while celebrating the establishment of a personal residence in the Muslim Quarter of the Old City, *Ha'aretz*, May 25, 1989.

10 Concerning these examples of extravagant and often embarrassing techniques to further the fetishization of expanded "Yerushalayim" see Dayan 1993, translated by the Joint Publication Research Service, NEA-93–080, July 9, 1993, 23–24; Landes 1995. The Covenant was largely ignored by Israelis but widely celebrated and endowed with special eschatological significance by evangelical Christians.

11 See, for example, Shamir 1995. The article was also distributed on the eretz-ysirael@shamash.nysernet.org listserv, October 13, 1995.

12 For an extended treatment of this fetishization project as a failed effort to establish the hegemony of politically profitable images of Yerushalayim, see Lustick 1996.

13 An "eruv" is a ritually acceptable fence, usually a combination of wire, existing walls, and other markers, which can be used to demarcate zones within which, according to *Halakhah* (Orthodox Jewish law), observant Jews are permitted to carry things on the Sabbath. For a map of the eruv as it divided the city in 2000, see Lustick 2000.

14 "Yisrael hitzi'ah la-reshut shlitah ezrahit bi-shkhunot tzfoniyot bi-Yerushalayim" (Israel Suggests the PA Exercise Civilian Authority in North Yerushalayim Neighborhoods), *Ha'aretz*, December 31, 1999; Susser 2000. According to the Oslo Declaration of Principles, Jerusalem would be negotiated as a final status issue after the transitional period of not more than five years was completed. The Oslo II agreement provided for three types of areas in the West Bank and Gaza during the transitional period: "A," in which the Palestinian Authority would govern; "B," where governing responsibilities would be shared between the PA and Israel; and "C," where Israel would govern. Although Jerusalem Arabs were allowed to vote in the Palestinian Authority elections, it was not until Barak's trial balloons in late 1999 that the Israel government appeared prepared to make portions of al-Quds as part of "Area B."

15 The bill was similar to a proposal advanced in 1995 by Likud and National Religious Party Knesset members worried about what they saw as Prime Minister Rabin's willingness to negotiate a change in the status or boundaries of Yerushalayim.

16 *Divrei ha-Knesset* (Knesset Record), debates during March–November 2000, *passim* (http://www.knesset.go.il/tql/mark01/H0005391.html).
17 Menachem Klein, an expert on Jerusalem and with numerous publications on the subject issued by the Jerusalem Institute for Israel Affairs, comments on this change: "Both sides now accept that the city cannot be divided again as it was between 1948 and 1967. They also recognize that the current municipal border cannot become an international boundary ... The only option open to both sides in the permanent status talks is a redefinition of the city's boundaries" (Klein 2001). See also Wasserstein 2001, 358–359.
18 http://www.cnn.com/2001/WORLD/meast/01/05/israeli.notes/#3.
19 Votes on the crucial individual parts of the legislation, prior to the final vote, featured majorities in favor of between 62 and 67 as against 13–18 opposed and the rest either absent or not voting.
20 *Divrei ha-Knesset*, November 27, 2000. See also http://www.mail-archive.com/ctrl@listserv.aol.com/msg56149.html.
21 If in fact the barrier is extended to include Maale Adumim, to the east of the city, the essential features of the "Eastern Gate" will have been implemented. Concerning the Eastern Gate Plan, see Moore 2005. For a map of the relevant area see http://www.fmep.org/maps/map_data/west_bank/e1_development_plan.html.

References

Baumol, Yossi. 2001. "Press Release, Jerusalem Reclamation Project—Ateret Cohanim." Text circulated by email, May 9.
Benvenisti, Meron. 1976. *Jerusalem: The Torn City.* Minneapolis: University of Minnesota Press.
Dayan, Arye. 1993. "Parchment under Glass." *Ha'aretz*, May 19.
Dinstein, Yoram. 1971. "Zion in International Law Will Be Redeemed." *Hapraklit* 27: 5–11. (In Hebrew.)
Divrei Ha'Knesset (Knesset Record).
Efrat, Elisha. 2000. "Why Should We Provide for Them?" *Ha'Tzofeh*, 28 (January 28).
Foreign Broadcast Information Service (FBIS), Daily Report: Near East & South Asia.
Foreign Broadcast Information Service (FBIS), Joint Publications Research Service.
Gazit, Shlomo. 1995. *The Carrot and the Stick: Israel's Policy in Judaea and Samaria, 1967–68.* Washington: B'nai B'rith Books.
——. 2000. "Divide Jerusalem." *Jerusalem Post*, February 1, 1.
Klein, Menachem. 2001. *Jerusalem: The Contested City.* Jerusalem: Jerusalem Institute for Israel Studies.
Landes, Yisrael. 1995. "Yerushalayim: haDavash ve ha'Okatz" (Jerusalem: The Honey and the Bitter Sarcasm). *Ha'doar* (September 22), 6–7. (In Hebrew.)
Laws of the State of Israel. 1966/67. Vol. 21, 5727–1966/67. Jerusalem: Government Printer.
Lustick, Ian S. 1981. "Israel and the West Bank after Elon Moreh: The Mechanics of De Facto Annexation." *Middle East Journal* 35.4 (Autumn): 557–577.
——. 1996. "The Fetish of Jerusalem: A Hegemonic Analysis." In *Israel in Comparative Perspective: Challenging the Conventional Wisdom*, ed. Michael N. Barnett, 43–72. Albany: SUNY Press.
——. 1997. "Has Israel Annexed East Jerusalem?" *Middle East Policy* 5.1: 34–45.
——. 2000. "Yerushalayim and al-Quds: Political Catechism and Political Realities." *Journal of Palestine Studies* 30.1: 5–21.

———. 2002. "In Blood and Fire Shall Peace Arise." *Tikkun* 17.3 (May/June): 13–19.

Makovsky, David. 2001. "Time Running Out on Clinton Proposals." *Peacewatch* 303 (January 11).

Moore, Molly. 2005. "Israeli Settlements to Reach Jerusalem." *Washington Post*, March 22.

Moratinos, Miguel. 2002. "Minutes of the Negotiations at Tabah—January 2001." *Ha'Aretz*, March 2.

Segal, Jerome M., Shlomit Levy, Nadar Izzat Sa'id, and Elihu Katz. 2000. *Negotiating Jerusalem*. Albany: SUNY Press.

Shamir, Yitzchak. 1995. "Haters of the Land of Israel." *The Jewish Press*, October 13.

Susser, Leslie. 2000. "You Say Jerusalem, We'll Say al-Quds." *The Jerusalem Report*, February 28.

Wasserstein, Bernard. 2001. *Divided Jerusalem: The Struggle for the Holy City*. London: Profile Books.

Appendix: Translation of official Israeli definition of the Jerusalem municipal boundary (June 28, 1967)

Grid reference = g.r.

Spot height = s.h.

From g.r. 1678613520 north along Wadi Issa to g.r. 1673613678 from there in a straight line north-east till the junction with the way in g.r. 1675413700 and from there eastward along the way till g.r. 1678813706 and from there in a straight line to s.h. 777.3 which is g.r. 1685413710 and from there in a straight line till the meeting with Wadi El-Akaba in g.r. 1690013694 and from there southeasterly along the northern part of Wadi El-Akaba till the junction with Wadi A-Sharki in g.r. 1699613604 from there northward along Wadi A-Sharki till g.r. 1705013712 and from there on northward till s.h. 703.2 which is located in g.r. 1705813848 and from there in a straight line to s.h. 793.5 that is in g.r. 1703613938 from there in a straight line north till the junction with the way in g.r. 1704213974 from there in a straight line to the center of g.r. 1704014062 from there till the junction with the way in g.r. 1701214114 and from there in a straight line northwesterly till the junction with the way in g.r. 1697014136 and from there north along the way till the crossroad that is in g.r. 1695414232 and from there in a straight line till g.r. 1697214294 and from there eastward by surrounding hill 826 from the north along the way till the crossroad in g.r. 1703814336 and from there in a straight line eastward till the junction with the road in g.r. 1710014332 and from there southeasterly till s.h.

straight line southerly till s.h. 700.5 that is located in g.r. 1740613002 from there in a straight line southeasterly till the junction with the way in g.r. 1747012936 from there south along the way till g.r. 1750412844 from there in a straight line southwesterly till the junction in g.r. 1748212830 from there in a straight line to g.r. 1747812826 from there in a straight line southwesterly till the junction with Kidron Valley in g.r. 1745612776 from there in a straight line southwesterly till the junction with the Wadi in g.r. 1739212736 from there south along the Wadi A-Luz till g.r. 1739212666 from there in a straight line till the junction with Wadi Al-Katz in g.r. 1737612590 from there in a straight line southwesterly till the junction with Wadi Al-Phaht in g.r. 1732012526 from there in a straight line south till s.h. 616 that is located in g.r. 1731212442 from there in a straight line till s.h. 604 that is located in g.r. 1727612412 from there in a straight line northwesterly till the junction with the way in g.r. 1720012448 from there northwesterly along the valley till g.r. 1717412500 from there in a straight line to g.r. 1713612516 from there in a straight line southwesterly till g.r. 1708412478 from there in a straight line northwesterly till s.h. 782.9 that is located in g.r. 1695012566 from there in a straight line till the crossroad in g.r. 1679812544 from there in a straight line till the crossroad in g.r. 1671212534 from there in a straight line northwesterly till g.r. 1657212664 from there in a straight line to g.r. 1646212672 from there in a straight line to g.r. 1643612712.

June 28, 1967   Signed Chaim Moshe Shapira

20 Sivan 5727   Minister of the Interior

18 Negotiating Jerusalem

Reflections of an Israeli negotiator

Gilead Sher

Introduction

This chapter contains excerpts of my own record[1] of the discussions, plans, and proposals on the issue of Jerusalem at the Camp David Summit in the summer of 2000, in which I had the privilege of playing a leading role as part of the Israeli delegation.

The Camp David Summit itself was something of a last-ditch attempt by President Clinton to wrap up a workable Middle East peace deal in the final year of his presidency. In the lead-up to it and in the course of it, he devoted unprecedented resources—both in human and material terms—to this end. The aim and hope was to create the physical circumstances whereby, after almost a decade of discussions, negotiations, and agreements, and in the most intensive round of negotiations to date, the leaderships of the respective parties could be guided, cajoled, and pushed toward settling the most intractable of the Permanent Status core issues which divided them. Among these were the future of Jerusalem, the final borders, and the issue of refugees. Probably the most sensitive and explosive of all of these was the issue of Jerusalem.

The future of the city of Jerusalem, in particular the future of East Jerusalem and the Old City, was an issue that lay at the very heart of the charged narratives of both sides of the conflict. It related, in particular, to the area within the Suleiman walls of the Old City, as well as the area that has come to be referred to as the Holy Basin, which extends from the north of the Old City southwards, encompassing most of the sites sacred to the three monotheistic religions, and including the Temple Mount (*Haram al-Sharif*), the Western Wall, the Church of the Holy Sepulcher, Gethsemane, Mount Zion, the City of David, the Mount of Olives, and the village of Silwan. Resolving the issue of the future of Jerusalem, therefore, meant, among other things, resolving the issue of the future of the holy places and the custodianship or sovereignty over these. Beyond these were other urban areas, to the north, south, and east, whose future remained in doubt and in dispute, and which were consequently also on the table at the negotiations.

In addition to being crowded with religious and cultural sites that were hotly contested, this area was also a densely populated one, particularly the Old City, within the Suleiman walls. At the time of the Summit, the population of the Old City was thought to be upwards of 30,000 (it has since grown to upwards of 40,000). The wider surrounding disputed areas contained populations that were double this figure. Any settlement would have to take into account the needs—including the political, traditional, ethical, historical, and religious needs of such populations—as well as their freedom and limitations on their movements.

Since the start of the secret talks between the parties at the beginning of the 1990s, through the Oslo Accords and after, the issue of the future of Jerusalem was one of those whose settlement the parties chose to postpone to the end—for the negotiations towards Permanent Status. On the one hand this was a logical ploy, as it enabled them to sidestep an issue loaded with potential deal-breakers, and to make progress on the other, less highly charged issues. On the other hand, it proved somewhat counterproductive and illusory, since any progress that could be made, and recorded, on the other issues, was progress only to the extent that this and the other core issues could be resolved. The approach taken at Camp David was to attempt to tackle the core issues head-on.

For those of us who took part in these historic negotiations, the sense of responsibility was immense. We were acutely aware of the significance of Jerusalem to our own people—its religious, historical, cultural, political, and strategic significance—and to this end approached the possibility of making concessions, any concessions, even in the interests of an historic agreement, with enormous trepidation. Yet we were mindful also of what had been created here—a once-in-a-lifetime opportunity, a moment in history, to be seized, or lost, with possibly calamitous consequences for our own country and the Palestinians themselves if we failed to reach an agreement. The stakes, therefore, as we embarked on these discussions, were very high indeed. And we knew it.

God bless you

Thus far in the summit, the Palestinians withdrew from all the understandings reached in the Swedish channel,[2] reopening everything for discussion, including the issues of refugees, the end of the conflict, and the finality of claims.

Robert Malley, President Clinton's Special Assistant for Arab–Israeli Affairs, and a member of the U.S. peace team, came to our cabin at around 11.30 p.m. on July 16. "Arafat will demand land swaps. Not symbolic ones," he told me. "Informally and implicitly he has agreed to leave eight to ten percent of the territories in Israeli hands, as you proposed," Malley added carefully. "But we have to get a deal on Jerusalem—putting all the alternatives and possible ideas on the table. Arafat needs a fig leaf. As for the eastern border, Palestinians should have all of the Jordan River," he continued, convinced that this was the right solution to the final delineation of the eastern borders of the Palestinian state. Malley knew that Israel was against this.

The Americans made it clear to us and to the Palestinians that they had no patience left. In a very tough conversation I had with Sandy Berger, who was the U.S. National Security Adviser under President Clinton between 1997 and 2001, he argued that Prime Minister Barak, who had wanted the summit and who had "pressed all of us," was now retracting from his previous positions, and was not showing enough flexibility. "As of tomorrow," he added, "I end my commitments to the peace process and start protecting the president." We did not let the blunt American pressure affect us.

In separate conversations with the respective leaders that afternoon, President Clinton proposed that each side select two representatives to engage in marathon secret talks unbeknown to the other delegation members and without interfering with the timetable for the negotiations. "We will make a brave and open attempt to conclude the ultimate package which constitutes an agreement on all issues," the President told Barak in their meeting. "And if it does not work out, we have lost nothing. We tried."

Barak designated "Amnon or Shlomo and Gilli"[3] (Amnon Lipkin-Shahak or Shlomo Ben-Ami, and Gilead Sher) to this back channel, Arafat nominated Mohammed Dahlan and Erekat (Sa'ib Muhammad Salih Uray-qat).[4] Ben-Ami, Shahak and, later, Israel Hasson were let in on the secret.[5] Yossi Ginossar,[6] as usual, knew from his Palestinian friends about the proposed format even before he found out from us.

"Use your heads," Arafat said as he sent Dahlan and Erekat off to the secret negotiations. "Bring back a good paper. Just do not budge on one thing: Al Haram is dearer to me than anything else."

At midnight, the four of us—Ben-Ami and myself along with Dahlan and Erekat—were called to the President. Clinton emphasized the importance of the unique event. "You are going off to the most important mission of your lives," he said simply, "to bring peace to your peoples. God bless you." Madeline Albright gave us each a hug. We felt like we were going off on a special ops mission.

It was pouring rain outside. The President's bodyguards led us to the central complex at Camp David, Laurel cabin. Security guarded the entrances to the cabin the entire night and would not let us leave. A continuous supply of sandwiches and coffee may not have relieved the fatigue, but it allowed us to continue. In the morning, Dahlan tried to leave the cabin in order to pray. A loud vocal exchange developed between him and the Americans. I snuck out the side door of the President's office, to shower and change.

The four of us began working at the corner of a huge table in the large conference room. It was the same place Clinton had launched the summit less than a week earlier. The first topic for discussion was Jerusalem. As the night dragged on, Ben-Ami and Dahlan worked in the conference room together with Israel Hasson, who joined them at around 4 a.m., while Erekat and I moved into the adjacent office of the President. A huge portrait of Winston Churchill adorned the wall. There were also a large desk, a computer, memorabilia-filled shelves, pictures, certificates, and badges. One black-and-white picture, in particular, was very touching: Bill Clinton, as a young teenager, shaking the hand of President Kennedy. The photograph was signed by JFK.

I had a long journey ahead of me in trying to convince Erekat to put what had already been agreed upon on paper in order to move forward. When we finally started drafting an agreement, it was a draining process, punctuated with short sermons by Erekat about why he refused to write that Israel was a Jewish state, why he would reject any attempt to limit the ability of the future state of Palestine to join international alliances, and a host of other arguments that did little to move us forward.

Nevertheless, we were slowly making progress, as both the negotiations and the drafting entered a more practical and relevant stage. The changes we made to the text were projected from the computer onto the wall in order to make us more efficient. But Ben-Ami and I were beside ourselves when we found out that the Palestinians intended to file a giant lawsuit against Israel for damages caused by the occupation since 1967, explaining, in fact, why they were avoiding an agreement. At 6 a.m. Erekat decided he must absolutely get some rest. "Are you crazy?" Ben-Ami shouted, bleary-eyed and disheveled. "This is our last chance and you're tired? This is how you work? Don't you want a state? And now you want to sue us for the occupation?" It was only with great effort that he calmed down. Rob Malley intervened, shook Erekat, and got him back to work.

Twelve hours after we had started, toward noon, we stopped. Meanwhile, we had heard other delegation members come and go for breakfast. We had to find a breakthrough. There was, however, no breakthrough to be had. We narrowed the gaps, especially on the issue of territory—the possibility of Israel's annexation of a small percentage of the West Bank in return for land within Israel proper (1949–67 borders)—and went in depth into the issue of Jerusalem. But this was far from being enough.

We reported these developments to the Prime Minister. Barak presented the concept of this exercise to the other members of the delegation: we were playing with ideas in order to see what a potential agreement could look like.

"The general concept presented last night," Barak said, "was as follows: separation from the southern and northern Arab neighborhoods of Jerusalem, and a special regime in the Old City which will be designed in accordance with its holy and unique character. There will be Israeli sovereignty, and complete management by the Palestinians of the Temple Mount. The Palestinians were very inflexible in their response," the Prime Minister continued. "There is no noticeable Palestinian movement in our direction. Decisions need to be made on both sides. If this is the situation, and this is all we have heard from the

Palestinians—we are probably headed toward conflict. This 'intellectual exercise' of Shlomo and Gilli"—as Barak named it—"had no validity or meaning without a Palestinian response."

Dahlan and Erekat's report to Arafat, on the Palestinian side, was laconic and bleak. "The Israelis have not moved forward on anything, except for the proposal to create a special regime in the Old City." They added that Israel demanded to annex four settlement blocs totaling 12 percent of the territory, and demanded control over another 10 percent in the Jordan Valley for an additional twelve to thirty years. Sixty-three settlements would remain in Palestinian territory.

At 2 p.m. the sides reported back to President Clinton. The report was loaded and emotional on the Palestinian side, and pessimistic on ours. "There is no package deal," we said. "The Palestinians are holding on to their tactical positions on all issues and are waiting for Israel to make all the concessions. Only then, maybe, under conditions they dictate, will they be willing to present their final positions. Moreover, who will assure us that those seated across from us are able and authorized to commit on behalf of Arafat?" Clinton thanked us for our effort. "I fully appreciate your brave effort. We'll move on."

"God, it's hard," the President said in an interview with the *Daily News*. "It's like nothing I've ever dealt with." Clinton later spoke with Arafat, in a meeting that began with a Palestinian warning. "If the Israelis insist on their demand to pray at al-Haram, an Islamic revolution will erupt." "You are welcome to present your objections, but if you do not move forward, we will leave here empty handed," Clinton said. "I think that Barak has in fact moved forward somewhat."

"This means nothing," Arafat replied. "It involves only the distant neighborhoods of Jerusalem, which he wants to get rid of anyway."

Clinton demanded clear answers from Arafat to three questions:

Will you agree to the Israeli demand to annex 10.5 percent of the territory?
Will you agree to a limited Israeli presence on the Jordanian border?
Will you agree to an agreement that constitutes an end of conflict, even
    though some issues remain unresolved?

It was a tense meeting. According to some of the American participants, Clinton actually yelled at Arafat. The President warned that if there would be no progress on at least one of the main points, there was no use in staying in Camp David, not even until Tuesday. The Palestinians have another version, claiming the meeting took place in a pleasant atmosphere.

It appeared that Clinton felt justified in placing the burden on the Palestinians, particularly having heard the reports from the two teams that were involved in the "theoretical exercise." According to the Americans, it was the Israeli report that changed the picture, placing responsibility for the dead end on the Palestinian side.

Even so, the Americans viewed this as the turning point in the entire summit and were still hopeful that an agreement could be reached and that a package deal that would bring an end to the conflict might be possible. The mooted agreement included a reasonable division of territory, with an 8 percent annexation of settlement blocs and strategic territory by Israel, no Right of Return for Palestinian refugees to Israel, the transfer of the peripheral and distant neighborhoods of Jerusalem to Palestinian sovereignty, and the eastern border—with Jordan—under Palestinian sovereignty. Although an explicit discussion had not yet taken place, security arrangements that would satisfy Israel also appeared attainable at this stage. Danny Yatom[7] noted that it was the first time that a Palestinian proposal was put on the table, which contends that eight to ten percent of the territory would remain under Israeli control. But although Arafat may have said this to Clinton, he would completely deny it.

Six days after the summit began and two days before he would leave for Japan, the President felt that he had an opportunity to "seal the deal," and prepared to shuttle between the leaders to ensure there was a concrete basis for this feeling.

It was against this backdrop that the Prime Minister convened a brainstorming session on the issue of Jerusalem on the afternoon of July 17. Barak began to systematically peel away at the outer shells and slogans, initiating a process that constituted the beginning of a dramatic conceptual change in the minds of many of the delegation members. This was a move of historic importance, and one whose originality and courage should not be underestimated. In opening up the subject of Jerusalem, Barak was forcing the delegation members to confront and challenge the underlying assumptions of the Israeli political discourse in the last three decades regarding Jerusalem. Later, this move by Barak would also mark the beginning of public debate and the adjustment of public opinion to ideas that had not been discussed seriously since the Six-Day War.

"The insight that policy making provides," opened Barak, "involves the ability to foresee and to recognize the wall against which we may crash. Today, the waters might be calm, but the iceberg is nearing. It is possible that a solution to the issue of Jerusalem will bring about the end of conflict and the success of the summit," the Prime Minister thought out loud. "Is Palestinian autonomy, while maintaining the settlement blocs under our sovereignty, indeed the solution, or will it begin a new problem? Is a painful break preferable to continued ambiguity? In any case Jerusalem is a central and critical issue, and I would like to consolidate a position together with you," he said, addressing all those now assembled in the room.

Israel Hasson commented first. "We must aim to perpetuate the existing situation and choose between an alternative of 'functional autonomy'[8] and the option of dividing Jerusalem on the basis of defined sovereign separation," he said. "The components that need to be addressed are municipal Jerusalem, the 'Holy Basin' and the Temple Mount. The greatest danger in functional autonomy is that many questions will become more pointed, and organizations such as the Waqf[9] will strengthen. We should consider mutually suspending the demand for sovereignty in the Old City because the ability to separate or divide is very limited.

"We have to narrow down to a minimum the area defined as the Holy Basin,"[10] he went on. "Anything that is not demographically clear and simple will not be sustainable. Regarding the Temple Mount," he concluded, "it's better to talk with the moderates today than with extremist groups such as the Islamic Movement or the 'Hamas' tomorrow."

Oded Eran, who headed the Israel Foreign Ministry's team in the talks with the Palestinians and later served as Israel's Ambassador to the EU and Jordan, noted that there were 130,000 Palestinians living along the outskirts of Jerusalem. "We have no historic or religious interest in the northern bloc which reaches up to Shoafat; in the southern bloc, east of Har Homa; and in the internal bloc. We have to avoid bringing thousands of Palestinians under Israeli sovereignty. Not doing so would be equivalent to accepting the Right of Return and would cost the Israeli Ministry of Finance US$200 million, annually. Regarding the Temple Mount, in accordance with what our chief rabbis have said, we have no intention of worshipping there. Nevertheless, we must maintain our sovereignty. We cannot divide the Old City into quarters. Instead, we should create a local, internal, and common administration to the Palestinians and us. Mount of Olives is, for all intents and purposes, under Palestinian sovereignty. It is where all their national institutions are located, and this is the way it should remain. It is the place from which Arafat has a direct and uninterrupted view of the Temple Mount. As for municipal management, two municipalities and a supra-municipality—the head of which will rotate—should be created."

"For the Palestinians, Jerusalem makes or breaks the agreement," Ginossar added. "There is a complete lack of understanding on their part regarding the significance of the Temple Mount to Israel and to the Jewish people. It's really quite amazing. We must rank our demands for sovereignty in descending order. First, the Temple Mount, followed by the Old City, the circle of adjacent neighborhoods, and finally the more distant neighborhoods." Ginossar warned that even Arafat's closest circle would not support a solution which does not yield some Palestinian sovereignty in Jerusalem, and more specifically, in the Old City.

Dan Meridor[11] recognized that once the principle of an undivided city[12] is violated, "the question is just—how much? It is difficult to draw the final line of withdrawal. If we breach the position of an undivided Jerusalem on the basis of demography, we need to be completely sure we have achieved a Permanent Status agreement. This should be the last step."

"It may be," I offered, "that the nucleus of our position and that of the Palestinian position do not intersect, in which case, the problem would not be solved and there would be no agreement. We could, in such a situation, forget about end of conflict and Permanent Status. If we cannot reach a full agreement, we should try to consolidate an agreed list of issues that remain disputed, and conclude a mechanism for resolving other issues, including timetables, as well as the level of continued negotiations. Jerusalem is the main part of the comprehensive package that 'seals' the agreement, and it would be a tactical mistake to discuss and conclude it separately."

"If we do not get the End of Conflict,[13] it will be wrong to go ahead with an agreement, both domestically and in terms of what could happen later in our relations with the Palestinians," agreed Amnon Shahak. "The issue of compromising over Jerusalem will not be easy to explain to the Israeli public, in the same way as the issue of compromising over the right of return for refugees will not be easy for the Palestinians to explain to theirs. We do not know if a deal that will bring about the end of conflict would be acceptable to the Israeli public. But, I would go for it anyway."

"This is one of the most substantial and most important moments that an Israeli prime minister has ever faced, at least since 1967," Shlomo Ben-Ami added. "This entire effort will ultimately fall squarely on the shoulders of Ehud Barak. We said from the onset that this summit is a conference on Jerusalem. Gilead and I could sense that this would solve the entire puzzle. We have made good use of the time that has passed since 1967, while the Arabs have lost and squandered theirs, and not only on the issue of Jerusalem. It is important that we decide today. There will not be a Permanent Status agreement if the Palestinians do not receive something in the way of a mythological element, which is not measured in territory. There will not be a solution without some Palestinian sovereignty in the Old City, or part of it, at least in the Muslim Quarter. We have to change the demographic balance, rather than fall prey or become paralyzed by slogans. Jewish Jerusalem has never been as big, and our control has never been as deep as it is now. Let us finally reach a decision regarding supra-sovereignty, for the sake of Jewish history. We can upgrade the infrastructure and image of the city."

"No to dividing the city, no to transfer of sovereignty," Meridor set off on a speech.

"There will not be an agreement without mentioning sovereignty for Arafat in some area of the Old City," concluded Ben-Ami.

Danny Yatom noted that we all knew how the municipal boundaries of Jerusalem had been drawn. "These are not holy, neither from a religious nor from a national perspective. These are boundaries that received more pomp and circumstance than substance. We need to adopt our real red lines. There must be signs of Palestinian sovereignty in the Old City, and it is important to finish this now—what is difficult today, will not become easier in a few years."

"What is Jerusalem?" Shahak asked rhetorically. "Large parts of the city are not 'my Yerushalaim.' The Israeli interest is to transfer as many Palestinian inhabitants to Palestinian control and leave the least number of Arabs under Israeli sovereignty. We cannot concede sovereignty on the Temple Mount. We cannot give Arafat the Jewish Temple, the cradle of the Jewish culture. But we cannot manage Al Aqsa either. Although I am unsure this will satisfy them, we must find a way of giving the Palestinians a defined area in the Muslim Quarter."

"This discussion is very difficult for me," Elyakim Rubinstein[14] said. "Legally, things are clear. There is a clear ability to provide for the needs on a human or religious level. But the internal cohesion of Israeli society is important."

Daniel Reisner[15] suggested minimizing the number of areas in which there is division between sovereignty and authority. "Such divisions do not hold over time. Look at the case of Hong Kong. We should choose functional solutions. They need sovereignty in the Old City, and therefore this is the only important question. Maybe we should think of sovereignty of both sides in the same area. We should not talk about a joint municipality, because this would then be applicable on the western Israeli part of the city. For the Old City, however, a joint administration—subject to both municipalities—for the special regime area could be useful."

Shlomo Yanai[16] made an analogy between Jerusalem and an onion that needs to be peeled. "What is this Jerusalem of ours that we really do not want to divide? The contours of this city allow us to exclude 130,000 Arabs that do not reside in historic Jerusalem, using a relatively simple definition by dividing sovereignty. We need a peace that will last longer than two days. Therefore, the day-to-day lives in these areas have to be simple rather than dictated by a complex and convoluted regime. Arafat looks at the historic-symbolic meaning, and it appears we can give this to him. As for the end of conflict, I believe we can reach this, although we need a formula, according to which he doesn't lose respect."

Barak returned to the heart of the argument. "I have no idea how we will leave here. But it is clear that we will be united as we face the world, if we find out that an agreement was not reached because of the issue of sovereignty over the site of our First and Second Temple. This is the center of our existence, the anchor of the Zionist endeavor, although this effort was largely secular. This is the moment of truth. We have been sitting here for over four hours, in a discussion that is tearing each of us apart on the inside. The issues are weighty, and we must decide, but not under the duress of fire and blood. This decision is very similar to the one taken on the partition plan or on the establishment of the State of Israel, or even the crisis of the Yom Kippur War. We are seated here, thirteen people, detached from the real world, and we are being asked to decide on things that will have an impact on the fate of millions. Postponing this process further is not an option. Prime Minister Begin understood well the importance of decisions he made in his time. Rabin and Peres knew exactly where certain formulations of Oslo, such as 'Single Territorial Unit,'[17] would lead. Rabin, in his time, made heart-wrenching decisions. I do not see him or any other prime minister transferring sovereignty to the Palestinians over the site of the First or Second Temple. Without separation and end of conflict, however, we are moving toward tragedy."

The Prime Minister moved on to discuss more practical tasks (such as collecting data, writing memoranda, preparing maps and reports, and so forth), professional opinions, and preparations for continued work. First, we would examine the mechanism necessary for two coordinated municipalities in the Zone of Jerusalem. After that, we would attempt to assess our minimalist position, which could be acceptable to the Palestinians, regarding the augmented area of Jerusalem. Then we would look into the different aspects of functional religious autonomy on the Temple Mount. Finally, we would work on preparing for separation—the border regime, the possible definitions for sovereignty, and arrangements on the Temple Mount.

With the help of the Ministry of Foreign Affairs and the IDF attorney's office we started preparing for the resolution of serious legal issues related to the framework agreement. The work was based, among other things, on precedents around the world, which focused on ending war, territorial claims, and finality of financial and property claims. In a document entitled "Legal Claims Regarding a Framework Agreement"[18] precedents were detailed, beginning with the Paris Peace Treaties, which ended the war between Italy and the Allies in 1947, through the agreement between Switzerland and Poland of June 1949 regarding financial claims, to the arrangements that were concluded in the agreement between Canada and Bulgaria in January 1966 and even the mechanism for settling mutual claims in the peace agreement between Egypt and Israel. In addition, we had inputs and professional opinions regarding the issue of settling inhabitants of one party to the conflict in territory which would come under the control of the other party; conflict resolution mechanisms relating to the implementation of agreements between the sides; and securing the interests of Israel, both during the transition period between agreements, and in the long term, in relation to the nature of the future Palestinian state and its commitments to previous agreements signed by the Palestinian side. Our deadline was 11 p.m.

The entire day, July 17, 2000, was dedicated to working on Jerusalem. Madeline Albright met with Abu Mazen and asked him directly how he would react if a deep disagreement were to emerge between him and Arafat on Jerusalem. "I will not go against him," Abu Mazen responded. "I would quit. You should remember that any concession on Jerusalem constitutes a death sentence for Arafat."

After meeting with Arafat and telling him that "tonight will be the night of Jerusalem," the President began to engage in shuttle diplomacy, marked by a meeting every three hours. Following a discussion with Barak and Ben-Ami, Clinton sensed an emerging possibility for moving toward concluding an agreement, and he wanted to examine if this was indeed so. Ben-Ami with the help of Gidi Grinstein[19] hastily drafted a document that included suggested talking points for the leaders to refer to. The aim was to clarify whether there was Palestinian willingness to move forward toward a final push. The document was presented as a draft for comments to Reisner, Rubinstein,

Yatom, and finally to the Prime Minister. The final version, of course, looked nothing like the original draft. Concurrently, Ben-Ami and I were asked to move forward with the overall negotiations, on all issues, with Saeb Erekat and Mohammed Dahlan, continuing to collect, integrate, and polish the documents, in tandem with the discussions.

An anxious and tired Albright met with Abu Mazen, Abu Ala, and Yasser Abed Rabbo.[20] "The Israelis presented ideas, initiated solutions, while you settle for a statement that Eastern Jerusalem is yours. This is not a way to negotiate," she contended. "We will not accept a solution that does not include Palestinian sovereignty over East Jerusalem," they responded. "What do the Israelis think, that they will continue to rule us, and give us only municipal authorities?" Abu Ala asked. "The Israelis cannot go as far as you would like, no one can," Martin Indyk[21] added. "Ben-Gurion established the State of Israel without Jerusalem. We can have an agreement in our hands tomorrow." "I'll bet you 10-to-1 that there will not be an agreement," Abed Rabbo said. "We are at a dead end. If we leave Camp David without an agreement there will be violence," Albright replied.

Close to midnight, most of the members of the Israeli delegation were working in the Prime Minister's cabin. Suddenly, those in the living room of the cabin heard loud sounds from the Prime Minister's office. There was hard pounding, screaming "Ehud, Ehud" and sawing, siren-like human sounds. Barak was choking on a peanut that was lodged in his esophagus. Yatom and Ben-Ami were chasing after him, tapping on his back, which actually increased pressure on his esophagus. Barak became dizzy and unbalanced, his arms were dangling in the air, and his mouth was open, grappling for air, his eyes wide open. Those in the living room arrived within seconds. Then Gidi grabbed Barak around his diaphragm, lifted him up in the air and brought him down with great force—the Heimlich maneuver. Barak let out a rasping, sharp, strangled shout and reached over to the sink looking for water. By this time the security had arrived and an American doctor was called. Rubinstein wanted to offer a Hagomel prayer.[22] The irony of the foolish, if real, threat of a peanut versus the magnitude of the inhuman stress the Prime Minister was under was not lost on those present. Word of the incident spread like wildfire throughout Camp David. Yasser Abed Rabbo, upon hearing about this incident, was quoted as saying "he who contrives to feed us peanuts, will choke on them himself."

Barak was over half an hour late to his meeting with Clinton. The President was furious. His impression was that the positions that were now being presented to him did not match the positions the Israeli team presented to him the day before. The President, who was so familiar with the details, did not find it difficult to identify the areas in which positions had hardened. "I cannot go to the Palestinians with the document you have presented to me," Clinton said as he began his 3 a.m. meeting with Barak. "You have to agree to special arrangements in the holy places; otherwise, I will not be able to reach a compromise between the two sides."

"I cannot allow myself, morally or politically, to go beyond that which is indicated in the document we have presented, on all the issues. However, Mr. President, do try to assess what you sense will genuinely create a convergence that will result in an agreement. I ask of you, ensure that Arafat does not document the Israeli position," Barak answered, civilly but clearly.

This was the first time that Ben-Ami and I would witness a process that would repeat itself a few times during the summit. The fear of being leaked to the press or being documented led to positions that were circumscribed and fortified beyond recognition. The mere fact that, in addition to those forming part of the Israeli delegation to the summit, documents and position papers were being reviewed and scrutinized by seven or eight others, inevitably led to slightly more hardened positions being presented to the Americans.

Ben-Ami urged Barak to entrust himself to Clinton, so long as the President promised he would not divulge the positions being presented. "There are things that are beyond the mandate I received from the voters," Barak said. "Deviating from this mandate would undermine my moral and political authority to sign any emerging agreement."

Eight hundred times Jerusalem

Following the Palestinians' presentation of their positions on the issue of territory, the President decided against convening a joint meeting for both sides, opting to try to bridge the gaps in the proposal the Americans decided to put forward.

At a meeting with Barak on Jerusalem that afternoon, we were joined for a short consultation by Reuven Merhav, the former director general of the Ministry of Foreign Affairs. Merhav was adamant about the need to provide the Palestinians with sovereignty somewhere in Jerusalem, but took into consideration opposition in the Christian world to Palestinian sovereignty in areas with sites sacred to the Christian faith. In the past, no national/religious connection had been made between the Palestinians and Jerusalem. "If we provide Arafat with secular symbols—such as a flag or guest house—on the Temple Mount, it would turn him into a kind of king," he argued. He also noted that there were no flags on mosques in any other Muslim country, including Iran.

In the Bible, Jerusalem is mentioned over eight hundred times as "Jerusalem" or as "Zion." In the Koran, it is not even mentioned once. Over sixty years ago, at the end of the 1930s, Ben-Gurion was willing to give up Jerusalem, turning it into an international zone under joint Jewish–Arab control. Later on, he changed his mind, largely under the influence of other Zionist leaders, who viewed the compromise of dividing the city as the only way of maintaining Jewish sovereignty in its western half. In 1949, Moshe Dayan suggested dividing the city between Israel and Jordan and allowing international forces to supervise areas such as the Mount of Olives and the Jewish Quarter.

Moti Golani, a historian in the Lands of Israel Studies Department at Haifa University, studied the retroactive Zionist fervor for Jerusalem (Golani 1998). "Until 1937 there was no Zionist claim to Jerusalem," he argued. It was actually in the Revisionist[23] circles of Jerusalem, that the idea of dividing the city was originally raised. In 1932, the Revisionists wanted to grant autonomy to the Jewish neighborhoods in the city. Most of the Jewish neighborhoods, with the exception of Talpiot, the Jewish Quarter, and Mount Scopus, were in the western side of the city. In 1947, it appeared that the temporary agreement to concede Jerusalem to internationalization was a price Zionism was willing to pay for the creation of an independent State of Israel. Since being exiled from Jerusalem by the Romans two thousand years before, the Jewish presence in Jerusalem had dwindled, but the religious and emotional ties of the Jews in the Diaspora to the city remained throughout the centuries of exile.

In 2000, there were more than 600,000 inhabitants within the Jerusalem municipal boundaries, of which 240,000 were Palestinians. Of those, 30,000 resided in the Old City. According to Barak, in areas in which Israel must maintain control, the number of Palestinians would not exceed 12,000. Among the "internal" neighborhoods were Sheikh Jarrah, Wadi Joz, Salah A Din (or Bab Az-Zahra), Sultan Suleiman, Musrara, As-sawana, A-Tur, Ras Al Amud, Silwan, Abu Tor. Within the outer perimeter of Jerusalem we identified Israeli interests that included Atarot airfield, Atarot industrial zone, the IDF's Central Command headquarters, Ma'ale Adumim-Ramot intersection, Givat Hatachmoshet ("Ammunition Hill"), the police academy, the Shepherd Hotel, the Tomb of Simeon the Just, the Tomb of Maimonides in Sheikh Jarrah, the monument of the convoy to Mount Scopus, Rockefeller intersection, the museum, and the Hadassah center in As-swana.

In the evening, Clinton called Ben-Ami and Erekat to his cabin to discuss, and hopefully reach, some agreement on Jerusalem. Ben-Ami pointed out Barak's significant deviation from his campaign promises regarding Jerusalem, hoping to underline the kind of compromises that were both necessary and expected, so as not to miss this historical opportunity to resolve our tragic century-old conflict. Erekat acknowledged Ben-Ami's remarks, using uncommonly hard words to express deep frustration at Arafat's prevarication over reaching concrete decisions on the Palestinian position regarding Jerusalem. There were still no answers from the Palestinians except for their insistence on sovereignty over the entire Old City, barring the Jewish Quarter and the Western Wall.

The President proposed three alternatives: first, postponing conclusions on the entire or part of the issue of Jerusalem for a later date (perhaps in five years). Postponement could include the "Holy Basin," only the Old City, or all of Jerusalem. Second, Palestinian custodianship on the Temple Mount alongside residual Israeli sovereignty; a special regime in the Old City, and decreased Palestinian sovereignty in the "internal" neighborhoods. Or, third, functional Palestinian autonomy in the internal neighborhoods; full Palestinian sovereignty in the outer neighborhoods; the Old City divided; the Muslim and Christian Quarters for the Palestinians, the Jewish and Armenian Quarters for Israel.

Clinton asked that Arafat, through Erekat, convey a response to the proposed alternatives. Ben-Ami left the meeting with little hope.

In the evening there was a feeling of crisis. It appeared that we had exhausted all the possibilities. Shahak, Ben-Ami, and I recommended to Barak that he approach Arafat, in a final attempt to examine, informally, the positions that were close to our real "red lines," and concurrently, to work with Mubarak to convince Arafat. The Prime Minister listened attentively, but no action followed. At dinner, the American team was discouraged. They claimed that the President had used up all his credit and time. He could invest no more in this process. In conversations, accusations were made against the "Old Man," Arafat. He was difficult, he was stubborn, and he would not move.

Rob Malley said that the Americans were very disappointed by what the sides presented in the meetings on borders/territory and refugees. The positions were still provisional and no progress had been made. They expected more. As did we.

It is possible, however, that the Americans had only themselves to blame for this. The history of Israeli–Palestinian negotiations shows that when both sides wanted an agreement, it could be reached directly. This was the case with regard to the Oslo Declaration of Principles during 1993, and the Beilin–Abu Mazen Understandings.[24] When one of the sides did not want an agreement, however, American involvement was critical. But for the mediation to successfully move the parties toward closing such a dramatic "deal," the process must be clearly defined and extremely strict. A rigid, binding agenda from which the parties cannot be allowed to deviate is needed in order to ensure progress. Unfortunately, the businesslike, practical atmosphere that had marked the beginning of the Camp David Summit quickly dissipated and returned only sporadically. There was no follow-up on the "assignments" given to each of the sides after the initial presentation of their respective positions at the start of the summit. The process was mismanaged, unclear, and disorganized, leaving the delegations without a map, so to speak.

Still, the Americans knew where the gaps were and where the areas of agreement lay. I urged Rob Malley, and the rest of his team, to stay the course as mediators and force the sides to talk within the confines of the issues that were now clear. We raised the possibility that the President issue a one-to-two-page paper, with instructions for further activity.

We had come prepared, and hoping, for the possibility of a real breakthrough toward the much talked about final permanent status agreement. At the end this still remained a distant prospect, with each side blaming the other for failing to deliver on their promises, or failing to accept the possibility of genuine compromise through negotiation. It was vital at this stage that the Americans not allow the general mood of defeatism to undermine the little that had been achieved.

On Tuesday morning, July 25, 2000, the members of the Israeli delegation gathered in Barak's cabin. There was a feeling of an end, of goodbyes. We took pictures to remember the moment. "I bear the full responsibility for the delegation and the results of the summit," Barak opened. "We engaged in a serious effort to make peace with the Palestinians—but not at any price—not by compromising Israel's vital interests. The developments of the past twenty-four to forty-eight hours thoroughly clarify that we do not have a partner. The process stopped with the other side's demand to transfer sovereignty over the Temple Mount. Even Clinton's proposal, in which we would have inconspicuous sovereignty on the Temple Mount and the Palestinians control over the mosques and on the ground, was rejected by Arafat." Amnon Shahak agreed. "The State of Israel did everything to reach a positive result. We have not been successful because of Arafat's position." "We touched our—and their—most sensitive nerves over the past two very special weeks," Ben-Ami said. "Although everything is null and void, we received a conditional agreement to annexing Arab land with 80 percent of the settlers. It's a historic break through deep-rooted Arab positions. Our negotiating partner had to make a historic decision—it turned out that he was unable to." "Our main problem now is how to avoid a violent confrontation and keep the dialogue alive," said Shahak. "I suggest you meet with Arafat," he turned to Barak. Israel Hasson agreed: "We have to create a situation of co-existence, knowing that we are divided on the principal issues."

Barak was agreeable to the idea of a possible meeting with Arafat but the meeting never took place. I was entrusted with preparing the main public messages. For the Israeli public we would have "full disclosure" of what we did at Camp David. In the United States we tried to convey Israel's commitment to Jerusalem and to its holy sites. In our message to the Arabs, we would focus on Israel's willingness to end the conflict even at a painful price, and on our commitment to acknowledge the Palestinian national aspirations, address their needs regarding Jerusalem, and find satisfactory resolutions to the plight of the refugees.[25]

Clinton, Barak, and Arafat parted formally from each other, with a warning. "We must do everything to prevent the region from deteriorating into a disaster," Clinton said. The two others nodded. The disappointment and fatigue were evident on all three.

In hindsight, and with Camp David now forming yet another milestone in the complex, turbulent history of the Arab–Israeli conflict, I have no doubt that Arafat—as a national leader—acted wholly irresponsibly. After decades of leading the Palestinians toward such a deciding moment, he failed once again to lead them to peace. He missed seizing the point after which the Palestinians could start living their lives as a people in their own sovereign state. Arafat simply damaged the long-term cause of the Palestinian people, thus determining the short-term fate of the people of Israel.

One factor in the ultimate failure of the Palestinians to move forward at Camp David was the lack of homogeneity in the Palestinian leadership present at the talks. More than could be said with regard to either of the other delegations at Camp David—the Israeli and American—the Palestinian delegation was characterized by two distinct groups, each pulling in different directions. There was the "young group" which consisted of second-generation Palestinian leaders, including Mohammad Rashid, Mohammad Dahlan, Hassan Asfour, and to a somewhat lesser extent, Saeb Erekat. Each was trying to push forward the gospel of compromise through treacherous waters, with the understanding that insisting on "all or nothing" would leave the Palestinian people stuck—with nowhere to go for a long time to come. But they were confronted with Abu Mazen, Abu Ala, and Akram Haniya, who encouraged Arafat to adopt uncompromising positions that ultimately proved unrealistic.

In the end it was these uncompromising positions that prevailed, and, as a result, almost inevitably, violence ensued. The beginning of the violence and hostilities in September 2000—the madness that accompanied the religious fanaticism behind such violence, the cynical Palestinian incitement, and the total collapse of trust—have all reduced the chances that those within the Palestinian leadership who supported a compromise might continue to push for an agreement.

With the close of the summit, the delegations packed up ready to leave, and our hosts removed all trace of the summit set-up. The speed with which the Americans did this was yet another example of the same American organizational efficiency that had marked the summit's beginning, and stood in sharp contrast to the summit's substantive management inefficiency. In less than an hour, the base was emptied, with no remnants of the American teams or the logistical set-up.

The President went off to a concluding press conference. Barak, too, prepared for a press conference immediately after, in which he stated: "The Government of Israel, and I as Prime Minister, acted in the course of the Camp David summit out of moral and personal commitment, and supreme national obligation to do everything possible to bring about an end to the conflict. . . .

"Israel," he continued, "was prepared to pay a painful price to bring about an end to the conflict, but not any price. We sought a stable balance, and peace for generations to come, not headlines in tomorrow's paper. Arafat was afraid to make the historic decisions necessary at this time in order to bring about an end to the conflict.

"Arafat's positions on Jerusalem," Barak stated, "are what prevented the achievement of the agreement. I, as Prime Minister, bear overall responsibility for the Israeli positions presented in the course of the summit; I stand behind them still, just as I would have stood behind any overall agreement, difficult as it may have been, had it been achieved."

"Mr. Prime Minister," came a question from one of the correspondents present, "you have failed in the Syrian track[26] and now in the Palestinian track—is Ehud Barak a disappointed man today?"

"Of course," Barak replied, "... but the primary responsibility of the Israeli government is to turn over every stone to ensure a way may be found to reach an agreement with our neighbors which would strengthen the security of Israel, and also to reach such an agreement, if possible. But two are needed to tango ... there is no way of forcing it on the other side."

Some members of our delegation remained in Camp David to document conclusions and prepare for departure. The Palestinians seemed to have vanished. In the afternoon, we left Camp David in the President's helicopter. Half a dozen American officers conducted a short and emotional military review for Barak, and saluted farewell.

Notes

1 Much of the account is based on excerpts from my book *Within Reach—The Israeli–Palestinian Peace Negotiations, 1999–2001* (Routledge 2006).

2 This refers to the back-track negotiation meetings held in Harpsund, Sweden, at the countryside residence of the Prime Minister of Sweden, in May and June of 2000, in preparation for the Camp David Summit. The participants included Abu Ala, Hassan Asfour, Shlomo Ben-Ami, and Gilead Sher.

3 Amnon Lipkin-Shahak is the former Chief of Staff of the Israeli Defense Forces and was later Israeli Minister of Tourism and Transport; Professor Shlomo Ben-Ami was at the time Israel's acting Foreign Minister and Minister of Public Security; Gilead Sher was Israel's Prime Minister's Chief of Staff and Policy Coordinator and co-chief negotiator with the Palestinians namely at the Camp David Summit.

4 Mohammed Dahlan was a member of Fatah-Revolutionary Council and leading Palestinian peace negotiator with Israel. He is also the former head of the Palestinian Authority's Preventive Security Service in the Gaza Strip. Erekat is Sa'ib Muhammad Salih 'Urayqat, who was the chief of the PLO Steering and Monitoring Committee.

5 Israel Hasson was the former Deputy Director of the Shin Bet (Israel's Security Service), and was closely involved in the negotiations leading to the Wye River, Taba, and Hebron memoranda.

6 Yossi Ginossar was a former senior official with the Israeli Shin Bet and key envoy of three prime ministers to the Palestinian Authority.

7 Danny Yatom was the PM chief of Policy and Security Staff and formerly the Director of the Mossad from 1996 to 1998.

8 Moshe Dayan was the spiritual father of this term, following the 1967 war. It meant that Palestinians would have daily control of their lives under Israeli sovereignty.

9 The Waqf is a religious endowment, a property giving revenues, conceptually similar to the common law trust, as regulated by Islamic law. The revenues from the Waqf finance mosques and other religious institutions.

10 The Holy Basin is the term used to denote the area encompassing most of the holy sites sacred to Islam, Judaism, and Christianity. It includes those sites in the Old City of Jerusalem as well as the area of Gethsemane, the site of the tombs of the Kings, the Jewish cemetery on the Mount of Olives, the area known as the City of David to the south of the Old City walls, and the Kidron Valley.

11 Dan Meridor served as Justice Minister, Finance Minister, and chair of the Knesset Foreign Affairs and Defense Committee.

12 The consensus in the Israeli political discourse over the previous three decades had been to regard the recently "liberated" East Jerusalem, including the Old

City, as an indivisible and inviolable part of the capital of the Jewish State. This principle was rarely challenged. The mantra of successive prime ministers after 1967 was to affirm the principle that Jerusalem, undivided, would always remain the capital of the State of Israel.

13 This is a major political notion in the negotiations. It refers to the Permanent Status Agreement which would mark in an official and binding way the end of conflict between the parties in addition to the finality of their respective claims.

14 Elyakim Rubinstein, a lifelong Israeli civil servant, took part in the negotiations at the Madrid Peace Conference in 1991, and subsequently headed the peace negotiations with Jordan. He was Israel's Attorney General from 1997 to 2004 and was then appointed to the Supreme Court.

15 Colonel Daniel Reisner was head of the International Law Branch of the IDF Legal Division.

16 Shlomo Yanai was the IDF Head of Southern Command and Head of the Planning Division.

17 This referred to the undertaking by Israel under the Oslo Accords to relate to the Gaza Strip and the West Bank as a "single territorial unit."

18 An internal memo prepared at the time for the negotiating team by the Ministry of Foreign Affairs and the IDF Attorney's office.

19 Gidi Grinstein served as Secretary to the Negotiating Team at Camp David on behalf of the Prime Minister's Office.

20 Abu Mazen was then the most senior member of the Palestinian delegation and later became the Prime Minister and subsequently the President of the Palestinian Authority. Abu Ala was the Speaker of the Palestinian Parliament and later became the Prime Minister. Abed Rabbo was Minister of Information and later became Minister for Cabinet Affairs.

21 Martin Indyk was U.S. Ambassador to Israel and formerly special assistant to President Clinton and senior director of Near East and South East Asia affairs at the National Security Council.

22 The Hagomel is the prayer normally said after someone has survived a potentially life-threatening ordeal.

23 Revisionist Zionism is a nationalist right-wing tendency within the Zionist movement. The ideology was developed by Ze'ev Jabotinsky who advocated a "revision" of the "practical Zionism" of David Ben-Gurion and Chaim Weizmann, which was focused on independent settlement of Eretz Yisrael. Revisionist Zionism was instead centered on a vision of "political Zionism," which Jabotinsky regarded as following the legacy of Theodore Herzl, the founder of modern political Zionism.

24 The Beilin–Abu Mazen Document—a framework for the conclusion of a final status agreement between Israel and the Palestine Liberation Organization (October 31, 1995).

25 The need for separate messages arose from the difference in tone needed when addressing such different audiences, although, of course, the public would be likely to have access to all three, particularly in a country with a free press such as Israel.

26 The reference here was to the attempt by Barak to restart the stalled talks with Syria over a political settlement.

Index

Page numbers in italics refer to illustrations

Abbas [Abu Mazen], Mahmoud 203, 290, 291, 293, 312, 313, 320n20
'Abd al-Malik (caliph) 86, 94–95, 97–98
'Abd al-Wahhab, Muhammad 158, 166n8
'Abdin, Shaykh 'Abd al-Qadir 274–75
Abdullah I, King of Jordan 10, 245–53, 255, 267
Abi Samra, Muhammad 162
Abraham and Isaac story 2, 3, 50, 95, 98
Abraham 2, 18–19, 27–28, 29
Abu al-Huda, Tawfiq 250
Abu al-Ma'ali al-Musharraf b. al-Murajja al-Maqdisi 88–89, 98
Abu Maizer, 'Abd al-Muhsin 272
Abu Sharakh, Faysal 277
Abu Zuluf, Mahmud 271
Acts of the Apostles 75–76
Abed Rabbo, Yasser 312, 320n20
Adrichom, Christian van 126–27, *127, 128, 135*
agricultural collectives 226
al-'Alami, Sa'd al-Din 271
Albright, Madeline 305, 312, 313
Alexander 70
Alexander Jannaeus (Hasmonean ruler) 33–34
Alexandria 72
alienation (*ghurba*) 162–63
All-Palestine Government 199
'*Amidah* (*Shemoneh Esrei*) 40
Amman, Jordan 10, 247, 254–55, 260
'Amru, Yasir 277
Anastasis *see* Church of the Holy Sepulchre

Anglo-Palestine Company 226
Antioch 72
Antiochus Strategos 67–68, 73, 81–82nn2–3
Antipater (father of Herod) 34
Antonia fortress 35, 37, 57
'Aql, Sa'id 160, 166n10
Aqsa *Intifada* 11, 12, 292–97
Aqsa mosque: and Abdullah I of Jordan 246, 261, 267; arson at 113; architectural style of 87; building of 86; and Camp David Summit 311; Christian traditions regarding 133; as holy site 86; and al-Khumsi 90; location of 21–22; on maps 129, 132–33; Muslim traditions regarding 91–93, 96, 133; in photographs *148, 149*; pilgrimage to 255; Qur'anic references 87, 96; and al-Wasiti 88
Arab League 246
Arab Revolt 228
Arab Studies Institute 276
Arafat, Dr. Fathi 277
Arafat, Yassir 12, 200–201, 270, 274, 278, 293; and Camp David Summit 304–18
Archelaus (Herod Archelaus; son of Herod) 36
archeology 7, 23–24, 35, 58
Area of Jurisdiction and Powers Ordinance 285
al-'Aref, 'Aref 271–72
Aristobulus (Hasmonean ruler) 33
Ark of the Covenant 28–29, 48, 63
Arlosoroff, Chaim 227–28
Asfour, Hassan 318
'Ashura ceremonies 175–76
Ateret Cohanimt 284–85, 298n3
Avi-Yonah, Michael 68

'*Avodah* 41
al-'Aysa, Sulayman 158

Babylonian exile 30–31, 48
Bakr, Ibrahim 272
Barak, Ehud 12, 200, 278, 291, 292, 305–19
Bar-El, Yair 115–16
al-Barghouthi, Salih 210
Basic Law: Jerusalem the Capital 237, 239, 283, 291, 292, 295
Beersheva 28
Begin, Menachem 234, 237, 239, 289, 311
Beilin, Yossi 290
Ben-Ami, Shlomo 306–7, 313–17
Ben-Aryeh, Yehoshua 208
Ben-Gurion, David 225, 226, 228–31, 233, 235
Berger, Sandy 305
Bezalel Art School 226
Bialik, H.N. 225
Blanquart-Evrard, Louis Désiré 144
Blenkinsopp, Joseph 31
Bnei Hezir (tomb) 34
Borculus, Hermanus von 132
Braun, Georg see *Civitates*
Breakdown and Bereavement (Brenner) 114, 116
Brenner, Joseph 114, 116
Breydenbach, Bernhard von 123, 132, 136, 140, *142*
British Mandate period 8, 9, 15, 226; and administration of holy places 257; effects of 226–27; and establshment of postal service 216; Jerusalem as capital during 229–30, 267; and Jewish Agency 242n11; memoirs of 210; political divisions during 267, 279n1, 280n9; and Supreme Muslim Council 271
British Ordnance Survey maps 123
Bush, George W. 294–95

Caesarea 72
Cairo meeting of Palestinian factions (2005) 201
Camp David Agreement (1978) 270
Camp David summit 10, 12, 200–201, 291, 303–19; aims of 303–4; and Aqsa mosque 311; and Church of the Holy Sepulchre 303; and East Jerusalem 303; and Holy Basin 294, 303, 308–9, 319n10; and Mount of

Olives 303, 309; and Old City 303, 309–10; proposals made at 306–8, 313–16; and Silwan 303; and Temple Mount 294, 303, 305–11, 314, 317; and Western Wall 303
Capture of Jerusalem by the Persians, The (Antiochus Strategos) 67–68, 73, 81–82nn2–3
Castle of the Pisans (*Pisanorum Castrum*) see Citadel
Central Military Cemetery 236
Chamber of Hewn Stone 37
Chamoum, Zulfa 157
Christian eschatology 97
Christian tradition, Jerusalem in 4–5, 15–16, 18–19, 20–21, 81
Church of the Holy Sepulchre (Anastasis) 82n5, 212; building of 69, 73; and cosmic stone 63; on maps 68, 132, 133, 134–35; as model for Dome of the Rock 176; in photography 149; sectarian claims to 23, 306; symbolism of 3; in travel accounts 71–72
Church at Siloam 68
Church of the Flagellation 213
Church of the Messiah 213
Church of the Nativity (Bethlehem) 108
Church of the Redeemer 213
Church of the Theotokos see Nea
Citadel (David's Tower) 58, 127
City of David 303
Civitates (Braun and Hogenberg) 135–36
Clinton, Bill 12, 294, 305–7, 312, 313–17
Cohen, Erik 115
coinage 33–34
collective memory 206
Constantine (Roman emperor) 21, 68–70, 80
Constantinople 22–23, 72
Construction Jihad (*Jihad-i Sazandegi*) 173
Council of Chalcedon (451) 72
Council of Nicea (325) 69, 72
Crusades period 5, 16, 22, 98–99
Cumanus (procurator of Judea) 37
Cyrus (Persian king) 30–31

Dahlan, Mohammad 305–7, 313, 318, 319n4
Dajani, Kamal 269, 271, 273
Damascus Gate 68, 149–50, *151*

Darwish, Mahmud 156, 158
David 2, 19–20, 28–29, 48–50, 91–93
Dayan, Moshe 314, 319n8
de Angelis, Antonio 130, 132–33
de Certeau, Michel 207
de Pierre map *130*, 131, 132
de Saulcy, Louis-Félicien Caignart 145, 149
al-Dhahabi, Shams al-Din 88–89
Diaspora and Diaspora Jews 28, 37, 40–44, 224–25
Diya' al-Din al-Maqdisi 98
Diyab, 'Amr 158
Dome of the Ascension 97
Dome of the Rock (*Qibbat al-Sakhra*): and Abraham and Isaac story 95; and the Aqsa mosque 21–22; architectural style of 86–87; building of 86, 94–95, 97–98; Church of the Holy Sepulchre as model for 176; and Iran–Iraq War 171, 175; in Islamic art 168–69; maquettes of 169–70, 175, 176–81; on maps 129, 132–33; and Muhammad 3, 21–22; and Muhammad's Night Journey 22; and Muslim sectarian conflict 7; name of 21; and pilgrimage 98; in photography 146, 148; and Shi'i grievances 175; as visual symbol 169–70, 171, 178
du Camp, Maxime 144, 153n3
Dusturiyeh (Constitutional) School 218–19

early Muslim tradition 63
East Jerusalem: and Camp David Summit 303; economic conditions 269; and Intifada 270, 294; under Jordanian rule 266–67; and Palestinian Authority 266, 274–78; Palestinian leadership in 266–79; and PLO, 270–71, 273–79; and Palestinian ownership of property 277; and Palestinian security services 277–78
Eastern Gate 37
Eder, Joseph *131*
Education Hill 236
Efrat, Elisha 291
Egeria 71
Egypte et Nubie (Teynard) 144
Egypte, Nubie, Palestine et Syrie (du Camp) 144
East Jerusalem 9–11, 266–79; conditions in 198, 201; control of

227, 228, 231, 237, 239, 242n15; Jewish population in 202–3
Eleh Ezkarah 41
Eliade, Mircea 1–2, 3
Eran, Oded 309
Erekat, Kamil 254, 259
Erekat, Saeb (Sa'ib Muhammad Salih Urayqat) 200, 275, 305–7, 313, 318, 319n4
Eretz Israel 19, 286–88
eschatology 103, 106–7, 113–14
Eudokia (wife of Theodosius II) 68–69
Eusebius 74, 80
Eustochium 72
Excursions Daguerriennes (Lerebours) 145

Fada'il (Religious Merits) genre 87–88, 90, 96
Fada'il (Diya' al-Din al-Maqdisi) 98
Fada'il Bayt al-Maqdis (The Merits of the Holy House) (al-Walid b. Hammad al-Ramli) 5, 88–98; date of 90; informants 89–90; and religious symbolism of Jerusalem 91–98; title of 100n8; transmission lines of 89, 90
Fada'il Bayt al-Maqdis wa-l-Khalil wa-fada'il al-Sham (The Merits of Jerusalem and Hebron, and the Merits of Syria) (Abu al-Ma'ali al-Musharraf b. al-Murajja al-Maqdisi) 88–89, 98
Fada'il al-Bayt al-Muqaddas (The Merits of Jerusalem) (Abu Bakr Muhammad b. Ahmad al-Wasiti) 88–89, 96, 98
al-Faryabi, Ibrahim b. Muhammad b. Yusuf 89
Fayruz 7, 155–65; albums of 158, 159, 161–62; and alienation (*ghurba*) 162–63; concerts of 164; documentary about 155–56; early career 156; films of 158, 165n3; "The Flower of the Cities" 155–60, 162, 165; and idea of return 163–64; and Lebanese Christian nationalism 156–57, 164–65; lyrics, language of 160, 161; musical characteristics 159; musical theatrical works 156–57, 161, 161, 165n1; and nostalgia (*hanin*) 155, 156, 162–63, 165; "Old Jerusalem" 156, 160–62; and Palestinian concerns 155–56; popularity in Syria 165n6; recipient of Jerusalem Award

156; and religion 157; and sense of
place 162; themes of 155; visit to
Jerusalem 161; "We Are Returning"
162–63; "We Shall Return One Day"
164–65
Festinger, Leon 117
figural art 33, 45n5
First Temple period 48–51
First Temple 19–20; destruction of 2–3,
97; in Islamic tradition 91–92, 99;
relationship to Temple Mount 92;
and *Shekhina* (presence) of God 2
Foucault, Michel 118–19
Foundation of the Oppressed and
Disabled People (*Bunyad-i Mostaza'fan
va Janbazan*) (Iraq) 189–90
Franciscans 22, 23
Frith, Francis 143–44, *143*, 149

Gabinius 34
Garabadian, Yessai 210
Gaza 202, 237, 266, 269–72, 274, 279
Gazit, Shlomo 291
German Colony 214
Ginossar, Yossi 305, 309, 319n6
Golani, Moti 315
Golden Gate 68
Government Hill 236
Grabar, Oleg 68
Greek Orthodox Church 22
Gregory of Nyssa 73
Grinstein, Gidi 312, 320n19

Hadassah Hospital 234, 236
Hadith collections 87–88
Hadrian (Roman emperor) 58
Hafiz, 'Abd al-Halim 158
hajj (pilgrimage) 24
Ha-Levi, Judah 44
Hamas 12, 173, 183, 201, 203
Ha-Mizrachi 225, 233
Hammer, Juliane 158
Haniya, Akram 318
Hanna, Yusuf 258
Haram al-Sharif see Temple Mount
Hasson, Israel 305–6, 308–9, 317,
319n5
Hebrew University (Jerusalem) 10, 227,
234, 236
Helena (mother of Constantine) 4, 68–69
Hellenistic culture 33–34
Heraclius (Byzantine emperor) 67, 81
Hermann, Haim 114, 116
Herod (king of Judea) 34–36, 57–58, 64

Herod Archelaus *see* Archelaus
Herodium 35
Herzl, Theodor 236, 320n23
Heschel, A.J. 44
Higher Committee for National
Guidance (*al-Lajna al-Ulya lil-Tawjih
al-Watani*) 268
al-Hindi, Amin 277
historical narratives 206–7
history and historiography 205–10
Hizbollah 173, 182–83
Hogenberg, Franz see *Civitates*
Hollerich, Michael 80
Holocaust museum (*Yad Vashem*) 105,
236
Holy Anastasis (monastery) 68, 70
Holy Basin 294, 303, 308–9, 319n10
holy cities 17–18
Holy Golgotha (church) 68
holy wars 18
Holy Zion (church) 68
Honi the circle-drawer 61
House of Prayer (religious community)
108–10, 111, 112–13
Hudson, Michael 226
Hussein I, King of Jordan 11, 245,
255–56, 261, 270
Hussein, Saddam 169, 171, 175
al-Husseini, Dr. Dawud 269, 272, 273
al-Husseini, Faysal 275–78
al-Husseini, Musa Kazim 252
al-Husseini, Sa'id 213

Iberian monastery 70
Ibn 'Abbas 92
Ibn al-Nahhas al-Ramli, Abu 'Umayr
'Isa b. Muhammad 90
Ibn Taymiyya 93, 99
Indyk, Martin 313, 320n21
intifadas 11, 12, 251, 270, 278–79, 292–97
Iran 7–8; and culture of martyrdom
170, 175, 181–87, 191–92; and
Islamic activism 169; and Palestinian
liberation 170; *see also* Iranian public
art
Iran–Iraq War 169; and Dome of the
Rock 171, 175; and Kermanshah
177; and martyrdom 175; and Shi'i
holy sites 169–70, 171; staging of
military operations 173–74
Iranian public art 168–93, *172, 174,
176–7, 179–80, 182–6, 188–90, 192*;
audience of 170; images of Dome of
the Rock 168–70, 171, 173–82, 185–93;

images of Khamenei 178, 187, 191;
images of Khomeini 174, 178, 187–
88, 190–91; in Kermanshah 176–78;
in Khuzistan and Ilam provinces 171;
in Mashhad 178–80; in Mehran 171–
73; and pilgrimage rituals 176; in
Tehran 170, 180–92
Iranian Revolutionary Guard Corps
(*Pasdaran-i Inqilab-i Islami*) 172–73
Irenaeus 74, 80
Iskandari, Iraj 191
Islam: *Fada'il* (Religious Merits) genre
87–88; Hadith collections 87–88; and
hajj 24, 91, 92–93; and Jerusalem as
first *qibla* (direction of prayer) 87;
Jerusalem as holy city of 96–99; and
Old Testament sources 91–92, 93–94,
95, 98; and Qur'an 15; Shi'as 7; *Sira*
(Life and Career of the Prophet
Muhammad) genre 87; Sunnis 7
Islamic architecture 86–87
Islamic eschatology 98–99
Islamic Jihad 173, 183
Islamic solidarity 7–8
Islamic tradition, Jerusalem in 3, 5, 7,
15–16, 18–19, 20–21, 86–99; Temple
Mount in 21–22
Israel: and Assyrian conquest 29;
Coalition Government 236; and
Eretz Yisrael 286–88; establishment
of 9; Khomeini's views on 169; Law
for the Protection of Holy Places
(1969) 23; Likud party 203; plans for
East Jerusalem 202–3; plans for Gaza
202; plans for West Bank 202–3;
political parties 225, 237; Settlers'
Movement 10; U.N. membership 233–
34; expansion into West Bank 283–86
Israel Museum 10, 236
Itinerarium Burdigalense (Pilgrim of
Bordeaux) 70–71

al-Jabali, Ahmad b. 'Abd al-Wahhab al-
Hawti 90
al-Ja'bari, Shaykh Muhammad 'Ali
268, 273, 274
Jabotinsky, Eri 235–36
Jabotinsky, Ze'ev 320n23
Jacob 28
James (brother of Jesus) 4, 58–59, 75
Jawhariyeh, Wasif 210, 214–15, 217–19
al-Jaza'iriyya, Warda 158
Jensen, Robin Margaret 81
Jericho palace complex 33–34

Jerome 71–72, 73
Jerusalem: and Abraham 27–28, 29;
and agency of native population 205–
6, 210, 221; as apostolic city 72; and
Aqsa *Intifada* 11, 12, 292–97; and
Arab population 11–12, 225–26,
241n6, 285–89, 294, 298–99n8; and
archeology 7, 23–24, 35, 205, 272; at
end of Crusades period 99; and
Babylonian exile 30–31; and Ben-
Gurion 225, 226, 228–31, 233, 235;
and biblical land of Moriah 19; and
biblical Salem 19; bishop of 72;
bouleterion 35–36; British
investments in 227; in Byzantine
period 67–70; and Caesarea 72; and
Camp David Summit 303–19; as
capital during Mandate period 229–
30, 267; and Cappadocia 73; in
Christian allegory 76–77; Christian
proselytzing in 109; in Christian
tradition 4–5, 15–16, 18–19, 73–81;
in Church Fathers 74, 78–81;
churches in 69–70, 213; City of
David 28–29, 42, 52; and Council of
Chalcedon (451) 72; and Council of
Nicea (325) 72; destruction of (70 CE)
39–40; during Crusades period 5, 98–
99; during Diaspora 40–44;
Europeanization of 226; expansion
into West Bank 283–86; and fall of
Constantinople 22–23; as first *qibla*
(direction of prayer) 87, 168, 174;
First Temple period 27–30;
formation of postal service 216;
Franciscan order in 133;
geographical setting 225; German
Colony 214; and Gospels 74–76;
Hebrew University 10; and
Hellenistic culture 33–34; Herodian
building projects 35–37; Herodium
35; historical discourse on 205;
historical narratives of 206–7; and
historiographical method 207–8; and
history 14–15; as holy city 2, 4, 17–
18, 20, 24; as holy city of Islam 96–
99; as idea 20; and ideology 15; as
imaginary city 6; industry in 213;
introduction of automobiles 215;
introduction of electricity 214–15; in
Iranian public art 168–93; and
Iranian rule 7–8; in Islamic
eschatology 98–99; and Islamic
pilgrimage 91, 92–93; and Islamic

solidarity 7–8; in Islamic tradition 3, 5, 7, 15–16, 8–19, 20–22, 86–99, 168; and Israeli law 11, 237, 239, 242n17, 283, 285–87, 291–92, 295–96, 298n5; and James, brother of Jesus 75, 77; and Jesus 74–76; in Jewish funeral services 43–44; in Jewish liturgy 224; in Jewish prayer 40–41; in Jewish tradition 3–4, 15–16, 18–20, 27–44, 47–58, 59–64; in Jewish wedding ceremony 42–43; and Jordanian policy 245–61, 267; in late Ottoman period 211–21; and limitations of traditional historiography 205–10; literature about 205; in Mandate period (1917–48) 8, 9, 16, 226–33, 246; in maps 123–36, *124, 127–31, 134–5, 141–2*, 298n1; in memoirs 9, 210; and memory 14, 40–44; in messianic movements 44; in modern Palestinian poetry 158–59; modernization of 9; monasteries in 68, 70; in mosaic in Sta. Pudenziana (Rome) 80–81; mosques in 133; and Mount Moriah 2; and Mu'awiya (caliph) 86; and Muhammad 3, 87; and Muhammad's Night Journey 87, 95–97, 99; Muslim conquest of 21; in Muslim tradition 3, 5, 7, 15–16, 18–19, 20–21, 86–99; names of 1, 29, 100n8; and national identity 199–200; in New Testament 28, 73–79; as official capital of Israel 230, 234–37, 240; in Old Testament 2, 27–30; as *omphalos* 68; and Oslo Accords 11; and Ottoman sources 208; Palestinian leadership 9–10, 11; and Palestinians 7–8; partition plans 226–33; period of Hasmonean rule 30, 31–34; period of Herodian rule 30, 34–39; period of Ottoman sovereignty 9, 22–23; period of Persian rule 30–31, 67; and Persian policies 31; and personal experience 198–99; and personal identity 8; photographic schools and firms in 210–11; in photography 6, 140–52, 210–11; and pilgrimage 28, 69, 70–72, 73, 80; in *piyyut* (religious poetry) 41–42; in poetry and song 155, 158, 224; political activism in 217; political and religious dimensions 29–30; prospect of a united city 203–4; and purity concerns 92; al-Quds

and Yerushalayim 11, 283–97; in responsa litertature 44; and return of Palestinian refugees 200–202; and Roman Catholic Church 24n4; schools in 218–19; Second Temple period 30–39; size and population 9, 31, 211–14, 229–30, 242–43n18, 304; St. Paul's relationship to 76–77; *status quo* decree (1852) 23, 252; and supercessionist argument 15; surrender to British 219–20, *220*; as symbol of loss 155; topography of 52–54, 57; in Torah readings 41; and tourism 213; and travelers' accounts 9; unification of 12; in visual arts 140–44; Yerushalayim 11–12; and Zionism 1, 8, 9–10, 19, 224–40, 296, 311, 314–15; and Zionist immigration 9, 225, 226; *see also* individual sites and institutions

Jerusalem, maps of 6, 68, 123–36, *124, 127–31, 134–5, 141–2*; audience of 125, 130, 136; by British Ordnance Survey 123; and Christian ideology 125–26, 130, 136; Church of the Holy Sepulchre on 132, 133, 134–35; concept of time in 126–28; Dome of the Rock on 129, 132–33; and imaginary elements 124–26, 136; and "mythic time" 129; and Orientalism 126, 135–36; and pilgrimage 123–25, 128–30, 135–36; and religious polemics 126, 132, 133–35; as representations of sacred space 130–33; Second Temple on 133–34; Temple Mount on 129, 132; *see also* individual mapmakers

Jerusalem Chamber of Commerce 235
Jerusalem Covenant 284, 289
Jerusalem Declaration 287
Jerusalem Economic Forum 235
Jerusalem (*al-Quds*) Force 173, 194n13
Jerusalem Institute for Israel Studies 293
Jerusalem Reclamation Project 284
Jerusalem Solidarity Encounter 284–85
Jerusalem Syndrome 5–6, 103–19; and anti-Christian sentiment 109, 112; and anti-Semitism 105, 107, 113; case studies 104–10; and cognitive dissonance 16–17, 120n14; and *communitas* 113; correlation with psychiatric hospitalization 117–18; early views of 114–15; and end times

106–7, 108–9, 111–12; as eschatological subculture 103, 113–14, 117–19; and "existential tourism" 115; and failed expectations 116–17; and healing powers 107–8; incidence and prevalence 104, 114, 115–17; and Israeli security concerns 112; and Jerusalem as holy city 103, 105, 107, 108, 109, 115, 117; and messianism 104–6, 110, 111; origin and definition of term 114, 119n2; and prophetic powers 107–8, 111; and racial purity concerns 106–7; and "rebuilding" of Second Temple 107; and religious denomination of subjects 103–4, 111, 115–17, 120n13; and social stigma 112; and tourist status 104, 114, 115–18, 119n1, 120n15; and visions 104, 106, 108, 110–11; and Zionist psychiatry 114, 116
Jerusalem Year 289
Jewish Agency 229, 231, 252
Jewish liturgy 53, 63
Jewish prayer 40–41
Jewish tradition 3–4, 15–16, 18–20, 27–44, 47–58, 59–64; and figural art 33, 45n5; Temple Mount in 23
jihads 16
Jiyerji, Zvar 211–12
John Hyrcanus (Hasmonean ruler) 33
John of Würzburg 133
John, Gospel of 75–76
Jordan 9, 10–11, 245–61; and access to holy sites in Jerusalem 11, 245–47; Amman 10, 247, 254–55, 260; annexation of West Bank 267; appointment of Custodian of the Holy Places and Protector of the *Haram al-Sharif* 247–53, 255; and other Arab states 258–60; efforts to incorporate Jerusalem into Jordanian kingdom 246–47, 266–67; and tax on Jerusalem's consular corps 253–54; and position of *muhafiz mumtaz* 256–58; view of Jerusalem as capital city 247, 254–61
Josephus 35–36, 39, 51, 55–58, 124
Judah Maccabee 33
Judas the Essene 37
Judeo-Christian eschatology 74, 76, 78–79, 82n20
Justin Martyr 74, 80
Justinian 68–70

Ka'b al-Ahbar 97–98
Kalian, Moshe 115–16, 118
Karbala (Iraq) 169, 171, 175, 176
al-Katib, Hasan 256–57
Kermanshah (Bakhtaran) 171, 174, 176–78
ketubah (marriage document) 34
Kfar Shaul (psychiatric hospital) 115
al-Khalidi, Dr. Hussein Fakhri 252
al-Khalidi, Yusuf Diya' 213
Khalife, Marcel 158
Khamenei, Ayatollah 169, 170, 178, 182, 187, 191
al-Khatib, Anwar 269, 271
al-Khatib, Ruhi 260, 268, 269, 272–73
Khomeini, Ayatollah: and 'Ashura ceremonies 175; and Construction Jihad 173; death of 170; image of, in Iranian public art 174, 178, 187–88, 190–91; and Iran–Iraq War 171; and Iranian Revolutionary Guard Corps 173; and Martyrs' Organization 183; views on Israel 169
Khorramshahr 171
al-Khumsi, Abu al-Qasim 'Abd al-Rahman b. Muhammad b. Mansur b. Thabit b. Istanibiyadh al-Farisi 90
Khuri, Ilyas 160–61
King David's Tower 283
King Hezekiah 29, 71, 149
King Josiah 30
Kitab al-Fitan (Book of Human Disasters) (Nu'aym b. Hammad) 98
Knesset 23, 202, 234–39, 270, 286–87, 291–92, 295–96
Kolek, Teddy 238
Krikorian, Grabed and Johannes 210
Kulthum, Umm 158

Labor Party 225, 237, 238, 239, 240, 242n13, 288, 289, 292
Labor Zionism 225, 226, 229, 237, 239
Law and Administration Ordinance 286
Law of Jerusalem's Unity 237
Le Secq, Henri 147
Lebanon and Lebanese nationalism 156–57, 164–65
Lekha Dodi 41
Letters of Paul 76–77
Liber Chronicarum (Schedel) 133–34
Likud Party 203, 225, 233, 237, 239, 291
Lipkin-Shahak, Amnon 305, 310, 316, 317, 319n3

Luke, Gospel, of 75

Madaba map 68, 123
Madrid Conference (1991) 251
Mahgrebi neighborhood 227, 237–38
Maimonides 44
al-Majjaj, Dr. Amin 277
Malley, Robert 304, 306, 316
Mamluk cemetery 199
Man qatala al-malik Abd Allah? (*Who Killed King Abdullah?*) (Nashashibi) 248, 249
Al-Maqasid Hospital 277
Mark, Gospel of 74
Martyrs' Organization (Iraq) 174, 183–85, 187
al-Masri, Hikmat 273
Massad, Joseph 157
Matthew, Gospel of 74, 76
Matza, Yehoshua 291, 292, 294–95
Mecca 24, 87, 91, 92, 98, 99
Medina 91, 92, 96, 99
Melchizedek 19, 27–28
Melito of Sardis 70
memoirs 9, 210
memory 14, 40–44
Merhav, Rueven 314
Merian, Matthaeus *142*
Meridor, Daniel 309–10, 319n11
messianism 41, 44
Micah 50–51, 52, 55
Ministerial Committee for Jerusalem's Affairs 240
Ministry for Jerusalem Affairs 289
miqva'ot (ritual baths) 32
Mishnah 59–61, 62
modernization narrative 208–9
Montanism 79–80
Motahheri, Ayatollah Morteza 186–87, 194–95n29
Mount Moriah 2, 19–20, 53
Mount of Olives: and Camp David Summit 303, 309; in early Christian period 68, 69, 71; on maps 131, 132; in Mishnah 60; in photography 143
Mount Scopus 227, 228, 229, 231, 234, 242n15
Mount Sinai 29
Mount Zion 29, 48, 49, 53, 55, 56, 69
Mountain of Remembering (*Har Hazikaron*) 236
Mu'ammal b. Isma'il 94
Mu'awiya (caliph) 86

Muhammad: burial place of 96; and Dome of the Rock 3, 21–22; and Jerusalem 3, 87; Night Journey and Ascension of 3, 5, 7, 20, 22, 87, 95–97, 99
al-Muhtasib, Shaykh Hilmi 271, 273
Municipal Corporations Ordinance 287
Münster, Sebastian 132
al-Musawi, 'Abbas 181–83, 185
Muslim Council (*al-Hay'a al-Islamiyya*) 268, 271–73
Muslim sectarian conflict 7
Mutran, Khalil 158
Muwasi, Faruq 158–59
myth and history 206–7

Nabulsi, Sulayman 261
Nahmanides 44
Najaf, shrine of (Iraq) 169, 171, 176
al-Nashashibi, Muhammad Zuhdi 277
Nashashibi, Nasser Eddin 248–51
Nashashibi, Ragheb 248–51
Nasir, Jamil 'Uthman 276
Nassar, Issam 142
Nasser, Gamal 258–59
national library 227
National Guidance Committee 270
National Religious Party 225
Nea (Church of the Theotokos) 69–70
Netanyahu, Benjamin 277
New Jew 224–25, 241n3
New Testament 28, 56, 58, 73–79
Nir, Yeshayahu 142
nostalgia (*hanin*) 155, 162–63, 165
Nu'aym b. Hammad 98
Nuseibeh, Anwar 259, 269
Nusseibeh, Sari 276, 277

Obeysekere, Gananathm 118–19
Old City 12, 213, 217–18, 226, 228, 233–34, 237, 250, 258, 276, 284–85, 290, 294; and Camp David Summit 304–11, 315–16
Old Testament 2, 27–30, 52–53, 55, 64n2
Olmert, Ehud 238, 284
Organization of the Martyrs of the Islamic Revolution (*Bunyad-i Shahid-i Inqilab-i Islami*) 169
Orient House 11, 275, 277–78
Origen 70, 74, 80
Orthodox Greeks 22
Oslo Accords 11, 201, 274, 277, 279, 291, 304, 311
Ottoman Parliament 213

Oz, Amos 198

Palestinian Authority (PA) 11, 266,
    274–78
Palestinian Center of Statistics 276
Palestinian Economic Council for
    Development and Reconstruction
    276
Paestinian-Israeli conflict 8, 11–13,
    169–70, 181–91, 198–204, 206, 239,
    267–79, 284–97, 303–19
Palestinian leadership 9–10, 11
Palestinian Solidarity Organization 187
Paula (mother of Eustochium) 72
Paulus a Milonis 128–29
Peel Commission 228–29
Peregrinatio (von Breydenbach) 123
Peres, Shimon 240, 311
Persia 67
personal identity 8
Philo Judaeus 38–39, 51
photography 6, 140–52; archeological
    and architectural 141–42; and
    Blanquart-Evrard publishing house
    144; calotype prints 143, 147, 153n3;
    Church of the Holy Sepulchre in 149;
    claims to truth 145–46; Dome of the
    Rock in 146, 148–49; French and
    English schools of 142–43, 147; and
    French nationalism 142, 145; and
    history 210; and idealized
    representations of Jerusalem 140–41;
    and imperialism 141; invention of
    140, 142–43; and Orientalism 141–
    42; photographic schools and firms
    in Jerusalem 152, 210–11, 213; and
    religious worldviews 143; techniques
    of mass reproduction 144; and travel
    literature 144–45; *see also* individual
    photographers
Pilgrim of Bordeaux 70–71, 72
pilgrimage 20–21, 28, 38–39, 52, 63, 69,
    70–72, 80, 91, 92–93, 98
Pines-Paz, Ofir 296
piyyut (religious poetry) 41–42
PLO (Palestine Liberation
    Organization) 11, 251, 266, 270–71,
    273–79
Pompey 34
Preventive Security Service (PSS) 277
Procopius 69–70, 72
Protestant School 214
Protevangelium of James 133
purity concerns 32–33, 55

Qabbani, Nizar 158
Qa'ida fi ziyarat Bayt al-Maqdis (Ibn
    Taymiyya) 99
Qibbat al-Sakhra see Dome of the Rock
Quaresmius, Francisco 130–31
al-Quds 11, 283–97
al-Quds University 277
Qur'an 87, 96–97

Rabbat Summit (1974) 270
Rabbinic literature 59–63
Rabin, Yitzhak 277, 290, 311
Ra'd, Khalil 210
Rafi' 94
Rahbani, Assi, and Mansur Rahbani
    155–65; *see further under* Fayruz
Raja' b. Haywa 95
Rajjub, Jibril 277
al-Ramli, al-Walid b. Hammad 5, 88–
    98
Ramon, Haim 292
Rashid, Mohammad 318
Reisner, Danny 311, 312–13, 320n15
responsa literature 44
"Reunification of Jerusalem" order 268
Reuwich, Erhard 132
Revisionist Zionism 225, 233, 315,
    320n23
Rock (*al-Sakhra*) sacredness of 93–95,
    99
Rohan, Dennis 113
Rome 72
Rubinstein, Daniel 259
Rubinstein, Elyakim 311, 313, 320n14
Russian Compound 214

Sabri, Shaykh 'Akrama 274–75
al-Sahir, Kazim 158
al-Sa'ih, Shaykh 'Abd al-Hamid 271,
    272
St. George (church) 68
St. Jacob (church) 68
St. James 76–77
St. John 76–77
St. John (monastery) 68, 70
St. Kiriakos (church) 68
St. Mary 133
St. Mary (monastery) 70
St. Paul 76–77
St. Peter 76–77
St. Serapion (church) 68
St. Sophia (church) 68
St. Thaleleus (monastery) 70
Sta. Pudenziana (Rome) mosaic 80–81

Sts. Cosmas and Damian (church) 68
Sakakini, Khalil 210, 215, 216, 217
Saladin *see* Salah al-Din
Salah al-Din 16, 22, 81, 99, 160
Salem 27–28
Salzmann, Auguste 6–7, 140–52, *143, 146, 148–51*; as archeologist 152; as architectural and archeological photographer 143–44, 146, 151; disenchantment with photography 150–51; early career 147; *Jérusalem: Étude et reproduction photographique des monuments de la Ville Sainte* 144; photographs of reservoirs 145, 147–48; photographs of city gates 149–50; photograph of Sultan's Pool 150; photographs of Wailing Wall 144, 146; and de Saulcy's theories 145; and scripture 147; use of calotype technique 147; work compared with Frith's 143–44, 149
Samaria 29
Sanders, E.P. 74
sanhedrin 37
Sapir, Pinhas 234–35
al-Saqati, Abu 'Abd Allah Muhammad b. al-Nu'man 89–90
Schedel, Hartmann 133–34, *134*, 140
Schneller Orphanage 214
Second *Intifada* 278
Second Temple period 39, 51–58
Second Temple: and Christian eschatology 97; in Christian tradition 74–75; date of 48; destruction of 27, 74–75, 133–34; and Jesus 74; and Jewish liturgy 53; in Josephus 51; and Judeo-Christian eschatology 74, 76, 78–79, 82n20; location of 32, 48–51; on maps 133–34; as *omphalos* 38; in Philo Judaeus 51; *Pterugion* 58; "rebuilding" of by 'Abd al-Malik 97–98; relationship to Temple Mount 54–55, 62; as ritual center 51–52, 55; site of 48–51; and murder of Zechariah 59
Sennacherib (Assyrian king) 29
Settlers' Movement 10, 239, 240
Seutter, Matthaeus *124*
Sextus Julius Africanus 70
Shahak, Amnon *see* Lipkin-Shahak, Amnon
Shakir, Hani 158
Shalabi, Elia (Evliya Tshelebi) 211
Shamir, Yitzhak 289

al-Shanti, Ibraham 255–56
Sharett [Shertok], Moshe 228–29, 231, 234
Sharon, Ariel 278, 292, 293–94, 296–97
Shatila refugee camp 155
Shekhina (presence of God) 2, 62
Sher, Gilead 305, 319n3
Shertok, Moshe *see* Sharett, Moshe
Shi'as 7
al-Shihabi, Mrs. Zalikha 273
Shrine of Imam Husayn (Iraq) 171, 185
Shrine of Imam Reza (Iraq) 178–80
Sidqi, Najati 210, 216–17
Sidr, Talal 277
Sieber, Franz Wilhelm 123
Silwan 303
Simeon b. Shatah 34
Simon (Hasmonean ruler) 33
Siniora, Hana 271, 276
Sira (Life and Career of the Prophet Muhammad) genre 87
Six-Day War 157, 266, 285
Socialist Zionism 225, 238
Sofer, Naim 254
Solomon 2, 19–20, 48, 49, 92, 93
Solomon's Portico 37
Solomon's Temple 48
Sophronius (Patriarch of Jerusalem) 86
Souresrafil, Behrouz 188
Spring of St. Elisha (monastery) 70
status quo decree (1852) 23, 252
Stephen (proto-martyr) 69
stone tablets 28–29
Sunnis 7
supercessionist argument 15
Supreme National Guidance Committee 272–73

Taha, 'Ali Mahmud 158
Tahbub, Hasan 271
Tamari, Salim 217
Tamir, Shmuel 239
Tarabulsi, Fawwaz 164
Tazzi, 'Ali 272
Tel Aviv 230, 231, 233, 235
Templum Salomonis see Aqsa mosque
Tertullian 74, 80
Teynard, Félix 144
Temple Mount (*Haram al-Sharif*) 22; and Abraham and Isaac story 50, 53; activities at 54; after destruction of Second Temple 58–64; Antonia fortress 35, 37, 57; and archeology 58; Ark of the Covenant 48; back-projection of

term 61–62; buildings on 57; and Camp David Summit 294, 303, 305–11, 314, 317; Chamber of Hewn Stone 37; concept of 55–57; Dome of the Ascension 97; in early Christian period 58–59, 63; in early Muslim tradition 63; Eastern Gate 37; "Foundation Stone" 62–63; functions of 36–37; Greek terms for 54, 55–56; and Hadrian 58; Hebrew terms for 54; and Herod 35, 57–58, 64; and idea of cosmic mountain 51, 53; Islamic architecture on 86; in Islamic tradition 21–22, 86, 93–94; and Jewish liturgy 63; in Jewish tradition 4, 23, 37, 47–58, 59–64; in Josephus 55–56; and Law for the Protection of Holy Places (1969) 23; maintenance of 38, 52; and Micah 50, 52; and Mount Moriah 50, 53; and Mount Zion 48, 49, 53, 55, 56; and movement of James, brother of Jesus 58–59; names of 55–56; in New Testament 56, 58, 64n7; as *omphalos* 22, 62–63; on maps 129, 132; origin of name 47–51, 56–57; in Old Testament 49–51, 52–53, 55, 64n2; Philo Judaeus on 38–39; in photography 146; and pilgrimage 38–39, 52, 63; and PLO 274–75; preaching on 37; prohibition against trees 60; and purity concerns 55; in Rabbinic literature 59–62, 62–63; rebuilding of 35–36; relationship to First Temple 92; relationship to Second Temple 54–55, 62; riots on 36–37; and ritual 60; as sacred site 2–3, 4; in Second Temple period 30; in Second Temple–era writings 54; and *Shekhina* (presence) of God 62; site of 68; Solomon's Portico 37; Solomon's Temple 48; sovereignty of 12; as symbol 47–48; and topography of Jerusalem 52–54, 57; walls around 58
tomb of Jason 34
Tosefta 62
Tower of David 68
Tractae Yoma 62
Tractate Kelim 61
Tractate Middot 59
Tuqan, Ibrahim 158
al-Turjman, Ihasn 210, 219
Turner, Victor 113

U.N. Resolution 181 10, 230–31, 233, 245
'Ubada 94
'Umar b. al-Khattab (caliph) 22, 81, 86
Umayyad dynasty 86
UNGA Resolution 194 245
'Uqba b. Abi Zaynab 96–97
Urban II (pope) 16

Vallat, F.A. 256
Villapando, Juan Bautiste 127–28, *129*
Voice of Palestine radio 7

Wailing Wall *see* Western Wall
Waki' b. al-Jarrah 94
al-Walid (caliph) 86
al-Wasiti, Abu Bakr Muhammad b. Ahmad 88–89, 96, 98
Weizmann, Chaim 226, 227, 241n5
West Bank 11, 202–3, 237, 239, 247, 250, 253–54, 266–79, 285–90, 284–97
Western Wall 7, 10, 108, 227, 303
Wilkins, Robert 80
Wilson, Charles 123
Wilson, Evan 253
Witztum, Eliezer 115–16, 118
Wolhgemut, Michael *141*
wuquf ritual 86

Yanai, Shlomo 311, 320n16
Yatom, Danny 310, 313, 319n7
Yazid b. Sallam 95
Yerushalayim 11–12, 283–97
Yishuv 227, 228, 231, 242n12
Yose, Rabbi 62–63

Zechariah 59
Ze'evi, Dror 207–8
Zevi, Shabbatai 44
Zionism and Jewish nationalism: and agricultural collectives 226; and Arab population 225–26; building projects 227; Commission to Palestine 226, 277; early history 224–25; goals of 224–25, 229; and immigration to Palestine 9, 225, 226; and Israeli statehood 231–32; and Jerusalem 1, 8, 9–10, 19, 224–40, 296, 311, 314–15; Labor Zionism 225, 226, 229, 237, 239; as modern project 225; and Mt. Scopus 228, 229, 231; and the *New Jew* 224–25, 241n3; Socialist Zionism 225, 238; and Tel Aviv 230,

233; and U.N. Resolution 181 230–31; and Western Wall 227, 237–38; and *Yishuv* 227, 228, 242n12

Zionist Commission to Palestine 226, 227
Zionist historians 209
al-Zuhri, Ibn Shihab 96–97

CPSIA information can be obtained
at www.ICGtesting.com
Printed in the USA
LVOW13s1247100718
583214LV00001B/1/P